The Spanish Empire
IN AMERICA

The Spanish Empire
IN AMERICA

C. H. HARING

A Harvest/HBJ Book
HARCOURT BRACE JOVANOVICH
NEW YORK AND LONDON

First Harbinger Books edition 1963
LIBRARY OF CONGRESS CATALOG CARD NUMBER: 47-1142
PRINTED IN THE UNITED STATES OF AMERICA

L M N

❦❧

Contents

❦❧

I The Beginnings of Royal Government in America
3

II Race and Environment
EL PUEBLO CONQUISTADOR
23

III Race and Environment
EL PUEBLO INDÍGENA
38

IV Territorial Organization
THE VICEROYALTY OF NEW SPAIN
69

V Territorial Organization
THE VICEROYALTY OF PERU
82

VI The Council of the Indies
94

VII Royal Government in the Indies
VICEROYS AND AUDIENCIAS
110

VIII Royal Government in the Indies
PROVINCIAL ADMINISTRATION
THE RESIDENCIA AND THE VISITA
128

IX The Cabildo
147

X The Church in America
166

XI School and Society
194

XII Literature, Scholarship and the Fine Arts
219

XIII Agriculture and Industry
235

XIV The Royal Exchequer (I)
256

XV The Royal Exchequer (II)
279

XVI The Spanish Commercial System
293

XVII The Last Phase
314

Bibliography
GENERAL MISCELLANEOUS
POLITICAL ADMINISTRATION
LEGISLATION
MUNICIPALITIES
INDIANS
NEGROES
THE CHURCH
EDUCATION
LITERATURE, SCIENCE, AND SCHOLARSHIP
THE FINE ARTS
TRADE AND INDUSTRY
MINING
THE EXCHEQUER
326

Index
354

Foreword

The following pages endeavor to bring together within the compass of a single volume what we know about the institutional history of the Spanish colonies in America from the Discovery in 1492 down to the Wars of Independence. They are concerned with the transfer of Spanish modes of government and society from the Old World to the New, and with their evolution in a remote and very different American environment.

The present state of research into the colonial annals of Spanish America does not permit of an adequate, systematic description of government and society based upon solid documentation. Political and economic policies in the various provinces of the Spanish Indies still await more thorough investigation. Literature and the fine arts are almost a virgin field. Several of our contemporaries have contributed much to the elucidation of the Indian problem, but we have yet to learn about the realities of daily life in these widely scattered and very diverse communities, the application of royal legislation in the several vice-royalties, and its observance or nonobservance. The long series of *memorias* or *relaciones* left by the various viceroys have been little utilized, and few of the more important viceroys have found a biographer. The needed preparatory studies, in short, if not altogether lacking, are often inadequate in range or maturity. Mountains of archival material in Spain and elsewhere await the investigator. This volume, therefore, does not pretend in any sense to be definite. Certain chapters suggest more questions than they answer, and but reflect the paucity of research in these areas.

As a history of institutions the volume leans more to description than to narrative. Throughout, however, the concept of development has been kept clearly in view. The reader need scarcely be warned against the common textbook error of describing Spanish American institutions as if they remained static through three centuries. Although under the later Hapsburgs colonial institutions did for a time seem to be suffering from an access of arterial sclerosis, the functioning of government in the days of Philip II was not the same as in the eighteenth century; nor may eighteenth-century institutions be taken as the norm for Spanish administration throughout the colonial era.

Resort to footnote references may appear to be somewhat erratic. In a volume of condensation so comprehensive in scope, reference to 'authorities' for every important statement would not only be irksome to the reader but would clutter the pages beyond all reason. Many matters, therefore, which the writer believes are not of uncommon knowledge among historians, are left undocumented, with the expectation that the curious reader will easily find further enlightenment in the bibliography. Other matters that in the writer's judgment are not so generally understood, call for more protracted treatment and the support of other invesigators in the field of reference to contemporary sources. Such, for instance, are many questions relating to the *encomienda,* the *cabildo,* the colonial Church, and the commercial system under the Bourbons.

The author has incorporated into several of the chapters the substance of earlier writings expanded and corrected by later information. For the chapter on the *cabildo,* he is deeply indebted to a manuscript by F. A. Kirkpatrick, *Regidores and Alcaldes Ordinarios,* entrusted to his care during the blitz in England, and used with Mr. Kirkpatrick's knowledge and approval. Indeed what value the chapter may have is due in considerable measure to his contribution.

This book had its inception in a series of twelve lectures delivered in the spring of 1934 at the Instituto Hispano-Cubano of the University of Seville in Spain. The Instituto's plans to publish the lectures were fortunately frustrated by the Civil War. In the intervening decade, numerous investigations have added to our knowledge, and the writer's grasp of the subject, it is hoped, has gained in breadth and maturity.

C. H. HARING

Harvard University
Cambridge, Massachusetts
January 1947

The Spanish Empire

IN AMERICA

I

The Beginnings of
Royal Government
in America

One of the most extended and spectacular movements in the history of
civilization has been that to which we commonly refer as the Expansion
of Europe. It was the process by which the European peoples, between
the fifteenth century and the nineteenth, made themselves for the time
being at least the heirs of the greater part of the surface of the earth.
Ushered in by the discovery of America by Columbus, and by achievements of the Portuguese in the science of navigation, it saw the rise and
fall of great colonial empires far distant from the centers in Europe, the
expansion of maritime trade into a world commerce, and the extension
of Christian missionary propaganda to the four corners of the world.
The area occupied by European races or dominated by European culture came to comprise vastly more than the old mother continent itself;
it embraced many continents: North America, South America, Australia,
and the greater part of Africa. Thereafter wars in Europe and Asia were
to be motivated largely by commercial and colonial rivalries and ambitions. For the first time in history the medium of the world's commercial
activity was the 'Ocean Sea,' which connects all lands of the earth; the
Atlantic became a new and grander Mediterranean.

In this process Spain and Portugal played the most dramatic role, and
pointed the way for other nations to follow. Their connection with the
New World began with the initial voyage of Columbus, and for a century they pre-empted virtually all of the western hemisphere as well as
the seas eastward to China and the Philippines. Before the seventeenth
century they were the great, in reality the only, colonial powers. Not
until after 1600 did the English, Dutch, and French seriously challenge
their supremacy. Portugal's imperial greatness was to be displayed chiefly
in the Orient; Spain reserved to herself the greater part of the two American continents. It was almost entirely under her auspices that the Western Indies were first explored and conquered. Within three generations

[1]

Spaniards discovered, subdued, and colonized the most extensive territorial empire the world had even seen, performed prodigies of valor and endurance, and created a civilized and sophisticated society in the midst of a virgin wilderness.

At the time of the discovery of America, Spain had achieved a considerable degree of political and religious solidarity, had gone far on the road to national organization—a necessary preliminary to war and adventure, discovery and exploration, in the New World. The two peninsular kingdoms of Castile and Aragon had recently been united by a dynastic marriage of the greatest significance. Prince Ferdinand, heir to the crown of Aragon, and Isabella, heiress of Castile, were married in 1469. A decade later each had come into full possession of his inheritance, and the history of modern Spain began. The two kingdoms, it is true, were joined only by a dynastic tie. Each retained its political and administrative personality, its own laws, parliaments, and other institutions. Isabella as queen in her own right reserved to herself the patronage and revenues of Castile, Ferdinand those of Aragon. In external affairs, however, the two sovereigns acted jointly for the whole of Spain. For purposes of war and diplomacy Castile and Aragon were thereafter a singe state.

Political conditions in the two kingdoms, moreover, were widely different. Aragon, the smaller, eastern kingdom, had an ordered, stable government under a limited monarchy. Rights of person and property were secure, and the *Cortes* had considerable control over legislation and finance, as much as had the Parliament in fifteenth-century England. In Castile, on the other hand, royal government was at lowest ebb. There had been frequent minorities and disputed successions, and the crown was generally defied by the aristocracy. Royal revenues were almost completely alienated, royal justice was venal and corrupt. The clergy were secularized and little better than the nobles. The principal towns, which in the Middle Ages enjoyed a large measure of autonomy, in the century before Isabella had been ruined by domestic quarrels, by strife with one another and with the country aristocracy. Royal government had lost all character and prestige. Private war was the rule; nobles fought over castles, lands, and honors, pillaged the churches, and devastated the country.

The new sovereigns left Aragon severely alone. They hesitated to tamper with its institutions. But they combined energy, ability, and resources to restore peace and security to Castile and to organize effective agencies of government. This was possible only by establishing the unquestioned supremacy of the crown. In so doing they laid the foundations of a royal absolutism which ultimately extended over the whole of Spain, and at the very time when Columbus was seeking financial backing for his enterprise. They were also unwittingly releasing the energies of Castile for the work of conquest and settlement overseas; and the institutions they created and developed in Castile were soon to be transferred to America and to prevail there for three hundred years.

The government of Castile in the fifteenth and sixteenth centuries, therefore, was rapidly becoming an absolute, patrimonial monarchy. Like other growing nation-states of Europe as they were consolidated in the age of the Renaissance, it escaped from the medieval limitations of Empire and Church and the feudal rights of the nobility—also from those acquired rights of municipal autonomy represented in Spain by the *fueros* of its principal cities. The superiority of the state over all longstanding customs, local privileges, and private jurisdictions was more and more accepted. Even subjection to the so-called Law of Nature of early political philosophers was questioned. All law emanated from the state. And in Spain, as in most countries of that time, the king became the sole beneficiary of these new political concepts.

One of the most ancient and enduring bases of government had been faith in its supernatural origin. The theory of the divine authority of a king's office was inherited from the Middle Ages, and in Spain as elsewhere it was used to strengthen and fortify the new patterns of royal absolutism. A religious sanction was added, while a loyal clergy inculcated the habit of passive obedience to royal command. Castilian sovereigns, therefore, were a divine institution. Every law came to be a concession of their will, every political organism existed only at their pleasure. Even the government of the Church, in its secular aspects, was subdued to their control, became but another branch of royal administration. They were themselves responsible to God alone.[1]

These concepts dictated the relations between the crown and its American provinces to an even greater degree than was possible in the government of Castile itself. In Spain there was no systematic attempt by the king to supersede or destroy all competing authorities, but merely to bend existing agencies to the royal will or to supplement them when necessary. This was accomplished, among other devices, by the use of commissioners—*corregidores, pesquisidores, visitadores,* they were called —royal agents possessing no independent legal competence, but acting

---

1 Many Spanish theologians and jurists of the sixteenth century, however, still maintained that the power of the Spanish sovereigns was circumscribed by all the fundamental limitations imposed by medieval theory. If political authority proceeded from God, it also imposed responsibilities. The prince was not absolute master of his kingdom, but only its administrator, bound to use his power for securing the spiritual and temporal welfare of his subjects. His actions were limited by the Law of Nature and by the usages and customs of the country. If he ruled unjustly, he was no longer a king but a tyrant, and his subjects might resist by force and even in extreme cases kill him to escape his unholy despotism. See Lewis Hanke, *Las Teorías políticas de Bartolomé de las Casas* (Publ. Instit. invest. hist., LXVII), Buenos Aires, 1935, 31-42.

solely in the name of the king. They soon assumed wide administrative tasks, undertook financial and judicial functions, and formed the basis of a centralized royal government.

America, however, presented to the Catholic kings a peculiar opportunity. Here was a virgin continent, occupied only by tribes of naked savages, or by the easily subdued semibarbarous native states of Mexico and Peru. Here was a New World free from the traditions and inhibitions of an Old-World society, a *tabula rasa* on which the Spanish sovereigns might impress their own conception of royal autocracy, without hindrance from institutional traditions or from class or regional rights and privileges inherited from earlier times.

The rise of national states in Western Europe in the fifteenth and sixteenth centuries, of large areas united under a single monarchy, implied consolidation in an economic sense as well. Industry and trade began to be organized for national objects, on a national basis. Gradually common weights and measures were introduced, a uniform coinage was imposed, a similar administration of justice, uniform customs burdens, etc.

This concentration of economic resources was also necessary for the task of expansion, of colonization and world trade, which was ushered in by the Age of Discovery. And in this direction Spain under the able leadership of Ferdinand and Isabella had gone far. In this she was as well prepared as any other nation of Western Europe to take advantage of the new opportunities offered for maritime and colonial enterprise overseas.[2]

2 On the other hand, it may be argued that the maritime and colonial supremacy of Spain and Portugal in the sixteenth century was largely a historical accident. Henry the Navigator, that remarkable royal prince who is given credit for being the founder of Portugal's imperial greatness, may perhaps be regarded as a biological accident. And certainly it was something of a historical accident that Columbus sailed under the patronage of the Queen of Castile. He had appealed earlier to the King of Portugal, and had sent his brother Bartholomew to England and France to seek the support of the authorities there. England under the first of the Tudors, who pursued the same methods as Ferdinand and Isabella in strengthening the monarchy and increasing the commercial and maritime prosperity of the kingdom, certainly was as well prepared for a colonial career as was Castile, and as the event proved produced better sailors and colonists. France, too, had an active seafaring population on the coasts of Normandy and Brittany. Her monarchy was strong and respected, and industrially she was more advanced than England. Columbus might conceivably have sailed as the client of the King of France, and French energies might have been diverted from the conquest of Italy and Jerusalem to the conquest of America. As a matter of fact, Frenchmen were the first to dispute Spanish and Portuguese claims to the Indies, and their corsairs appeared in American waters as early as 1506.

Columbus first won the ear of Isabella, however, or rather of her intimate advisers, and the Indies once discovered, Spain's rights there were generally accepted. When John Cabot sailed from Bristol, he turned toward the north; and as the northern coasts of America proved to be unattractive, projects of English expansion westward were temporarily abandoned, to be resumed later partly as a consequence of the religious feud between Elizabeth and Philip II.

The first expedition of Columbus was authorized and financed as a venture of Queen Isabella, and the profits of the venture accrued to her and her heirs as the sovereigns of Castile. And from the outset the Indies were treated as the direct and exclusive possession of the crown. They were not, strictly speaking, Spanish. They were not even an integral part of the Castilian kingdom. Mexico and Peru were kingdoms, combined with the kingdoms of Spain under a common sovereign, bound to Spain only by the dynastic tie. They were not colonies, strictly speaking, although they were colonized by Spaniards. The king possessed not only the sovereign rights but the property rights; he was the absolute proprietor, the sole political head, of his American dominions. Every privilege and position, economic, political, or religious, came from him. It was on this basis that the conquest, occupation, and government of the New World were achieved.

This theory continued until the eighteenth century to be a fundamental maxim of American policy. It was a theory that toward the end of the colonial period, under the Bourbon dynasty, Spanish statesmen were apt to forget or ignore. But it was re-asserted by the colonists themselves to justify their demands for political autonomy.

Moreover, under the Hapsburg kings the Indies, as has been intimated, were held to belong to the crown of Castile alone, not to that of Aragon. In the beginning apparently only subjects of Castile were allowed to go to the Indies without special royal license. Queen Isabella in her will declared that as the islands and mainland of the west had been discovered and conquered at the cost of Castile and by her subjects, the trade and profit of these regions should be confined to them. And down to the death of the Queen it seems that few inhabitants of the eastern kingdoms were granted the privilege of emigration and settlement; although after 1506, when Ferdinand became regent of Castile, the restrictions were considerably relaxed in favor of his own Aragonese subjects. It was not till the year 1596, if we are to accept the evidence of the *Recopilación de leyes de las Indias,* that the inhabitants of all the other Spanish kingdoms were legally given the same privileges of emigration to the New World.

Consequently the laws and institutions of Spanish America were modeled on those of Castile, often modified in form and in function to meet local needs, but always emanating from the crown and kept under royal control. Philip II makes a specific statement to the effect in a code of ordinances issued for the Council of the Indies in September 1571, when he says:

And because the kingdoms of Castile and the Indies belong to one crown and their laws and manner of government ought therefore to be as alike as possible, the members of our council shall try, in the laws and institutions which they may establish (*ordenaren*) for those states, to reduce the form and manner of their government to the style and order by which are ruled and governed the realms of Castile and León so far as may be permitted by the diversity and difference of the lands and peoples.[3]

As Merriman has remarked in his *Rise of the Spanish Empire,* geographical conditions may have accounted for something—the fact that the Indies were so far distant from the metropolis and therefore might more easily escape royal control. But a 'far more fundamental explanation of the unwillingness of the sovereigns to permit any of the political methods of the eastern kingdoms to percolate to the Indies was their dread lest the new territories should be contaminated by coming in contact with the "Aragonese liberties" which they had not been able wholly to subvert.' Consequently, in matters of government and administration the realms of the crown of Aragon were almost completely excluded from participation in American affairs, although, as Merriman points out, the eastern kingdom had hitherto enjoyed far the largest measure of imperial experience.[4]

From the every beginning the crown and jurists in Castile were much exercised over the theoretical question raised by the conquest in regard to the king's 'just title' to dominion in America. Had the new-found lands been wholly unoccupied, a title might have been established in 'natural law' by virtue of prior discovery and occupation. But they were already inhabited, and the need was felt of discovering reasons in sacred or profane law by which war against the infidel Indians and the conquest of their land might be justified. This question was the occasion for a number of famous debates among missionaries, theologians, and lawyers, and council after council was assembled by the crown to determine its rights and duties in the New World. Involved was the allied question whether the Indians were rational beings, or more like beasts of the field as indicated by their cannibalism, idolatry, and other vices. If they were rational beings, could they with justice be deprived of their lands and freedom? If they were utterly barbarous—inferior by nature according to Aristotelian doctrine—justification for their conquest might be found in the Christian duty of raising them to a higher plane of human dignity. The passions aroused by this dispute and the notable part played in it by Bartolomé de las Casas are too well known to call for recapitulation here. The controversy, beginning in the time of the Catholic kings, far outlived the sixteenth century.[5]

3 *Colección de documentos inéditos,* 1st, ser., XVI, 415.
4 Roger Bigelow Merriman, *The Rise of the Spanish Empire in the Old World and in the New,* 4 vols., New York, 1918-34, II, 221-2.
5 Lewis Hanke, *The First Social Experiments in America,* Cambridge, 1935, ch I; Ricardo Levene, *Introducción a la historia del derecho indiano,* Buenos Aires, 1924, 45 ff.: Silvio Zavala, *New Viewpoints on the Spanish Colonization of America,* Philadelphia, 1943, chs. 1-4.

Out of these inquiries—the crown's title to dominion in the Indies and the just cause of war against the natives—emerged the famous *Requerimiento,* so often referred to as an instance of the notorious legalism and religiosity of the Spaniards. This proclamation, full of legal technicalities, began with the Biblical creation of the world, and, passing in review the origins of the Roman hierarchy and the donation of Alexander VI, called upon the bewildered aborigines to acknowledge the supremacy of the Pope and of the kings of Castile, on pain of enslavement and confiscation of wives and goods. Every Spanish *conquistador* was required to have it read to the Indians by a notary and through an interpreter, before their territory could legally be taken or hostilities against them be started. 'Having promulgated the *Requerimiento* in due form, the Spanish captain sent the official report back to Spain with the necessary signatures and his conscience was clear.' [6] But in any event the consequences were often tragic or grotesque.

That there was ever any question in the minds of Isabella and her successors about their sovereign rights in the New World is very doubtful. Dominion was of course based in the first instance on the famous bulls of Pope Alexander VI between May and September 1492, after Columbus's first voyage, which granted to the crown of Castile all islands and mainland found west and south of a fixed meridian [7] toward the Indies, provided they were not already possessed by another Christian prince. Other European states bordering on the Atlantic refused to recognize this supreme jurisdiction of the Pope and never accepted the bulls; and in fact the Castilian monarchs themselves were generally disinclined to admit papal interference in temporal matters. Yet it is clear that they sought and accepted this award as a basis for opposition to the vague and extended claims of the Portuguese and other possible rivals. It is evident from the terms of the documents that the Papacy did dispose of the lands and peoples of America in favor of the Castilian crown. And although rejected by theologians and jurists of another school of thought, such as Las Casas and Francisco de Vitoria, this interpretation was commonly assumed by later Spanish writers.

The first European settlements were made on the island of Haiti or Hispaniola in the West Indies, and Hispaniola remained for several decades the center of Spanish authority and enterprise. From its shores the work of exploration and colonization was carried forward in every direction, and with great rapidity considering the resources available

---

6 Lewis Hanke, 'The *Requerimiento* and its interpreters,' *Revista de historia de America,* no. 1, 28.

7 Later established by the Treaty of Tordesillas between Castile and Portugal, 7 June 1494, at 370 leagues west of the Cape Verde Islands. This Line of Demarcation falls between 48° and 49° west of Greenwich.

and the difficulties involved. The occupation of the islands surrounding Hispaniola was mostly the result of local enterprise, but soon concessions were made by the crown for settlement along more distant coasts. Expeditions sailed north, south, and west to the continental shores beyond, the outlines of the Gulf of Mexico were definitely determined, and efforts were made to occupy the mainland from the Carolinas to Panama and Peru, till Cortés and Coronado in the north and Pizarro and his companions in the south had traced the ultimate limits of Spanish expansion in the New World.

The variety and size of the territories to be encompassed and the competition of rival adventurers for the glory and lucre of conquest were the reasons for division of the land into numerous and often conflicting jurisdictions—jurisdictions out of which were evolved the colonies or 'kingdoms' of a later time, from which in turn emerged the republics of today. The earliest essays in royal government, however, were made in the Antilles, or West Indian islands. There the Spanish crown first encountered the novel experience of trying to control a frontier community thousands of miles from the home base, at a time when primitiveness and uncertainty of communications by land or sea made distances many times greater than they are today.

The first royal agent in the New World was Christopher Columbus. In the celebrated capitulations with the Queen of Castile in April 1492 he was accorded the hereditary title of viceroy of the lands he expected to discover, together with those of governor, captain-general, and admiral. As admiral, he was to have the dignities and privileges pertaining to an Admiral of Castile, and the right to be sole judge in cases arising in connection with the trade of the new-found territories. As viceroy and governor, he was to have a tenth of all the royal revenues accruing from the Indies, and the right of presenting three candidates for any post of profit or emolument under him, from whom the crown was to select one. He was also given the privilege, if he contributed an eighth to the cost of the expedition, to receive an eighth of the profits resulting therefrom. But these extended powers and privileges had been granted rather hastily to still the importunities of a visionary sailor. And doubtless they were an inverse measure of the degree of faith which the crown placed in Columbus's grandiose scheme.

As the magnitude and importance of these new regions slowly dawned upon the consciousness of the sovereigns, they were disinclined to honor their original contract. Columbus, unsuccessful in his management of the colonists on the island of Hispaniola, was permanently removed from the government in the year 1500. Whether his failure as an administrator was due to weakness or inadaptability, or merely the result of circumstances beyond his control, will probably never be determined. It is manifest from the eloquent narrative of Las Casas that this Man of

[8]

Destiny was unable to cope with the greed and evil passions of the more unscrupulous of his followers. Perhaps he made a mistake in not allotting lands earlier to individual colonists; farming in the beginning apparently was on a community basis. At any rate, specific authority to assign freeholds, on condition of four years' continuous occupancy, was vouchsafed to him in July 1497, before his third voyage; [8] and it is significant that when allottments were made to the rebel Roldán and his associates two years later, the most serious opposition to Columbus's rule subsided. The Admiral was accused of arrogance and impatience in dealing with his followers. True humility was never conspicuous in the Columbus temperament, either in the Discoverer or in his heirs. Nevertheless, the state of the first colonists at best was one of idleness, intrigue, and rapine, which even a better man would have found extremely difficult to control. Whatever were the vicissitudes of pioneering in the tropics—something new in European experience—they were invariably charged against the governor.

Columbus in 1499, after his humiliating peace with Roldán, wrote to Ferdinand and Isabella urging them to send out to his assistance an experienced lawyer to administer justice on the island, and to designate two virtuous persons to serve as an advisory council.[9] The sovereigns, it seems, had already decided to replace the viceroy himself. The recurrent charges against him were having their effect upon the loyalty of the queen, as was his stubborn insistence upon developing an Indian slave trade. In the spring of 1499, on receipt of the first news about the Roldán insurrection, they had chosen a special commissioner, *juez pesquisidor,* to investigate the disorders and bring the guilty to justice. Francisco de Bobadilla, knight commander of the Order of Calatrava and officer in the royal household, was selected, a man commended by both Las Casas and Oviedo for his honesty and disinterestedness. At probably the same time, a patent as governor of the Indies was issued to him, for two months later a letter, addressed to all those in authority in the New World, commanded implicit obedience to his rule.[10] Most of Columbus's biographers, taking their cue from Las Casas, infer that Bobadilla's powers as governor were to be proclaimed only in case of necessity; but it is clear that the sovereigns intended him to supersede the Discoverer from the outset, for in their original commission to Bobadilla as *pesquisidor* they refer to Columbus simply as Admiral, not as in all previous communications as 'Admiral, viceroy, and governor.' In the covering letter

---

8 *Col. doc. inéd.,* 1st ser., XXXVI, 174.

9 Bartolomé de las Casas, *Historia de las Indias,* 5 vols., Madrid, 1875-6, lib. 1, cap. 160. Columbus offered to defray the judge's salary himself.

10 Martín Fernández de Navarrete, *Collección de los viages y descubrimientos, etc.,* 5 vols., Madrid, 1825-37, II, 237.

of credence issued to Bobadilla on 26 May, Columbus is again addressed merely as Admiral of the Ocean Sea.[11]

The story of Bobadilla's dealings with Columbus is too well known to warrant retelling here. Deceived perhaps by reports of interested witnesses, he let zeal outrun discretion, and after a lengthy inquest in which Columbus rather than Roldán was the culprit, the Discoverer and his brothers were shipped manacled to Spain. But apart from the crown's disavowal of Bobadilla's overhasty actions, his rule in Hispaniola was even more disastrous than that of his predecessor. The stern measures of Columbus and his brother Bartholomew had failed to bring peace and well-being to the island. The indulgent policy of Bobadilla turned disorder into unbridled license, with terrible consequences for the unhappy Indians. And without warrant from the crown, the royalty collected from the output of the gold-washings and mines was greatly reduced. A new governor was therefore speedily selected, Nicolás de Ovando, to continue the well-nigh hopeless task of creating a stable society in the American colony. His commission and instructions, of September 1501, vested him with virtually absolute authority in the New World. He was empowered to appoint and remove subordinates, including municipal *alcaldes, regidores,* and *alguaciles,* and even, if need be, to replace royally designated officials of the exchequer. He might expel undesirables from the colony, and from his decisions there was no appeal to the sovereigns in Spain. He was also to conduct a *residencia* of Bobadilla and his deputies, to last for thirty days, the first recorded use of this institution in the New World.[12]

Ovando's instructions in other respects were carefully detailed and embodied principles of government that were to be adhered to throughout three centuries of colonial administration. No one was thereafter to seek or operate mines without express permission, and one-half of the yield (reduced later to one-third, then to one-fifth) was reserved to the crown. Moors, Jews, and recent converts were to be strictly excluded from the Indies,[13] as were any foreigners who appeared there on voyages of trade or discovery. Ovando was to assure the native chiefs that they and their people were under the crown's especial protection. They were to pay tribute only as the rest of the king's subjects, were to be treated with mildness, and for their labor must be given reasonable wages. Twelve Franciscan friars accompanied the new governor to instruct the Indians in the elements of the Christian religion.

The expedition that sailed in February 1502 was the largest yet dis-

---

11 *Ibid.* p. 240.

12 *Col. doc. inéd.,* 1st ser., XXX, 12, 520; XXXI, 13; XXXII, 22.

13 Evidently some were already there, or later slipped through the net at Seville, for the proctors sent to represent the colonists in Spain in 1508 complained that the natives were being corrupted by their teachings!

patched to the new lands: 30 small vessels and over 2,500 persons, including 73 families—a tremendous addition to the 300 survivors in the colony. Bartolomé de las Casas was among the number, and Hernando Cortés would have been had he not received a severe wound from an outraged husband a few days before departure. After weathering a severe storm near the Spanish coast, Ovando arrived at Santo Domingo on 15 April, and immediately assumed the government. As for his followers, most of them were intent only on securing gold and returning rich to Europe; instead of planting corn, they rushed off in search of mines. They were unprepared for the hard labor involved or for the subtleties of a West Indian climate. Provisions failed them, fevers seized them, and within a short time over a thousand of the twenty-five hundred miserably perished —so fast, says Las Casas, that the clergy had not time to conduct their funerals.

Governor Ovando seems to have retained throughout the six years of his administration the confidence of the crown. When he arrived in America he was about 42 years of age, a man, according to Las Casas, of prudence, integrity, and justice, untainted by avarice. He was courteous and affable, but of great firmnness, and ambitious to command. Under his guidance, life in the colony first assumed an ordered form. Some of the more troublesome settlers he either shipped to Spain or deprived of their *encomiendas*. Several new towns were established upon the island, and in the capital, Santa Domingo, removed to a more healthful site across the river, was begun the construction of a fortress and a hospital of masonry. The farmers were fairly prosperous, raising cattle and swine, and cultivating cassava, yams, and perhaps a little sugar. The extraction of gold rapidly increased. During the first decade after 1492 the remittances of this precious metal to Spain had been in sorry contrast to the expectations engendered by Columbus's reports. Only after the coming of Bobadilla were the gold-washings on Hispaniola developed to any extent, and this continued under Ovando when, in spite of the reduction of the percentage of the king's royalty, the revenues from this source began to excite the cupidity of Ferdinand. Production reached its zenith probably toward the end of the second decade of the century, after which it rapidly declined. The maximum annual yield was perhaps as much as 450,000 pesos.

Nevertheless there were occasions for disgruntlement on the part of the king. The governor's authority was comprehensive and the Atlantic was both wide and deep; yet a more regular correspondence than Ovando maintained with the crown Ferdinand felt to be desirable. The governor's supervision over the administration of royal finances was somewhat erratic; his treasurer (Santa Clara) proved a defaulter, and for that the comptroller was, unjustly it seems, imprisoned. Instructions to the effect that the colonists be required to keep arms and attend periodical musters were not carried out, nor were orders that each town in the colony be endowed with common lands sufficient for its needs. Many of the settlers complained of the governor's arbitrary conduct toward them, and of his refusal to permit the transmission of their correspondence to Spain.[14]

These grievances were of course brought to a head in the *residencia* of Ovando, conducted by his successor in 1509, and should be accepted with reserve as an expression of the malcontent minority found in every community. On the whole his government must have been satisfactory to most Spaniards. His policy, however, toward the natives who still lived in semi-independence under their own chiefs was harsh in the extreme; the system of *encomiendas,* which he first definitely established, became merely a cloak for heartless exploitation to which he opposed no effective restraint; kidnapping expeditions to the Bahamas became in his time a regular practice.

As there was no prospect that the Discoverer would ever be reinstated in his honors and dignities, Diego Columbus, his son and heir, in 1505 memorialized the crown to be given the administration of the Indies in requital of his father's great services; and the latter wrote also to Ferdinand in support of Diego's petition.[15] This appeal presumably received no more attention than had its predecessors, and after Columbus's death in the following year Diego immediately pressed the crown for a restitution of his inherited rights. His claim to a tenth of the royal revenues from the Indies was promptly recognized, first by Philip of Burgundy, who shared the Castilian throne with Isabella's daughter Juana, and later by Ferdinand as regent; but it was not so promptly enforced. In 1508 Diego brought suit before the royal council. Meanwhile his marriage to María de Toledo, niece of the Duke of Alva and cousin of Ferdinand, worked powerfully in his favor, and he was in the same year accredited as governor of the Indies, though without the title of viceroy. Diego arrived at Santo Domingo in July 1509, acompanied by his wife, his brother Fernando, and his two uncles, besides a numerous retinue of persons of both sexes belonging to distinguished Castilian families. He was therefore enabled to maintain a sort of viceregal state in the little capital, in sharp contrast with what must have been rather primitive conditions of living.

Ovando was directed by the crown before his departure from America to draw up for the information and guidance of Diego Columbus a detailed statement or 'memorial' of the methods his experience had shown most adequate in the government of the colony, a copy of which he was

14 Cf. royal *cédulas*, mostly addressed to Diego Columbus, Ovando's successor, in *Col. doc. inéd.*, 1st ser., XXXI, 436, 475, 492, 494, 500, 501, 519, 522, 549.
15 Las Casas, *op. cit.*, lib. II, cap. 37.

to bring with him to Spain for the perusal of the king.[16] It was the first instance of a state paper of this sort in the history of the Spanish Indies. A similar memoir or *relacion* was prepared by Antonio de Mendoza, first viceroy of New Spain, for the assistance of his successor in 1550, and the precedent was followed by later viceroys in both North and South America. Ovando had more than once appealed to Ferdinand to be allowed to retire from his government, and, assured in advance of his sovereign's favor, he returned immediately to Spain to live at Alcántara as *comendador mayor* of his Order. He died there, rich and honored, in 1511.

The government of the Indies was entrusted to Diego Columbus on much the same terms as to his predecessor, and in his early correspondence Ferdinand displayed the greatest cordiality to this new colonial ruler. Disciplinary authority over the exchequer officers, however, was now specifically reserved to the crown, a reasonable precaution in view of the extensive claims of Diego upon the American treasury. The new governor was also expected to keep in much closer touch with the authorities in Spain, advising them of problems as they arose and guiding his actions by the advice received from king and council.[17]

It was understood in Spain, if not elsewhere in Europe, that Columbus first discovered the mainland of America as well as the islands, and part of that mainland he had been the first to explore. Diego Columbus, like Ovando his predecessor, was appointed to rule over the 'islands and mainland' in the Western Indies. But, except in the small duchy of Veragua, the crown was loath to admit the rule of the Columbus family over the mainland. The suit instituted by Diego, apparently with the collusion of King Ferdinand, resulted three years later in what appeared to be a favorable decision. The royal council in May 1511 declared that

To the said Admiral and to his successors belong the government and administration of justice . . . of the island of Española as well as of the other islands which the admiral don Christopher Columbus his father discovered in those seas and of those islands which by the diligence (*por industria*) of his father were discovered, with the title of viceroy as a legal and hereditary right forever . . .[18]

No mention, however, was made of the mainland, and when Pedrarias Dávila arrived on the Isthmus of Panama as captain-general and governor in June 1514, it was to set up a regime independent of the viceroy

---

16 'Real cédula para que Frey Niculas Dovando dé a Don Diego Colón una puntual noticia del modo con que a governado las Indias,' 3 May 1509, *Col. doc. inéd.*, 1st ser., XXXI, 410.

17 'Ynstrución que se ymbió al Almirante Don Diego Colon,' 3 May 1509, ibid. 1st ser, XXXI, 388. See also royal *cédulas* of 14 August and 14 November 1509, ibid. XXXI, 436, 494. Diego, in addition to his tenth of the net revenues, was allowed a salary of 366,000 *maravedís*, but out of this he had to pay a *merced* of 200,000 *maravedís* annually to Hernán Tello, member of the royal council. Ibid, XXXI, 407; XXXII, 87.

18 Ibid. 2nd ser., VII, 42.

Diego, although till then the tiny isthmian settlement had for all practical purposes taken its orders from Santo Domingo. And all the jurisdictions subsequently carved out of the mainland were dependent directly upon the crown and its officers in Spain.

The verdict of the council placed other limitations upon the vague and extended powers and privileges granted to the Discoverer. The general right to nominate officials in the Indies was not respected.[19] In the early summer of 1508, at the very time when Diego Columbus was given the administration of the Indies, the crown was conferring upon Alonso de Ojeda and his new associate, Diego de Necuesa, the privilege of colonizing and governing those portions of Tierra firme known as Urabá and Veragua; and in the following year it appointed Ponce de León governor, and later 'captain,' of the island of San Juan (Puerto Rico). Diego protested against these appointments as infringing on his rights,[20] but the council in 1511 in this manner maintained a discreet silence. On the other hand, it was specifically declared that the crown might appoint judges of appeal in any of the islands, and that the appointment of notaries, *regidores*, and other minor officials belonged to the king alone. Thereafter, as indeed had been the practice while Ovando was governor in the New World, it was clear that, except when specifically delegated, the nomination and appointment of colonial officials lay with the crown and its council in Spain.

The tithe of all profits from the newly discovered regions, promised to Christopher Columbus in 1492, had evidently been interpreted to apply to the revenues of the crown in gold, pearls, and other articles of value obtained by way of royalties from mines and fisheries or from the king's estates.[21] Diego, however, demanded a tenth of all net profits acquired anywhere west of the Line of Demarcation, whether by the crown or by private individuals, including royal taxes, ecclesiastical tithes, and ju-

---

19 Ever since the discarding of Columbus, the crown had assumed the practice of appointing subordinate governors to outlying islands and mainland areas in the Indies. As early as June 1501, Alonso de Ojeda had received a commission as governor of the island of 'Coquivacoa' and its environs in the Gulf of Urabá, as recompense for his services of discovery in the well-known voyage of 1499. Three months later a similar commission was given Vicente Yáñez Pinzón for the government of the coasts he had first explored to the north and south of the Amazon. Pinzón was, in fact, the first appointed European governor of Brazil. And when Ovando's commission as governor-general of the Indies was issued in the same month, his immediate authority was extended everywhere 'ecebto en las Islas do tienen la gobernacion Alonso de Oxeda e Vicente Yáñez Pinzón, por otras Nuestras cartas.' Ojeda's rights in Urabá were renewed or confirmed in 1504 and again in 1508. In the latter year, however, it was specifically stated that judicial appeals should go to the governor at Santo Domingo, and it is evident from the general tenor of these documents that supervisory powers lay with Ovando and his successors.

20 'Primera petición del Almirante D. Diego Colón al Consejo' etc., *Col. doc. inéd.*, 2nd ser., VII, 2.

21 'Real cédula encargando al Gobernador de la Isla Española el complimiento de lo estipulado con el Almirante' etc., 24 August 1507, ibid., 1st ser., XXXIX, 153.

dicial fines. These modest claims could scarcely be admitted by the king, but until 1536 the Columbus family did receive a tenth of the royal profits, other than taxes, of the West Indian islands. Of significance also is the declaration that the assignment of Indians in *repartimiento* belonged to the crown alone, not to the Admiral;[22] the first clear statement of a theory maintained throughout the colonial era, although the right was usually granted to the first conquerer of a new region, and was specifically delegated later to governors, viceroys, and other high executive officers.[23]

The conclusions of the royal council, approved by the crown in June 1511, and confirmed by a decree of the following November, did not settle the questions at issue so far as Diego Columbus was concerned. In January 1512 his attorney in Spain sought a declaration from the council that the government of the new settlements on the Isthmus of Panama belonged of right to the Admiral; and in December Diego himself, from his distant frontier capital of Santo Domingo, entered a vigorous protest and denunciation of the entire verdict. The lawsuit was therefore resumed, centering now about the question of jurisdiction over Darién; while the aspirations of the Admiral rose higher and higher as the contest progressed.

As early as 1508 proctors chosen to represent to the king the needs of the inhabitants of Hispaniola had requested that a judge of appeals be appointed to obviate the necessity of carrying lawsuits overseas to Spain.[24] At that time the crown was noncommittal, but three years later the council's verdict provided that judicial appeals should be carried from local *alcaldes* to the Admiral or his deputies, and thence to the king or to persons to whom the king gave jurisdiction over such appeals. In conformity with this decision, Ferdinand, in the autumn of the same year, established at Santo Domingo an *audiencia e juzgado de apelación* of three judges, the first institution of its kind in the New World, and one destined to play a dominant role in the government of the Spanish Indies.[25] Here was a new source of dispute and dissatisfaction for the

---

22 Governor Ovando, and Diego Columbus as his successor, had formerly been entrusted with the administration of *repartimientos*. Cf. letters of the king to Diego Columbus and to the treasurer-general, Miguel de Pasamonte, 14 and 15 August 1509, ibid. 1st ser., XXXI, 449; XXXIX, 188.

23 Solórzano, *Política indiana*, lib. III, cap. 5. As a matter of custom by the seventeenth century it had come to be exercised by most governors in the Indies. Cf. León Pinelo, *Tratado de confimaciones reales*, pt. I, caps. 6, 7.

24 *Col. doc. inéd.*, 1st ser., XXXII, 13.

25 Rodrigo de Aguiar y Acuña, 'Sumarios de la Recopilación de las Leyes de Indias,' tit. XIV, ley I, reprinted in Maúrtua, *Antecedentes de la Recopilación de Indias*, p. 218, gives reference to a cédula of Burgos, 6 October 1511. The first ordinances for this primitive American *audiencia* are dated 15 October 1511, *Col. doc. inéd.*, 1st ser., XI, 546. The first three justices were Marcelo de Villalobos, Juan Ortiz de Matienzo, and Lucas Vásquez de Ayllón. The tribunal had attached to it a proctor for poor suitors and a notary, but no bailiff (*alguacil*) or other officials.

Admiral. He protested not only against the creation of an *audiencia*, but against the allowance of any appeal from him in his judicial capacity as governor and viceroy even to the crown itself! If the judges must remain, at least let them serve as a sort of viceregal council and hear appeals jointly with him—an interesting anticipation of the relations between viceroy or president and *audiencia* in the next generation.[26]

The ordinances issued for the new tribunal in 1511 authorized it to take cognizance in first instance of suits to which the crown was a party (*casos de corte*), as was the rule later for all the American *audiencias*. When the Admiral protested that this was another infringement of his all-embracing privileges, the jurisdictions were made concurrent; yet conflicts between Diego Columbus and the judges seem to have been continuous throughout the former's lifetime. In a long memorial of December 1515, comprising some 42 chapters, Diego revived his most extreme claims to the absolute government of the Indies, from the exclusive administration of justice to the appointment of all officials in the New World. At the same time he revealed the endless sources of friction at Santo Domingo, whether due to jealousy of the king's officers for this 'Hispanicized Italian' whom chance had placed as viceroy over them, or to the favoritism and irregular practices of the Admiral and his followers.[27] To face his enemies' accusations and innuendoes and to press his suit before the royal council Diego was twice recalled to Spain, in 1515 and again in 1523. The first visit dragged through five weary years, in which the Admiral 'negoció poco e gastó mucho,' but in the end he received provisional recognition of his pretensions in a royal decree issued from Coruña on 17 May 1520, just three days before the young emperor's departure for Flanders. Diego was confirmed in his rights as governor and viceroy over the West Indian islands as laid down in the council's declaration of 1511, and a limited right of nomination to minor offices in the colonies was recognized. For certain municipal posts the Admiral and the judges of appeal were jointly to name three individuals from whom the crown would appoint one. The offices excepted, those of *alcalde, escribano,* and *procurador,* were reserved to the king or were to be filled by election in the *cabildos*. In other respects the restrictions imposed upon the viceroy's authority in 1511 were retained and reiterated. Appeals were to go as before from the local *alcaldes* to the viceroy or his deputy, thence to the *audiencia,* and ultimately to Spain; and the

---

26 'Testimonio de reclamación y protesta de D. Diego Colón,' etc., 29 December 1512, ibid. 2nd ser., VII, 232; 'Resumen de las peticiones del Almirante' etc., ibid. VIII, 236.

27 Cf. correspondence of the judges with the crown, February 1513, ibid. 1st ser., XXXIV, 155 ff., and August and October 1515, ibid. XXXVI, 372, 375, 430. The memorial of Diego Columbus is in the 2nd ser., VIII, 244-304.

Admiral's right to a tenth of royal taxes gathered in the Indies was again categorically denied.[28]

The question whether a viceroy in the New World was subject to the judicial process called the *residencia* was debated early in the history of Spanish colonial administration. The royal council in 1511 had declared that the crown might at any time order a *residencia* to be taken of the Admiral and his officials in conformity with the laws of Castile. This Diego had persistently denied, on the grounds that the procedure had not been applied to viceroys in Castile and León, and that his own office, moreover, was perpetual. In 1520 the formal immunity of the viceroy seems to have been tacitly admitted; but he was declared subject to investigation by *comisarios* appointed by the crown, upon whose report the king or his council would take appropriate action—which was merely the *residencia* under another name. And in fact from the very beginning this institution, developed by the Catholic kings as a means of control over the office of *corregidor* in Castile, was universal in Spanish American administrative practice, all public officials from the viceroys of Mexico and Peru to the ordinary municipal *alcaldes* submitting at the end of their term of office to the *residencia*.

The meager concessions of 1520 were as unsatisfactory to Diego Columbus as had been the council's declaration nine years earlier, and on 23 August, in Seville, just before sailing for the New World, he entered another formal protest and appeal from the decision. And so the dispute persisted, as a legal battle in Spain, and in America in the revival of the old quarrels with the treasury officials and the *audiencia*. As Diego's enemies became increasingly bitter, they accused him of unlawfully granting annuities payable by the colonial treasury, giving pardons and privileges for money, arrogating to himself as Admiral many cases which did not properly fall within the admiralty jurisdiction, and enforcing his disputed financial and judicial rights by means of decrees issued in the emperor's name and with the royal seal.[29] They left no stone unturned to create the impression, expressed by Lope de Conchillos, secre-

28 'Real provisión ordenando la forma en que se han proveer los oficios en Indias por resultado de la vista de los privilegios del Almirante en el pleito pendiente,' ibid. 2nd ser., VIII, 331 ff. Whether or not because of a confusion in the minds of the council, Diego's authority as Admiral is represented in the decree as extending to the islands and mainland, his powers as viceroy and governor to the islands only; yet the right of nomination to local offices and to one-tenth of the royal profits from mines, etc., presumably associated with his position as viceroy, were recognized as applying to the entire area of his admiralty jurisdiction. Whatever the explanation, the result could only be to make confusion worse confounded, and to confirm Diego in his determination to push his claims to their uttermost limit.

29 'Relación presentada por el fiscal de las cosas que se han innovado por el Almirante, después que llegó a las Indias contra lo que se solía y acostumbraba hacer y contra lo que está proveído por el Rey Católico y por S.M.,' 2 September 1524, ibid. 2nd ser., VIII, 361.

tary of King Ferdinand, some years before, when he felt constrained to call attention to the fact 'quel Rey e la Reyna, Nuestros Señores, son sus Señores naturales, e non el Almirante, como fasta aquí lo an creido allá algunos.' [30] Yet the Admiral must have felt that the decree of 1520 justified his insistence upon his high pretensions; and certainly the practice most resented, the issue of writs in the king's name, had been specifically enjoined upon him by Charles V at that time.

In 1523 Diego was summoned again to Spain to answer charges preferred against him by Lucas Vásquez de Ayllón, one of the judges of appeal who had himself returned to seek a concession for colonizing the coast of Carolina.[31] There the Admiral remained, following the court in vain efforts to secure a final vindication of his inherited rights. With the formal establishment of the Council of the Indies in August 1524, the lawsuit seems to have been pressed with renewed vigor, but no fresh developments occurred till after Diego's death, which took place at the village of Montalván near Toledo, 23 February 1526. He had ben viceroy of the Indies for fifteen years. His body was interred in the Carthusian monastery of Las Cuevas near Seville by the side of his father, whence both were later conveyed to Santo Domingo.

Some sixteen m   .ns after the Admiral's death, in June 1527, a committee of the new council formally withdrew the decisions of 1511 and 1520 and proceeded to judge the entire case *de novo;* [32] while Maria de Toledo, Diego's widow, journeyed to Spain to continue the suit in behalf of her eldest son, Don Luis, then five years of age. There was another lean interval of seven years, and in 1534 and 1535 the right of heirs of Christopher Columbus to the offices of admiral, viceroy, and governor in perpetuity was again recognized, with jurisdiction not only over the islands but also on the mainland coasts of Paria and Veragua which the Discoverer had been the first to explore. Still the Columbus family was dissatisfied, demanding virtually sovereign powers over all the western continent, until in June 1536, by the arbitration of Cardinal Loaysa, president of the Council of the Indies, and Dr. Gaspar de Montoya, of the Council of Castile, a compromise was effected. Don Luis might retain the title and privileges of Admiral of the Indies, but he renounced all other rights accorded to his house in return for a perpetual annuity of 10,000 ducats, the island of Jamaica in fief, and an estate of twenty-five

30 Ibid. 1st ser., XXXIV, 175.

31 Gonzalo Fernández de Oviedo, *Historia general y natural de las Indias,* 3 vols., Madrid, 1851, lib. IV, cap. 5; *Col. doc. inéd.,* 1st ser., XIII, 494.

32 'Sentencia declarando que . . . las sentencias y declaraciones y provisiones fechas y dadas en Sevilla y la Coruña . . . se dan por ningunas,' 25 June 1527, ibid. 2nd ser., VIII, 431.

square leagues on the Isthmus of Panama, with the titles of Duke of Veragua and Marquis of Jamaica.[33]

The labor of discovery, conquest, and settlement in Spanish America was from the time of Christopher Columbus pre-eminently the achievement of private enterprise. The individual or group that organized the venture made a *capitulación* or contract with the crown—often a negotiable instrument that might be sold or exchanged—in which were set down the rights reserved to the king in the new territories to be occupied, and the privileges conceded to the participants in recompense for their investment and the personal risks involved. Very rarely did the king contribute to the cost of the undertaking. The *concessionaire* might be the military leader of the expedition, but sometimes as in the case of the Welsers in Venezuela, was merely the impresario or organizer. In any case the *capitulación* constituted a kind of primitive charter for the newly established community.

The founders and early governors of new colonies on the islands and mainland frequently bore the title of *adelantado*. Apparently the first to be promised it by the crown was Juan Ponce de León in 1512, as a reward for his projected discovery of the land of 'Bimini.' Pedro de Alvarado received it as *conquistador* in Guatemala, as did Pedro de Mendoza, who brought out the first European colony to the Rio de la Plata, and Francisco de Montejo in Yucatan—to cite only a few instances. Of the seventy or more individuals who in the sixteenth century contracted with the crown to subdue or colonize new areas in America, the rank of *adelantado* was vouchsafed to somewhat less than half.[34]

The office of *adelantado* was an old one, belonging to the medieval polity of Castile. At least from the time of Alfonso X its incumbent was a kind of royal deputy placed over an extensive territory and endowed

---

33 Ibid. 2nd ser., VII, vi-xii. Don Luis returned to Santo Domingo in 1540 with the title of captain-general, and remained there till 1551—but by virtue of a royal appointment, not by hereditary right. He evidently inherited the contentious spirit of his father, and lawsuits touching one point or another of the settlement of 1536 continued till the accession to the Spanish throne of Philip II. In 1556, after ineffectual attempts to colonize the province of Veragua, Don Luis was constrained to abandon everything but the honorary titles of duke and admiral for an additional pension of 7,000 ducats. His case had without doubt been weakened in the Council of the Indies by the scandals of his private life, and after several polygamous marriages he was imprisoned and eventually condemned to exile in the penal settlement of Orán. There he died in Februray 1572. His nephew Diego, fourth Admiral of the Indies and second Duke of Veragua, was the last of the Columbus family in the direct male line.

34 R. R. Hill, 'The Office of *adelantado*,' *Polit. Sci. Quart.*, XXVIII, 654-5. Actually the first *adelantado* in America was Bartholomew Columbus, to whom the office and title were granted by the Discoverer in 1497 (Herrera, dec. I, lib. 2, cap. 15, referred to by Hill, 652). The crown was somewhat annoyed by this assumption of authority by the Discoverer, but ratified the appointment.

with civil and judicial functions. He was charged with the supervision of public order, and with keeping the king informed of conditions within his territory, and he reviewed judicial cases appealed from lesser magistrates. But in the age of the *Reconquista,* there were also *adelantados de frontera,* military and civil governors of frontier towns or districts, holding their outposts against the infidel Moslems. The *adelantado de frontera* was a sort of *Markgraf* or count of the march, the direct representative of the king, who because of his exposed position, and in return for services rendered, was entrusted with very extensive military, executive, and judicial powers. In later times, after the *Reconquista,* the office fell into disuse. But the title persisted as an honorary one in certain noble families, down to the time of the discovery of America.

With the Discovery, it is interesting to observe, this medieval office was revived in the New World. For these newer regions overseas were now the frontier of Castile. In fact this new frontier was thrust upon the Castilians just at the moment when the Moorish frontier completely disappeared in the peninsula, with the capture of Granada by the armies of Ferdinand and Isabella in 1492. The distant American frontier, then, required to be settled and defended; it was exposed to dangers from the infidel as was the Christian frontier in medieval Castile. And as the office of *adelantado* had been used to stimulate the conquest of the Iberian Peninsula from the Moslems, so it now served to stimulate discovery and conquest beyond the Atlantic.

The dignity of *adelantado* in America was granted for one or two lives, or sometimes in perpetuity. Early patents expressly stated that its powers and prerogatives were to be the same as those of *adelantados* of Castile. It carried with it the governorship of the territory subdued, with proprietary rights, which also was often transmissible by inheritance to a second generation. The *adelantado* enjoyed certain special privileges, such as the receipt of a specified income out of the revenues of the province, the assignment of a great landed estate within the area, and sometimes a monopoly of trading and fishing rights, as well as exemption for life from sundry taxes such as the *alcabala* and the *almojarifazgo.* He had authority to nominate certain municipal and ecclesiastical officials, and the privilege of distributing land and water rights as well as *encomiendas* of Indians among the soldiers and settlers who helped to found the colony.[35] To what degree these powers and privileges accrued to him as *adelantado,* or as governor, is not always clear, for the two offices were evidently regarded as separate and distinct; and yet many colonial impresarios who were not *adelantados* were granted in the royal capitulations much the same authority. Apparently an *adelantado* was held to be in somewhat more ample measure the direct representative of the

---

35 According to the *Ordenanzas . . . para los nuevos descubrimientos, conquistas y pacificaciones* of 1573, the *adelantado* might choose an *encomienda* for himself in the neighborhood of each new Spanish settlement. *Col. doc inéd.,* 1st ser., XVI, 160.

sovereign. In return he usually bore the entire cost of the enterprise,[36] and was required to transport to America a stated number of settlers, together with at least two qualified priests or friars, and to establish within a specified time two or more towns and forts. Over the latter he was usually appointed perpetual *alcalde,* and he sometimes received by separate patent the posts of captain-general and high sheriff or *alguacil mayor.*[37]

These extended powers and privileges were granted by the crown to compensate for the contribution, personal and pecuniary, which the impresario made to the expense and labor of conquest and settlement. It created a sort of temporary lordship or seigniory, somewhat analogous to that of the colonial proprietor in the English colonies or to the captain donatory in colonial Brazil. And it was used by the crown as the cheapest and surest means of bringing about the reduction and colonization of its far-flung transatlantic dominions. Thus the great conquests in America were achieved at little or not direct cost to the sovereign. Adventurers avid of fame and fortune amid the seemingly boundless opportunities afforded by a new world, ambitious to carve out a manorial or semifeudal domain based upon royal patent and their own strong right arm, made contracts with the king, or very occasionally with his representative in America, and bore alone the burden of financing and organizing projects of empire of which the crown in the end was to be the chief if not the sole beneficiary.

The *adelantados* were of significance only for the early period of Spanish settlement in the sixteenth century. Most of them survived but a few years, and their career was often a short and violent one. Many of them were killed in wars with the Indians, or assassinated by turbulent and envious associates, or deprived of authority by the crown because of royal jealousy of their influence in the colony they had created, sometimes after long and bitter lawsuits. Few of them transmitted the office to their heirs. As in the case of the viceroyalty of Columbus, the sovereigns were ever fearful of the overweening independence of their powerful subjects overseas, determined to consolidate in America the nascent absolutism of Castile; and once the initial steps of conquest and settlement were achieved, they speedily limited or revoked the authority and privileges earlier granted. Sooner or later a royal governor was appointed who was removable at the pleasure of the crown, and the colony was administered as a royal rather than as a proprietary province.[38] And

---

36 The more important of those who took service with the *adelantado* in the expedition, however, generally supplied their own horses and equipment, and some of them might contribute companies of soldier-colonists at their own expense.

37 Hill, *loc. cit.* 661.

38 For an excellent discussion of the matters reviewed in the preceding paragraphs, see Robert S. Chamberlain, 'Spanish Methods of Conquest and Colonization in Yucatan, 1527-1500,' *The Scientific Monthly,* XLIX, 227-44, 351-9.

so, the claims of the Columbus family finally disposed of, and new provinces created one by one on the mainland from Mexico and New Galicia in North America to Chile and Paraguay in South America, the crown was able before the middle of the sixteenth century to erect two vast political entities in the New World, the viceroyalty of New Spain, established in 1535, and that of Peru, organized in 1544.

II

❧❧❧

Race and Environment

❧❧❧

EL PUEBLO CONQUISTADOR

The Spaniards of the fifteenth and sixteenth centuries had acquired certain national idiosyncrasies which were exemplified in the conquest and occupation of the New World, and which are explained at least in part by their history and environment. No part of Europe had suffered more from the shock of conquest or felt the impact of more diverse races and cultures than had the peninsula of Spain.

In ancient times, after the Punic Wars, with the expansion of Roman imperialism in the Mediterranean, the peninsula was slowly conquered by Roman armies, and became one of the most distinguished and flourishing of the Roman provinces. With the disintegration of the empire in the fifth century, the peninsula was invaded by Vandals and Visgoths, and a rude Germanic kingdom was imposed on a Celt-Iberian and Roman population, which lasted nearly three hundred years, until it was overthrown by a Moslem horde from across the Straits of Gibraltar in the year 711.

During the next twenty years Arabs and Berbers subdued virtually the whole peninsula, and extended their power beyond the Pyrenees into Aquitaine and Provence. The Moslem capital, Córdova, became the center of a civilization which rivaled that of Damascus and Bagdad.

A Christian remnant, however, in the mountains of Astrurias and Galicia soon found their highland valleys too narrow for their abounding warlike energies. A struggle began with the conquering Moslems which continued at intervals for five hundred years, from the middle of the eighth to the middle of the thirteenth century. From one generation to another the military frontier swayed back and forth, but in the long run the advantage lay with the Christians.

Meanwhile behind the battle line small semifeudal, Christian states were taking shape: Portugal in the west, León-Castile in the center, and Aragon in the east. In parallel columns their armies pressed southward, until by 1248 the decaying Moslem power was confined to the small kingdom of Granada. There it survived for 250 years, till driven across the straits into North Africa by Ferdinand and Isabella in 1492, the year of the discovery of America.

In the early history of the Iberian Peninsula, therefore, even more than in the rest of western Europe, the chief interests had been war and religion. The five centuries of struggle between Christians and Moslems, an almost continuous crusade against the infidel, had engendered a vigorous military spirit and love for an irregular and venturesome mode of life—together with something of a contempt for the less spectacular peacetime arts, which could safely be left to the Mors and Jews; also, in the crusade against the Moslems, an ideal of religious solidarity that was easily transformed into intolerance and fanaticism.

In other respects the Castilian people furnished excellent material for the pioneer work of exploration and settlement. Except in the far south, most of the peninsula was a high plateau with a somewhat rigorous climate and a none too productive soil. These conditions produced a sober, robust race, endowed with endurance and tenacity, to whom the opportunity for wealth and adventure abroad made a peculiarly strong appeal. At the same time the national temper displayed a hardness that sometimes amounted to cruelty, as well as a certain intellectual indolence which perhaps in part explains the exaggerated attachment to tradition.

Nevertheless intellectual life in Spain had been vastly enriched by the mingling of races and cultures—Roman, Visigothic, Hebrew, and Moslem. The University of Salamanca, founded in 1215, was one of the earliest in Europe, and shared with Oxford, Paris, and Bologna the distinction of being one of the great centers of medieval learning. Spain made important contributions to medicine, mathematics, astronomy, and physics, and the first two centuries of Spanish settlement in America saw the foundation of numerous colleges and universities both in the colonies and in the mother country. The celebrated University of Alcalá de Henares (moved in the nineteenth century to Madrid) was established by Cardinal Jiménez de Cisneros in 1508, and produced the famous edition of the Bible known as the Complutensian Polyglot. These same centuries also comprised the Golden Age of Spanish literature and art. Writers of diverse temperament and interests, from Fray Luis de León to Cervantes, and from Lope de Vega to Gracian, adorned the intellectual life of their time and had a profound influence upon the literature and thought of neighboring nations. El Greco Velázquez, Ribera, and Murillo were painters whose work made a deep impact upon later generations. Theologians and jurists of Spain—Vitoria, Suárez, Vázquez— were pioneers in the realm of international jurisprudence.

The astounding fact of the discovery of a new world impinged very slowly on the imagination of intellectuals and men of letters. It made in the beginning no appeal at all to the upper aristocracy of Spain, who took little or no part in the expeditions of discovery and colonization that followed on the heels of Columbus. Secure in their lands, honors, and privileges at home, they did not feel the call to adventure either as leaders or as financial backers. They did come out later, when the burden and heat of conquest were over, as viceroys and governors, and many after a few years returned home, like the Anglo-Indian nabobs of a later century to England. As has been noted before, the conquest and occupation of Spanish America was a work 'eminently popular' in character. In nearly every instance it reflected private, individual initiative and effort, rather than official action by the state.[1] By and large the Spaniards who came to America were a race of warriors, legists, peasants, and priests. Members of the gentry, soldier adventurers, missionary friars, and younger sons of the nobility made up the personnel of the early colonizing enterprises, and they comprised the greater number of the emigrants later on.

It has been remarked that more than all the other peoples of the modern world the Spaniards of the sixteenth century displayed the characteristics of the ancient Romans. They revealed in the conquest and settlement of America the same courage and enterprise, the same military qualities, the same patience under hardship, that distinguished Roman soldiers and colonists in the times of Scipio Africanus and Julius Caesar. And like the Romans they were pre-eminently creators of laws and builders of institutions. Of all the colonizing peoples of modern times, the Spaniards were the most legal-minded. They speedily developed in the new empire a meticulously organized administrative system such as the world had rarely seen. And the famous *Recopilación de leyes de los reynos de las Indias,* promulgated in 1680, in spite of defects visible to the wider experience of a later day, remains one of the most notable documents of modern colonial legislation.

At the same time it must be admitted that, with all their great martial and legalistic qualities, the Spaniards had not emerged, as Brooks Adams has said, from the 'imaginative' period. They had not developed the economic type. In Spain the soldier, the legist, and the priest reigned supreme, at a time when the mercantile and skeptical type had begun to predominate in the other nations of western Europe. Spaniards showed the same incapacity for industrial development and for the higher branches of finance, the same intellectual rigidity, that characterized the imperial Romans. There was little attainment in agriculture or trades. And so Spain, possessed of the richest and most magnificent colonial empire in the world's history, for a time declined, as Rome declined, from internal decay. Without a flourishing industry and the means of maintaining and increasing an active commerce—unable to retain therefore the control of the sea—the empire spread over two continents

---

1 José María Ots Capdequi, *El Estado español en las Indias,* Mexico, 1941, 15-16, 21.

became ultimately an economic and military liability rather than an asset.

In the eighteenth century, under a new dynasty, exposed to the influences of eighteenth-century rationalism, and guided by a series of distinguished and patriotic statesmen who were imbued with the economic ideas and principles prevalent in England and France, Spain recovered some of the ground she had lost. At the close of the colonial era the Spanish empire was more prosperous, and more profitable to the mother country, than it had ever been before. Intellectual activity in the American colonies was greater than ever before; the newer scientific ideas and methods of Europe were penetrating the universities. In spite of the strength of the scholastic tradition, there were a number of scholars who gradually emancipated science from theology and began to cultivate it in an independent manner. The laws barring all foreigners from the Indies were greatly relaxed in practice. Distinguished foreign scientists were sometimes invited to visit the Spanish American provinces, under official auspices—Frenchmen, Italians and Germans—as explorers, mining experts, and naturalists. But the very progress and increasing well-being of the colonies made for discontent. The leading men among the colonists, inspired by the political philosophy of the revolutions in France and North America, desirous of the wealth that would flow from complete liberty of trade with the world at large, and ambitious for self-government to the exclusion of all European interference or control, seized the opportunity offered by the Napoleonic invasion of Spain to strike for home rule. It was a manifestation of that same spirit of regionalistic independence that has been a constant factor in Spanish history from the Middle Ages to the present day, and that Spain's sons carried with them overseas to the new communities in America.

The history of European colonization does not begin with the discovery of America. There was colonization in ancient and in medieval times, by the Phoenicians, Greeks, and Romans, and by the Teutonic peoples and the Crusaders. But there were important and obvious differences between colonial enterprise preceding the Discovery and that which followed. The former was confined to the shores of the Mediterranean and the Baltic seas, it was carried on among allied races, in a similar climate, and at a short distance from the home base. Modern colonization presented entirely new problems. It took place at great distances from the metropolis, which made communications slow and often dangerous. It encountered new and strange conditions of environment, often a crudely tropical climate, and relationship with curious and uncongenial races. Greater opportunity was offered for mutual misunderstanding, contempt, and open hostility. At the same time exploitation of the economic possibilities of the newly occupied lands often involved the necessity of reducing these 'inferior' native races to serfdom or slavery.

In America, therefore, lay an immense area isolated for ages from Europe and Asia, virtually unexploited, inhabited by aborigines relatively few in number and still in a state of savagery or barbarism, unable to present effective resistance to the European invaders. Here was an opportunity to establish new homes, new societies overseas, in an environment relatively free from the social restrictions and inhibitions of the older societies in Europe.

Historically speaking, European colonies in the New World in the sixteenth and seventeenth centuries may be divided into two general classes, which have been designated by some economists as farm colonies and exploitation colonies.[2] A brief consideration of their significance may serve as a useful background to a study of the institutions of the Spanish empire in America and will make clear that physical or geographical circumstances in the New World, and the kind of natives found there, conditioned the formation of settlements and to some extent the types of society created. It will help also to account for the kinds of institutions developed, or at least for the spirit in which these institutions were permitted to function. And it will go far to explain the difficulties encountered by the authorities in Spain in governing so vast an area three thousand miles distant from the center of political control.

The 'farm colonies' were generally established in regions that produced the same commodities as were produced in Europe, i.e., they were situated in the temperate zone. They possessed no special advantage in the way of producing exports for which there was a large European demand, whether by agriculture or by mining. Many of them were, therefore, founded by settlers who were anxious chiefly to find a refuge from the political and social discontents in the home country. These settlers came out not primarily to produce or acquire wealth; exportable products were a secondary objective. They were content with the satisfaction of moderate wants. Such colonies were most of those established by the English in North America, and to some extent those created by the Spaniards in Chile and Buenos Aires, and by the Portuguese in southern Brazil.

The 'exploitation colonies,' on the other hand, were nearly always situated in the tropics, or in regions rich in mineral wealth; areas, that is to say, which produced commodities not easily obtainable in Europe, or to be had only in small quantities; commodities moreover, for the production of which the soil and climate, or the geological formation, of these colonies presented peculiar advantages. There the industry of the settlers was turned primarily to the production and export of a few staple articles: sugar, cotton, indigo, gold, and silver; the impulse to colonization was chiefly economic, the accumulation of wealth. Such were practically all the tropical colonies on the continent, whether Span-

---

2 Albert Galloway Keller, *Colonization*, Boston, 1908, 4 ff.

ish, Portuguese, or English; all the European establishments in the West Indies; and the great mining communities of Peru, Mexico, and New Granada on the Spanish American mainland.

Out of these differing economic conditions naturally developed different types of society, as expressed in the systems of landholding and in social and political organization. The typical property in the temperate farm colony was the small freehold, developing out of the clearing made in the forest by the more or less isolated pioneer. In the exploitation colony, whose commodities were few in number, and where production became highly specialized and therefore soon established on a capitalistic basis, a start was generally made with a larger unit of land, and the great estate became the prevalent form of landholding—estates often owned to absentee proprietors, and therefore managed by stewards. In most of the English colonies of North America where the system of great proprietors was tried, it soon failed; and it was scarcely more successful in the Spanish communities established in the temperate zone, except possibly in Chile.

There were, as might be expected, consequent differences in social organization. In the exploitation colonies an ample supply of common labor was an absolute necessity. Europeans were too few in number to supply the needed labor, or they were deterred from it by the tropical climate. If the Europeans *could* not work, the natives generally *would* not, for a foreign master. The result was compulsion. As a matter of fact, all such colonies secured their labor by forcible means—either from within the colony, by reducing the original inhabitants to a condition of serfdom, or from outside by importing Negro slaves from Africa. Exploitation or plantation colonies in the past have regularly been the seats of human slavery, open or disguised, whether on the English islands in the West Indies, among the mines of Peru and Mexico, or in Africa in the nineteenth century.

In the areas the Spaniards chiefly settled in America—central Mexico, Guatemala, the Andes—they found an aboriginal population in an agricultural, sedentary stage of development, living in cities and towns with public edifices of stone, trained to regular industry, and possessing a relatively advanced political and religious organization. At the time of the Spaniards' arrival these Indians were scarcely civilized, it is true; they still lived largely in the stone age, with no coined money and with a very rudimentary kind of writing; but they had attained a level on the brink of 'civilization.' They were skilful hoe-culture farmers, who terraced and irrigated their lands and cultivated corn, beans, potatoes, squash, cotton, and other crops. Such a population could easily be reduced to the status of a dependent laboring class, parcelled out among the conquerors to work in mines and factories, or attached to the soil like the peasantry in medieval Europe. Moreover, as the cultural levels of these semicivilized Indians and their European conquerors were not very widely separated, and as the number of women among the immigrants was small, interracial unions were frequent, and a large intermediate mestizo class soon made its appearance. Immigrants, moreover, were not attracted to a community of landlords and serfs, and the natural increase of the white population was slow.

Under such circumstances, a servile laboring population on large estates and a mestizo proletariat led naturally to the creation of a system of castes or classes, and to the concentration of wealth in the hands of a few, that is, to an aristocratic type of society repeating the extremes of social gradation found in the Old World. This was the case in the wealthier Spanish colonies, and also in the English colonies of the West Indies; and it was all the easier, of course, inasmuch as the European societies from which the colonists came were still semifeudal in organization and social and legal traditions.

The gold and silver mines of Spanish America constituted one of the principal reasons for the divergence between Spanish and English colonial life—the immense stores of minerals easily available and of the sort most valued. They made European society in the Spanish colonies one of great wealth and luxury, and intensified the aristocratic character of that society. They account for the sharp contrast between the opulence and splendor of Lima, or Potosí, or Mexico City, and the frugal simplicity of Philadelphia or New York in the eighteenth century.

These conditions were reversed in the colonies of the temperate zone. Here there was no specialization in products, and therefore no exploitation of labor. The forest and prairie Indians, moreover, were relatively few in number, and in a low stage of barbarism. Far less advanced in agriculture than the plateau Indians of Mexico and Peru, they lived chiefly by hunting and fishing, with no regular habits of industry, yet were fierce fighters, proud and stubborn. It was not practicable to make serfs of them, or to extract regular labor; and so the Indians were slowly exterminated, or they retired to the mountains and woods of the remote interior.

In the temperate colonies, which happened to be largely English, the laboring classes therefore remained more nearly European and the population in general more homogeneous. Immigrants were not deterred by the presence of servile labor in the community, and were largely drawn from the middle classes at home: small farmers, artisans, and middle-class burgesses. Under the Stuarts, when English colonization really began, settlers went out as a rule not to seek mines, or to exploit inferior races, or to set up trading stations (as did the Dutch and French), but to establish themselves as independent farmers, and they generally took their women with them. Rather than to the West Indies, they went mostly to the northern colonies, regions that did not produce the colonial staples, but where land was cheap, where climate and farm products were the same as in England, and where labor was white and respected. Small holdings and an abundance of land made men independent of the landlord or employer. Rents were low and wages high, for labor was at a premium, and there was consequently neither depressing poverty nor much luxury. Although social gradations of course existed, resting upon differences of wealth and breeding, conditions were little fitted for the development of a real aristocracy. The trend was to an equalitarian society, to democratic institutions.

These observations apply to a considerable degree to the Spanish communities in the temperate zone as well as to the English. In the region of the Rio de la Plata, where climate and other physical conditions were much like those encountered in Europe, and where the prairie Indians were few and warlike, the population remained more generally white, but relatively poor, without the extremes of wealth found in Peru and Mexico, and it displayed a disposition to a more equalitarian form of society. In short, when the Spaniards settled in regions analogous to those of the English mainland communities, the type of colonization, in spite of great differences of political organization, approximated more nearly that found in the latter. It remains true, however, that no other European nation could rival England in the quantity of its colonists of pure European stock, and in the 'domestic quality' of the emigrants.

In the temperate farm colonies, consequently, there was usually a more general spread of elementary education, but less care for the higher branches of learning; a strong sentiment of individual independence, self-reliance, but often a lack of the refinements of courtesy in the upper classes or of inherited loyalty in the poorer classes. In a sense they were closer to the frontier. The characteristics of the wealthy plantation or mining colonies were just the opposite: a highly sophisticated, courtly society, given to extravagance and display, and below the surface often tainted with cruelty and libertinism; a society achieving all the outward signs of opulence, imposing public buildings, universites and hosptals, magnificent churches and monasteries, but founded upon the exploitation of inferior races.

Economic differences were also a reason for some tendency to political divergence. The colonies of the temperate zone, producing a variety of commodities like those in Europe, mostly necessaries of life for local consumption, were economically more independent. They could survive without much outside aid, and not being of a capitalistic exploitation type, they were frequently allowed to do so. The exploitation colony, however, specialized in the production of one or two staples for export, was in greater economic dependence on the outside world for the trade to which they gave rise; a circumstance which meant in those days dependence upon the mother country. And economic dependence spelled political dependence. These communities, because of their vast exploitable resources, were as a rule more constantly subject to interference, regulation, by the metropolis than were the temperate colonies, and were therefore given less opportunity to gain political experience and training in self-government. Such was the situation of most of the Spanish provinces in America. Although the Castilian monarchy from the outset was prepared to create in the New World a paternalistic despotism, which implied also the organization of society along the aristocratic lines prevalent in Spain, much the same development would probably have taken place had the political tendencies been, as in England and in Aragon, in the direction of popular control.

It is true that national policy was also a determining factor. The Spanish American empire was founded at a time when Ferdinand and Isabella were laying the bases of absolute monarchy in Castile. In the New World they found a clear field in which they and their successors could establish the royal authority without let or hindrance. All powers were vested in the crown, and were exercised directly by royal ordinances and decrees, or through the viceroy and other royal officials. State and Church were closely united, and the ecclesiastical power was almost equal to the civil. The Church was an immense and omnipresent force, with great influence over the masses of the people, in a society saturated with clericalism. Yet it too was ultimately responsible to, and controlled by, the crown, and became merely another instrument of royal despotism. Lucrative posts in Church and State were ordinarily reserved to European Spaniards, and from the outset a close watch was kept on emigration. In contrast to England, which never made an effort to sift prospective colonists, Spanish emigration was put through a fine-meshed sieve to keep out undesirables. The motives were religious, to maintain purity of the Faith; economic, to deny to foreigners access to American wealth, and therefore to any direct knowledge about the American empire; and social, to keep the standards of colonization high.

The English colonies, in contrast to the Spanish, were left in the main to govern themselves. The English, as Sir John Seeley has said, 'seemed to have conquered and peopled half the world in a fit of absence of mind.'[3] There was nearly everywhere some kind of colonial assembly, and a local assembly of town or country; and justice was popularly administered by juries. Representative government was seldom expressly granted in the early colonial charter. It was assumed by the colonists as a matter of right, and possibly it was so assumed by the authorities at home. As in the beginning of Spanish colonization, settlements were generally founded by private 'adventurers' at their own risk and expense, and broad economic and political rights were conceded in first instance

---

3 *The Expansion of England*, London, 1883, 8.

to the proprietors, as they were to the *adelantados* in Spanish America. But disputes arose between colonists and proprietors, or between the latter and the crown. The rights of the proprietors were apt to be ignored, and except in a few instances, their government soon disappeared and the colonies were thrown back upon the king.

Royal governors sent out from England, however, on the whole interfered little with the power of the colonists to regulate their own affairs. No thought was seriously entertained of creating in America the elements of aristocracy or of a state church as understood in the Old World. Virginia was the only province in which the Church of England was established, and there it received little support and rapidly decayed. The Puritans enjoyed undisturbed their peculiar notions of ecclesiastical government, and when they expelled dissenters from the colony England took no steps to interfere. And if the crown did occasionally assert its prerogatives, it generally provoked resistance and only emphasized the general adherence to principles of self-government. The chief ambition of the English Government was to regulate the trade of the colonies in the imperial interest. Only in this respect were the ultramarine provinces fenced round with restrictions and watched with increasing jealousy.

It is always well to keep in mind, however, that in the English plantation colonies on the West Indian islands, where economic conditions were similar to those in tropical Spanish America, an aristocratic and often improvident planter class soon appeared supported by Negro slavery, and as the number of slaves increased there was less and less room for the small freeholder. Royal governors sent out from England exercised more authority, and the colonists generally less, in the regulation of local affairs. In short, government and society tended to assume forms analogous to those in New Spain and Peru.[4]

A more extended comparison between Spanish and English colonization in the New World may not be without significance and interest. The Spaniards and the English, as already intimated, have historically speaking been the great empire-builders of modern times—that is, in the age of the Renaissance and since. And by and large they have been the most successful colonists. The Dutch were never more than traders, although they acquired what ultimately came to be a great territorial empire in the East Indies; an empire, however, which was never colonized in the sense that America was colonized, and which could not be because it was already occupied by teeming millions of Orientals far advanced in civilization. The French for a short time in the eighteenth century possessed extensive territories in North America, but they showed no inclination to leave home in large numbers to settle these empty

---

4 Cf. Lowell J. Ragatz, *The Fall of the Planter Class in the British Caribbean, 1763-1833*, New York, 1928, 3-36.

spaces, and they contributed little to the development of effective or significant institutions of government in the New World. The English and the Spaniards, however—and Spain's cousins, the Portuguese—did subdue, occupy, and administer effectively vast virgin areas, and gave the impress of their race and their civilization to a galaxy of nations which today play an increasingly important role in world affairs.

The motives for colonization were much the same in both peoples, whatever nationalistic writers in one country or the other may have said to the contrary. The desire for *adventure* was obvious enough, and as a rule came earliest in point of time. It was a motive, however, that influenced individuals rather than governments or corporations, and as such need not detain us. Elizabethan England produced its generations of explorers, treasure hunters, and pirates, as did sixteenth-century Spain.

The *desire for wealth,* on the part of both of those who emigrated to America and of those in the government at home, is equally obvious, and was shared by Englishmen and Spaniards alike. Except for the discovery of vast stores of the precious metals, the Spanish occupation of America would doubtless have been much slower than it actually turned out to be. As it was, Spain sent out colonists in larger numbers than did any other European country except England: younger sons of the aristocracy, prevented by the rules of primogeniture in a stereotyped Old-World society from sharing the patrimony of their elder brothers; merchants and artisans who hoped to improve their lot in new countries where land and opportunity were more plentiful than in the crowded towns and villages of Europe.

But it also impelled the governments and the merchant princes at home to encourage and support colonization by every means in their power, and led to system and permanence in colonial undertakings. The desire to obtain a more abundant supply of goods than was earlier available, especially the luxuries supplied by tropical and subtropical lands, and to make a profit therefrom, induced the formation of merchant gilds, chartered companies, and the development of other forms of cooperative enterprise. In a mercantilist era considerations of commerce, goods, and markets were always a principal objective. Before the nineteenth century, however, they furnished a preponderant motive only in the acquisition of tropical colonies and of areas rich in mines, especially mines of gold and silver. Since then they have been an even more compelling motive: in the imperialism of the nineteenth and twentieth centuries when industrialized Europe, no longer able to feed and clothe itself, was forced to depend upon the wheat and corn, the beef, mutton, and wool, of newer countries overseas.

Yet before the nineteenth century as well, the desire for wealth—for more direct access to and control of sources of tropical luxuries and precious metals—formed a principal incentive to exploration and settlement, whether by the sons of Spain or of England. This in turn disclosed fresh tropical areas and new products, and introduced new luxuries which soon became necessities. It also brought great riches to the nations that controlled these new areas, and stirred other nations to compete for them, as evidenced by the long series of colonial wars which characterized the age under review.

A third motive of colonization was without question the *zeal for propaganda*—religious propaganda, and in a sense 'political' propaganda as well—the zeal of European peoples to impose their modes of civilization upon as large a part of the world as possible. It first took the more obvious form of religious proselytism, and was especially evident in the fine crusading spirit of the Spanish and Portuguese missionaries in the New World, from California and New Mexico in the north to Chile and Paraguay in the south. It appears also in French America, in the explorations and ministrations of the Jesuits in the valleys of the St. Lawrence, the Mississippi, and the Great Lakes. It was a motive—this of religious conversion of the natives—least apparent in the colonization by the English and the Dutch, among whom, except in a few individual cases, the missionary motive was strangely absent. The Puritans with all their intense religious earnestness, their desire to establish a new society on a scriptural basis, were content to trade with the natives but made no very serious effort to civilize or convert them. In this splendid endeavor Spain everywhere stood supreme, as the ruins of Spanish mission stations on every American frontier today attest. The story of the Spanish and Portuguese missionaries in America, their self-sacrifice, heroism, and martyrdom, is an epic which has few if any parallels in the history of western Christendom.

A very important motive of emigration to and settlement in the New World was *discontent* with conditions, political, social, and religious, in the older societies of Europe. In a sense this motive underlies and conditions all the other reasons that have been suggested for the colonizing impulse. The military adventurer, the soldier of fortune, the disinherited younger son, the missionary enthusiast were all imbued with a discontent, divine or mundane, with life as they found it at home. But apart from this personal or individual discontent—which may be interpreted as ambition to do or be something more than was afforded them by the limited opportunity of the communities in which they had been born and raised—there was active dissatisfaction with the political and religious and social institutions of the old country, and the impulse to fly away to distant lands where they might create a society in accord with their own desires. Often they were forced by active persecution—because they refused to conform to the social and religious standards of the majority—to seek refuge in the vast open stretches of America, where they hoped to find an escape from the long arm of the government or of the Church at home.

This impulse was less apparent in the colonizing of the Spanish empire in America than in that of English America. The religious motive was obvious enough in the first settlement of New England, in the theocracy of the Puritans of Massachusetts and Connecticut, and in the founding of Rhode Island by Roger Williams. Religious convictions also had an influence in the planting of the colony of Maryland by Sir George Calvert, and of Pennsylvania by the Quakers. In both Spain and England there was active persecution of religious non-conformists; but whereas the English crown permitted religious dissenters to live and worship as they liked in its distant American provinces, the Spanish crown, more logical and consistent in its determination to enforce conformity, immediately applied in the new communities overseas the same rigid orthodoxy it demanded in Europe. Jews, Moors, and heretics were from the very beginning—from the days of Christopher Columbus—excluded from the New World. And while some managed to slip through the fine meshes of the net set for them at the seaports of Spain, and many managed to live unmolested in the loosely organized communities of the American frontier, life at best for them was almost as uncertain and dangerous as it had been at home, and at any moment they might be subjected to a bitter persecution.

Political discontent, too, drove many Englishmen as colonists to America during the seventeenth-century struggles between crown and Commons in Great Britain. But these struggles had no counterpart in the Spain of those days; the disturbing notion of the sovereignty of the people was not to be heard there for many generations. Spaniards were suffused with a loyalty to king and Church—and the two ideas were inextricably bound together—which was perhaps without parallel among the nations of Europe, and which helps to account for the ease with which the Spanish crown held together so vast a territorial empire for three centuries. Even during the wars of independence in Spanish America, a great part of the population retained its traditional loyalty to the crown, and at most could be galvanized only into fitful outbursts of resistance against it. The wars of independence were essentially civil wars—Spanish Americans fought on both sides of the conflict—and as in the case of most of the great revolutions of the world's history, they were the work of an active, energetic, determined radical minority.

Yet even to Spanish America in the sixteenth and seventeenth centuries came many restless and discontented elements who were led to prefer an uncertain future in distant lands to the established order into which they had been born at home. Spanish *conquistadores* obtained from the crown permission to carve out new provinces on the frontier, which they undertook to settle and fortify, on condition that they became governors for life with certain large perquisites in the way of lands, Indians, and the right to nominate local officials. Here they hoped to live as great, independent feudal barons, the lords of all they surveyed, ruling arbitrarily over the fortunes of the colonists beneath them, often disposing at will of the resources of the royal patrimony, and so far removed in space and time from the authorities in Spain that they need fear no effective interference. Such were certainly the motives of a Pedro de Valdivia in Chile, or of a Juan de Oñate in New Mexico, or of a Francisco de Montejo in Yucatan.

Nor did these considerations move merely the great *conquistadores,* founders of modern states and provinces. Men of lesser fame and ambition might, for instance through the possession of *encomiendas* of Indians in distant mountain valleys, acquire a relatively large opulence, and enjoy a similar freedom from the restraints and inhibitions of an Old-World society. And the same exhilarating prospect of escape from supervision and restraint might induce royal officials, and even the clergy, to seek posts or benefices in the colonies, where they could cast the conventional moralities to the four winds and live in a world more in accord with their own sweet but selfish desires.

All of the circumstances enumerated above serve as a significant background for the study of the organization and functioning of Spanish colonial society in America. As we remarked at the outset, they help to account for the kinds of institutions that developed and the spirit in which they were administered. And they also account for many of the problems with which the Spanish crown had constantly to contend in governing its far-flung ultramarine empire.

It was the circumstances of environment in the New World, both physical and racial, that explain in large measure the growth of an extravagant, sophisticated but fascinating colonial society in Mexico and Peru, based upon the possession of mines or huge estates and upon the exploitation of human labor, and perpetuated by the purchase of *mayorazgos* and titles of nobility. They also explain the more democratic societies of Buenos Aires and Paraguay, with their greater economic equality and their spirit of independence, but prevailing provincialism and rusticity. They serve to interpret the concentration of interest by the Spanish crown on the tropical and mining regions, and the close political supervision and regulation exercised over all that concerned them; just as they explain, at least in part, the consistent official neglect of farming or pastoral areas like the Rio de la Plata and Venezuela, whose products had small demand or promised little profit in Europe, or the development of whose trade might be inimical to the economic interests of the major areas of Mexico and Peru, and of the mercantile interests in Spain that depended upon them. And above all, the circumstances related account in large measure for the libertinism, the official corruption, and the lack of social restraints which, if we are to believe Spanish as well as foreign observers, permeated many sections of colonial society and administration and made the task of just and effective government so difficult. But this was not peculiar to colonial Spanish America. It was equally characteristic of Portuguese Brazil, and to a large extent of English and French America. It was a common phenomenon of the frontier, and is still so wherever the frontier persists today.

III

✦

Race and Environment

✦

EL PUEBLO INDÍGENA

Reference has already been made to the problem of labor supply, as one of the earliest and most difficult to solve of the questions which faced the Europeans in tropical America. In all frontier regions free labor is hard to come by; for where land is abundant and profit for oneself easy to make, few are willing to enter the employ of others. The Spaniard's aversion to manual toil in those days complicated the situation still further. Europeans could not, or would not, work in a West Indian climate. Native labor was to be had only under compulsion. Yet if settlement was to be maintained, life there must be made attractive and profitable. Consequently in tropical lands or in mining communities where production was soon on a large scale, capitalistic basis, forced labor or a disguised slavery of weaker races was the inevitable result.

The problem goes back to the very earliest days of Spanish settlement, when Columbus came out to Hispaniola on his second voyage in 1493. The colonists were many and food was scarce. Most of the newcomers apparently, instead of settling down to planting, either lived on royal doles, for which the supplies sent out from Spain were quite insufficient, or expected the aborigines to support them out of their own meager resources. The Indians at first acquiesced; but primitive peoples are rarely able to accumulate a store beyond their immediate needs, and as the demands made upon them became intolerable, they revolted. Foraging expeditions by the colonists only resulted in plunder and bloodshed. In any case, the aborigines suffered the fate usually meted out to primitive races under like circumstances. When later they were made to work on farms and in the mines, their lot was no easier, and extermination, at least in the Antilles, was just as sure.

Meantime the first colonists themselves suffered from sickness, poverty, and disappointment. They were ex-soldiers, adventurers, convicts, attracted only by the prospect of sudden riches, men to whom agriculture was a demeaning occupation. Gold, however, was not to be picked from the trees, not even in the golden Indies, although there was plenty to be had by labor in rock and river-sands, as the next few decades were to reveal. The situation indeed was not peculiar to the Spanish settlement of the Antilles. Sickness and death from scanty food and inadequate shelter were to be the fortune of the first settlers in nearly every American colony, whether it was Spanish, French, Dutch, or English. That sixteenth-century Castilians should find the West Indian climate trying, and be ignorant of the simplest rules of right living in the tropics, is not remarkable. Only in the twentieth century is medical science making such regions truly habitable for the white man. Nor is the story unique in so far as it affected the relations between the colonists and the aborigines. It was to be repeated to the last detail in every settlement made by Spaniards in the New World.

Columbus, we are told, after the great rebellion of 1494-5, tried to regulate matters by prohibiting foraging expeditions and imposing a tribute or tax on the whole Indian population over fourteen years of age—a small amount of gold or cotton four times a year. If they were unable to pay, they were permitted to furnish a certain amount of labor instead. That must have been the thin edge of the wedge. Columbus's intentions were doubtless good, although, as we well know, he had no objection to Indian slavery. But it gave to the colonists the leverage they wanted. And when in 1499 the rebel Francisco Roldán and his associates submitted on condition that they receive allotments of land and the services of the Indians living upon them, the principle of the *repartimiento* was fairly established. Thereafter the alternative of service was apparently the rule. And under Bobadilla, when the worst elements got the upper hand, the exploitation of the aborigines went unchecked.

Reports in Spain of this state of affairs must have been very disconcerting to the queen. The papal bull of 1493, which gave to the kings of Castile dominion over the Indies, imposed one supreme obligation: to spread the gospel and draw the pagans into the Church of Christ; and Isabella to the day of her death regarded the welfare of the American natives as a major responsibility. When, therefore, the new governor, Nicolás de Ovando, came out to America in 1502, he was instructed by Isabella to assure the native chiefs that they and their people were under the crown's especial protection. They might go in entire freedom about the island, and no one was to rob them or harm them in any way, under severe penalties. They were to pay tribute only as the rest of the king's subjects. Only in the royal service in mines or on public works might they be compelled to labor. These orders were followed to the letter. But left to themselves, the Indians refused to work, which in view of their recent experience is not surprising. They withdrew from all association with the colonists, with results that from the European point of view were disastrous. Within a few months Governor Ovando wrote to Spain protesting that the only effect was the falling off of tribute, lack of labor, and inability to carry forward the work of conversion to Christianity.

The sovereigns replied with the famous orders of March and December 1503, which legalized the forced labor of free Indians but attempted at the same time to protect them from uncontrolled exploitation. The natives must be made to work, if necessary, on buildings and farms and in the mines, but in moderation and for reasonable wages. At the same time, to insure their being civilized, they must be gathered into villages, under the administration of a patron or protector, and provided with a school and a missionary priest. Each adult Indian was to have a house and land which he might not alienate. Intermarriage of Spaniards and Indians was also to be encouraged. And in everything they were to be treated 'as free persons, for such they are.' Only cannibal Indians from neighboring islands if taken in war might be sold into slavery. The crown, however, as in the original instructions to Ovando, was not oblivious of its special interest in the increase of gold production. The governor was ordered to give particular attention to the regulation of native labor at the mines, and in a secret instruction he was directed to place the Indian villages as near the mines as possible, so that more gold might be extracted.

Ovando's interpretation and enforcement of these orders took the form of the *encomienda*. The device may have been suggested to him by his association with the military Orders. He was himself a *Comendador* of the Order of Alcántara. The *encomienda* had been a temporary grant by the crown of jurisdiction and manorial rights over lands conquered from the infidels, made to knights as a reward for services in the Moorish wars. The peasants on these lands presumably were crown tenants, and life rights to their services were given to the *encomenderos*.[1] As developed in the Indies, the *encomienda* was the patronage conferred by royal favor over a portion of the natives concentrated in settlements near those of the Spaniards; the obligation to instruct them in the Christian religion and the elements of civilized life, and to defend them in their persons and property; coupled with the right to demand tribute or labor in return for these privileges. So far as we know, no grant of land was involved, although references in some of the early documents are ambiguous. The recipients of *encomiendas* were to be *conquistadores* and meritorious settlers so rewarded for their contribution to the founding of new colonies.[2] It was an attempt to reconcile the crown's determination to deal kindly with the natives and the need for a stable and continuous labor supply, and it became the basis for Spanish-Indian relations over a period of two and a half centuries. The practice was legalized by Ferdinand as regent of Castile in 1509, in a decree which provided that immedi-

[1] Robert S. Chamberlain, 'Castilian Backgrounds of the Repartimiento-encomienda, *Carnegie Institution of Washington Publication*, no. 509, 35.

[2] For two years, 1509-1511, the crown exacted one *castellano* in gold for each Indian granted in a *repartimiento*. *Col. doc. inéd.*, 1st ser., XXXI, 438, 472; 2nd ser., V, 333.

ately upon the pacification of a region, the governor or *adelantado* might divide the natives among the conquerors.

If we are to believe Las Casas, the *encomienda* in the Antilles under Ovando and his successors was little more than the *repartimiento* [3] of Columbus under another name. The Indians were assigned in lots of fifty, a hundred, or more, by written deed or patent, to individual Spaniards to work on their farms and ranches or in the placer mines for gold dust. Sometimes they were given to officials or to parish priests in lieu of part of their annual salary. The effect was simply to parcel out the natives among the settlers to do with as they pleased. In theory, the royal orders of 1503 were obeyed; in practice the obligations of the *encomendero* as patron and protector became a mere gesture. Wages were nominal and instruction was limited to a perfunctory service of baptism. The term of service in the mines at first was six months, later eight months. But in any case the results were disastrous. Men and women were worked beyond their strength, infant mortality was high, the birth rate declined. If the Indians fled to the hills and woods, they were hunted down like fugitive slaves. And the consequence was the rapid disappearance of the aborigines from the American islands.

The two attorneys sent to Spain in 1508 to plead the cause of the colonists reported that the natives were rapidly dying out, and recommended that the Indians be brought in from smaller neighboring islands. The regent Ferdinand, less tender of the natives' welfare than Isabella, gave his approval, but with the proviso that the kidnapped Indians were not to be enslaved, but to be paid wages and otherwise treated like the 'free' natives of Hispaniola. The traffickers in Indians received according to some contracts a fourth of the natives brought in, and according to others a third or a half, the remainder going to the crown for labor in the royal mines; for as the king righteously observed, 'since Our Lord has begun to give us such good prospects in these mines, it is fitting that I should assist and see to it that nothing is left undone that can reasonably be done.' [4] The king also was thoughtful enough to suggest that if the natives of Hispaniola were better workmen than those

---

3 The words *repartimiento* and *encomienda* were sometimes used interchangeably to mean the same institution. The terms, however, should not be confused. The *encomienda* implied a *repartimiento* or distribution of Indians. But 'repartimiento' was also used as a general term to denote division or distribution of anything; lands, houses, goods, services, troops, taxes, etc. *Repartimiento de indios* also referred to the allotment of Indians for necessary tasks in the Spanish community, such as building, mining, agriculture, or transport of goods. It also denoted the Indian labor gang itself. As regulated by law in Peru, this periodical conscription of Indians for manual work was called the *mita*. Another frequent and more specific use of the word was to denote the distribution or forceable sale of goods to the Indians by the *corregidores*. F. A. Kirkpatrick, 'Repartimiento-encomienda,' *Hisp. Amer. Hist. Rev.* XIX, 372-97.

4 Royal *cédula*, 15 June 1510, *Col. doc. inéd.*, 1st ser., XXXII, 81.

from other islands, a certain number of the former be taken from colonists possessing *repartimientos* in exchange for Indians imported. The kidnappers first resorted to the Bahama Islands, and when these were depopulated, they extended their operations to the South American mainland. As always happened on slaving expeditions, the mortality from exposure and starvation was high, and in fact became a public scandal.[5] In 1511 the king ordered that thereafter a third of all the Indians on the island be kept working in the mines, a rule sanctioned in the Laws of the Burgos of 1512. There were a thousand or more in those operated for the crown alone.

The Indians also suffered from the evils of absenteeism. After the Admiral was deprived, by the verdict of 1511, of the right to distribute *encomiendas,* there were sent to Santo Domingo in 1514 two *repartidores de indios,* Pero Ibáñez de Ibarra and Rodrigo de Albuquerque, to make a new distribution of the natives. This was done entirely in the interest of the king's secretary, Lope de Conchillos, and his friends, the permanently settled married colonists losing many or all of their Indians, and large *encomiendas* being assigned to government officials and to courtiers in Spain. In this fashion the ascendent Aragonese element at the court proceeded to exploit the patronage and revenues of a Castilian colony. And it would seem that it was in these *encomiendas,* managed by irresponsible stewards for absentee proprietors, that the natives suffered most cruelly, for the resident colonists realized that their permanent interest was bound up with the survival of the Indian laborers. Absentee ownership was not finally outlawed until the issue of the New Laws of 1542, and even thereafter did not entirely disappear.

The *encomienda* system as carried to the continent by the *conquistadores,* by Cortés to New Spain, and by Pizarro and his companions to Peru, was modified somewhat by the new conditions they encountered. Here the natives were semicivilized, living in permanent towns and villages, accustomed to the systematic labor of an agricultural economy. Here the natives could be more easily reduced to the status of a dependent, semiservile peasantry. Many of them were already in that condition under their own kings or chiefs. The transition to the *encomienda* therefore was possible without a violent break with previous custom, for often it involved merely a change of master. Moreover a feudal element was introduced on the mainland which seems to have had no counterpart in the Antilles. In New Spain and Peru the *encomendero* owed a military obligation to the king in return for the favor received. He was required to present himself with horse and accoutrements, alone or with a stated number of armed retainers, depending upon the size of his

5 Silvio Zavala, 'Los Trabajadores antillanos en el siglo XVI,' *Rev. Hist. Amer.,* no. 2, 44-9.

encomienda, whenever called upon for the defense of the community. And by law military musters were required from time to time, at the summons of the captain-general. We are told that in the Mixton War 150 *encomenderos* furnished as many as 500 horsemen for the campaign, as well as men for the defense of Mexico City.

The rapid decline in numbers of the aboriginal population was not confined to the West Indian islands, although there it was most spectacular; nor was it due wholly to destructive wars with the European conquerors or to overwork in the mines. It was also due to epidemics, often of diseases imported from Europe against which the natives had built up no protective immunity and to which therefore they were particularly susceptible. Smallpox was especially destructive in the early years of the conquest; also measles and, later on in the tropics, malaria and yellow fever.

It has often been observed that whenever in modern times adolescent races have come into contact with more mature peoples, the same phenomenon has occurred—as witness the South Sea islanders. Yet in spite of famine and pestilence, the hardier, more civilized races of the mainland of America survived the shock of conquest. And in most of the continental states of tropical America, aboriginal blood, in the mestizo and the Indian, still forms the preponderant strain in the population.

As already remarked, the question of the juridical status of the Indians was one that agitated Spanish theologians and legal theorists for over a century. The controversy began when the Dominican friar Antonio de Montesinos mounted the pulpit in Santo Domingo on Advent Sunday of 1511 and preached a flaming denunciation of the enslavement of the natives. And the first clash of the opposing forces in Spain was in the juntas assembled by King Ferdinand in 1512, which resulted in the framing of the celebrated Laws of Burgos.

The first Dominican friars, a group of six under the leadership of Pedro de Córdoba, had arrived at Santo Domingo in 1510, and filled with a Christian charity which was unblunted by familiarity with West Indian conditions, soon raised their voices in protest against the exploitation of the aborigines. The sermon of Montesinos threw the town into an uproar. The colonists protested to the governor Diego Columbus and demanded a retraction by the Dominican community. Promised another sermon by Montesinos on the same theme the following Sunday, they flocked to the church only to hear themselves castigated even more passionately for their inhumanity and greed. The upshot was that the settlers sent a friar of the rival Franciscan order to Spain to lodge a complaint with the crown, and Montesinos himself returned to plead his cause with the king.[6]

---

6 Bartolomé de las Casas, *Historia de las Indias*, 5 vols., Madrid 1875-6, lib. II, cap. 4.

Ferdinand was greatly disturbed because the friars discussed the rights of Spain over the Indies and its inhabitants, and he ordered Diego Columbus to put a stop to any further controversy by the Dominicans on such matters in public or private, on pain of their expulsion from the colony.[7] At the same time he ordered a commission of clergymen and officials to study the situation and propose plans of reform. After long debate the junta, while recognizing the liberty of the Indians in principle, concluded that the *encomienda* system was necessary. The 32 Laws of Burgos emanating from these deliberations were promulgated by the crown on 27 December 1512. With some additions in July 1513 and in 1518, them sum up the legislation of the Catholic kings, and constitute the first general code for the government and instruction of the American aborigines.

The Laws of Burgos reflect a comprehensive effort to regulate relations between Spaniards and Indians, and they laid down principles never entirely abandoned by the Spanish government. They included specific rules regarding labor, instruction, and food of the natives, and provided that those who showed themselves desirous of becoming Christians capable of governing themselves should be set free. The ablest Indians were to be chosen as future teachers, and Latin was to be taught to the sons of *caciques*. On the other hand, there was no appreciable relief from the labor *corvés*. A third of all Indians must still be kept at work in the mines, and all Indians must give at least nine months of the year to service for the Spaniards. The ordinances in fact did little more than sanction the system devised by Governor Ovando, while attempting to check more effectually the tendency to unlimited exploitation. And it was speedily discovered that although laws might reflect the best of intentions, distance and defective communications made it virtually impossible to enforce them.

Montesinos was soon overshadowed by a clergyman of greater genius, Bartolomé de las Casas, missionary, diplomat, historian, and chief source for what we know of the Indian problem during the generation following the discovery of America. His long and arduous career has called forth a considerable literature,[8] and need not be related here except in so far as it touches our immediate inquiry. Las Casas came out to Hispaniola with Ovando in 1502, following his father who had already acquired an 'estate' there. He had apparently taken holy orders and in 1510 celebrated his first mass at Santo Domingo. In the following year he accompanied Velázquez in the occupation of Cuba, and with a partner received an *encomienda* of Indians, like other settlers lay and ecclesias-

---

7 Lewis Hanke, *Las Teorías políticas de Bartolomé de las Casas* (Publ. Instit. invest. hist. LXVII), Buenos Aires, 1935, 13, n. 2.

8 For the best short statement with regard to Las Casas, see Hanke, op, cit. There are two rather uncritical biographies in English, by Arthur Helps, Philadelphia, 1868, and by F. A. MacNutt, New York, 1909.

tical. There he came to the conclusion that the system was a terrible blunder, and the rest of his life he spent in ceaseless endeavor to win justice and freedom for the Indians.

He began by renouncing the share in his *encomienda,* and preaching manumission from the pulpit. Finding no response, he sailed for Spain in September 1515 to lay the matter before the crown. Rodríguez de Fonseca, still chief counselor for American affairs, was hostile or indifferent, Ferdinand was ill, and died the following January. But the regent, Cardinal Jiménez de Cisneros, was more sympathetic. In the absence of the viceroy Diego Columbus from America, he commissioned three Hieronymite friars, chosen by Las Casas and accompanied by Alonso Zuazo, as legal adviser and chief justice, to govern the Indies. They were instructed to enforce the laws in the interest of the natives, and to make a thorough investigation of the whole Indian problem to serve as a basis for future policy. They were also ordered to set at liberty all 'capable' Indians under their own chiefs, to live alone as free subjects of the king.[9] Las Casas sailed for America at the same time, fortified with the title of Protector of the Indians.

The arrival of the friars at Santo Domingo in December 1516 caused a general alarm among the colonists. But the commissioners conducted themselves with great prudence and caution. They set at liberty all Indians assigned to absentee courtiers in Spain, and tried to do away with abuses; but after an extensive inquest among the settlers, they reported to the Cardinal-Regent that the natives must work or the colony be abandoned, for the Spaniards were too few in number to maintain it alone. They urged that immigration be encouraged not only from Andalusia but directly from all the ports of Spain, that new settlers be married men, mostly farmers, and that they be assisted with gifts of seeds, cattle, and implements. Las Casas, completely disillusioned, returned to Spain in 1517 to continue his campaign for Indian freedom. He got little sympathy from the official class, but he did gain the ear of the young king Charles, then 17 years of age. And Charles was to remain his best ally.

---

9 The friars, while given the widest latitude in the application of their instructions, were ordered to try an experiment already foreshadowed in the Laws of Burgos. Indians found capable of living by themselves were to be removed into villages of their own, about 300 to each community, and were to pay a certain fixed tribute to the crown. Each village was to have a church, a hospital, and common lands, and was to be governed by its chief assisted by a priest and a Spanish administrator who were to induce the natives to adopt European habits of life. The two Spanish officials would be paid salaries contributed half by the crown and half by the Indians. Spanish colonists thereby deprived of their Indians were to be compensated by a portion of the tribute or in some other way. If the scheme failed to work, things were to remain as provided in the Laws of Burgos with certain suggested improvements. See Gonzalo Fernández de Oviedo, *Historia general y natural de las Indias,* lib. IV, cap. 2; Lewis Hanke, *The First Social Experiments in America,* Cambridge, Mass., 1935.

In 1518 Rodrigo de Figueroa, successor to the Hieronymites, was ordered to pursue the investigation further, and meantime to liberate all civilized and Christianized Indians in the manner prescribed to his predecessors. Figueroa did install in three pueblos some of the Indians from *encomiendas* he had been ordered to suppress, i.e., from those belonging to the crown, to the Admiral and other officials, and to absentees in Spain; but the experiment soon proved to be a fiasco.[10]

Two years later Las Casas obtained from Charles V consent to a new scheme. To prove that the problem of Indian labor could be solved without Indian serfdom, he would establish a self-supporting European community on a free labor basis, Spanish and Indian. And he went about Castile trying to persuade fifty Spaniards of good character to subscribe 250 ducats apiece and go out with him, together with a larger number of Spanish farmers and artisans. He was assigned territory on the coast of Venezuela near the later town of Cumaná; but the choice of site was unfortunate since for years it had been the haunt of Spanish slave-catchers from the islands. The settlement, started after great effort in 1521, soon ended in disaster. Within a few months, during Las Casas' absence at Santo Domingo, the Indians, unable to distinguish between good Spaniards and bad, attacked his followers and killed or scattered them. Las Casas then entered the Dominican order and for eight years lived a secluded life within his monastery at Santo Domingo.

Although all of these experiments proved to be a complete failure, the emperor Charles, on the eve of sailing from Coruña for the Low Countries in May 1520, apparently capitulated completely to the champions of Indian freedom. King and Council decided that the *encomienda* as chief source of the Indians' misfortunes should be eliminated, and orders were sent to Figueroa and other authorities in the islands to speed the program earlier outlined to them. For the Antilles the decision came too late to be of practical consequence, but in the vast regions on the mainland it was to have serious repercussions. Cortés apparently had been moved not to allow the introduction of the *encomienda* in his newly conquered provinces, but had been forced to give way before the importunities of his followers. When the emperor heard of it, he forbade the assignment of any more *encomiendas* in New Spain and ordered those already granted to be revoked.[11] He also forbade the conversion of the Indians by force or intimidation. The errors that had caused the destruction of the natives of the islands must not be repeated on the main-

---

10 Hanke, op. cit. 42-8. It was at this time that both Las Casas and the Hieronymite friars suggested the importation of Negro slaves into the West Indies to save the natives from destruction. The friars at the same time gave warning of the danger to the Spanish community from the association of Negroes with the great number of hostile Indians.

11 Instructions to Cortés, 26 June 1523, *Col. doc. inéd.*, 2nd ser., IX, 167-81.

land. But petition after petition from the settlers was sent to Spain in protest. Cortés withheld publication of the order, and wrote home that its enforcement would entail the dissolution of the colonies, by depriving the Spaniards of labor and therefore of subsistence, and by discouraging immigration. The government thereupon yielded and the order was withdrawn. And so the crown continued in its vacillating course, torn between the need of preserving its distant empire and the desire to save the natives from destruction. General ordinances, for instance, issued at Granada in November 1526 to regulate the conduct of captains and other officials on expeditions of discovery and settlement, stated that the natives must not be required against their will to labor for private persons, that if they worked voluntarily they must be paid, and that in all other respects they must be well treated and their property respected. Yet if it was thought necessary for their conversion, the Indians might be distributed in *encomiendas* 'as free persons,' with the advice and consent of the religious who accompanied the expedition.[12]

The question of the right of inheritance of an *encomienda* was from the days of King Ferdinand of deep concern to the crown as well as to the *encomenderos* themselves. It had been brought to the attention of Ferdinand even before the coming of Diego Columbus to Santo Domingo, when the king was constrained to warn the governor that the assignment of *encomiendas* was not for life but for two or three years only, with the possible privilege of renewal.[13] Such insecurity of tenure, however, aggravated the misfortunes of the Indians, since the Spaniards with no assurance as to the future 'used them like borrowed property' and worked them to the limit of endurance. In reply to the interrogatory of the Hieronymites in 1517 the colonists urged for these reasons that the *encomiendas* be made perpetual; and Cortés did the same in his correspondence with the emperor after the conquest of Mexico, as did the bishop Zumárraga in 1529. Perpetuity would be a guarantee of social stability, encourage planting, prevent emigration of the colonists, assure prosperity and therefore the increase of the royal revenues, and provide the community with a permanent source of military protection. An *encomendero* dependent upon the natives for his support would have greater regard for their welfare than a temporary proprietor or a royal overseer.

The emperor was evidently convinced by these arguments, for in his instructions to the first *audiencia* of New Spain in 1528 the promise of *encomiendas* in perpetuity, with rights of jurisdiction over the natives, was held out to *conquistadores* and other meritorious settlers after a general census of the country had been taken. And this was repeated in a

12 Ibid. I, 450-5.
13 Ibid. XXXI, 436-9.

decree of 8 October 1529.[14] Yet in this very year Charles called together another junta at Barcelona to pass upon the legality of forced Indian labor, and its verdict was again that the *encomienda* was unjust in law and practice. Secret instructions, therefore, to the second *audiencia* in 1530 once more called for the gradual eradication of this institution, along the lines laid down for the Hieronymites and Figueroa a decade earlier; although the Indians must not be permitted to relapse into idleness but must be persuaded to work on farms and in the trades.

This attempt of the *audiencia* faithfully to carry out these instructions not only worked injustice to many deserving colonists; agriculture ceased when former *encomenderos* no longer had Indians to work for them, while those having Indians sent them to the mines and worked them to death in the short time remaining to them. Trade took a tailspin and many colonists were leaving the country. So the judges reported, and so again the process of abolishing the *encomienda* came to a stop, and was not to be renewed for a decade. In fact, a decree of 16 June 1535 established the right of succession to *encomiendas* by wife or child for one life, and in the following year the order was made general for all the Indies. The instructions for Antonio de Mendoza, first viceroy of New Spain, marked definitely the return of the *encomienda* into royal favor.[15] It may not be without significance that this coincided with the foundation of Lima and the extension of Spanish sovereignty over another great continental area to which Spanish settlers needed to be attracted.

There were from the beginning two kinds of unfree Indians in the colonies: chattel slaves, presumably prisoners captured in a 'just war,' that is, when they refused submission to the Spaniards, and 'free' Indians held in *encomienda*. As early as 1495 Columbus sent to Spain several shiploads of natives taken in the recent war of pacification on Hispan-

---

14 At the same time, in December 1528 and August 1529, a series of ordinances was addressed to the authorities in New Spain for the protection of the *encomienda* Indians. They were not to be used as burden-bearers under any circumstances, with or without pay, or employed in any way in the operation of mines or in building houses for sale. Indian women used in domestic service must not be separated from husband and children. Tribute must be just and reasonable in amount and kind, and vagabond Spaniards who traveled about living on the natives and robbing them of provisions and other goods were threatened with expulsion from the colony. The hiring out of Indians was absolutely forbidden; and from all of these rules there was to be no appeal. *Col. doc. inéd.* 2nd ser., IX, 386, 425, 427; Genero V. Vásquez, ed., *Doctrinas y realidades en la legislación para los indios*, Mexico, 1940, 211. The necessity for the issue of such orders by the crown is clearest evidence of the rapacity and tyranny of the Spanish colonists.

15 These instructions (25 April 1535) once more held out the prospect of *encomiendas* granted in perpetuity with rights of jurisdiction as in a feudal fief; but the suggestion was withdrawn in royal orders of a year later. *Col. doc. inéd.*, 1st ser., XXIII, 423-45; 2nd ser., X, 245-63; 323-8.

iola for sale as chattel slaves. His brother Bartholomew shipped another batch to Cadiz in the following year. Queen Isabella at first apparently took no definite stand in the matter,[16] but at least from the year 1500 the enslavement of Indians was in principle forbidden. Exception was made only in the case of the cannibal Caribs, and later of Indians taken in 'just war,' exceptions which opened a wide door to abuse. This continued to be the general policy of the crown throughout the colonial era. But as pacification became general, the legitimate supply of Indian slaves from such sources naturally decreased, while the demand became greater, especially in the new and richer mines on the mainland. For years slave-catching expeditions were common along the shores of the Caribbean on the flimsiest pretext of Indian hostility.[17] Pánuco in New Spain, under the governorship of the notorious Nuño de Guzmán, also became a center for the capture of Indians for export as slaves to the islands. In 1528 Charles V ordered the *audiencias* of Santo Domingo and Mexico to make a thorough investigation of such scandals, examining and registering all slaves then held. And in November 1526, and again in August 1530—the year in which the crown was momentarily reverting to the program of abolishing the *encomienda* system—a decree forbade Spaniards thereafter to reduce any natives to slavery under any pretext, even though taken in 'just war,' and revoked all earlier rules to the contrary. Anyone who did so, or who possessed such slaves by purchase, exchange, or by any other title, was liable to the confiscation of all his property.[18]

Again, however, the crown retreated. Enslavement seemed the most appropriate means of punishing Indian rebellion, and the mining industry called for labor. Shortage at the mines, in fact, and the rise in the price of slaves was an irresistible temptation to kidnappers and to unscrupulous *caciques* and *encomenderos*. So the decree of 1530 was reversed four years later,[19] only to be resurrected in the New Laws of 1542. And even thereafter enslavement was sometimes permitted in specific

---

16 Lesley Byrd Simpson, *Studies in the Administration of the Indians in New Spain*, IV. *The Emancipation of the Indian Slaves and the Resettlement of the Freedmen*, 1548, 1555, Berkeley Cal., 1940, 20-24. Rodríguez de Fonseca was instructed to sell the Indians in Andalusia, but a few days later, apparently as an afterthought, was ordered to impound the proceeds until the legal aspects of the case could be settled. Finally on 20 June 1500 the Indians were ordered released and returned to their country of origin. *Col. doc. inéd.*, 1st ser., XXX, 331; XXXVIII, 439; Fernández de Navarrete, *Viajes*, II. 173.

17 In the beginning a few slaves were also obtained by barter (*rescate*) from Indian chiefs.

18 *Col. doc. inéd.*, 2nd ser., X, 38-43.

19 With the exception that women and children under 14 years at the time they became slaves, could not legally be held in bondage.

cases of Indian resistance to Spanish authority, or as a punishment for Indian crimes and misdemeanors.[20]

A special class of natives were the *yanaconas* in the viceroyalty of Peru.[21] They were hereditary Indian servitors attached to the soil, generally as agricultural laborers or as household servants, and were said to number in Peru in the time of the viceroy Francisco de Toledo about fifty thousand. The origin of the *yanaconas* is obscure. They may have been an inheritance from pre-conquest times; or they may have had their origin in 'vagabond' Indians who had fled from their villages or *encomiendas*, and were persuaded to settle on a Spaniard's estate, or who were placed there by a Spanish magistrate. They and their families went with the land when it changed hands, but they could not leave the land or be removed from it. They were supposed to receive from the *partón* clothes, wages, and sometimes a small plot to cultivate for their own support, in return for a stipulated number of days of work. Like other Indians they owed tribute to the crown. Apparently many of them were skilled workmen, and some labored for their masters on a commission basis.

The continuance of this semiservile class was forbidden in the New Laws of 1542 and in later decrees as being inconsistent with the principles of Indian liberty. *Yanaconas* might not be granted in *encomienda* or render services except of their own free will and for reasonable wages. The institution was recognized, however, in the legislation of the viceroy Francisco de Toledo, and by the decree of 1601 regulating the personal service of the Indians, and ordinances were issued to insure just and merciful treatment. Probably the lot of the *yanaconas* was somewhat easier than that of most of the other tributary Indians. But Solórzano, who did not approve of the institution, asserts that the protective laws were of no effect, and that the evils inflicted on the Indians outweighed any benefits to them or to the Spanish community.[22]

The next important step in the history of Indian bondage was a series of momentous declarations by Pope Paul III in 1537, at the instigation of the Dominican friar Bernardino de Minaya, that the Indians were rational beings capable of becoming Christians. They were therefore 'not to be deprived of their liberty or the possession of their property even though they be outside the faith of Jesus Christ . . . nor should

---

20 Silvio Zavala, *Spanish Colonization of America*, Philadelphia, 1943, 65-7.

21 A somewhat analogous class in the West Indian islands and in New Spain were called *naborios, laborios,* or *gañanes.* As laborers they were apparently free to come and go as they wished, but were probably in most cases attached to their place of employment by some form of peonage.

22 Juan de Solórzano Pereira, *Política indiana*, Madrid, 1647, lib. II, cap. 4; Philip Ainsworth Means, *Fall of the Inca Empire and the Spanish Rule in Peru*, 1530-1780, New York, 1932-164-5.

they in any case be enslaved.' [23] Anyone who disregarded these injunctions was to be denied the sacraments of the Church. This proved to be the most important papal pronouncement of the century on Indian serfdom. The emperor, it appears, was seriously embarrassed by these declarations, especially by the threat of drastic ecclesiastic penalty for those who disobeyed. They seemed to encroach upon the crown's ecclesiastical privileges under the *Patronato*. In the following year the Pope was prevailed upon to revoke at least the penalties if not the bulls themselves, although Las Casas and the other reformers who so triumphantly cited the Pope against their enemies were either unaware of or ignored the fact.[24] Thereafter the government endeavored, but without great success, to prevent the Pope from making further pronouncements and to keep Spanish ecclesiastics disposed to agitate reforms away from the papal court.

Las Casas is said to have translated the bull into Spanish and to have sent copies to many parts of the Indies, and when he returned to Spain in 1539 he had the backing of a new ally, the Papacy. It seems to have been partly due to his influence that in the years 1542-3, [25] after lengthy discussions, were promulgated the famous New Laws of Charles V, the *Leyes y ordenanzas nuevamente hechas por S. M. para la governación de las Indias y buen tratamiento y conservación de los Indios*. They set the seal of royal approval on the bulls of 1537, however embarrassing this papal declaration may originally have appeared to be.

After laying down rules relating to the functions of the Council of the Indies and of the American *audiencias,* the New Laws were occupied chiefly with the condition of the Indians. There was again a formal declaration that the American natives were free persons and vassals of the crown of Castile, and that no one might make use of them in any way against their will. The New Laws forbade all further enslavement and branding of the Indians under any pretext, as prisoners of war or otherwise, and ordered the release of slaves to whom title could not be proved. They also forbade the granting of any new *encomiendas* under any circumstances. Colonists who had ill-treated their Indians, and all ecclesiastics, religious Orders, and royal officials were to give up their *encomiendas* immediately and never thereafter to possess them.[26] Other

23 Lewis Hanke, 'Pope Paul III and the American Indians,' *Harvard Theological Review*, xxx, 65-162.

24 Apparently to the very end of Spanish rule in America some of the clergy refused the Eucharist to the Indians on the ground that they were inferior beings. Ibid. 96.

25 The New Laws were issued on 20 November 1542 as a result of an inspection (*vista*) of the Council of the Indies and its administration by the emperor begun earlier in that year. Additional, amplifying ordinances were issued on 4 June 1543.

26 León Pinelo in his important treatise, *Tratado de confirmaciones reales,* Madrid, 1630, pt. i, cap. 10, gives the following list of officials who might not possess *encomiendas;* members of the Council of the Indies, viceroys, presidents, *oidores, alcaldes del*

settlers who could establish legal title to their *encomiendas* might retain them, but not transmit them by inheritance; their wives, children, or other heirs were to be provided for out of the tributes paid to the crown. Compulsory personal service by the Indians was forever abolished, and the Indians remaining on the islands of Hispaniola, Cuba, and Puerto Rico were especially singled out for relief. They were not to be molested with tributes or any kind of service beyond that to which Spaniards were subject, and were free to go about the islands as they pleased. *Encomenderos* were to reside in the province in which their *encomiendas* were located, and might receive only the tribute owed by the natives to the crown. This was to be fixed in each district, so that the natives might not be overtaxed. And finally 'protectors' of the Indians were to be appointed in each colony to watch over their interests. The New Laws, if carried out, meant the ultimate disappearance of the *encomienda* system, and indeed threatened the complete elimination of the Indian as a source of cheap colonial labor.

This legislation, as is well known, could not be enforced in its entirety in any of the American provinces. Everywhere, in New Spain and Peru, Guatemala and New Granada, the colonists rose in their wrath and threatened rebellion. The *encomiendas* had been made inheritable for a generation, and had even been promised in perpetuity, and now everything was taken from them, even their chattel slaves. High officials were sent out from Spain in 1544 to enforce the decrees, Francisco Tello de Sandoval, member of the Council of the Indies, as *visitador* to New Spain, and Blasco Núñez Vela as first viceroy to Peru. New *audiencias* were established at Lima and in Guatemala with the same purpose in mind. In Peru the outcome was a bloody civil war which involved the death of the viceroy. In New Spain the colonists were in an ugly mood— the secular clergy in part, the regulars solidly, opposed the liberation of the natives—and in the face of popular tumult the *visitador* and the viceroy Mendoza decided that discretion was the better part of valor and withheld the promulgation of the decrees. Meanwhile the *cabildo* of Mexico City sent attorneys to Spain to present the grievances of the colonists and obtain the revocation of the legislation affecting the *encomenderos*. Their mission was a success, and in 1545 and 1546, in spite of

---

crimen, *fiscales, cantadores de cuentas, oficiales, reales, gobernadores,* and other officials of justice and the exchequer; also, with certain exceptions, their relatives to the fourth degree, servants, and 'familiares y allegados.' *Corregidores, alcaldes mayores,* and deputy governors were permitted to hold *encomiendas.* All clergymen, churches, monasteries, and other religious establishments were excluded except by special concession of the crown. Solórzano tells us that such concessions were made frequently, especially to nunneries and hospitals for the poor, as well as to viceroys and other high officials whom the king delighted to honor, and even in his own time to absentees in Spain. Lib. III, cap. 6, par. 6, 39, 40, 51.

the protests of Las Casas and the reformers, the more obnoxious decrees were revoked.

The result was a compromise. The laws forbidding future enslavement of the Indians and those abolishing enforced personal service remained, but those which operated as a confiscation of *encomiendas* already existing were rescinded. The right of succession by the wife or child of an *encomendero* was re-established. And after much shilly-shallying back and forth in the Council of the Indies, the crown between 1548 and 1551 reaffirmed and extended certain provisions of the earlier legislation. All female slaves and all males under 14, as well as slaves to whom no legal title could be proved, must immediately be set free;[27] and by a decree of 22 February 1549 the rule was established that personal service might in no case be demanded of free Indians as tribute. The *audiencias* were instructed to assign attorneys to institute judicial process for liberating the Indian slaves. As in most cases proof of legal title was almost impossible to establish, the *audiencias* of Guatemala and Santo Domingo emancipated all the slaves within their district. In New Spain the procedure was slower, but within the following decade some 4,000 were set free.[28] Many of the mines faced disaster, as the viceroy himself warned the emperor, especially those on the margin of utility.[29] But the industry survived and continued to flourish, for other means were found of reducing the Indian to a *de facto* if not a legal servitude.

And so the *encomiendas* continued as a permanent institution, although in the course of time private *encomiendas* tended to decrease in number while those that reverted to the crown increased.[30] Indeed they seemed essential to the perpetuation in the New World of an aristocratic society organized on the lines of that in the Old. As the Dominican chapter wrote to Tello de Sandoval, 'there could be no permanence in the land without rich men, or rich men without *encomiendas,* because all industry was carried on by Indian labor, and only those having Indians were able to carry on commerce.' Moreover, they continued, 'it was necessary to have rich men as a defense against enemies and as a pro-

---

27 Orders to this effect had already been sent to the *audiencias* of Guatemala and Santo Domingo in 1545 and to the governor of Cuba in 1548. Zavala, op. cit. 37-8; *Contribución a la historia de las instituciones coloniales de Guatemala,* Mexico, 1945, 28.

28 Zavala, *Spanish Colonization of America,* 63-4.

29 Simpson, op. cit. 11-12.

30 In 1568 the crown ruled that large *encomiendas* should be limited to an income of 2,000 pesos, the remainder of the income being distributed by the government in pensions to worthy colonists, these pensions being likewise limited to a maximum of 2,000 pesos. *Recopilación,* lib. VI, tit. 8, leyes, 30, 31.

The crown also legislated repeatedly against the tendency of the colonial authorities, when *encomiendas* were vacated, to break them up into smaller units, often to the detriment of the Indians. Ibid. lib. 6, tit. 8, leyes 21-7.

tection for the poor—as was the case in Spain and in every well regulated republic.' [31] The crown, however, never departed from the fundamental purpose of treating the Indians as free persons and vassals of the king. The *encomendero* was subject to certain religious, military, civil, and economic obligations, but his proprietary right in the *encomienda* was never recognized. Nor did he possess any judicial authority over his Indians. The *encomienda* continued under the administration of the governing authorities of the province, who fixed the amount of tribute in money or produce and exercised general political and judicial supervision.

The second viceroy of New Spain, Luis de Velasco, was permitted by decree in 1555 to extend the *encomienda* to a third generation, but by subterfuge (*por via disimulación*).[32] In 1607 possession was extended to a fourth life, and later sometimes even to a fifth. Thereafter, or earlier in defect of succession, the *encomienda* escheated irrevocably to the crown. In Peru the rule of two lives persisted until 1629 when, in return for a heavy composition, inheritance for a third was permitted; but *encomiendas* that fell vacant were more generally reassigned by the viceroy than seemed to be the case in New Spain.[33]

Although the crown never surrendered its rights of ultimate reversion, one of the major problems throughout the sixteenth century was whether or not the *encomiendas* should be changed from a temporary grant into a permanent manorial fief. Some of the clergy in New Spain had urged this step when protesting against the New Laws in 1544, as had the attorneys representing the *cabildo* of Mexico City. In 1546 the crown again, as in 1528, promised that the *encomiendas* would be assigned in perpetuity, but without power of jurisdiction. Although the matter continued to be discussed in the Council of the Indies, nothing came of it. Early in the reign of Philip II, the king's need of money was so pressing that he almost yielded to the importunities of the Peruvian *encomenderos* who offered a large *servicio* for the privilege of perpetuity. The Council of the Indies strenuously objected, but when the Conde de Nieva went to Peru as viceroy in 1560, three commissioners accompanied him with instructions to investigate the matter and with power to grant perpetuity if the *servicio* was forthcoming.[34] The com-

---

31 Lesley Byrd Simpson, *The Encomienda in New Spain*, Berkeley, Cal., 1929, 168.

32 By the *Ordenanzas* . . . *para los nuevos descubrimientos, conguistas y pacificaciones* of 1573, *encomiendas* in newly settled districts might be assigned by the *adelantado* for three lives. *Col. doc. inéd.*, 1st ser., XVI, 159.

33 León Pinelo, op. cit. pt. 1, cap. 4, par. 45-9; José María Ots Capdequi, *Instituciones sociales de la América español en el periodo colonial*, La Plata, 1934, 82-9. The crown frequently recompensed the heirs of former *encomenderos* with pensions drawn from the Indian tributes vacated (*tributos vacos*).

34 Royal instructions, dated 23 July 1559, in *Nueva Colección de documentos inéditos para la historia de España y de sus Indias*, VI, 1-35.

missioners amassed a quantity of evidence and visited many Indian towns to ascertain the native view of the proposal. The Indians, instigated by the clergy, opposed it, even to the extent of having representatives in Spain offer the bait of a larger *servicio* than that suggested by the *encomenderos*. Also opposed were the poorer Spaniards in the Indies who had no *encomiendas,* for fear that the rule of perpetuity would exclude them forever from this source of wealth and well-being. The commissioners wrote to the king that if the *encomenderos* were conceded this right, their descendants or other successors, born in the Indies and unacquainted with the mother country, would soon lose all sense of loyalty to the crown. So in spite of pressure from *cabildos,* officials, and individual colonists, the commissioners decided against the innovation. But this did not prevent later efforts to the same end both in New Spain and in Peru.[35]

Meanwhile, and to the end of the colonial era, efforts were made by the crown and often by the viceroys [36] to prevent abuses. Laws and instructions were issued with weary reiteration to protect the lives and interests of the natives, but with varying degree of success. Those of the Hapsburg era are found summarized in the *Recopilación.*[37] *Encomenderos* must fulfill in person the duties attending their position; they must not leave the district without permission of the governing authority, and then their duties must be delegated to a responsible agent. They must not hire out the natives, or pledge them to creditors, under penalty of fines and forfeiture of the *encomienda.* They might not maintain a residence in the Indian villages, or a workshop, or any other building except a granary, or keep pigs or cattle within the confines of the *encomienda.* Itinerant merchants or other Spaniards might not tarry more than two or three days in a village, and Negroes, mestizos, and mulattoes were entirely excluded. Tribute must be just and reasonable, and in return the Indians must be protected and receive Christian instruction. And elaborate rules were devised governing the assessment of tribute, in New Spain by the first viceroy, Antonio de Mendoza, in Peru by the viceroy Francisco de Toledo.

When Las Casas returned to the West Indies with the Hieronymite friars in 1516, he had been fortified with the title of Protector of the Indians. The office was revived in New Spain in 1528 in the person of the first bishop of Mexico, Juan de Zumárraga. With the judicial support

---

35 See Ernesto Schäfer, *El Consejo real y supremo de las Indias,* Seville, 1935, 168-9.

36 Ordinances dictated by the authorities in America, who tried to conciliate realities as they found them with the general norms established by legislation sent out from Spain, are an important source of information concerning official policy with regard to the Indians. See documents in Genaro V. Vásquez, *Doctrinas y realidades en la legislación para los indios,* 226 ff.

37 *Recopilación,* lib. VI, tit. 9.

of the *audiencia* he was to see to the enforcement of all orders for the defense of the natives. Entrusting this function to ecclesiastics, however, proved to be unsatisfactory, and within five years the office was for a time abolished. Protectors were later appointed in Peru, and the viceroy Toledo issued ordinances for their guidance that were still recognized as basic when the *Recopilación* was published a century later. A defender of the Indians was to be placed in every considerable community to protect them from exploitation by legal pettifoggers or from extortion by their own *caciques,* and to settle minor Indian disputes with fairness and dispatch. Under no circumstances was he to collect any fees or levy any costs against his Indian charges. Toledo also appointed a special attorney (*abogado*) for Indian suits. But Rynaga Salazar tells us that the Protectors, appointed by the viceroy, were too frequently changed, and without sufficient personal prestige to withstand the wealthy landowners and miners, or to carry influence with the judges. The *abogados,* too, were poorly paid, and their salaries generally in arrears. Consequently they devoted their time to private law practice, to the neglect of the Indians.[38] Solórzano reports that these officials did little but collect their salaries and abuse the confidence reposed in them by the natives.

Defense of Indian rights in cases brought before the *audiencia* was also one of the duties of the *fiscal;* but because of the increasing burdens of office, in the first quarter of the seventeenth century viceroys and presidents were directed to choose for each *audiencia* a special solicitor (*procurador de indios*) who shared this responsibility with the *fiscal.*[39] About 1573 an extraordinary court was created by the *audiencia* in New Spain, the *juzgado general de indios,* which apparently served as an official check upon the abuses of Indian service. It was a court of appeal from the acts of *corregidores* and *alcaldes mayores* in all cases involving Indians, its jurisdiction covering every phase of contact between natives and Spaniards. According to Bernabé Cobo, a similar institution was established by the viceroy Velasco in Lima in 1603.[40]

The *encomienda,* contrary to common belief, was not a landed estate. As early as the Laws of Burgos, Indians belonging to an *encomienda* were declared to be proprietors of their houses, lands, and animals, and neither the *encomendero* nor anyone else might dispose of them. And later on the mainland of America this principle was well defined from

38 *Memorial discursivo sobre el oficio de protector de los indios del Piru,* Madrid, 1626, 1-9.

39 *Recopilación,* lib. VI, tit. 6; Solórzano, lib. II, cap. 28, par. 42 ff.; Simpson, op. cit. 95-6, 117-18. In New Spain a half real was collected annually from each Indian to pay the salary of the Protector and cover other legal expenses.

40 Lesley Byrd Simpson, *Studies in the Administration of the Indians in New Spain,* III. *The Repartimiento System of Native Labor in New Spain and Guatemala,* Berkeley, Cal., 1938, 22-4; Bernabé Cobo, *Historia de la fundación de Lima,* Lima, 1882, cap. XXVIII.

the early years of the conquest.[41] There were, in fact, ample precedents in the manorial organization of Spain. A *señor* had the right to receive rents and tributes from his vassals, but they in turn as against him had the right to the property and use of their land, and to dispose of its produce in so far as it was not absorbed by tribute. There is no evidence that Spanish legislation ever combined title to an *encomienda* with territorial proprietorship. On the contrary, it often prohibited the usurpation of lands by the *encomendero,* although the latter might acquire by purchase, gift, or other legitimate means lands within the limits of his *encomienda.*[42] Lands abandoned by the Indians by flight or decease passed by law to the community or to the crown. On the other hand, examples of usurpation and of lawsuits resulting therefrom were not uncommon in sixteenth-century New Spain, and may have been more frequent in later times.

The laws forbidding forced personal service, although they remained on the statute books, were entirely without effect.[43] The Indians, whether held in *encomienda* or not, were in practice held to all sorts of exactions. The Spanish magistrate, the parish priest, the native *cacique,*[44] each came in for his share, and they often worked in collusion. Vagabond Spaniards and half-castes wandering about the country 'sponged' on the

41 On this subject see the important essay by Silvio Zavala, *De Encomienda y propiedad territorial en algunas regiones de la América Española,* Mexico, 1940, which covers the situation in New Spain in the sixteenth century.

42 This was forbidden by Philip IV in 1633, *Recopilación,*A lib. VI, tit. 9, ley 17.

43 Controversy over the use of Indians as carriers goes back to the days of King Ferdinand, who in 1511 outlawed the practice as one of the causes of the depopulation of Hispaniola and the other islands. In New Spain, where before the conquest all transport of goods for lack of beasts of burden had been on the backs of Indians, the custom was revived on an enormous scale, and it seems with great cruelty. The carriers, we are told by Bishop Zumárraga, were loaded with excessive burdens, treated like pack animals, and not even fed. By ordinances of December 1528, therefore, the Indians were permitted to carry burdens only with their consent and for pay. The second *audiencia* drew up a schedule regulating load, pay, and length of journey, and this compromise was accepted by the emperor. According to the New Laws carriers might be used only in places where the practice could not be avoided, i.e., where there was a lack of pack animals. These restrictions, however, remained a gesture, and although in later times much of the heavier transportation was doubtless performed by mule trains, this form of exploitation of the Indians continued down into the nineteenth century.

44 In regions on the continent where the Spaniards found Indian communities with a social organization compatible with their own, they adopted such native institutions as they found feasible in incorporating the Indians into the orbit of their own civilization. One was the institution of the native chiefs (*curacas or caciques*), who were retained in many regions and protected by legislation in their hereditary rights against encroachment by the colonial authorities. These chiefs exercised a minor judicial authority over their clansmen, and played an important part in the apportionment of labor and the collection of tribute. To them the Indians also owed personal service, later changed by law to a tribute fixed by the Spanish government. Cf. *post,* p. 215.

defenseless natives, demanding food and shelter, or squatted in their villages. Moreover, both in New Spain and in Peru the tendency persisted in the sixteenth and seventeenth centuries—although about this we as yet know little—to commute part of all the tribute for labor, especially in the case of very small *encomiendas*.[45] Local officials were sometimes punished for their exploitation of the natives, through the *residencia* or the *pesquisa*, and occasionally the natives were successful in lawsuits against their oppressors in the Spanish courts. But this, as might be expected, was exceptional rather than the rule.

Even so-called free labor of the natives, for which they were regularly hired and paid wages, was not all free in the sense that they were free to accept or reject it. Very soon after the abolition of Indian slavery and of service tributes, the practice appeared of requiring the Indians to give a certain amount of their time to work in mines and factories, on farms and ranches, and on public works. *Corregidores de indios,* officials who were in charge of crown Indians and collected their tribute, had in the past often rented them out to anyone needing labor in order to help raise the tribute or for their own private profit. In this practice was found a useful precedent. Relays or shifts of labor gangs came to be regularly conscripted to work in turn for a limited period fixed by law. Forced paid labor replaced forced tributary labor.[46] In Peru it was systematized by the viceroy Toledo in the form of the *mita,* said to have been suggested in part by a study of the economic organization of the Incas. His legislation had been foreshadowed in ordinances issued by his predecessors in Peru, but Toledo revised, completed, and codified the rules and gave them a definite form which lasted to the end of the viceroyalty. Thereafter all adult males, except craftsmen and Indian magistrates, in every village or pueblo were subject to these requirements in addition to the tribute, a seventh being always so employed at any one time. The *mitayos* were brought to the nearby Spanish town, where they might be engaged for a specified period, generally one or two months, by anyone who needed them for their farms, vineyards, textile or sugar mills, etc.[47] Those assigned to the mines were taken only from certain districts, and

---

45 Only in Chile and the provinces of the Rio de la Plata was this legally permissible because of the small number of Indians available for work on the farms and ranches. See *Recopilación*, lib. VI, tit. 16, leyes 16, 37; Ricardo Zorraquín Becú. *La Reglamentación de las encomiendas en el territorio argentino,* Buenos Aires, 1946, 13.

46 Zavala rightly points out that the presumed congenital 'idleness' of the Indians was due rather to the introduction of a more advanced European economy calling for a huge increase in the demand for labor, an economy in which the Indians had little interest or participation, or adequate remuneration, and to the agricultural techniques of which they were unaccustomed. ('Orígenes coloniales del peonaje México,' *El Trimestre económico*, X, 717.)

47 Personal or domestic service after 1542 was usually excluded, but the law was often disregarded.

served for ten months or a year. Presumably they worked for a week at a time, with a fortnight's interval for rest.

In New Spain there soon appeared an analogous institution called the *repartimiento* or *cuatequil*, which was given definitive organization by the viceroy Martín Enríquez, contemporary of Toledo, in 1575-80. Ordinarily the number drawn upon at any one time varied from 4 or 5 per cent for the mines to 10 per cent or more for agriculture during the weeding and harvest seasons.[48] A *repartimiento* might be granted only at the express command of the viceroy or *audiencia*, or in New Spain of the *juzgado de indios*. It was administered by *jueces repartidores* and, later, by the *corregidores* and *alcaldes mayores* with the collaboration of the Indian *principales* or chiefs.

A person wishing a repartimiento filed a regular form petition, to the effect that he had a wheat farm (or cattle ranch, or what not) from which he supplied the country with necessary food or goods (the good-of-the-state principle), and that to plant and harvest his crops he needed the services of so many Indians for such a length of time. He promised to pay them the standard wage and to treat them well.[49]

Apparently in some instances the Indians of a district subject to the *repartimiento* were gathered together in a central place and hired by those who needed their services, as was the custom in Peru. The legal work period was one or two weeks,[50] generally three or four times a year, and wages, which were somewhat less than those paid for free labor, varied from a customary real or real and a half per day in the sixteenth and seventeenth centuries, to three or four reals in mining in the eighteenth century.[51] Artisans were sometimes included in the *repartimiento*, but with double pay.

The system was intended to be reasonable and just, but as under the earlier *encomienda* there was abundant room for abuses. The *oidor* Alonzo de Zorita tells us (c. 1575) that the natives in New Spain were often taken long distances from their homes, sometimes on a journey of four or five days. They received pay for only a week's work, but spent

---

48 By the Ordinances of 1609 in an ordinary *repartimiento* one-seventh of the tributaries of a given *pueblo* might be taken at one time, but in 1614 the quota for work in the mines was reduced to 4 per cent, as apparently had earlier been the custom. Between seasons the quota for the farms might be as low as 2 per cent. Simpson, op. cit. 13 n., 17, 49, 98; Vásquez, op. cit. 260-65, 'Instruccion a don Augustin Manuel Pimentel, juez comissario de los aquileres de Tulancingo,' issued by the viceroy Marquis of Montesclaros, 6 September 1606.

49 Simpson, op. cit. 94-6.

50 In some regions four or five weeks in the mines. Miguel O. de Mendizábal, 'Los Minerales de Pachua y Real del Monte en la época colonial,' *El Trimestre económico*, VIII, 266.

51 By the mining ordinances of the viceroy Toledo, *mitayos* assigned to the mines in Peru were to be paid two and a half reals a day, free laborers three and a half reals.

an additional week or more traveling to and from their villages. They had to provide their own food, and sleep on the ground in all sorts of weather. They were often flogged, or had their blankets taken from them as security against their running away, and consequently died of exposure.[52] The crown endeavored by numerous devices to alleviate the burden of forced labor,[53] especially by a code embodied in the important decrees of Philip III, 24 November 1601 and 26 May 1609.[54] The earlier of these decrees put an end to the existing system of *mitas* and *repartimientos*. In its place, a fourth of the able-bodied Indians of any village or district at any one time were to gather in the plaza or other public place, where they might freely hire themselves to whomsoever they pleased, for the number of days or weeks they wished. Vagabond Spaniards, Negroes, mestizos, and other half-castes were subject to the same rules. In short, labor remained compulsory in so far as it had to be rendered, but was free in so far as a free choice of employer was permitted. The new regulations also identified the system in New Spain more nearly with that of the *mita* as practiced in Peru.

Indians were forbidden to work in sugar mills, textile factories (*obrajes*),[55] pearl fisheries, as carriers, or as rowers on the rivers; and there were numerous regulations regarding the payment of wages, hours of labor, the provision of food, clothing and shelter, the distance Indians

---

52 Alonso de Zorita, *Breve y sumaria Relación de los señores de la Nueva España,* Mexico, 1942, 140-50.

53 From the reign of Philip II it was absolutely forbidden to use Indians in the cultivation of indigo in Central America and Yucatan, even on a voluntary basis. *Recopilación,* lib. vi, tit. 14, ley 3. The crown also issued elaborate instructions for the protection of Indians employed on the coca plantations in the montaña of Peru, ibid. lib. vi, tit. 14, ley 2. Proprietors of mines and *estancias* who employed *mitayos* were required by law to provide adequate housing for the Indians, clergy to attend their religious instructions, and hospitals for those who fell ill, ibid. lib. vi, tit. 15, leyes 1, 10, 17.

54 *El Obraje embrión de la fábrica,* Documentos para la historia económica de México. Publicaciones de la Secretaria de la economia nacional, xi, Mexico 1963, 18-42.

55 The *cédula* of 1601 absolutely forbade the employment of Indians in the textile mills because of the 'extortion and abuses' they suffered there. They were to be replaced as quickly as possible by Negroes or other workers. These mills consumed the wool produced on the large sheep ranches to manufacture coarse textiles for the domestic market; and the workers, including many Chinese brought from the Philippines by way of Acapulco, lived a life of virtual servitude, with long hours and close confinement to the mill premises. In Peru at least, the Indian *caciques* were sometimes the culprits, exploiting their people by forcing them, especially women and children, to labor in the *obrajes* on the pretext of collecting tribute.

The *cédula* of 1609 withdrew the prohibition, but endeavored to regulate conditions. Indians might be hired only of their own free will with hours and wages fixed by the viceroy, and in such mills already established in the principal cities which were necessary to supply the community. Labor conditions in the textile factories, however, continued to be a scandal. Simpson, op. cit. 15, 18, 129-40; Vásquez, op. cit. 181-2- 233-42.

might be taken from home, etc. Royal officials forbidden to possess *enco-miendas* were prohibited from employing Indians except on a voluntary basis. If necessary to maintain the operation of mines, however, the older system might be continued in such case for one year only, until the miners could obtain Negro slaves or accommodate themselves to the new order. Under all circumstances employers should be urged to purchase Negroes, so that with the increase of slave and of voluntary workers it might ultimately be possible to abolish forced labor altogether.

It was an ambitious reform, and the viceroys were given discretionary power in its enforcement so as to avert great discontent and commotion. As a matter of fact the new rules were executed only in part, various American authorities suggested amendments, and in the supplementary decree of 1609 the crown receded somewhat from its earlier position. Rules for the protection of the Indians were repeated, but the *reparti-miento* was restored for service on ranches and farms and for certain tasks in the mines. Moreover the new rules were gradually modified by the viceroys to guarantee a specified number of laborers to important private employers or public institutions, or for public works in particular areas or towns, and the larger quotas demanded at harvest time remained in force.[56] In short, the older system survived in many respects and strongly modified the new.

Although fifteen years elapsed before the *audiencia* of New Spain passed an enabling act, the new code remained in force, on paper at least, to the end of the colonial regime. Yet later decrees, in both the seventeenth and eighteenth centuries, revealed that virtually none of the ordinances was observed and that exploitation continued in every conceivable form.[57] Especially in the more remote corners of the empire, legis-

---

56 The *repartimiento* for agriculture was definitely abolished as an institution in New Spain by the viceroy Marquis of Cerralvo in December 1632, but continued substantially in practice.

57 Simpson, after reviewing the records of the *juzgado de indios* in New Spain, sums up the situation as follows: 'The most general complaint is that the magistrate abuses his authority by forcing the Indians to serve him personally, in violation of the law, paying them either less than the prescribed wage or nothing at all. Floggings, jail sentences, and exposure in the stocks are their punishment for refusing to serve, or for complaining. The magistrates also interfere in the Indian elections, going against Indian tradition and violating the law, in order to put in young men who will be their tools in the exploitation of the others. The magistrates force the Indians to sell them foodstuffs and other goods at a low figure and then resell these same goods in the cities for their own profit. The magistrates keep herds of cattle and horses which they pasture in the grainfields of the Indians. The magistrates assess the Indians for all sorts of irregular services, such as fishing, the use of their pack animals, the use of their women as *molenderas* (tortilla makers). They assess fines against the Indians on any pretext for the purpose of exorting money. They oblige the Indians to supply pack animals and carriers to convey their goods to the capitals. They assess the Indian villages with the expenses of the *visitas*, which they make as often as pos-

lation regulating both the *mita* and the *encomienda* seems to have been largely ignored in daily practice. The failure of the *visitador* Francisco de Alfaro sent by the *audiencia* of Charcas to the provinces of the Rio de la Plata in 1611-12, to impose uniformity with the rest of the Peruvian viceroyalty, is a striking case in point.[58]

Reformers fought for the abolition of enforced personal service without success, and the controversy persisted down to the days of independence. For as Fernández de Oviedo had written back in the sixteenth century: 'Sobre este servicio de los indios ha avido muy grandes altercaciones en derecho entre famoses legistas é canonistas, é theólogos, religiosos, é perlados de mucha sciencia é conciencia; diciendo si deben servir ó no estos indios . . .' And he adds significantly, 'Pero como han seydo muy diferentes en las opiniones en esta disputa, ningun provecho se ha seguido á la tierra ni á los indios.' [59]

The *mita* and the *repartimiento* were always considered by the authorities in Spain to be a makeshift, with the hope that they would ultimately be supplanted by free labor or Negro slavery. And there is evidence in New Spain of the early rise of an independent wage-earning class, especially in the cities and in the mines. In fact free wage labor always existed side by side with the *repartimiento*.[60] The miners found the constant shifting of *repartimiento* Indians to be unprofitable because skilled labor was needed, and so a class of free workers appeared attracted by the relatively high wages.

There are also signs of peonage even in the second half of the sixteenth century, i.e., advances of money and goods which bound the Indian to the farm or mine by placing him in debt to his employer. 'It was inevitable,' as Dr. Zavala has said, 'that the farmers, to assure themselves of labor on their lands, would begin to try by all means available to induce Indians with their families to abandon their native pueblos and settle permanently on the farms.' [61] And although the decrees of 1601 and 1609 forbade landowners by any device to attach Indians to their properties or retain them against their will, there is no evidence that

---

sible, in violation of the law. The magistrates force the Indians to buy from them set quantities of certain necessities, such as soap and salt, at exhorbitant prices. A few magistrates (not many), being of a choleric temper and free from immediate restraint, were able to indulge their appetite for gratuitous floggings and tortures. Others seized Indian lands and rented or sold them for their own profit.' Simpson, op. cit. 42-3.

58 Enrique de Gandia, *Francisco de Alfaro y la condición social de los indios. Rio de la Plata, Paraguay, Tucumán y Perú. Siglos XVI, y XVII*, Buenos Aires, 1939.

59 *Historia general y natural de las Indias*, lib. IV, cap. 2.

60 Mendizábal, loc. cit. 259 ff.

61 Zavala, op. cit. 720-21. It was just as inevitable that the Indian pueblos would oppose this tendency, since it threatened to reduce the number of laborers available for the requirements of the *repartimiento* and of the tribute owed by the Indian community.

these practices ceased. Such Indians were still subject to the *reparti-miento,* but they were usually allowed to do their stint for their employer, who deducted their time from the *repartimiento* allotted to him. From time to time limits were established by law to the amount which might be advanced to the peon and the length of time by which he might be bound for repayment. By the Mining Ordinances of 1783 operators were forbidden to discount more than a fourth of the worker's daily wage in repayment of debts to the mineowner. By and large in the eighteenth century, however, the Bourbon viceroys were inclined to lay stress on the economic freedom of the Indians, and lend more support to the pretensions of the farmers and miners. To increase production became a major concern of the authorities. And more and more the system of debt peonage came to be frankly recognized as the predominant labor institution of the colonies. Even in the mining areas growing native discontent because of the difference in the treatment of free labor and that of the *repartimientos,* and sometimes open rebellion, forced wages to a level approximating those of the free workers.[62]

The situation in Chile was somewhat different from that in the other Andean provinces. The Indians found by the *conquistadores* in the central valley north of the River Biobio had diminished alarmingly in number owing to frequent epidemics, brutal treatment, and heavy labor in the placer gold mines. The landowners therefore depended more and more upon natives captured in the interminable wars against the Araucanians in the south. Repeated royal decrees and ordinances of the local authorities against personal service went unheeded, and gratuitous and obligatory labor by the Indians was universal. Captives were sold, exchanged, or shipped to Peru, and were slaves in all but name. In view

62 At the Real del Monte mines in the eighteenth century, free labor was paid a fixed wage of four reals for a day of 12 hours, alternating with 24 hours of rest. This amounted to a 48-hour week. In addition there was the *partido,* or right to half the ore mined after the minimum quantity assigned for the day was extracted. If the vein was rich the *partido* was less than a half, depending upon agreements between the workmen and the operator, and there were various deductions for the conveyors of Pachuca and for medical and other services.

The *partido* system had existed since the sixteenth century, later became very common in New Spain, and was recognized by the Mining Ordinances of 1783. It was used to attract free labor when the *repartimiento* was insufficient, or when a degree of specialization was desirable that was not possible with the weekly labor shifts. It was also resorted to by miners with little capital to supplement or even replace the daily wage. An attempt by the Conde de Regla to abolish the *partido* at Pachuca in 1766 caused the laborers to desert the mines and start a veritable proletarian insurrection in which the *alcalde mayor* was killed and the Conde de Regla himself narrowly escaped. And although the movement was sharply repressed by the authorities, it created a state of anarchy in the mines which lasted for several years. Mendizábal, loc. cit. 297 ff.

A practice somewhat analogous to the *partido* was also in effect in the mines of Upper Peru. Jorge Basadre, 'El Régimen de las mitas,' *Letras,* 1937, 345.

of the resistance of the Araucanians south of the Biobio, the crown in 1608 conceded that Indians taken in war might be reduced to chattel slavery. Four years later the Peruvian viceroy, in a vain effort to appease the Araucanians, suspended the order and prescribed the substitution of tribute in money or kind for personal service. This was expanded by the viceroy Esquilache in 1620 into a body of ordinances which, save only the abolition of slavery, was confirmed by the crown two years later. By law only the *mita* survived as obligatory service. A third of the Indians at a time were to be employed in agricultural labor for nine months in each year, or at the discretion of the authorities all of the Indians, a third serving every three months in turn. After some vacillation on the part of the crown and sudden shifts of policy, this became the legal norm, and ultimately found its way into the *Recopilación* of 1680.[63]

None of these royal precepts, however, was ever observed in practice. Later efforts to equate the custom in Chile with that prevailing in the other colonies failed equally before the tenacious opposition of the *encomenderos*. Under Charles II, in 1662, 1674, and 1679, the enslavement of natives taken in war was again prohibited, and all those held in bondage were ordered to be liberated. But the practical effect upon the condition of the Indians was nil. Obligatory labor for all the natives remained the rule. Only by slow degrees in the eighteenth century, as the rural laboring population changed from Indian to mestizo, and as Chilean society lost some of the frontier rudeness of earlier times, did the *inquilino* attached to the great agricultural *fundos* as we find him in the nineteenth century gradually emerge.[64]

To ensure that all the aborigines were reduced to Christian faith and governance, and that the royal tribute and other services were forthcoming, the crown from the days of Queen Isabella ordered that scattered Indians be concentrated in towns and villages, each with its church and school and simple form of local government. So it appears in the instructions issued to Nicolás de Ovando in 1503, in the Laws of Burgos of 1512, and in the program entrusted to the Hieronymite friars six years later. Similar instructions were sent to the *audiencia* of Peru after the close of the civil wars there, although they were not enforced systematically until the time of the viceroy Toledo (1569-82). Even in

---

63 Lig. VI, tit. 16. Also in the provinces of the Rio de la Plata (Tucumán, Paraguay, and Buenos Aires) the rules for the *mita* differed in detail from those prevailing in Peru. It is interesting that each of these remote and backward areas, Chile and the Rio de la Plata, merits a separate *titulo* in the *Recopilación* regulating the amount of tribute and the forms of Indian service.

64 For a fuller account of the Indian problem in colonial Chile, see Guillermo Feliú Cruz, *Las Encomiendas según tasas y ordenanzas* (Publ. Instit. invest. hist., LXXVII), Buenos Aires, 1941.

remote Chile there were efforts to reduce the seminomad woodland aborigines to village life under Spanish *administradores,* and lengthy ordinances were issued for their governance. In New Spain some slight
attempt to collect the dispersed Indian population in settlements was
made by the first viceroy, Antonio de Mendoza.[65] In response to prod-
dings from Madrid, a much more ambitious effort followed in the last
years of the sixteenth century, under the viceroy Luis de Velasco II and
his successor, Gaspar de Zúñiga y Acevedo, Count of Monterey (1590-
1603). In 1598 Monterey sent out a number of expeditions to survey
all the territory of New Spain from Tampico and Guadalajara southward—i.e., all the area of the civilized Indians—and report back on the
reductions or 'congregations' it seemed advisable to make. A large number were established during the next few years, especially in the mining
districts. It was prescribed that the Indians must not be coerced, and that
lands abandoned by them in their former locations were not to be taken
from them. Once the reductions were created, the Indians might not
leave for another pueblo, nor might the site of the new pueblos be
moved. But the wisdom of such a wholesale and violent uprooting of the
native population was very doubtful. Torquemada tells us that the
operation was accompanied by much carelessness and stupidity, if not
outright injustice and corruption, and that it worked cruel hardships
on many of the Indians involved.[66] They were torn from their homes
often to places where inadequate protection from the elements was
provided, and many of them died or ran away.[67] Wherever in Spanish
America this policy was followed it must also have broken up or weakened the old clan relationships, and left to the Indians little but the
bond of a common agrarian interest.

For reasons that are not always clear, the condition of the Indians in
Peru seems generally to have been worse than in New Spain. Especially
in the silver mines of Potosí and elsewhere in the Andean highlands the
situation was completely disastrous.[68] In 1657, during the viceroyalty
of the Conde de Alba de Liste, one of the *oidores* of Lima, Juan de

65 Arthur Scott Aiton, *Antonio de Mendoza, First Viceroy of New Spain,* Durham,
N. C., 1927, 94. By *cédulas* of 1551 and later years such Indians gathered into mission
pueblos by the friars were exempted for ten years from the payment of tribute, and
were promised that they would never be allotted in *encomiendas,* Vásquez, op. cit. 220-
25. Other Indians so reduced to village life were relieved, if they were Christians, of
half of the tribute for the first two years. *Recopilación,* lib. VI, tit. 5, ley 2.
66 Juan de Torquemada, *Monarquía indiana,* Madrid, 1732, I, 686-90, quoted by
Lesley Byrd Simpson, *Studies in the Administration of the Indians in New Spain,* II.
The Civil Congregation, Berkeley, Cal., 1934, 35.
67 On this general subject see Solórzano, *Política indiana,* lib. II, cap. 24; *Recopilación,* lib. VI, tit. 3; Simpson, op. cit. 31-46; Vásquez, op. cit. 245.
68 For the evils of the *mita* at its worst, see Arthur Preston Whitaker, *The Huancavelica Mercury Mine,* Cambridge, Mass., 1941, 18-20.

Padilla, drew up for the crown a well-known report on the wretched situation of the natives, with an appeal for reform. New regulations were issued, excellent in themselves, and a new viceroy was sent out to enforce them. And for a time there was probably some mitigation of the evils described.[69] Yet when Antonio de Ullo journeyed through Peru a few generations later, conditions apparently were as bad as ever. Tribute was exacted from those under 18 years of age and over 50, contrary to law, and even from the crippled and deformed. The *corregidores* in many places, instead of the statutory seventh, dragged off all the men of the district to the factories or mines, leaving only the women and children behind. Wages were unpaid, hours in the textile factories were incredibly long, and children of six or eight years of age in defiance of the regulations were forced to work in them.[70] There seems also to have grown up a practice of kidnaping Indians, while the system of peonage or debt servitude was already fully developed.

It was this oppression which caused the terrible Indian insurrection of Tupac Amaru in 1780; and although the *mita* as an institution was generally abolished by law after the emergence of the new republics, as inconsistent with the newly discovered principles of liberty, equality, and fraternity, for a long time in the nineteenth century the treatment of the aborigines saw little practical improvement. The Wars of Independence had not been fought for the Indian, nor by him. Only in the past generation or two, notably in Mexico, has the Indian come into his own as the rational being he was declared to be by Pope Paul III four hundred years ago.

To return to the story of the *encomienda*—in the seventeenth century, as the Hapsburg kings became more and more straitened financially, they began to exact from the *encomenderos* a part of their revenue from the tribute. In Peru, from the early years of the reign of Philip IV, the recipients of reassigned *encomiendas* of an annual value of over 800 ducats were required to turn a third of the tribute into the royal exchequer.[71] In 1687 the crown demanded of all *encomenderos* half of

69 In the eighteenth century the practice spread of commuting personal service of the *mita* for a money payment made by the *curaca* or the *corregidor* responsible for supplying the labor quota. The *corregidor* preferred to keep the Indians at home for his own use, and the miner was able to substitute hired labor which was generally more efficient.

70 By a Royal decree of 7 June 1729 the *mita* as a source of labor for the mines was abolished in New Granada, presumably because of reports of the ill-usage of the Indians. As a consequence many of the mines, both of silver and of gold, were abandoned, Vicente Restrepo, *Estudio sobre las minas de oro y plata de Colombia*, 2nd ed., Bogotá, 1888, 177. As there was no real evidence of exhaustion of the country's mineral resources, evidently mining methods were so primitive and uneconomical that they could not bear the added cost of free, contractual labor.

71 Gasparo de Escalona y Agüero, *Gazophilatium regium perubicum*, Madrid, 1647, lib. II, pt. 2, cap. 18; *Recopilacion*, lib. VI, tit. 8, leyes 38, 39.

the annual income (*media anata*) for four years from the following January, and later extended the requisition to January 1695. In 1703 the *media anata* was again exacted for two years.[72] A decree of 1701 directed that all *encomiendas* held *in absentia* should revert to the crown upon the death of the occupant. And as these inroads upon the system increased, the *encomienda* became a less and less desirable privilege except for the opportunity it offered for illegitimate profits. After the War of the Spanish Succession, Philip V continued in the same policy. A general decree of 13 November 1717 removed from viceroys, presidents, and *audiencias* the right to grant *encomiendas,* which thereafter was reserved exclusively to the king. And finally on 23 November of the following year the order went forth that thereafter every *encomienda* vacated by the death of a holder or for other cause should be administered for the crown. It was confirmed in other decrees of 1720 and 1721,[73] but was never consistently enforced. The *encomenderos* of Yucatan were exempted from its operation in the latter year, and those of Chile in 1724. And we have record of confirmations in many scattered regions such as New Granada and Buenos Aires in the second half of the century. *Encomiendas* in Yucatan were suppressed by royal decree of December 1785, those in Chile by order of the captain-general Ambrosio Higgins in 1789, but in some remote, outlying areas the institution probably survived to the end of the colonial regime.

The disappearance of the *encomienda* did not, moreover, necessarily imply an improvement in the lot of the aborigines. The *pueblos* and villages merely reverted to an administration of the *corregidor de indios,* or in New Spain to the *alcalde mayor,* who took over the functions of the *encomendero* and collected the tribute for the royal treasury. The *corregidor* was generally on limited appointment with an insufficient salary, and became an instrument of exploitation not only in the exaction of forced labor and illegal tributes, but by excessive fees and fines in judicial suits, and through the privilege of commercial monopoly within his *corregimiento.*[74] Under cover of this concession called *repartimiento,* he introduced goods to double or triple the amount allowed by law and through the native *cacique* forced upon the Indians objects which were often unnecessary or entirely useless to them. The system was not abolished until the establishment of the *intendencias* in the last quarter of the eighteenth century.

However, such conditions were not peculiar to the eighteenth century or to the Spanish colonies. Nor were they equally bad in all of the

72 Silvio Zavala, *La Encomienda indiana,* Madrid 1935, 332-5.

73 J. M. Ots Capdequi, *Instituciones sociales de la América española en el período colonial,* La Plata, 1934, 88.

74 On the oppression of the Indians by the *corregidores* see Jorge Juan and Antonio de Ulloa, *Noticias secretas de América,* London, 1826, pt. II, ch. 1.

American provinces. It is the age-old problem, which has persisted since the days of Columbus: the problem of finding a stable economic basis for European occupation and development of new, productive lands, and a problem which has not yet been satisfactorily solved.[75] Cheap native labor can be had only under compulsion. Yet if the settlements are to be maintained, life in them must be made both attractive and profitable to the European pioneer. In Spanish America the problem involved a direct conflict between juridical theory and the pressure of vested interests, between the good intentions of the crown and the spirit of exploitation which dominated a new frontier society.

[75] Not many years ago serious charges were brought in the Parliament of Belgium against officials of the Congo in Africa, that Negroes were forcibly recruited for public labor even when in a dying condition, and that mortality figures among the natives were almost equal to the casualty rate of Belgium during World War I. And we read that in Kenya Colony in East Africa the native tribes have been deprived of a third of their land capable of cultivation, which has passed into the hands of a small number of white settlers, while the native population in thirty years has decreased from four to three millions. The statement that possession of great tracts of land does not profit the white settler unless he has cheap labor, and that the natives refuse to work for him except under stress of dire necessity, has a familiar ring.

IV

Territorial Organization

THE VICEROYALTY OF NEW SPAIN

In the long history of political organization and control in Spain's American empire, several periods may easily be discerned. They are reflected both in the colonial institutions created and in the spirit in which these institutions were administered. The first period, comprising the years from the initial enterprise of Columbus to the conquests on the mainland in the 1520's and 1530's, was the age of the *adelantados*.[1] As already pointed out, the expeditions of discovery and colonization were left to private enterprise, and their leaders were rewarded with wide political and economic privileges in the lands they occupied, privileges which harked back to the seigniorial regime of the Middle Ages. Nevertheless, in spite of these privileges so lavishly bestowed, colonization and administration in America were conceived from the very beginning as a function primarily of the state.

In the second period, extending to the middle years of the reign of Philip II, the crown, stimulated by the magnitude of the conquests in Mexico and Peru, abandoned its earlier cautious policy and undertook to recover all the attributes of sovereignty in its overseas territories. Dr. Ots Capdequi has admirably summed up the situation.[2] Most of the great privileges conceded to the first discoverers and their descendants were withdrawn or limited, often through long and complicated lawsuits sustained with tenacity by the interested parties. Jurists gradually formulated a complete picture of the regalia inherent in the monarchy in the so-called Western Indies. The political incorporation of the colonies in the crown of Castile was formally asserted. Organs for the governance of the new empire were created in the metropolis, and upon it was projected the whole complex of the official bureaucracy of the peninsula: viceroys and judges, captains-general and governors, *corregidores* and officers of the exchequer. Minute and systematic rules were drawn up for new dis-

---

1 Cf. *ante*, pp. 19-22.

2 José María Ots Capdequi, 'Algunas Consideraciones en torno á la política económica y fiscal del estado español en las Indias,' *Rev. de las Indias, Bogotá, época 2, no. 6, 174-7, of which this and the two following paragraphs are a free adaptation.

coveries, and settlements which culminated in the celebrated ordinances of 1573. The juridical and social condition of the Indians was definitely fixed, after a long period of doubts and contradictions punctuated by the bitter polemics of theologians and jurists. It was the age of great experiments in government, during which institutions were forged which were to remain almost unaltered until the great reforming efforts of the eighteenth century.

A stability, one might almost say petrifaction, of institutional life, which may already be observed in the second half of the sixteenth century, is the characteristic feaure of Spanish policy in the Indies throughout the rest of the Hapsburg era. The creative vigor of earlier times seems to have been wholly exhausted. The town councils in the Indies, with the sale of municipal offices and the implanting of the *corregidores,* entered upon a period of frank decadence. The descendants of the *conquistadores,* the Creoles, found themselves debarred from all high posts of administration by the old aristocracies of the metropolis, which had been notably absent earlier during the hard and critical period of conquest and colonization. The tendencies to centralization and uniformity were accentuated. A mistaken policy in Spain was matched by a colonial bureaucracy marked by extreme complexity and routine. The history of the Spanish state in the Indies became little more than a collection of more or less picturesque anecdotes; jurisdictional conflicts and questions of etiquette absorbed the life of judges and viceroys. It was nevertheless in this epoch that the greatest commentators on Spanish American law flourished, and that the celebrated *Recopilación* of 1680 was promulgated.

The important reforms of the eighteenth century, especially those undertaken by Charles III and his ministers, marked the final period to be discerned within the colonial era, a period that lasted, with diverse results in the various spheres of administration and government, until the days of the first struggles for independence in America.

This sequence of institutional development was clearly reflected in the territorial organization of the American empire. The Castilian sovereigns governed their overseas possessions through the instrumentality of viceroys, captains-general, and *audiencias.* With the lapse of the early viceroyalty of Columbus in the West Indies, and the rapid extension of Spanish conquest over the highland areas on the mainland, the crown was enabled to create two vast political jurisdictions which together embraced most of the territory of the western hemisphere. One, with its capital in New Spain, included all the Spanish provinces north of the Isthmus of Panama; the other, centered in Peru, covered all of Spanish South America except the coast of Venezuela.

These two great viceroyalties remained unaltered for two centuries, until the coming of the Bourbons. They were divided, partly for historical reasons, partly for administrative convenience, into a number of extensive subordinate areas, each of which constituted a kingdom among the innumerable territorial possessions of the Hapsburg sovereigns, and they were so referred to in royal decrees and other official documents. Over each was placed a governor assisted by an administrative and judicial tribunal called the *audiencia*. Over the kingdom in which the viceroy had his residence the viceroy himself acted as governor. The other kingdoms within the viceregal jurisdiction were not all of the same grade or status with respect to the authority of the viceroy. Over some he ruled directly as governor; over others his authority was of a more vague and supervisory character. The former came to be called presidencies, the latter captaincies-general. The viceroy served as president of the *audiencia* established in the viceregal capital, and also in the very beginning as president of the *audiencias* created for the other areas which were fully subordinated to his authority. But in the reign of Philip II all of these subordinate *audiencias* came to have presidents of their own—hence the name *presidencia*—the viceroy reserving only the title and functions of governor. In the seventeenth century such a president was as a rule also appointed governor of the immediate province within which he resided, or even of a larger area under the *audiencia's* jurisdiction, but in any case he remained subject to the supervision and direction of the viceroy in all questions of policy. Only matters of routine administration were left to the governor and *audiencia*.

The captaincy-general, although regarded as part of the viceroyalty, was for most practical purposes independent of viceregal intervention. The president of the *audiencia* was also the governor, and within his own jurisdiction he exercised virtually autonomous powers. Although theoretically subordinate to the viceroy, he was answerable for his acts only to the king and the Council of the Indies in Spain. The dignity and salary of the captain-general were less, but as time went on, and especially in the eighteenth century, captains-general came to be more and more regarded as little viceroys. Their official title always ran as 'president, governor, and captain-general.'

The title 'captain-general' consequently appears in Spanish colonial America in two senses. It denoted first of all and primarily, of course, a military rank. The viceroy was almost invariably the captain-general as well within his immediate jurisdiction. And the president of one of the subordinate *audiencias* was sometimes given this military title, if local circumstances such as war with the Indian savages on the frontier warranted, although the area was not, in the political sense indicated above, a captaincy-general. Even the governor of a frontier province like Florida was sometimes called a captain-general if his training and experience justified it. On the other hand, the term 'captain-general' after the middle of the sixteenth century was also used with this special connotation of the royal governor of a region independent of the viceroy and subject to the king and council in Spain.

The first permanent viceroyalty to be erected in America was on the mainland, that of New Spain. When Hernando Cortés, conqueror of Mexico, returned to Europe in 1528 to plead his case before the emperor against the charges and calumnies of his enemies, he was overwhelmed with honors in recognition of his immense achievement in the New World, but he was not reinstated in the civil government of the area he had conquered. The course of events had demonstrated that the great *conquistadores* might grow too powerful and too independent to be controlled by the authorities at home. As Professor Merriman has pointed out,

the Hapsburgs did not, as a rule, take kindly to subordinates of the brilliant or inventive sort, who wanted to strike out on lines of their own. The official whom they preferred was the hard-working, competent, but obedient type, who would faithfully discharge the duties laid upon him, and send back for fresh instructions in any case of doubt . . . The distance from Spain, the slowness of communications, the new conditions of which Europe was necessarily in densest ignorance, all rendered supervision from home exceedingly difficult, and offered the greatest temptation to independent action; it was therefore doubly essential that the crown be certain of the men that it placed there.[3]

Even before Cortés' arrival at the Court, a royal tribunal of five persons had been appointed—the first *Audiencia* of New Spain—to take over his government. But it proved to be a fiasco. Its president, the notorious Nuño de Guzmán, was a rapacious and cruel tyrant, and a flood of complaints flowed to Spain. Consequently in November 1529, at a joint meeting of the Councils of Castile, Finance, and the Indies, it was recommended that the difficult situation be solved by the appointment of a royal representative endowed with fullest powers. Ten days later Antonio de Mendoza, brother of the celebrated Diego Hurtado de Mendoza, and scion of one of the most distinguished families of Castile, was selected as the first of the Spanish viceroys on the American mainland. For reasons that are not entirely clear, it was nearly six years before Mendoza could get his instructions and sail for his post; and in the interval a second *audiencia* was sent out to New Spain to replace the first as custodian of the royal authority. Cortés by these means was permanently excluded from the government of Mexico. When he returned to America in 1530 he was forbidden to enter the capital, and the clergy were even reproved for praying for him in the churches.

The crown never had reason to regret the selection it made of its first

----

3 Roger Bigelow Merriman, *The Rise of the Spanish Empire*, III, 649.

viceroy. Mendoza already had been employed in various diplomatic capacities in Europe. As viceroy he displayed qualities of firmness and decision, devotion to the king and to the church, together with a generosity and liberality that made him one of the greatest and most popular of Spain's rulers in the New World. He was viceroy of New Spain from 1535 to 1550, and it was he who really laid down the lines—within the compass of his voluminous instructions from the Council of the Indies— along which the viceregal institution was to develop in America.[4]

The viceroyalty of New Spain in the time of the Hapsburgs embraced the central kingdom of Mexico or New Spain proper, and the outlying areas of New Galicia, Central America, the Antilles, and, after their conquest by Miguel de Legaspi, the Philippine Islands.[5] Each of these jurisdictions was a captaincy-general, except New Galicia, which was a presidency. Each was provided with a royal *audiencia,* which exercised administrative as well as judicial functions, under a president who was governor of the region.

The central kingdom of New Spain was under the immediate jurisdiction of the viceroy himself, who served as president, governor, and captain-general. Its *audiencia,* as we have seen, antedated the arrival of the first viceroy, but after 1535 it was subordinated to him. The ecclesiastical government was vested in a bishop, first appointed in 1525, but within a decade raised to the rank of archbishop. Eventually there were eight suffragan bishops. The University of Mexico, the most celebrated of all the colonial universities, was founded by royal decree in 1551, and formally inaugurated by the second viceroy, Luis de Velasco, eighteen months later.

The authority of the viceroy as president, governor, and captain-general covered all the area of the present republic of Mexico, save for an enclave in the west which embraced the domain of the *audiencia* of New Galicia. It extended northward to the Californias and New Mexico, and beyond into that *terra incognita* which is now the center of the United States; also eastward along the shores of the Gulf of Mexico around to the tip of the peninsula of Florida (*hasta el cabo de la Florida*).[6]

---

4 For the best account of Antonio de Mendoza, see Arthur Scott Aiton, *Antonio de Mendoza, First Viceroy of New Spain,* Durham, N. C., 1927.

5 The Philippine Islands, ruled by a governor appointed in Spain, were erected into a captaincy-general in May 1583 (*Recopilación,* lib. II, tit. 15, ley 11). Their political organization and general administration, both central and local, were in all essential respects the same as in a captaincy-general in America. See Ordinances of 1583 in Blair and Robertson, *The Philippine Islands,* 1493-1898, Cleveland, 1903-1909, V, 274 ff.

6 *Recopilación,* lib. II, tit. 15, ley 3. See also Merriman, op. cit. III, 643, n. 5. Augustine, a frontier dependency of New Spain and supported by an annual subsidy (*situado*) from Mexico City, was immediately subordinate to the *Audiencia* of Santo Domingo; but because of its isolation and remoteness as a military outpost, it seems to have been rather independent, often negotiating in frontier matters directly with the Council of the Indies.

The region west and northwest of Michoacán, comprising the province or kingdom of New Galicia, had first been overrun in the years 1530-1 by Nuño de Guzmán, president of the first Mexican *audiencia*. After his removal from the government of New Spain he prudently withdrew to his recent conquests, over which he exercised jurisdiction as the first royal governor. Later retired in disgrace and imprisoned, he was succeeded by Francisco Vásquez de Coronado who from New Galicia as a base undertook his famous expedition to the Seven Cities of Cibola, an enterprise which discovered the Grand Canyon and the Colorado River, first explored New Mexico, and penetrated through northern Texas into the valley of the Missouri River.

New Galicia remained attached to the government in Mexico City until 1548 when an *audiencia* of four judges was established in the squalid little village of Compostela. Its political and judicial control extended over a vague frontier region reaching to the crests of the western cordillera,[7] and ultimately northward through New Biscay (Durango and Chihuahua) to the Rio Grande. The viceroy retained authority as president and governor, however, for another twenty-five years, when the *audiencia* was raised to the rank of a *chancillería*[8] with a president of its own. In the interval the new tribunal was subordinated to the viceregal *audiencia* in Mexico City to a degree that was unique in American annals. Civil cases were appealed from the lesser to the higher tribunal. According to the original ordinances of 1548 certain important crown cases (*casos de corte*) might at the discretion of the plaintiff be carried directly to the Mexican *audiencia*; and by a royal decree of 1550 all suits in which the judges failed to reach an agreement were to be referred there. Judges of the provincial *audiencia* might be dispatched by the viceroy on inspection tours (*visitas*) to any part of New Spain, and might even be called upon to assist in the judicial labors of the superior tribunal, although this privilege apparently was not much used by the viceroy. In 1560 the *Audiencia* of New Galicia was moved to the more important town of Guadalajara where it remained to the end of the colonial era.

All the rest of modern Mexico remained subject to the *Audiencia* of New Spain. As the savage, semidesert north came slowly to be subdued and occupied by the Spanish miner, the rancher, and the missionary friar, military governments were organized: New Biscay (1562), New Leon (1579), New Mexico (1598), Coahuila (1687), Texas (1718),

---

7 The older settlements on the Pacific slope were not added until 1574. For the best short statement about the beginnings of the *Audiencia* of New Galicia, see John H. Parry, 'The Ordinances of the *Audiencia* of Nueva Galicia,' *Hisp. Amer. Hist. Rev.* XVIII, 364-75.

8 In Spanish history a supreme court of appeals whose written decisions were sealed with the royal seal placed upon them by a *chanciller* or his deputy.

Sinaloa (1734), New Santander (1746), California (1767); until in the eighteenth century Spanish authority was carried eastward to the banks of the Mississippi River, and northward to Monterey and San Francisco on the Pacific.

To the southeast of the land of the Aztecs lay the picturesque and fertile area of Central America, the seat of the most interesting and probably the most civilized culture produced by the American aborigines in pre-Columbian times. In a medial position with reference to other and earlier areas of European occupation, it was invaded and subdued by the Spaniards simultaneously from three directions, from Panama, Mexico, and Santo Domingo; and for many years it was subject to shifting or conflicting jurisdictions. The *conquistadores* themselves, as they established settlements in the new and vaguely outlined provinces of Nicaragua, Honduras, and Guatemala, fought with one another like feudal barons in a tropical wilderness; and as neighboring *audiencias* were created, these too strove to extend their authority over this focal region. The *Audiencia* of Santo Domingo, the first to be set up in the New World, endeavored to exert its political jurisdiction over the agents of Cortés in Honduras and of Pedrarias Dávila in Nicaragua, with no great success; although for two years, from the arrival of the first royal governor, Diego López de Salcedo, until the establishment of a continental *audiencia* in Mexico City in 1528, the province of Honduras was subject nominally at least to the authority of Hispaniola. The new Mexican *audiencia* in the beginning received administrative control over Honduras and Guatemala; but beyond, in Nicaragua to the southward, the island tribunal retained control until the installation of a new continental *audiencia* at Panama in 1538-9.[9]

A seperate *audiencia* for Central America was first announced in the celebrated New Laws of 20 November 1542, and it was formally installed at the interior town of Gracias a Diós, in what is now the republic of Honduras, a year and a half later.[10] Its jurisdiction covered the territory of all the present Central American republics, besides the isthmus of Panama or Castilla del Oro, and the provinces of Chiapas and Yucatan which now belong to the republic of Mexico. The *audiencia* established only four years earlier on the isthmus was at the same time abolished. But for several decades both the residence and the territorial jurisdiction of this new tribunal—called the *Audiencia de los Confines* because, says López de Velasco, it was first set up on the boundary of Nicaragua and Guatemala, without a definite place of abode—remained very uncertain. Panama was in 1550 separated from Central America and joined to the

---

9 Formally created by royal decree in February 1535.

10 The formal decree of erection was issued on 13 September 1543, and called for a tribunal of four judges, one of whom was to serve as president. *Recopilación*, lib. II, tit. 15, ley 6; Antonio de Remesal, *Historia de la provincia de S. Vicente de Chyapa y Guatemala*, Madrid, 1619, lib. IV, cap. 11, par. 2; cap. 14, par. 1, 5, 6.

Audiencia of Lima in Peru; in 1563 it once more became part of the Central American jurisdiction; but in 1567 it was finally reunited with the viceroyalty of Peru, again with an *audiencia* of its own. For over a decade Yucatan with its related provinces of Cozumel and Tabasco shifted uneasily back and forth between the *audiencias* of Central America and New Spain, until in 1560 they became permanently attached to the latter. The residence of the Central American *audiencia* itself was in 1549 moved to Santiago de los Caballeros de Guatemala, today La Antigua, and fifteen years later was shifted down to Panama with a jurisdiction which included Honduras, Nicaragua, Costa Rica, and the Pacific coast of New Granada. Guatemala and Chiapas were at the same time temporarily annexed to New Spain. But not for long. Within five years, 1570, the *audiencia* was back again in Guatemala City, and there it remained until the end of Spanish rule in the nineteenth century.[11] It is generally referred to as the *Audiencia* of Guatemala.

These kaleidoscopic changes over a period of a quarter-century, covering the later part of the reign of Charles V and the early years of Philip II, are interesting as evidence of the difficulties involved in the effort by the crown to set up institutions of royal government in an American wilderness 4,000 miles from the metropolis and in regions the exact geography of which could be only vaguely surmised.

Apparently in the beginning the president of the *Audiencia* of Guatemala was not given the powers of a governor. In other words, the executive authority was placed in commission, in the hands of the whole board of judges, as in the first *Audiencia* of New Spain. But in September 1560 president Juan Núñez de Landecho was named sole governor, with all the powers of the viceroy in Mexico City. This evidently marks the beginning of the captaincy-general of Guatemala in the special sense indicated above.[12] Difficulties of transportation between Mexico City and the Central American provinces made communications extremely slow and unsatisfactory. Continuous and effective consultation with the Mexican viceroy was out of the question; the latter could not possibly keep in touch with changing conditions and problems so far distant from his capital, nor could the local authorities be dependent upon instructions from headquarters which when they arrived might no longer be applicable. It is not surprising therefore that Philip II felt impelled to set up a local executive in Guatemala with virtually independent authority responsible directly to the crown. Somewhat similar circumstances of

---

11 *Col. doc. inéd.* 1st ser., VIII, 36; León Fernández, ed., *Colección de documentos para la Historia de Costa Rica*, 10 vols., 1881-1907, IV, 290-92; F. de P. Garcia Palaez, *Memorias para la historia del antigua reyno de Guatemala*, 3 vols., Guatemala, 1851-52, I, 164-7 238-9; Manuel M. de Peralta, ed., *Costa Rica, Nicaragua y Panamá en el siglo* XVI, Madrid, 1883, 132-3, 416, 431.
12 García Pelaez, op. cit., 238-9.

distance and isolation prevailed in the great interior plateau region of New Granada south of the isthmus, and here too a captaincy-general was created shortly after that in Guatemala. It was indicative of a slow process of administrative decentralization of the extremely extended territorial jurisdictions of the viceroys which was to see its logical fruition in the age of the Bourbons in the eighteenth century.

Ecclesiastical government in Central America was entrusted to a bishop resident in Guatemala City and subordinated until the eighteenth century (1743) to the archbishop of Mexico, when the bishopric was raised to archepiscopal rank with three suffragan bishops. The Dominican college of Santro Tomás in Guatemala City, founded by the first bishop Marroquín, was in 1676 raised to the dignity of a royal and pontifical university, the Universidad de San Carlos Barromeo, and achieved some distinction in the New World as a school of theology. But although the fertile and well-cultivated upland regions supported a numerous and prosperous Spanish population, there was relatively little pursuit of learning and of letters as compared with New Spain or Peru. Colonial life, though punctuated at times by Indian revolts, earthquakes, and pirate raids, was generally tranquil, sequestered—a somewhat bucolic and intellectually untroubled existence which some of us in this present age may regard with no little envy.

The oldest Spanish jurisdiction in the New World, as related in an earlier chapter, was that established in the West Indian islands, with its center in the city of Santo Domingo. And here in 1511 was set up the first American *audiencia,* at the same time that the rights of Diego Columbus as American viceroy were formally recognized by the crown.[13] This tribunal was instructed to meet at regular intervals with the viceroy Diego and the officials of the royal exchequer to open the king's letters and draw up replies, and in general to discuss and decide all matters of public policy. Intended to curb the extended powers and pretentions of Don Diego, and the occasion for numerous conflicts during his lifetime, the practice nevertheless became firmly established at Santo Domingo. And so from the beginning the *audiencia* in the New World became something more than, as in Spain, a mere court of law; it was also a council of administration advisory to the governor of the district, and shared many responsibilities with him. Indeed in 1520 Charles V referred to the court at Santo Domingo as 'nuestro consejo real.'

Temporarily suspended in 1517, it was revived three years later, with four judges and a president—which came to be the conventional membership of the smaller *audiencias* in America—and with an increase of salaries, although the tribunal had no president for nearly a decade. When the office of president was created, it was evidently intended to be

13 See *ante,* p. 18.

merely a judicial post as in the *audiencias* of Spain. The definitive re-call of Diego Columbus to Spain in 1524 enabled the crown to unite the offices of president and governor, and they remained so permanently thereafter.

After the return of the viceroy Diego to Spain, the *audiencia* assumed the general administration of the Indies—again a government in com-mission—until the arrival of a president and governor in 1529, the bishop Sebastián Ramírez de Fuenleal. He was the first president actually to exercise his peculiar functions in the New World; and his government was so satisfactory to all parties concerned that when the new *audiencia* in Mexico was reorganized in 1530 Ramírez, while retaining his island bishoprics, was transferred to the presidency of the mainland tribunal. Meanwhile in 1526 the *Audiencia* of Santo Domingo was elevated to the status of a *chancillería,* and this step was ratified by a new code of ordinances for its governance issued from Monzón on 4 June 1528. From the arrival of the first Mexican viceroy Mendoza in 1535, the An-tilles apparently were recognized as a government within the viceroyalty of New Spain, but virtually independent of it in all matters except those of military and naval defense. It therefore was a captaincy-general in the later acceptance of this term, the first in the New World.

Diego Columbus had persistently endeavored, but without success, to secure recognition of his authority as viceroy over the mainland of Amer-ica. After his recall the jurisdiction of the *Audiencia* of Santo Domingo over the mainland came to be so recognized, until the creation of the continental tribunals already referred to. In the ordinances of 1528 its judicial competence as a court of appeals was extended over Central and South America, from Nicaragua southward to Peru. And the judges made vigorous efforts to establish their political authority as well, intervening actively in the quarrels between Governor Velázquez of Cuba and Her-nando Cortés, between Cortés and Francisco de Garay, and in the com-plicated three-cornered struggle for possession of the province of Hon-duras. Special investigators (*jueces pesquisidores*) were also sent to Venezuela and to Peru, to keep the peace between warring factions and conserve the interests of the king. The new *audiencias,* however, first that of New Spain and later those of Panama and Lima, soon with-drew these mainland areas from Santo Domingo's jurisdiction—every-where except on the Venezuelan coast to Rio Hacha, which remained until the eighteenth century attached to the captaincy-general in the Antilles.[14]

European wars, and the intrusion into America of Spain's maritime rivals, the English, French, and Dutch, affected the history of the West

---

14 For the early history of the *Audiencia* of Santo Domingo, see C. H. Haring, 'The Genesis of Royal Government in the Spanish Indies,' *Hisp. Amer. Hist. Rev.,* VII, 141-91.

Indies more closely than that of any other part of Spanish America. From the days of the emperor Charles V to the French Revolution every war in Western Europe had its immediate repercussions in the New World; in the sixteenth and seventeenth centuries often in the form of raids by privateers upon Spanish settlements in the Antilles and upon the neighboring shores of Tierra firme; in the seventeenth and eighteenth centuries in local wars between the Spanish islands and those more recently seized and colonized by competing European nations.

It was in the seventeenth century that these adversaries first seriously contested the claims of Spain and Portugal to exclusive territorial dominion in the New World. Most of the Lesser Antilles, which the Spaniards, attracted by the richer provinces on the continent, had never seen fit to occupy, were settled by the English, Dutch, and French between 1625 and 1650. Jamaica was seized by a naval and military expedition sent out from England by Cromwell in 1655; a decade later the French took formal possession of the western end of the island of Hispaniola, which later became the flourishing French sugar colony of Saint Domingue, a division perpetuated in the two present-day nations of Haiti and the Dominican Republic.

After 1739, when the captaincy-general of New Granada in South America was raised to the dignity of a viceroyalty, the coasts of Venezuela were temporarily removed from the political and military jurisdiction of Santo Domingo and attached to that of Bogotá, although judicial appeals still went to the *audiencia* on Hispaniola. Later, in 1763, the province of Florida was lost by cession to Great Britan; and in the following year, after France had ceded to Spain the vast area in the Mississippi valley called Louisiana, the island of Cuba was set up as an independent captaincy-general to which the new province was attached.[15]

In these ways the ancient captaincy-general of Santo Domingo gradually decreased in size and importance, until in 1795 Spain, in making peace with the regicide French republic, ceded to it the eastern end of the island of Hispaniola as well. From that time forward the focus of Spanish authority in the West Indies remained at Havana, and the old *Audiencia* of Santo Domingo was formally transferred to Cuba, to the town of Puerto Príncipe, in 1797.

The only other important territorial innovation in the eighteenth century was the establishment of the *Provincias Internas* in northern Mexico. Schemes for a separate government for these northern frontier regions, exposed to constant raids by the Seri, Pima, and Apache Indians, had several times been considered. The viceroy in Mexico City was overworked, and too remote from the frontier to understand its real needs. Aggression from the north and east by the Russians, the English, or the

---

15 Also Florida after its reversion to Spain by the Treaty of Paris in 1783.

French was a constant preoccupation of the Spanish authorities. As early as 1751 the creation of an additional viceroyalty in northern Mexico had been suggested, stemming from the presidency of New Galicia [16] —as had been done in South America in the recent erection of the viceroyalty of New Granada. In 1760 the plan, it seems, was given serious consideration. But the viceregal institution could scarcely be supported by the meager resources of that area, and it was wholly inappropriate to a semidesert wilderness dotted with a few mission stations and mining camps and largely occupied by savage nomads.

The question became one of the major preoccupations of José de Gálvez, the last and greatest of the *visitadores* or inspectors-general sent out to New Spain,[17] and he recommended an independent military government or commandancy-general. This reform he was able to execute in 1776, after his return to Spain where he was promoted to the post of Minister of the Indies. What are now the northern states of the Mexican Republic,[18] together with California, New Mexico, and Texas, were placed under the military and political government of a Commandant-General of the Internal Provinces, independent of the viceroy and responsible directly to the king. His capital was first in the town of Arizpe in Sonora, later removed to Chihuahua.

The autonomy of this new territorial entity, however, was somewhat less than that of the captaincies-general. Occasionally as circumstances seemed to warrant, the authority of the viceroy was for a short period partially or wholly revived. In 1785-1786 the commandancy-general was split into three units under the supervisory power of the viceroy. In 1787 this was renewed, the commandancy-general being now divided into two units each with its own commandant-general. Five years later the independent military government was restored, but now divested of the three provinces of California, New Leon, and New Santander. Finally a decree of 1804 (not wholly enforced until 1812) divided what remained into two independent commandancies-general, of the east and the west respectively.[19]

The commandancy-general, moreover, possessed no *audiencia* of its own, and judicial appeals from its *alcaldes mayores* and other magistrates were carried from the provinces of New Leon and New Santander to the *Audiencia* of Mexico, from the other provinces to Guadalajara.

16 In a memorial by Fernando Sánchez Salvador. Charles E. Chapman, *The Founding of Spanish California . . . 1687-1783*, New York, 1916, 37.

17 For José de Gálvez, see Herbert Ingram Priestley, *José de Gálvez, Visitor-General of New Spain*, 1765-1771, Berkeley, Cal., 1916.

18 Sinaloa, Sonora, Lower California, New Biscay (Durango and Chihuahua), and Coahuila, to which were later added New Santander and New Leon. See Eusebio Ventura Beleña. *Recopilación sumaria de todos los autos acordados de la real audiencia y sala del crimen de esta Nueva España*, 2 vols., Mexico, 1787, I, 290-91.

19 Chapman, op. cit. 426.

As its resources were inadequate to maintain the military establishments needed for its defense, it was always dependent financially upon the viceroyalty in Mexico City.

The viceroyalty of New Spain with its dependencies of New Galicia and the Internal Provinces, together with the captaincies-general of Guatemala and Havana—these constituted the general territorial organization of Spanish America north of the isthmus of Panama at the opening of the nineteenth century. From it were shortly to spring the republics of Mexico and Central America, the latter destined to distintegrate into the five nations which today represent old provincial divisions of the Spanish captaincy-general.

V

❧❦❧

Territorial Organization

❧❦❧

THE VICEROYALTY OF PERU

The viceroyalty of Peru in South America was more extensive in area than its North American counterpart, embracing all of the continent except Portuguese Brazil, the Guianas, and the Caribbean coast of Venezuela. And although it was created a decade later than the viceroyalty of New Spain, for two centuries it was regarded as the more important of the two jurisdictions. Peru appeared as the most precious of the crown's American possessions, the source of most of its wealth. Many of the Peruvian viceroys had previously occupied the post of viceroy in New Spain, and translation from Mexico City to Lima was considered to be the last step of promotion in the imperial hierarchy.

This pre-eminence of Peru in the minds of Spaniards was due to the profusion of its mines of gold and silver. Throughout the length and breadth of the cordilleras of the Andes, from the northern part of the present Peruvian republic south to Chile and the borders of Argentina, silver deposits were abundant. They had been worked by the aborigines, as was attested by the immense stores of silver ornaments and utensils seized by Pizarro and his companions in the conquest of the Inca empire, to the amount of over 266,000 marcs, or nearly two and a half million dollars; [1] and after the conquest they were exploited on a much larger scale by Spaniards with the aid of forced Indian labor. The richest mines were found in present-day Bolivia, especially those of the famous Cerro de Potosí discovered by an Indian in 1545, and producing during the following century over 400 million pesos in silver bullion. How much silver was extracted which failed to be registered at the government assay offices in order to escape payment of the royalty due to the crown, it is impossible to say.

Gold too was found within the bounds of ancient Peru. The golden plunder of the Spanish *conquistadores* was greater in value, although not in volume, than the silver—over 1,900,000 *pesos de oro,* the equiv-

---

[1] American dollars of current value. The purchasing power of gold in Europe in the middle of the sixteenth century was approximately ten times as great as in recent times.

alent of more than three million dollars. But the more abundant source of gold after the conquest was New Granada, today the republic of Colombia, and the principal cities of that region, from Medellín to Popayán and Pasto, owed their early wealth and importance to the mines in their neighborhood. New Granada also produced emeralds in abundance, and has continued to be the principal source of these gems.

The importance of the southern viceroyalty in the production of the precious metals was reflected in the remittances of bullion to Spain from the 1550's onwards. The amount that entered Spain on the account of passengers and merchants before the eighteenth century was always greater than that from Mexico, although the trade in European goods was less; an indication that it represented the greater profits of private mine owners, whether Spaniards or colonists, in the viceroyalty of Peru.

This great southern viceroyalty in the sixteenth century embraced the central kingdom of Peru proper—or New Castile as it was called in the early days of the conquest—together with the kingdoms of Panama, New Granada, and Quito to the northward, and Chile and Charcas, including the area of the Rio de la Plata, in the south. All of these regions were presidencies, with one exception, New Granada, which early in the reign of Philip II was raised to that stature and dignity of a captaincy-general. This was in contrast to New Spain, in which all the subordinate areas were captaincies-general except one, New Galicia. In the eighteenth century under the Bourbon kings, as will be seen later, this administrative setup was considerably altered.

Over the central region of Peru the viceroy himself ruled directly as president, governor, and captain-general. He was also governor in the two adjoining jurisdictions of Quito and Charcas, when they received a separate organization. The first viceroy was the ill-starred Blasco Núñez Vela, who came out from Spain in 1544 with a special mandate to enforce in Peru the New Laws intended to abolish Indian servitude. With him came the first royal tribunal to be established in South America, the viceregal *Audiencia* of Lima.

The whole southern continent had in the beginning been regarded as subject to the quasi-political jurisdiction of Santo Domingo, as already related, until the erection of Panama in 1538. The territorial limits of the latter were made to include the area from Nicaragua and the coasts of Cartagena southward to the Strait of Magellan—a fantastic concept! That judicial appeals from the provinces of the Rio de la Plata, for instance, which are mentioned specifically in the decree of erection, should be carried to the isthmus of Panama, was an incredible expectation. It may have been intended to be but a temporary expedient, until more reasonable administrative arrangements could be agreed upon. At any rate it survived only four years, for the 'New Laws' of 1542 provided for the erection of two new *audiencias,* in Peru and Guatemala, and at the same time abolished the *Audiencia* of Panama. During the next twenty-five years political control over the isthmus shifted uncertainly from one authority to another. The region was twice for a short time annexed to Central America. Finally in 1567 it was permanently attached to Peru, again with an *audiencia* of its own, and organized as a presidency subordinated to the viceroy, but with territorial jurisdiction limited to the isthmus and to the Pacific coast south to Buenaventura. And so it remained until the middle of the eighteenth century. Meantime, after the arrival of the first *audiencia* at Lima in 1544, all of Spanish South America was placed under its jurisdiction, except New Granada and the settlements on the Caribbean coast, which were once more attached to Santo Domingo—until the organization one by one of the other regional *audiencias* on the periphery of the viceroyalty.

The first of these was the tribunal at Santa Fe de Bogotá in New Granada, erected by decree in 1549, and installed in April of the following year. Ever since the conquest a decade earlier by Gonzalo Jiménez de Quesada, this colony had been torn by factions among the colonists, and petitions to the crown urged the establishment of a local *audiencia* to restore order and put an end to the excesses and scandals of the *conquistadores*. Moreover, communications between the interior plateau of Cundinamarca and the *audiencia* at Lima or at Santo Domingo had proved to be extremely difficult and costly, and appeals from local magistrates redounded only to the interest of the wealthy settlers. Even in preconquest times, the aboriginal Chibcha tribes had lived in isolation from the Incas in the south and from the tribes on the coast of the Caribbean. Another *audiencia* was an evident necessity. Its foundation in reality marked the end of the period of the conquest and the beginning of the colonial regime. Its territorial jurisdiction covered the coast of Cartagena, the valleys of the Cauca and Magdalena Rivers, and the lands eastward to the great plains.

Government by the new tribunal, however, did not give the satisfactory results anticipated; public administration was paralyzed by quarrels between judges and *visitadores,* and by an endless chain of *residencias.* Government by commission, in other words, was not a success. In 1563, therefore, the crown appointed a president with authority as governor and captain-general, independent of the viceroy in Lima, and with similar powers in matters of *encomiendas,* military affairs, ecclesiastical patronage, missions, protection of the natives, and economic and financial administration.[2] This marks the beginning of the captaincy-general of New Granada, analogous in authority and importance to the captaincies-general of Guatemala and Santo Domingo in the northern viceroyalty. The first captain-general, Dr. Andrés Díez Venero de Leiva, gave the

2 José Antonio de la Plaza, *Memorias para la historia de la Nueva Granada,* Bogotá, 1850, 210-11.

country for the first time a government which we are told was firm, prudent, diligent, and just. He ruled for the unusually long period of ten years, and his administration was called the golden age of the colony. Returning to Spain in 1547, he was rewarded for his eminent services with membership in the Council of the Indies.

With political independence the new captaincy-general secured ecclesiastical independence as well. The first bishoprics south of the Caribbean were those of Cuzco and Lima, established in 1534 and 1539. Six years later, in 1545, Lima was erected into an archbishopric, and among its component dioceses was that of Santa Fe de Bogotá, which received its first resident bishop in 1553. But in 1564 the bishopric of Santa Fe was itself raised to the rank of an archbishopric, with eventually four suffragan bishops. By the middle of the seventeenth century the colony had been provided with two colleges of university grade, both located in the city of Bogotá.

The two extremities of the great Inca empire over which a Spanish viceroy now presided were Quito in the north and Charcas (modern Bolivia) in the south. Both were too far distant from Lima to be effectively served by the viceregal *audiencia*,[3] and Philip II early in his reign set them up as separate jurisdictions. After discussions in the Council of the Indies covering several years, an *Audiencia* of Charcas was formally established by royal decree in June 1559,[4] and installed two years later in the town of La Plata, the oldest Spanish settlement in the region. In colonial days this town also went by the Indian name of Chuquisaca, and today it is the city of Sucre. It lay in a rich silver-producing area that attracted great numbers of adventurers, especially after the discovery of the mines of Potosí in 1545, and it became the center of an extravagant, contentious, and not overly law-abiding, frontier community. The need of strengthening the arm of the law amid such circumstances was obvious. The decree creating the *audiencia* of Quito was issued in August 1563, in response to petitions from the municipal council setting forth the abuses of justice and the weakness of royal government in that remote province.[5]

The territorial jurisdiction of the *Audiencia* of Charcas, at first fixed vaguely as extending a hundred leagues about the city of La Plata, was within a few years pushed eastward to the settlement of Santa Cruz de la Sierra, on the borders of that wilderness called the Gran Chaco, and southward to include Tucumán, Paraguay, and the settlements on the Rio de la Plata. Until 1568 it included also the city and district of Cuzco

---

3 It was also averred that many highland Indians, when forced to resort to the court at Lima, fell ill and died from the results of the change of climate.

4 Enrique Ruíz Guiñazú, *La Magistratura indiana*, Buenos Aires, 1916, 149-50.

5 Federico González Suárez, *Historia general de la república del Ecuador*, 7 vols., Quito, 1890-1903, III, 9, 14 n,

in southern Peru, a source of bitter quarrels with the Lima *audiencia;* but in that year Cuzco was returned to the administration of Lima, and in 1573 the district was divided between the two jurisdictions.

The territory of the *Audiencia* of Quito was much more extended in area than the present-day republic of Ecuador which is its modern counterpart. It stretched from above Paita in northern Peru to Buenaventura midway up the Pacific coast of modern Colombia, and in the interior as far north as Buga, beyond the city of Cali. It embraced therefore the wealthy and fertile region of Popayán and the upper Cauca valley, which till then had been subject to the *Audiencia* of New Granada. In the interior southward, it extended to the limits of the Peruvian towns of Piura, Cajamarca, Chachapoyas, and Moyabamba, to the banks therefore of the Marañón River.

In ecclesiastical government both Quito and Charcas belonged to the province of Lima until the seventeenth century when they were themselves elevated to archepiscopal rank. At the same time Quito achieved three schools with the degree-granting privileges of a university, but none of them equaled in importance the Royal and Pontifical University of San Marcos in the viceregal capital created by royal decree in 1551 and organized and endowed by the viceroy Toledo twenty-five years later. A more distinguished provincial institution was the university at La Plata in the presidency of Charcas, founded in 1623, at which later were trained many of the leaders in the Argentine movement for independence.

Both districts, Quito and Charcas, were presidencies and remained so throughout the colonial era. Over Charcas presided the senior judge with the title of regent until 1563, when the regent Ramírez de Quiñones was invested with the rank of president. Quito had a president from the outset, appointed in the same year, 1563. But in neither area did the president in the sixteenth century normally exercise the functions of governor. The governor and captain-general in each was the viceroy at Lima. The *audiencia* and its president were entrusted with wide administrative functions, but only in matters of routine; the appointment of officials, the assigning of *encomiendas,* and other important decisions were reserved to the viceroy-governor. These subordinate administrative authorities, however, might take action in urgent cases, such as an invasion of insurrection, without awaiting orders from Lima, as was logical and reasonable.[6] And the president of Quito, because of the great distance from Lima, was apparently accustomed to exercise this discretionary power more frequently than his analogue at La Plata. In the event of a vacancy in the viceregal office, the *audiencia* at Lima exercised the vice-

---

6 The celebrated Ordinances of Monzón, of 311 articles, issued to the *Audiencia* of Charcas in October 1563, comprised a code that served as a model for those of all later *audiencias.*

roy's authority *ad interim,* and this included the powers of governor in the subordinate presidencies—as happened after the assassination of the Count of Nieva in Lima in 1564.

Such arrangements, as might be expected, were the source of frequent quarrels and conflicts of jurisdiction between the local *audiencia* and the distant viceroy. The *audiencia,* jealous of its prerogatives, was always quick to assert an independent executive authority, and in the event of an interim government to ignore letters or instructions from Lima. As the governor of Charcas or Quito resided as viceroy in Lima, the *audiencia* could not meet with him in *acuerdo* or executive session, but could communicate only by correspondence and make recommendations. The fact, moreover, that the viceroy was also president of the Lima *audiencia,* and doubtless consulted with it on the affairs of the subordinate presidencies, made for jealousy between the tribunals. And this was probably intensified by the rule that appeals against the edicts of the viceroy-governor had to be carried to the central *audiencia* at Lima, rather than to the local judges. If the viceroy happened to be of a forceful temperament, active and vigorous in the conduct of affairs, occasions for conflict multiplied. And if the local president was not of a complacent disposition, complaints from both sides poured into the Council of the Indies. Such was the situation during the twelve years' rule of Francisco de Toledo. Toledo was apparently inclined to usurp many of the borderline functions of the *Audiencia* of Charcas, especially by the exercise of his right to decide if matters at issue were administrative or judicial in character. As the friar Rodrigo de Loaisa wrote in a memorial of 1586, 'Don Francisco de Toledo jamás tuvo paz con ninguna audiencia.'

Similar difficulties occasionally arose in the northern realms of New Spain, between the viceroy and the presidency of Guadalajara. But Guadalajara was close to Mexico City, with which communications were easy and constant. Conflicts of authority and of personalities were never so continuous or so bitterly contested as they were in the southern viceroyalty, between Lima and Charcas and Quito.

In the seventeenth century, the presidents of both Charcas and Quito were given the titles of governor and captain-general, but they always remained subject to the political authority of the viceroy in Lima, to a degree that was not true of the captaincy-general of New Granada.

During the course of the sixteenth and seventeenth centuries experiments were made elsewhere on the periphery of the viceroyalty, by the organization of regional *audiencias* in Chile and Buenos Aires. Chile ever since the conquest by Pedro de Valdivia had been under a government more military than civilian. In southern Chile the Spaniards came into contact with a warlike race celebrated in history as the Araucanians. A tall, muscular people, divided into more or less independent tribes inhabiting a heavily forested country, they alone among the aborigines of

South America by their obstinacy and valor proved a match for European weapons and discipline. The destruction of Valdivia himself in an Indian ambuscade in 1553 marked the beginning of a war waged almost continuously for a hundred years and ending in the recognition of the virtual independence of the Araucanians.

Philip II in 1565 decided to erect an *audiencia* in the town of Concepción on the Indian frontier, with three judges and a president, and entrusted with the direction of military as well as civilian affairs. It was not installed till two years later, and it survived less than a decade. Continued military disasters and factional disputes persuaded the crown to invest the president, Bravo de Saravia, with sole powers. But as the situation did not improve, decrees of 1573 suppressed the *audiencia* and directed that thereafter judicial appeals be carried to the tribunal in Charcas. It finally disbanded in 1575.[7]

Chile was again under a military governor until the beginning of the following century, when the experiment was tried anew. In 1609 the second *audiencia* came into residence, this time in the city of Santiago, where it remained thereafter. Its jurisdiction extended over the territory of the modern republic from Copiapó southward to the Strait of Magellan, and included a region east of the Andes about the settlements of Mendoza and San Juan called the province of Cuyo, today part of the Argentine republic. There was a president, who was also governor with the military rank of captain-general, but he remained subordinate till near the close of the eighteenth century to the viceroy of Peru. Because of its military responsibilities and its remoteness from Lima, the presidency of Chile, like that of Panama, seems to have been permitted greater independence of action than were the governments of Charcas and Quito.

Chile, however, as a Spanish colony remained until the eighteenth century economically poor; there was some agriculture and grazing, and a little mining, but for a long time most of its energies and revenues were absorbed in frontier Indian wars. Expenses were greater than receipts, and under the Hapsburg kings the colony was always a charge upon the treasury at Lima. In ecclesiastical government there were two bishoprics belonging to the province of Lima.

Before the eighteenth century the territory covered by the Argentine republic was, like Chile, impoverished and relatively backward, with a scant population dependent chiefly upon a trade in cattle, mules, and hides. The region south of Buenos Aires was an unconquered wilderness, and even to the west and north wild pampas Indians roamed unmolested, plundered *estancias,* and attacked caravans travelling between the iso-

---

7 Diego Barros Arana, *Historia general de Chile,* 16 vols., Santiago, 1884-1902 II, 372 ff.

lated settlements. The most populous civilized area was the semitropical northwest, the province of Tucumán, where numerous sedentary Indian tribes provided a source of labor, and where was developed a local textile industry which supplied the markets of Upper Peru and Chile. Cattle, mules, and wheat, too, went to support the mining cities of the Bolivian plateau.

The inhabitants of the Rio de la Plata, however, early sensed the future importance of that region, and in 1607 and later years, after the crown had decided to re-establish the *audiencia* in Chile, the *cabildos* of Buenos Aires and Córdoba petitioned the king to locate it in one or the other of these towns instead. Córdoba especially, because of its central position, its resources in cattle and grain, and its importance as a commercial entrepot between Paraguay, Chile, and Peru, was urged as the most appropriate and desirable residence for the new tribunal.

Nothing came of these importunities, but sixty years later the provinces of the Rio de la Plata did for a few years possess an *audiencia* of their own. It was set up by royal decree in 1661. The reasons alleged were the distances separating these regions from the *Audiencia* of Charcas to which they had until then been attached, and above all the determination to put an end to the contraband trade by foreign ships, especially English and Dutch, with the port of Buenos Aires.

In accord with the crude bullionist ideas of that age, and in deference to the monopolistic pretensions of the merchant houses of Seville and of Peru, throughout most of the colonial period the port of Buenos Aires was almost completely closed by law to maritime trade of any kind. European merchandise introduced by way of the Rio de la Plata into the interior provinces would, it was believed, reduce still further the already declining trade of the galleons to Tierra firme, to say nothing of providing a channel for the clandestine extraction of silver bullion from Upper Peru. This prohibitory legislation, however, condemned Buenos Aires to the utmost poverty and decrepitude, and an active contraband trade was inevitable if the colony was not to vanish altogether. Yet it was this relatively small stream of trade that the projected *audiencia* was expected to dry up.

After debates in the Council of the Indies extending over many years, Buenos Aires in 1661 became a presidency, like Chile or Panama, with jurisdiction as well over Paraguay and Tucumán, these provinces being detached from the *Audiencia* of Charcas. But the innovation did not effect the results anticipated. Contraband under the conditions created by Spanish legislation could not in the very nature of things be suppressed without inviting disaster. Buenos Aires, moreover, was a miserable town of 4,000 inhabitants, mostly mestizos, Indians, and Negroes (although containing four monasteries), leading a crude, rustic existence, with little or no cash in circulation, and not even provided, at times, with the services of a doctor or a druggist. It could hardly be expected to maintain the tribunal with the dignity and decorum which such a royal institution merited. In 1671, therefore, the presidency and *audiencia* were abolished, and the provinces of the Rio de la Plata for another hundred years returned to the jurisdiction of the *Audiencia* of Charcas.[8]

The advent of the Bourbon dynasty to the throne of Spain produced in the course of the eighteenth century many radical changes in the political administration of Spanish South America. Territorial frontiers were altered, and a new spirit was injected into the government of the empire. Under the Austrian dynasty, as has elsewhere been said, government had been 'narrow, usurious, unenlightened, fettered by red tape and routine; that of the Bourbons was much more liberal, more scientific and progressive.' In becoming more efficient, it also centralized political controls more narrowly in the government at Madrid.

Throughout the sixteenth and seventeenth centuries there was but one viceroy, resident at Lima, responsible for the government of all the vast territories of Spain in the southern continent. In the eighteenth century this huge area was divided into three viceroyalties, along lines already anticipated by the faltering administrative experiments of the Hapsburgs. The captaincy-general of New Granada was momentarily raised to the rank of a viceroyalty by royal decree of April 1717, with political jurisdiction over the territories included within the modern republics of Colombia, Ecuador, and Venezuela, i.e., the Caribbean provinces of Guayana, Cumaná, Caracas, Maracaibo, Santa Marta, and Cartagena, and the interior governments of Antioquia, Santa Fe, Popayán, and Quito. The *Audiencia* of Santo Domingo, therefore, was deprived of its authority over the coasts of Venezuela, while the presidency of Quito was entirely suppressed. It is true that within six years, for reasons of economy chiefly, the new arrangements were revoked, and the former administrative organization was restored. But in August 1739 the viceroyalty was again established, to last until the end of the colonial era. It included the same territories assigned in 1719,[9] with the addition of the *Audiencia* of Panama; but this time both Panama and Quito were left intact as presidencies, now subject to the new viceroy instead of to the authorities at Lima. The Venezuelan provinces, however, still carried their judicial appeals to Santo Domingo. In 1751 the presidency of Panama finally came to an end, owing apparently to endless discords and official irregularities, and perhaps also to the discontinuance of the galleon trade, and its judicial business was added to the already large responsibilities of the *Audiencia* of Santa Fe.

---

8 *Historia de la Nación Argentina*, III, 489-90.

9 By royal decree of 12 February 1742, however, the province of Caracas was again separated politically from the new viceroyalty. José Gil Fortoul *Historia constitucional de Venezuela*, 2nd ed., 3 vols., Caracas, 1930, I, 83.

A reform of even greater significance was the creation of the viceroyalty of Buenos Aires in 1776, for it marked the beginning of the importance of modern Argentina as a center of material and intellectual progress. With this event was also closely associated the age-long struggle between Spain and Portugal over the frontiers between their respective empires in South America, a struggle that was finally to culminate in the creation of the independent republic of Uruguay in 1828, to serve as a buffer between Argentina and Brazil.

The boundary between Spanish and Portuguese America had presumably been established soon after the Discovery by the Line of Demarcation drawn in the Treaty of Tordesillas of 1494. This line gave to Portugal the eastern part of Brazil, although owing to the lack of adequate maps and the inability in those days to measure longitude accurately, its exact location for generations remained uncertain. Both Spaniards and Portuguese claimed the estuary of the Rio de la Plata, and their first settlements in that region were inspired by the determination of each to hold it against the other. For years, however, there was no open collision. Spaniards in the sixteenth century were chiefly interested in the Andean regions on the Pacific side of the continent, and the Portuguese chiefly in the sugar colonies of Baía and Pernambuco in the north. Conflict was further postponed by the union of the crowns of Spain and Portugal between 1581 and 1640, although Brazilian colonists, the famous *Mamelucos* of Sao Paulo, were raiding and destroying the Spanish Jesuit missions on the Upper Parana River, in territory that was clearly Spain's.

Not till 1680 was a settlement made on the eastern banks of the estuary, by Portuguese from Rio de Janeiro, who built a fort called Colonia del Sacramento directly opposite Buenos Aires. Although the governer of Buenos Aires promptly crossed the river with a force of Creoles and Indians and captured the place, it was soon restored by the Spanish government to Portugal; and thereafter whenever the two crowns were involved in war with one another in Europe, Spaniards from Buenos Aires crossed over and expelled the Portuguese, and by the terms of peace in Europe were as regularly compelled to retire. Not till 1729 was a formal Spanish settlement established in the Banda Oriental, at Montevideo, on an excellent harbor conveniently close to the sea.

A better understanding of the physical geography of that part of the world led to a treaty between Spain and Portugal in 1751, which gave to Brazil approximately the southern and western boundaries she possesses today. It was based in part on actual possession, in part on the physical configuration of the country. But the Spanish colonists protested, the Indians of the Spanish missions in territory released to Portugal, encouraged by the Jesuit fathers, rebelled; and eventually, when Spain entered the Seven Years' War in 1761, the treaty was annulled. At the end of the war the *status quo ante* was once more restored, but the Spaniards failed to give up the Brazilian province of Rio Grande do Sul, which they had occupied during the war. And the forcible seizure of that region by the Portuguese in 1775 induced Charles III of Spain to take steps to settle the whole issue once and for all. In 1776 he sent to the Rio de la Plata a military and naval expedition of 10,000 men on a fleet of over 100 vessels, under command of Pedro de Cevallos, who came out with the title of viceroy of Buenos Aires and president of the *Audiencia* of Charcas. Cevallos was proceeding rapidly with the reconquest of the disputed areas when word was received that the quarrel had been settled in Europe. The treaty of San Ildefonso, of October 1777, virtually renewed the terms of the repudiated agreement of 1751.

It was an obscure conflict over an unoccupied wilderness, but on its issue depended the question whether the future republic of Uruguay was to be Spanish or Portuguese. It also gave to Buenos Aires the political importance which its inhabitants had long craved, and made it the capital of a new viceroyalty.

Another and no less significant reason for placing in that region an official of viceregal authority and prestige was the question of Patagonia and the Falkland Islands. The temporary seizure of the islands by the English during the previous decade had almost led to war with England, and there was real fear that the French and the English, attracted by the whale fisheries of the South Atlantic, might establish themselves permanently on the coasts of Patagonia.

The dispatch of Pedro de Cevallos as viceroy in 1776 was a provisional step, inspired by the military needs of the moment. The permanence of the viceroyalty was assured by the appointment of his successor in 1778, Juan José de Vértiz y Salcedo, who had earlier been governor, and who as viceroy for over a decade cemented the foundations of the new regime. The territory of the new jurisdiction included the governments of Buenos Aires, Paraguay, and Tucumán, the presidency of Charcas which was detached from Lima, and the province of Cuyo which till then had belonged to Chile. For the first time the Andes became the dividing line between Spanish jurisdictions on the Atlantic and Pacific slopes of the continent. Judicial appeals, however, continued to be carried to the presidency of Charcas until 1783, when a viceregal *audiencia* was established at Buenos Aires for all the provinces save those of the old presidency itself. Such was the general organization of the Argentine provinces at the opening of the nineteenth century.

The tendency of the Bourbons to decentralize the territorial administration of their American empire was doubtless due in general to an increasing appreciation in Spain of the geographical conditions and difficulties involved, accompanied by a rapid development of the science of cartography, and by an enhanced interest in mathematics and the physical sciences. It was also due to the spirit of economic and political reform that animated the Spanish monarchy to a degree unknown since the days of Ferdinand and Isabella, and that was especially evident in the reign of that enlightened monarch, Charles III. This decentralizing tendency is observable in the growing independence of the captaincies-general in the eighteenth century, and in their increase in number as well. Venezuela, which had consisted of a group of small governments subordinated at one time or another either to the captaincy-general of Santo Domingo or to that of New Granada, was itself in 1777 organized as a captaincy-general,[10] and in 1786 was provided with its own *audiencia* resident in Caracas. Chile, too, in 1778 was raised from the rank of presidency to that of captaincy-general. The captains-general, moreover, were treated more and more as little viceroys, with authority equal in every respect to that of the viceroys of New Spain and Peru—only in dignity and salary did any discrimination appear.

The last *audiencia* to be created was that of Cuzco in southern Peru in 1787. Its establishment was inspired by the sanguinary Indian rebellion of Tupac Amaru earlier in the decade, and was designed to afford greater protection to the aborigines against exploitation by their governors and tribal chiefs. It was, however, merely a judicial tribunal, and its creation had no great political significance. It was the thirteenth *audiencia* in Spanish America.

This brings to a close the long and somewhat complicated story of the development of Spanish territorial organization of the South American continent during three centuries of colonial history. Beginning with the rule of a single viceroy over an area covered today by eight large republics, there gradually emerged new and independent jurisdictions within the older unity, until at the close of the eighteenth century the ancient viceroyalty of Peru was confined within the limits occupied by the modern republic of that name. All the rest of the continent had been set up as new viceroyalties or independent captaincies-general. Yet much of the historic prestige of the viceroys of Peru remained; the old families of Peru were more closely allied by marriage and sympathy with the aristocracy of Spain than were the inhabitants of any of the other colonies; and Peru was the last of the South American communities to be induced to throw off its allegiance to the crown of Spain.

---

10 The 'governor and captain-general' of Caracas, in 1742 relieved of all dependency on the viceroyalty of Santa Fe, in 1777 had added to his jurisdiction the Venezuelan provinces of Guayana, Cumaná, and Maracaibo, and the islands of Trinidad and Margarita. Gir Fortoul, op. cit. I, 83-4.

VI

The Council
of the Indies

Throughout most of the several centuries of Spanish rule in America, the administration of imperial affairs in Spain itself was vested, not in a single minister or secretary of state, but in a council called the *Real y Supremo Consejo de las Indias.* It owed its separate and legal existence to a decree of the emperor Charles V, issued on 1 August 1524.

In the very beginning, as early as May 1493, shortly after the return of Columbus from his first historic voyage to the westward, Isabella chose a member of the Council of Castile, Juan Rodríguez de Fonseca, archdeacon of the cathedral of Seville and the queen's chaplain, to take charge of all matters relating to the newly discovered lands, and to co-operate with Columbus in preparing for his second voyage. And he remained until his death in 1524 the chief counselor of the crown for American affairs.

Fonseca was a cleric of noble family, a protégé of the queen, but not an administrator of outstanding ability. He apparently was a man of impatient, domineering temperament, jealous of his equals, and an implacable enemy, as Columbus and Cortés found to their cost; [1] but it is to his credit that he retained the favor and confidence of his sovereigns to the very end, and was promoted in turn to the bishoprics of Badajoz, Córdoba, Palencia, and Burgos. The establishment of the *Casa de Contratación* in 1503 took from him the immediate superintendence of commercial and allied matters, although he was probably in some measure responsible for the creation of that institution and for the ideas it embodied. But he continued to be practically the colonial minister until the time of Charles V, and the chief of an informal administrative organization.

From 1504 Fonseca was assisted by one of the secretaries of the crown, and after 1508 from time to time by various members of the *Consejo Real;* but royal orders and decrees were signed by the bishop alone and

---

1 For the character and early career of Rodríguez de Fonseca, see Ernesto Schäfer, *El Consejo real y supremo de las Indias,* Sevilla, 1935, 2 ff.

countersigned by the secretary. As Professor Schäfer has shown in his splendid monograph,[2] after Ferdinand's death the cardinal-regent Jiménez de Cisneros substituted in Fonseca's place two councilors of Castile, Lic. Luis Zapata and Dr. Lorenzo Galíndez de Carbajal. And shortly after the arrival in Spain of the young king Charles, there appeared a *junta* for Indian affairs composed of certain members of the Council, to which Bishop Fonseca returned as chairman. In 1520 there was added a solicitor (*procurador*) and a reporter (*relator*), and a year later an *abogado de los pleitos de las Indias*. This group very soon became known as the Council of the Indies, corresponding to its real character. But the new entity in the beginning was charged only with administrative functions; for all matters of justice supreme authority still lay in the Council of Castile. Later, with the conquest of the mainland territory by Cortés and the increasing volume of colonial business, it was desirable that the Council of the Indies receive autonomous rank as a 'royal and supreme council'; and shortly before the death of the aged Fonseca, in the middle of 1524, the emperor gave it a definitive organization with complete administrative and judicial authority.

The first president under the new dispensation was the emperor's confessor, Fray García de Loaisa, bishop-elect of Osma, general of the Dominican Order and later cardinal-archbishop of Seville.[3]

The personnel of the Council in the beginning consisted, besides the president, of four or five councilors who were generally lawyers or members of the clergy, a secretary, a *fiscal* or crown attorney, a reporter, a clerk of accounts, and an usher.[4] In 1528 a grand chancellor was appointed [5] whose duties were performed by a deputy. Other officials were added from time to time before the end of the century: a treasurer (*receptor*), three additional accountants, two solicitors attached to the office of *fiscal*, an attorney and a solicitor for poor suitors, two additional reporters, a chaplain, various notaries, several ushers, and a bailiff. In 1571 was created the post of historian and cosmographer (*cosmógrafo-cronista mayor*), the functions of which were twenty years later divided between two individuals,[6] and in 1595 was added a professor of mathe-

---

2 Schäfer, op. cit. 31 ff.

3 Ibid. 46.

4 For the salaries of these officials, see ibid. 46-50, 120-29, 249-61.

5 Mercurino de Gattinara, who was already grand chancellor of Castile. The office lapsed in 1575, but was revived in 1623 as a hereditary honor for the Count-Duke of Olivares, chief minister of Philip IV.

6 The first *cosmógrafo-cronista mayor* was Juan López de Velasco, who compiled the very useful *Descripción de las Indias Occidentales*. The most distinguished was Antonio de Herrera y Tordesillas, appointed *cronista* after the separation of the two offices in 1596 and author of the monumental *Historia general*, the first great official chronicle of the Indies. In the eighteenth century the functions of these two officials were incorporated in the Academy of History founded in 1735. Cosmographers appointed to compile and study all information relating to geography and navigation in America had been attached to the *Casa de Contratación* for many years.

matics. In 1604 the number of secretaries was increased to two, one for the viceroyalty of New Spain, the other for the viceroyalty of Peru. The number of councilors was also increased to six and later to nine or ten.[7] Many of the councilors were promoted to that position from the Chancelleries of Valladolid and Granada, from among the *alcaldes de corte,* or less often from those who had filled important offices in the Indies so as to have the benefit of their experience and advice. As the Council of the Indies ranked second in order of honorific importance under the crown, its members were frequently promoted to the Council in Castile, in the seventeenth century too rapidly to permit of much continuity in the labors of colonial administration.

Philip II displayed a lively interest in promoting a scientific knowledge of America. About 1570 he dispatched Dr. Francisco Hernández as *protomédico* to New Spain on a special mission to investigate the medicinal virtues of American plants, and a few years later he sent the Valencian cosmographer and mathematician Jaime Juan to make astronomical observations in New Spain and the Philippines.[8] The king, anxious to have as comprehensive a description as possible of his trans-Atlantic possessions, from time to time had questionnaires sent to the viceroys, *audiencias,* and other officials asking for complete information on the history, geography, flora, fauna, and population of all the settlements in the Indies. Such an inquiry was dispatched to the exchequer officials in 1569, and another in 1577 broader in scope and addressed to all important political officers in America. The program, incidentally, may not be unrelated to Juan de Ovando's 'visitation' of the Council of the Indies in 1569 and his revelation of the shocking.ignorance of the Council regarding colonial matters.

The resultant reports of *relaciones,* most of them drawn up between 1579 and 1582, and in many cases accompanied by maps and plans, remain one of our richest sources of information regarding both Spanish and Indian communities in the New World before 1600. In many instances Indian elders and *caciques* collaborated in providing important information otherwise unknown about their aboriginal past. The *relaciones* were intended to be used in the compilation of a General Description of the Indies by the *cronista mayor,* but this plan was never realized on the scale contemplated. They were turned to account, however, in the composition of analogous works, notably by Antonio de Herrera in his *Historia general.*[9]

---

7 On the other hand, members of the Council were frequently absent on special missions either to America or to the *Casa de Contratación* in Seville, Schäfer, op. cit. III.

8 Ibid. 118 and n. 4.

9 Many of the *relaciones* have been printed, those relating to Peru by Marcos Jiménez de la Espada, 4 vols., Madrid, 1881-97; those for Yucatan in *Col. doc.*

Under the later kings of the House of Austria, and with the appearance of rank favoritism in the royal court, the number of officials in the Council of the Indies vastly increased. Instead of the 9 councilors of the later years of Philip II, the number varied from 12 to 19, and was no longer confined to *letrados* (men trained in the Civil Law), but included many *de capa y espada*. The subordinate personnel and the expenses of the Council increased at the same time in corresponding ratio. Shortly after the death of Philip IV the total number connected with the Council was three times what it had been at the beginning of the century, although the state was completely bankrupt, conciliar business had not increased, and the salaries of officials were long in arrears. In the reign of Charles II several attempts were made at economy and reform, but without perceptible results.[10]

Under the Hapsburg kings, as stated in an earlier chapter, the Indies were held to belong to the crown of Castile, to the exclusion of Aragon, for it was under the auspices of Queen Isabella that they had first been discovered and explored. Consequently the laws and institutions of Spanish America were modeled on those of Castile, although changes in form and function developed to meet local needs. Moreover the Indies were treated as the direct and absolute possession of the king. Mexico and Peru were kingdoms, joined with the kingdoms of Spain under a common sovereign, bound together only by a dynastic tie.

The Council of the Indies, therefore, was a 'real y supremo consejo,' independent of and coordinate with the other royal councils of State, Finance, War, etc.[11] It had the same jurisdiction over Spanish communities in America and the Philippine Islands as was possessed within the Spanish peninsula by the Council of Castile. The latter had been brought to a high state of importance and efficiency by Ferdinand and Isabella, and served indeed as a model for the administration of all the great divisions of the empire outside the peninsula.[12] The competence of the Council of the Indies extended to every sphere of government: legislative, financial, judicial, military ecclesiastical, and commercial. All other officials and tribunals were solemnly forbidden to meddle in its affairs.[13] The king was absolute lord of the Indies and the Council

inéd., 2nd ser., XI and XIII; and some of those for New Spain in vols. IV-VII of *Papeles de Nueva España* published by Francisco del Paso y Troncoso. Cf. Federico Gómez de Orozco. *Relaciones historico-geográficas de Nueva España*, Mexico, 1931; Jiménez de la Espada, op. cit. vol. I, lvii ff.

10 Schäfer, op. cit. 275-85.

11 León Pinelo, *Tratado de confirmaciones reales*, pt. I, *ch.* VIII, par. 20.

12 As the royal council par excellence, it apparently for some years retained the right to nominate the councilors for the Indies; but in every other respect the Council of the Indies was coordinate and independent.

13 Philip II in 1556-7, however, very soon after his accession to the throne, unified fiscal organization by confiding to the Council of Finance the administration

was his mouthpiece. It resided at the court, wherever that might be, and its deliberations were secret. A formal body of ordinances for the Council was not issued, however, until November 1542, as the first nine chapters of the celebrated New Laws.[14]

All laws and decrees relating to the administration, taxation, and police of the American dominions were prepared and dispatched by the Council, with the approval of the king and in his name; and no important local scheme of government or of colonial expenditure might be put into operation by American officials unless first submitted to it for consideration and approval. In consultation with the crown, it traced the territorial division of the American empire. It proposed the names of colonial officials whose appointment was reserved to the king, and to it all such officers were ultimately accountable. It corresponded with the authorities in the New World, lay and ecclesiastical, and kept jealous watch over their conduct. Since by early papal bulls the tithes and the patronage of the Church in America were reserved to the crown of Castile, the supervision of ecclesiastical matters also fell within the Council's jurisdiction. Nominations to all important benefices were made in this tribunal, and no papal letters or decrees might be published in America without its exequatur. Significantly enough, it was only with respect to the Spanish Inquisition and its agents that the supremacy of the Council was sometimes called into question.

In its judicial capacity, the Council sat as a court of last resort in important civil suits appealed from the colonial *audiencias,* and in civil and criminal cases from the judicial chamber of the *Casa de Contratación.* Reserved to it in first instance were all other cases arising in Spain and concerned with the Indies, as were all matters relating to *encomiendas* of Indians. Supervision of the interests of the aborigines was indeed one of its special concerns; for their conversion and civilizing was always regarded as the crown's peculiar responsibility. The Council in a semijudicial capacity also made arrangements for the *residencias* (judicial review of an official's conduct at the end of his term of office) of

of all royal funds including receipts and expenditures on the account of the Indies. This greatly reduced the administrative autonomy of the Council of the Indies, for thereafter all its requisitions for outfitting the fleets or for general colonial administration had to be approved by a royal order issued by the Council of Finance. State funds thus centralized were much more at the mercy of an autocratic king living from day to day, with no concept of a budget, and weighed down by ever increasing political expenses. The new arrangement also caused frequent conflicts of jurisdiction and long delays. Schäfer, op. cit. 102-10.

14 Following a *visita* of the Council in 1569-70 by Juan de Ovando, later appointed president, the crown on 24 September 1571 issued a second and much more elaborate body of ordinances that remained unchanged until the reign of Philip IV. In 1636 appeared a new edition of the ordinances incorporating the innovations since 1571. The number was doubled, from 122 to 245, especially because of the vast expansion of the offices of Secretariat and Accountancy. Ibid. 129-37, 234-44.

viceroys, governors, judges and other important colonial officers. From time to time it sent to the Indies inspectors-general (*visitadores*) to investigate every phase of colonial life and administration and report back to the Council. In the sixteenth century it audited the accounts of colonial treasurers and comptrollers of the exchequer. But owing to distance and to the difficulty of securing a regular remission of accounts, in 1605 courts of audit were set up in the New World, at Lima, Mexico, and Santa Fe de Bogotá, from whose decision there was no appeal.

Powers of censorship were also exercised by the Council. No book treating of the Indies might be printed in Spain or in the colonies without its previous inspection, approbation, and license, and no books might be introduced into the Indies without its express permission. Although the ideas and principles behind colonial administraton doubtless emanated from the crown, especally in the formative period of the sixteenth century, the influence of the Council of the Indies upon legislation must have been considerable. It also provided a pattern for government in the colonies themselves. The *audiencias* in America bore much the same relation to the viceroys, as consultative councils sharing in administration, as the Council of the Indies bore to the sovereign in Spain.

Like most Spanish councils, the Council of the Indies was a hard-working body. It was required to meet from three to five hours every day except holidays, three councilors constituting a quorum.[15] Important matters were decided by the Council as a whole; minor questions were assigned to smaller committees by the president. From time to time, especially after the accession of Philip II, special commissions or juntas were delegated by the king to deal with new or difficult problems of colonial administration, such as Indian policy, finance, or naval defense. These commissions, to which occasionally were added members of the Councils of Castile, War, or Finance, sometimes carried on for many years.

Matters relating to royal patronage in the Indies had in the beginning been within the competence of the Council as a whole. For twenty years, betwen 1571 and 1591, nominations made to the king were reserved to the president of the Council alone; but in the year 1600, after the accession of the weak and indolent Philip III and the beginning of the disastrous era of government by royal favorites, a permanent commission was set up called the *Consejo de cámara de las Indias*. Consisting of the president and three councilors, as a smaller body it was presumably expected to be more amenable to the exigencies of the omnipotent Duke

---

15 To ease the overcrowded docket of the Council, after 1528 the rule was applied that petitions from private persons in the Indies must be accompanied by the opinion of the judicial authority of the district in which the petitioner resided. Judicial appeals from the colonies would be entertained only if followed up within eight months after their receipt by the Council. Ibid. 53.

of Lerma. It proved to be so riddled with venality and favoritism that it was abolished in 1609, but was revived again by Philip IV in 1644.

Military and naval affairs after 1600 were reserved to a *Junta de guerra de Indias*,[16] consisting ultimately of the president and three councilors of the Indies and four members of the *Consejo de guerra* of Castile. It had supervision over all matters of military government and justice, including the dispatch of armadas and fleets, as well as the nomination of important naval and military officers and of those charged with the expenditure of military and naval funds. Assignment to membership in the Junta was usually reserved to councilors *de capa y espada*.[17]

An institution such as this, responsible collectively to an autocratic king, possessed the defects inherent in a conciliar system of government: on the one hand, absence of individual responsibility, on the other, growth of a spirit of routine which paralyzed procedure and made rapidity of decision and action difficult. Like other councils of Hapsburg Spain, it deliberated interminably. Matters were referred to the king, from the king back to the Council, and to the king again. There were instructions after instructions, memorials upon memorials, an endless accumulation of documents, useful as preserving precedents, and enlightening to the modern historical investigator, but serving only to clog the wheels of government. Moreover, the conciliar system threw greater responsibility back upon the sovereign, in whom alone resided any unity of control such as might have been exercised by a single minister of state. If the king lacked energy, character, decision, or was absent from the kingdom, the inevitable result was perpetual debate, procrastination, suspended judgment. These defects were especially visible in the time of the later Hapsburgs, *les rois fainéants* of the seventeenth century. During this later period, it should be added, the authority and prestige of the Council of the Indies noticeably declined. Other royal councils such as those of Castile and Finance were often allowed to ride roughshod over its long-established powers and prerogatives, even encroaching upon its competence in the sphere of colonial justice. The funds of the Council were pilfered to provide gifts and subventions for the friends and relatives of those in authority, and in most matters of

16 The origins of a special committee for military and naval affairs go back to 1583 or 1584, when there appeared a *Junta de Puerto Rico* to consider the fortifications of San Juan and other important West Indian seaports. Ibid. 170-71.

17 For the jurisdiction of the *Junta de guerra* see *Un manuscrito desconocido de Antonio León Pinelo*, Lewis Hanke, ed., Santiago, 1937.

In 1595 also appeared a special committee of finance or *Junta de hacienda*, to which were added two members from the Council of Finance of Castile. Formally established in 1600, at the same time as the *Cámara* and the *Junta de guerra*, it apparently lasted only a few years, dropping out of sight in 1604 or 1605. Schäfer, op. cit. 170-74; 203-06.

personnel the Council was forced to accede to caprice of the royal favorite.

Under an absolute and paternalistic monarchy, legislation for the Indies soon became very columinous, touching every aspect of the duties, rights, and responsibilities of the colonists and of the officials set to rule over them. This legislation was intended to carry over into America the spirit and intent of the law of the metropolis, as Philip II explicity declared in 1571. It implied the transplanting of society and institutions from an old world to the new. Yet the legislation of Castile itself had in the colonies the force only of supplementary law. From the very first the crown had to 'adapt the distinct physiognomy acquired by traditional institutions' to circumstances both geographical and historical which were radically different from those in the metropolis.[18] The peculiar conditions prevailing in America called for the elaboration of a new legislation with a distinct character of its own. Moreover, in spite of the centralist and unifying tendencies of Hapsburgs and Bourbons, the crown was forced to take into account, both in legislation and in its application by viceroys and governors the great differences between one region in America and another. A surprising amount of autonomy was often permitted to colonial authorities. There likewise grew up a substantial amount of customary law in the overseas dominions derived from the jurisprudential practices of the times, which had a recognized legal force if accepted by the crown and if no written legislation was applicable.[19] Much of this customary jurisprudence developed from the modifications of royal orders by viceroys and captains-general to meet the exigencies of a local situation.

Finally, the crown tried to incorporate into its American legislation some of the juridical customs of the aborigines—especially of those, such as the Incas and the Aztecs, who had evolved a strong political and economic organization—customs which were not in contradiction to the fundamental precepts of Spanish organization and control.[20] These had to do, naturally enough, with the life of the lower orders of society: the regulation of labor, the succession and the privileges of native chiefs, Indian village organization, agricultural practices, etc. A striking example may be found in some of the celebrated ordinances of the viceroy Toledo in Peru. The most difficult problems in fact were those arising from the government of an Indian population which could not be reduced to the norms of Spanish law. Juan Matienzo, judge in the *Audiencia* of Charcas and intimate adviser of Toledo, in his celebrated text-

18 José María Ots Capdequi, *Estudios de historia del derecho español en las Indias,* Bogotá, 1940, 5-6; León Pinelo, *Tratado de confirmaciones reales,* pt. I, ch. VIII, 49 vto.

19 *Recopilación,* lib. II, tit. 2, ley 21.

20 Ibid. lib. II, tit. I, ley 4.

book of Peruvian administration, *Gobierno del Perú* (*c.* 1570), warns the Spanish authorities not

to try and change the customs abruptly and make new laws and ordinances, until they know the conditions and customs of the natives of the country and of the Spaniards who dwell there, for as the country is large so customs and tempers (*temples*) differ. One must first accommodate oneself to the customs of those one wishes to govern and proceed agreeably to them until, having won their confidence and good opinion, with the authority thus secured one may undertake to change the customs.[21]

Basically, however, people in the Indies, especially in the domain of private law, lived according to the same judicial criteria as in Spain.[22]

In the course of time much of the superabundant legislation emanating from king and council became obsolete or contradictory. More than a century of efforts to compile and systematize it resulted eventually in the publication in four folio volumes of the well-known *Recopilación de leyes de los reynos de las Indias.* This compilation, in spite of many technical deficiencies, is a notable monument of colonial legislation. True, it lacks the organic character of a modern code in the distribution and coordination of the statutes; the latter are not always formulated with the precision one would desire; contradictions or inconsistencies abound; marginal references are frequently in error. And as one Spanish scholar has remarked, it reveals

as a consequence of the concentration of power in the absolute monarchy, a constant confusion between the fundamental laws and the details which in the modern age have been entrusted to the regulatory power . . . laws which provide that there be a clock in the Casa de Contratación of Seville and that the doorkeeper of its Sala de Gobierno receive appropriate gratuities; that powder should not be wasted in salutes; or that the judges of Manila should not receive as gifts the chickens they consume or even purchase them at low prices. With some precepts very exalted, others very detailed, the Laws of the Indies constitute an unequal system, with assertions of high ideals surrounded by a network of mistrust.[23]

Nevertheless the *Recopilación*, in spite of defects visible to the wider experience of a later day, and in spite of the restrictive, paternalistic spirit which dictated it, is altogether one of the most humane, and one of the most comprehensive, codes published for any colonial empire.

---

21 *Gobierno del Perú*, Buenos Aires, 1910, 118, quoted by Levene, *Introducción a la historia del derecho indiano*, Buenos Aires, 1924, 34-5.

22 Ots Capdequi, op. cit. 5-6.

The shortcomings of Spanish colonial legislation often lay rather in the lack of observance than in the intention of the legislator. In the words of an Argentine historian,

the harsh realities in America, the conflict of sordid interests and unmeasured ambitions, the individualist and rebellious spirt, the crudities of colonial society, the variety and the mixture of diverse races, all combined to invalidate many of the written regulations and to subvert the established legal regime. This unobservance of the law was a liberating factor in the life of the colonists, when it was a question of eluding the enforcement of absurd prescriptions regarding commerce, the exchequer, the admittance of foreigners, and the publication and diffusion of books; but it was deplorable in so far as it perverted the organization of justice and corrupted the administration and government of the Indians.[24]

Smaller collections of ordinances, printed or in manuscript, had been compiled from time to time in the sixteenth and seventeenth centuries, but they generally referred to a particular subject or institution or geographical area. In 1552, for example, was published for the *Casa de Contratación* a code of all the laws in force respecting trade and navigation with the New World. In 1573 were issued ordinances governing discovery, conquest and settlement, a general compilation systematizing and crystallizing preceding legislation and earlier capitulations.[25] And a decade earlier was printed in Mexico City the well-known *Cedulario* of Vasco de Puga, member of the *audiencia* of New Spain, a collection in chronological order of laws and royal decrees in force within the jurisdiction of that tribunal. It did not include all the *cédulas*, and there were errors in names and dates, but it remains one of the rarest and most valuable of American incunabula.[26]

The need of a general compilation, however, was more and more felt, and in 1570 Juan de Ovando of the Council of the Inquisition, who in the preceding year had made a celebrated inspection of the Council of the Indies, was charged by Philip II with the task. Ovando had reported that the Council did not and could not have information about affairs in America over which it was supposed to take administrative cognizance; and that neither in the Council nor in the Indies was there adequate knowledge of the laws and ordinances by which those provinces were governed. As a matter of fact, the great mass of colonial legislation

---

23 Niceto Alcalá Zamora, *Impresión general acerca de las leyes de Indias,* Buenos Aires, 1942, 21-2.

24 Ricardo Levene, *Notas para el estudio del derecho indiano,* Buenos Aires, 1918, 81-2.

25 *Col. doc inéd.,* 1st ser., XVI, 142-87.

26 Vasco da Puga's labors were continued somewhat later by his colleague in the *audiencia,* Alonso de Zorita, but the work remained in manuscript.

was inscribed in the Registry Books of the Council in chronological order only, without any arrangement by subject matter, and in the colonial *audiencias* the situation was probably worse. Of the forty councilors who had served up to that time only six had personal knowledge of the Indies derived from actual residence in the New World.[27]

Ovando himself examined all the Registry Books, some two hundred volumes he tells us, and drew up a classified catalog divided into seven books of the laws and instructions then in force to serve as the basis for a complete compilation. One book was finished, covering the ecclesiastical government of the Indies, and the first chapter of Book II relating to the organization and functions of the Council of the Indies. But unfortunately the project so brilliantly conceived and initiated by Ovando was never carried out. Only the ordinances of the Council of the Indies received royal confirmation in September 1571. At the same time Ovando was promoted to the presidency of the Council.

The Council of the Indies never lost sight of the need for a general code for the American empire, although with the characteristic Spanish procrastination of those times a century elapsed before it was finally achieved. Councilors to whom the task was assigned would not accept it because of the time and difficulties involved, until in 1582 it was undertaken by an old and experienced clerk of the Secretariat, Diego de Encinas. After more than a decade of conscientious and laborious effort, he produced a collection in four closely printed folio volumes.[28] The legislation was arranged in chronological order, roughly divided under three or four general subjects; and the organization was so faulty that only sufficient copies were printed for use by the Council and by a few private individuals.[29] It is supremely useful, however, to students of the early history of the Spanish empire in America.

After 1624 the labor of compilation rested chiefly on the shoulders of the zealous and indefatigable Antonio León Pinelo, who earlier in Peru had begun on his own initiative to draw up a code for the Indies; although he worked under the formal direction of one of the councilors, first Rodrigo de Aguiar y Acuña [30] and later Juan de Solórzano Pereira. Solórzano, one of the most learned and distinguished jurisconsults of his day, had been a judge in the *Audiencia* of Lima, and during his residence in Peru had also been engaged on the collection and elaboration of a colonial code.

---

27 Schäfer, op. cit. 131.

28 *Provisiones, cédulas, capitulos de ordenanzas, instrucciones y cartas . . . tocante al buen gobierno de las Indias . . .* 4 vols. Madrid, 1596.

29 Schäfer, op. cit. 306-08.

30 Aguiar y Acuña published in 1628 his *Sumarios de la recopilación general de las leyes, ordenanzas,* etc., which was merely an extract of the first book of the work contemplated.

León Pinelo reduced the laws of the Indies to over 11,000, extracted from some 400,000 royal *cédulas*.[31] His labors were completed in October 1635, and approved by Solórzano the following May. But another forty-five years were to elapse before the work was printed, owing chiefly to the disastrous penury to which the crown was reduced. The *Recopilación de leyes de las Indias*, largely reorganized by Fernando Jiménez Paniagua, one of the reporters of the Council, and edited to bring it into conformity with more recent legislation, finally saw the light of day in 1681.[32] The crown ordered that copies be sent to the viceroys, presidents, and governors in America for distribution to the *cabildos* of all the cities and towns, each *cabildo* being required to pay thirty pesos for the set.[33]

The *Recopilación* in its final form contains approximately 6,400 laws arranged in nine books [34] of very unequal length, divided into chapters or categories (*titulos*) within which the statutes are grouped and classified. Marginal annotations indicate when the laws were originally issued, were repeated or were modified. The text, however, does not reveal the changes introduced from one time to another, giving only the substance of the law in force at the time the *Recopilación* was published. Nor does it include earlier legislation, some of it contained in previous compilations, which though once in effect had since been abrogated. By the student of the history of colonial institutions, therefore, it must be used with caution. Moreover the *Recopilación* soon became antiquated, for new laws continued to be issued in profusion. Under the Bourbon kings, especially after the middle of the eighteenth century, political and administrative reforms were introduced which wrought important changes in the institutional life of the colonies, and superseded in large measure the laws contained in the *Recopilación*. A decree of Charles III addressed to the Council of the Indies in 1765 envisaged a revised edition of the work. Nothing was done until 1776 when a commission of two jurists was appointed to prepare an entirely new code.[35] Only Book I

31 José Torre Revello, *Noticias históricas sobre la Recopilación de Indias*, Buenos Aires, 1929, 20, 23.

32 Charles II, in sanctioning publication, 18 May 1680, ordered that all decrees and ordinances issued to American *audiencias* should continue in force if not contrary to the new code.

33 Santiago Montoto, 'D. José de Veitia Linaje y su libro: Norte de la Contratación de las Indias,' *Bol. Centro Estud. Amer. de Sevilla*, nos. 44-5, p. 10.

34 Briefly stated, the contents of the nine books are as follows: I. ecclesiastical government; II. Council of the Indies and colonial *audiencias*; III. political and military administration, viceroys, and captains-general; IV. discoveries, colonization, and municipalities; V. provincial government and justice; VI. Indians; VII. penal law; VIII. royal exchequer; IX. commerce and navigation.

Five reprintings have appeared, three in the eighteenth century (1756, 1774, 1791) and two in the nineteenth (1841, 1889-90). See Schäfer, op. cit. 322.

35 The secretary of the commission for several years was Manuel Josef de Ayala, native of Panama and member of the Council of the Indies, who had gathered together

was completed, by Juan Crisótomo Ansótegui. It was presented by the king to the Council for review in 1780, returned to the crown ten years later with many needed revisions of form, and approved by Charles IV in 1792, but it ·· as never published. Other projects as late as the time of Ferdinand VII were of as little effect. And so the *Recopilación* of 1680 in spite of its manifest shortcomings remained in force until the Spanish-American wars of independence.

Our respects should also be paid to the other important juristic works of León Pinelo and Solórzano Pereira, especially the *Tratado de confirmaciones reales* of the former, and that great monument of historical jurisprudence, the *Política indiana* of Solórzano.[36] It is interesting to remember that both men secured their early training and experience in the *Audiencia* of Lima, León Pinelo as *abogado* and Solórzano as *oidor*. And in writing these treatises they inevitably formulated in their own minds principles that bore fruit in the *Recopilación*. Through them and their work the jurisprudence of the American *audiencias* influenced the development of legal theory and practice in Spain itself, and helped to make the seventeenth century the golden age of Spanish juridical studies.

To a certain extent the type of colonial government embodied in the Council of the Indies was applied to the rule of the Portuguese colonies in Brazil and the Orient during the union of the two crowns of Portugal and Spain. Indeed it was to this era of Spanish control, between 1580 and 1640, that Brazil owed most in the way of the development of colonial administration. Till then the Portuguese crown had done little or nothing to create institutions specifically for the colony. At Lisbon there was neither a colonial council nor a colonial minister of state. The government of Brazil was in most respects identified with that of Portugal itself, and in America the new communities, like the early English colonies, were permitted to develop along their own lines without much interference from the crown.

It was under Spanish influence that special institutions of colonial government were created, and special codes of law devised, which naturally approximated to those of the colonies of Spain. The establishment in 1591 of a Council of Finance divided into four sections for the government of Portugal and its dominions, was followed by the creation in 1604 of a Portuguese Council of the Indies which shared the govern-

an extraordinary collection of notes and documents, and who prepared a Dictionary of Government and Legislation of the Indies and Spain in 26 volumes still in manuscript. One hundred and twenty ms. volumes in all still survive, constituting one of the richest sources for the historical study of colonial institutions, especially during the later days of the American empire. J. M. Ots Capdequi, 'D. Manuel Josef de Ayala y la historia de nuestra legislación de Indias,' *Hisp. Amer. Hist. Rev.* III, 281-322.

36 This is a Spanish translation and adaptation of an earlier Latin version, *De indiarum jure disputationis*, published in 1629-39.

ment of the colonies with the Council of Finance. In 1608 was also established a royal court of appeals, or *audiência, for* Brazil at Baía, the first tribunal of this sort in Portuguese America, and the only one until the middle of the eighteenth century, when a second was created at Rio de Janeiro.

Although the Portuguese Council of the Indies possessed many of the powers, executive, judicial, and ecclesiastical, of its Spanish prototype, for various reasons it never enjoyed as much authority as the latter. After the recovery of Portuguese independence in 1640, the new Braganza dynasty preserved these institutions which it had inherited. But they were managed with much less consistency and unity of control, and even the recognized attributes of the Council were not respected by the king or his ministers, who often intervened directly in colonial affairs, and appointed or dismissed officials at pleasure.

When Bourbon princes came to occupy the Spanish throne, in the beginning of the eighteenth century, they brought with them the administrative experience and practices of France, and in the course of time many innovations were introduced into the political organization of the state, in Spain and in America. Cabinet ministers were appointed, among them a Secretary or Minister of Marine and Indies in November 1714, just after the close of the War of the Spanish Succession. To this Minister were transferred all matters relating to war, finance, navigation, and commerce, and the nomination of all but purely political and judicial officers, including members of the Council of the Indies and of the *Casa de Contratación.* He was himself frequently President of the Council or of the *Casa de Contratación.* Much later, by a decree of 8 July 1787, a second Minister of the Indies was appointed, with jurisdiction over justice and the patronage associated with it, both civil and ecclesiastical; but within three years, in April 1790, the two portfolios were suppressed, and their functions were distributed among five ministers who presided over the respective departments of government for the peninsula: Foreign Affairs, War, Marine, Justice, and Finance. The older Hapsburg theory of the relation between the crown and its American possessions was forgotten or ignored.

As a matter of fact, the far-reaching reforms in colonial government implanted by the Bourbon kings, especially in the reign of Charles III, were consciously aimed at the unification and coordination of the metropolis and the American provinces in a single organism, political, economic, and juridical. As the king stated in his instructons to José de Gálvez, the last and greatest of the *visitadores* to New Spain, his purpose was

the commendable idea of adjusting this great kingdom and making its political and economic system uniform with that of the metropolis, from which would result, among many other advantages revealed by time, the fact that its government would be calibrated with the higher government in Spain, and that those who come out to take office would not have to learn rules contrary to, or at least very different from, the rules which are observed at home.

The Bourbons, however, never succeeded in accomplishing this purpose. It is very doubtful if they would have been able to achieve it had they been given sufficient time—the distractions of war during the French Revolution and the age of Napoleon cut short their efforts. And it is equally doubtful if the ideal aimed at was in every respect desirable. As a matter of fact, not only time but circumstances militated against it. Geography, diverse economic influences, different types of social organization, and the heterogeneous ethnic composition of the population in America combined to produce fundamental divergences in the various sections of the overseas empire, divergences that account for the destruction of the old Spanish unity in the nineteenth century, and the rise of many independent republics.

After the French invasion of Spain in 1808, and the forced abdication of Carlos IV and Fernando VII, the *Junta Central,* which aspired to rule in the name of the legitimate dynasty, in January 1809 issued a decree declaring that the American colonies were an integral part of the Spanish kingdoms, that they belonged to the Spanish nation. And from this it deduced the right to rule the colonies, in the name of the sovereign, as if they were part of the peninsula. For the moment most of the colonies acquiesced. Both Creoles and Spaniards in America rallied with enthusiasm to the support of Ferdinand VII and the patriot juntas in Spain, and against the foreign usurper. But with the conquest of all the peninsula by French armies, and the more or less honorable decease of the *Junta Central* in 1810—in other words with the complete disappearance of all visible signs of legitimate national government—the American provinces proceeded to set up governing juntas themselves, reviving the older theory that the Indies were the property of the crown of Castile. If the crown was the only link between them and the metropolis, with the disappearance of the monarchy they claimed the right to establish provisional governments of their own, as the Spaniards did in Spain. If they came into conflict with the junta or the *Cortes* in Spain, they asserted their freedom from its authority. And from this position to the theory that with the disappearance of the monarchy the sovereignty reverted to the people, was not a very long or difficult step. In 1810, therefore, the autonomist movement in South America unfolded itself on a vast scale, and with an apparent unity of impulse and of action that attracted to it the attention of the world.

Meantime, after the radical change of 1790, the Council of the Indies continued to serve in an advisory capacity to the king, shorn of many of its former powers, but proud of its traditions. Several changes in its organization and prerogatives were introduced in the reign of Charles III, notably by decrees of 1773 and 1776, which divided it into three chambers—two of government and one of justice—and increased the number of councilors to fourteen. The *Cortes* of Cadiz, in which natives of America participated, abolished the Council, along with other old councils and tribunals, by a decree of 17 April 1812. It was re-established by Ferdinand VII after his restoration in 1814. After the loss of the major part of the Spanish-American empire, it was finally abolished by a law of 24 March 1834. Except for the short interval between 1812 and 1814, it had enjoyed a continuous and distinguished career of 310 years.

VII

❦

Royal Government
in the Indies

❦

VICEROYS AND AUDIENCIAS

The Council of the Indies was the highest legislative and administrative authority for the American empire after the king. Its most important political and judicial agents in America were the viceroys, the captains-general, and the *audiencias.*

The viceroys and captains-general each exercised supreme authority within his jurisdiction as the direct representative of the sovereign. Each was the chief civil and military officer within his immediate province. He also had supervision over justice, the exchequer, and the secular aspects of church government. He was specifically charged with the maintenance and increase of the royal revenues, and he nominated most of the minor colonial officials both lay and ecclesiastical. The welfare of the Indians was presumed to be his special care, and he was expected to devote a part of two or three days each week to the consideration of Indian petitions. He might hear in first instance suits in which Indians were involved. He also reallotted *encomiendas* that had fallen vacant, a practice that gave rise to much jealousy and discord.

The *audiencias* were the highest royal courts of appeal within their respective districts, and they served at the same time as a consultative council to the viceroy or captain-general. To him they stood in much the same relation, saving only the ultimate authority of the crown, as the Council of the Indies bore to the king in Spain.

To both executive officials and *audiencias* was conceded a limited degree of legislative power as well. From the very beginning of colonization, authorities in America were permitted by the crown to issue ordinances of local application, subject to ultimate royal approval. Columbus and his immediate successors in the government of the West Indian islands exercised this power especially with reference to the relations between Indians and Spaniards, as did the leaders in the conquest of the mainland, such as Cortés in Mexico and Pizarro and his satellites in

Peru. Later, when the administrative organization of the empire assumed form and substance, similar authority was exercised by viceroys and captains-general, occasionally to a lesser degree by the *audiencias,* and even by provincial governors and by *cabildos* or municipal corporations. The bulk of this regulatory legislation related to the government of the Indians; but other important aspects of colonial administration were also from time to time included, matters that could not readily be formulated by the authorities in Spain. The well-known ordinances of the viceroy Toledo in Peru are perhaps the most celebrated, covering not only Indian affairs but mining, finance, irrigation, and municipal organization. The second viceroy of Peru, Antonio de Mendoza, in 1552 had drawn up regulations for the *Audiencia* of Lima, based upon the New Laws of the previous decade, and later viceroys both of Peru and New Spain issued ordinances for the management of mines, craft guilds, Indian 'reductions,' and similar matters.[1] All ordinances issued by viceroys, *audiencias,* or lesser authorities required royal confirmation. But while those of viceroys or *audiencias* might be put into effect immediately, those of governors or municipalities required first the approval of the viceroy before enforcement and ultimately royal sanction.[2]

In spite of the apparent centralization of authority in the hands of viceroys and captains-general, as the system worked out they found their power considerably restricted both in theory and in practice. It was limited by the following circumstances:

(1) All the more important officers in America—governors, judges, exchequer officials, etc.—were appointed and removed by the king and council in Madrid, and might correspond directly with the central authorities in Spain over the head of the viceroy or captain-general. The latter consequently could exercise little effective control over subordinates whose mandate of authority and tenure of office were independent of them.

(2) While matters of routine administration were delivered entirely into their hands, these routine activities were often regulated in detail by the voluminous legislation of a paternalistic monarchy. The extent and minuteness of these regulations command the admiration and sometimes the despair of modern investigators. And it appears with the very beginnings of colonization. The fixing of prices, the ferry charge on the river at Santo Domingo, the right to own fishing boats, permission to import from Spain cattle and foodstuffs necessary for the subsistence of the new overseas communities, the right to engage in local trade

1 Rafael Altamira, 'La Décentralisation législative dans de régime colonial espagnol (XVIe-XVIIIe siécles),' *Bull. du comité internat. des sci. hist.,* no. 43, 182-4.
2 León Pinelo, *Tratado de confirmaciones reales,* pt. II, cap. XXIII, VGC, *Recopilación,* lib. II, tit. 1, ley 32.

with nearby settlements, or to build vessels for such a trade; the exact manner in which towns must be laid out, the width of the streets and their direction in relation to the sun, the size and subdivision of the city blocks, the location of the church and the town hall—all these and countless similar matters often remained with the crown or its council in Spain for decision.

(3) In larger matters of policy—not routine administration—the viceroy or captain-general as time went on was more and more reduced to playing the role of a mere royal commissioner charged with the execution of royal orders. No large project or change of local policy might be undertaken, no unaccustomed expenditure might be made from the royal treasury except in time of emergency, without first referring it to the Council of the Indies for approval. This was frequently long in forthcoming, either because of the slow-grinding mechanism of conciliar procedure, or because of the desire for more information and further consultation with agents in the New World. And when the scheme was finally approved, the conditions in the American colony that prompted it might in the meantime so have changed that the proposal was no longer applicable or demanded further modification—which in turn required the sanction of the authorities in Spain. Viceroys in the eighteenth century, under the jealous, centralizing regime of the Bourbon kings, complained that they were even debarred from bestowing necessary favors and rewards upon deserving subjects, but could only make recommendations to the crown. For the common run of appointments to minor offices they made selection from lists of three candidates provided by the *intendentes* or by the chiefs of the various government agencies.[3]

(4) Finally there was the fact that the viceroys and captains-general shared virtually all their powers with the *audiencia* as a council of state. And while the ultimate decision lay in most cases with the viceroy, a recalcitrant or hostile *audiencia* might make an infinite amount of trouble for its presiding officer, and at times effectively clog the wheels of royal government.

It was apparent, therefore, that two principles were characteristic of Spanish imperial government in America: a division of authority and responsibility, and a deep distrust by the crown of initiative on the part of its colonial officials. These circumstances often prevented adequate and effective administration in the colonies. Through the necessity of constant reference to the home government, procrastination, delay, red tape were the rule. The only real centralization was in the king and his council in Spain. Spanish imperial government was one of checks and balances; not secured as in many modern constitutional states by a

---

3 Revillagigedo, *Instrucción reservada . . . a su sucesor en el mando, Marqués de Branciforte . . .*, Mexico, 1831, par. 12.

division of powers, legislative, judicial, executive, but by a division of authority among different individuals or tribunals exercising the same powers. There was never a clear-cut line of demarcation between the functions of various governmental agencies dealing with colonial problems. On the contrary, a great deal of overlapping was deliberately fostered to prevent officials from unduly building up personal prestige or engaging in corrupt or fraudulent practices.

It was a government, as someone has said, that was not intolerably bad, but that was also never vigorously good. And given the antecedent conditions—a territorial empire covering two continents, whose centers of authority were three or four or five thousand miles from the home base, ruled by an absolute sovereign jealous of his authority and zealous to oversee and determine every aspect of colonial life and government, at a time when communications were extremely slow and uncertain, when there were no steamships and telegraphs, and sailing ships were small and unwieldy—it was probably the only type of government that could be devised that met squarely all these circumstances and that at the same time possessed the elements of permanence and security. However, as a system it was both cumbersome and costly. The shortcomings of Spanish administration in the New World lay not in any lack of good intentions on the part of the sovereign and his councilors, but in the delinquencies of their American agents, in the physical conditions of time and distance, and in the circumstances of social and political organization which in those days were accepted as axiomatic. The success or failure of European colonization in the sixteenth and seventeenth centuries must be judged, not by the standards of experience today, but by those of the people who were forced to face and solve the difficult problems involved.

This suggests another aspect of Spanish colonial administration that deserves especial emphasis. In spite of the theoretical centralization of the Castilian monarchy, and because of the distance of the colonies from Spain and from one another—sometimes even in the eighteenth century it took eight months for news from Europe to reach Lima in Peru—colonial authorities from the viceroy at the top to provincial governors and local magistrates frequently acted with a degree of freedom and independence which may seem inconsistent with the principles of government so far discussed. The right was accorded to viceroys and other officials to stay the execution of orders from the metropolis which in view of special circumstances in the region concerned might prove dangerous or inopportune, produce conflicts or injustice.[4] In such cases they must report back to the king and council the reasons for their action, and presumably suggest appropriate modifications. In this way they were able

---

4 *Recopilación*, lib., II, tit. 1, ley 24.

in many cases to disregard the injunctions of the authorities in Spain, or the course of action laid down by the Council of the Indies. Decrees that were impossible or inconvenient to execute were shelved with the famous Spanish formula, 'I obey but do not execute,' and were referred back to Spain again for further consideration.

This conception of the law, as written and as applied, was well understood by that great Spanish jurist Castillo de Bodavilla, who says in his magnum opus, *Política para corregidores*:

By laws of these realms it is provided that the royal provisions and decrees which are issued contrary to justice and in prejudice of suitors are invalid and should be obeyed and not executed ... and the reason for this is that such provisions and mandates are presumed to be foreign to the intention of the Prince who, as Justinian has said, cannot be believed to desire by word or decree to subvert and destroy the law established and agreed to with great solicitude.[5]

This question, however, of the breach between the written law and its application goes even deeper in the consideration of Spanish administration in America. Not only special royal mandates, but also general rules and regulations for the routine conduct of office were often ignored in practice by colonial officials in the hope or expectation that, with distance and isolation in their favor, and the delays in communications, they 'could get away with it.' And they often united with other officials in the neighborhood in a common conspiracy to disregard restrictive laws. As Solórzano so wisely wrote in the seventeenth century:

For it is clear that there cannot fail to be vices and iniquity whatever and as long as there are men; and especially in provinces so remote and isolated from their kings; in which ... the mandates of the princes themselves may be foolish, or some without warrant, and open a wide field to those who inhabit or govern them, to judge and hold lawful everything to which their whim urges or persuades them. For human temerity easily disregards that which is very distant.[6]

In other words, restriction of initiative by the Spanish crown, in an endeavor to maintain an effective control over its colonial officials, sometimes served merely to prevent efficient and honest administration. At the same time it engendered a disrespect for law which some would claim was characteristic of government in the Spanish colonies, but which, I suspect, has been characteristic of all new or frontier communities in all ages of history, whether they be Spanish or English or of any other nationality.

---

5 Lib. ii, cap. x, sect. 74, 440, ed. Barcelona, 1616.

6 Quoted from Ricardo Levene, *Introducción a la historia del derecho indiano*, Buenos Aires, 1924, 32 note.

Among the viceroy's more important functions were those of captain-general. He issued instructions for the defense of the coasts and Indian frontiers and made tours of inspection as occasion warranted. General military regulations required ultimate approval in Spain, but from the very nature of his office he often acted with more freedom and initiative than in any other capacity. As commander-in-chief he had full charge of military justice, and sat as a court of appeal in civil and criminal cases concerning persons who enjoyed the military *fuero* or privilege. On such occasions he was advised by a legal counsel or *asesor*, who was generally one of the judges of the *audiencia*, called the *auditor de guerra*. From the captain-general reappeal might be made to the *Junta de guerra* [7] of the Council of the Indies in Spain.

It was in the eighteenth century, after the creation of a standing army in the American colonies following the Seven Years' War, that the military attributes of the viceroy assumed increased importance. Until then, Alamán tells us, in New Spain the only permanent troops had been the guard of halberdiers of the viceroy, reinforced later by a company or two of infantry called *compañías de palicio*. Both in New Spain and elsewhere, however, merchants in some of the principal cities, and occasionally several of the craft guilds, maintained a small private armed force, a kind of urban militia; and in the seaports and on the frontier there were separate companies subject only to local service and composed of Negroes, mulattoes, or mestizos. But these latter represented little in the way of training or discipline, and generally did not even have uniforms. In time of danger from Indian uprisings or foreign corsairs, local forces were usually raised and armed for the emergency.

A professional army was first organized in New Spain in 1762, partly with regiments from the peninsula, partly with colonial levies, for defense against the English when Spain was drawn into the war in Europe; but the army as ultimately constituted was almost wholly maintained by local impressment.[8] At about the same time there was created a regular colonial militia, distributed by battalions throughout the provinces and districts.[9] The officers were wealthy miners and landed proprietors, among whom the rank of colonel or lieutenant colonel became a source of social distinction, and who paid dearly for the office. In New Spain this militia, apart from local companies on the coast and frontier, constituted on a war footing between twenty and twenty-two thousand men. But the ranks were rarely if ever completely filled. With the 6,000 reg-

---

7 Cf. *ante*, p. 108.

8 In New Spain it consisted of four line regiments and one battalion (5,000), two regiments of dragoons (1,000), a brigade of artillery (720), a small company of engineers, and the local companies stationed at minor seaports. As one regiment was kept at Havana, the actual number in New Spain was about 6,000. Lucas Alamán, *Historia de México*, 5 vols., Mexico, 1883-5, I, 107-8.

9 Indians were by law exempt from military service.

ulars, the viceroy of New Spain at the end of the colonial period had at his disposal an armed force presumably of nearly 28,000 men.[10]

It was the custom, and indeed the duty, of each viceroy at the end of his term of office to draw up and transmit to the king, for the information and enlightenment of his successor, a detailed report or memorial of the state of affairs within the viceroyalty, and of the most important events that had occurred during his tenure of office. Antonio de Mendoza prepared such a memorial at the end of his fifteen years as the first viceroy of New Spain, and when transferred to Peru he introduced the practice there during the few remaining months of life allotted to him. These valuable state papers have most of them been preserved—some in recent times have been reprinted—and they form one of our most important sources of information for the history of the Spanish empire in America.[11]

We read in the *Recopilación de Indias* that the term of office of the viceroys was three years, as had been more or less the practice in the Mediterranean dependencies of Sardinia, Naples, and Sicily. As a matter of fact in the beginning they were appointed for an indefinite period, or during the pleasure of the king. Antonio de Mendoza, as stated above, was kept at his post in New Spain for fifteen years, and then was transferred to Peru where he died shortly after. His successor in New Spain, Luis de Velasco, governed for fourteen years and died in office. On the other hand, Mendoza's successor in Peru, the Marquis of Cañete, was appointed for a term of six years only (probably the conventional formula thereafter), while Francisco de Toledo, who came out a decade later, remained in Peru for twelve years before he was allowed to retire. Even after 1629 when the three-year rule was established, little if any attention was paid to it, many of the viceroys serving during a much longer period; and the same lack of uniformity holds true of the age of the Bourbons. Apparently the customary term of appointment was five years at the close of the colonial era.[12] The appointment of a captain-general was stated in the *Recopilación* to be for eight years, and this, certainly in later times, seems to have been nearer to the general practice.

The salary of Antonio de Mendoza in New Spain was 6,000 ducats (approximately 8,270 pesos of eight reales [13]), 3,000 as viceroy, and

---

10 Ibid. I, 109-10.

11 Apparently this *memoria* was not always forthcoming, for a law of 1628 imposed a penalty of forfeiture of the last year's salary upon viceroys who failed to prepare it. *Recopilación*, lib. III, tit. 14, ley 32.

12 Alamán, op. cit. I, 82.

13 A ducat was worth 375 marvedis, a silver peso 272 marvedis. For salaries of other officials in the sixteenth century, see C. H. Haring, 'Ledgers of the Royal Treasurers in Spanish America in the Sixteenth Century,' *Hisp. Amer. Hist. Rev.*, II, 173-87.

3,000 as president of the *audiencia*, besides various perquisites which probably raised his income to double that amount. He also drew 2,000 ducats additional for the maintenance of a horse and foot guard, which at that time consisted of a captain, ten horsemen, and twenty footmen.[14] The stipend of the second viceroy, Luis de Velasco, who came out in 1550, was increased to 10,000 ducats. In Peru the viceregal salaries were higher. Mendoza was assigned 20,000 ducats on his translation to Peru in 1551, and his successors in the southern viceroyalty until 1615 received 40,000. In the seventeenth century the stipends were reduced. That of the Mexican viceroy came to be fixed at 20,000 ducats (approximately 27,000 pesos), that of the viceroy of Peru, always considered to be the highest grade in the official hierarchy, at 30,000 ducats (approximately 41,000 pesos). As the salaries of judges of the *audiencia* and of exchequer officers were also generally higher in Peru than in New Spain, the disparity may reflect a difference in the cost of living in the two viceroyalties. Under the Bourbons, when New Spain came to be the most prosperous, and financially the most valuable to the crown, of all the American kingdoms, the salary of the viceroy in both New Spain and Peru was raised to 60,000 pesos a year, and in some instances even higher. The increase is readily accounted for by the decrease in the purchasing power of money. And always there were perquisites and expense allowances that made the emoluments of these officials considerably larger. Their official income therefore compared favorably with that of a president of the United States today. In the newer viceroyalties of New Granada and Buenos Aires, which were much poorer in material resources, the viceroys received a salary of 40,000 pesos. The stipend of the captains-general and presidents in the seventeenth century ranged from 3,500 to 6,000 ducats, and in the following century were somewhat higher.

The viceroy was assisted in his administrative duties by a secretariat that increased the size and importance with the increase of business. Consisting in the beginning of one or two secretaries and their clerks, in the eighteenth century the secretariat expanded rapidly until there were five or six, and the second Revillagigedo tells us that in 1790 there was a total staff of thirty divided into five departments.

The long succession of viceroys over a period of nearly three centuries —41 ruled in Peru and 62 in New Spain—included many from Spain's noblest and most distinguished families. In Peru five were supplied by the house of Mendoza alone. Many of the viceroys were men of intelligence and good intentions, who endeavored to improve the material

---

14 According to the *Recopilación*, the viceroy of Peru was permitted by law to have a palace guard consisting of a captain and fifty halberdiers; in New Spain he might have only twenty halberdiers. *Recopilación*, lib. III, tit. 3, ley 67.

and moral welfare of the country they governed by means of public works and useful foundations, tried to purify the administration of justice, enforce the laws for the protection of the aborigines, and restrain the avarice and cruelty of Spanish settlers and local officials. Some of them were statesmen of the first rank, especially in the early years when everything had to be done to organize a durable European society on the American frontier, to stabilize the various social classes, and consolidate the royal power against the egotism and restlessness of the *conquistadores*. Such were Antonio de Mendoza in New Spain, his successors Luis de Velasco and Martin Enríquez, and in Peru the Marquis of Cañete and Francisco de Toledo. A few of the viceroys were scholars, founders of colleges, interested in literature and the arts, who held salons in the viceregal palace. But most of them ruled indifferently, leaving little behind but their portraits, which may be seen today in the museums of Lima and Mexico City .

Their efforts, even when well-intentioned, were frequently crossed and hindered by the unruliness of powerful colonists, by the pride and arrogance of the higher clergy, by the jealousy of royal judges and other officials, or by the distrust of the government in Spain. They were frequently in conflict with the ecclesiastical power, with the *audiencias,* or with exchequer officers over questions of precedence or jurisdiction. Rules promulgated for the guidance of local authorities or for the defense of the Indians remained a dead letter. And endless demands for money from an ambitious or impecunious government at home tied their hands against any permanent improvement.

Eleven of the 62 viceroys of New Spain were drawn from the Episcopal hierarchy, 8 of them archbishops of Mexico. Curiously, in the history of Peru there were only 3 ecclesiastical viceroys, an archbishop of Lima (1678-81), a bishop of Quito (1710-16), and an archbishop of La Plata (1720-24), all within a short space of 46 years.

Of the 41 viceroys of Peru, nine had previously occupied that exalted position in New Spain, all of them in the Hapsburg era before 1700. From the middle of the eighteenth century there was a change in the class of men selected for the post of viceroy. They were apt to be chosen not so much for their high rank and lineage, but from experienced military and naval officers who had served their apprenticeship in other parts of the Indies—in Cuba or Louisiana in the northern viceroyalty, or in Chile in South America. Five of the viceroys of Peru after 1745 were translated from the captaincy-general of Chile, two from the recently created viceroyalty of New Granada.

One of the most distinguished by his achievements of all the viceroys was Francisco de Toledo, who ruled in Peru from 1569 to 1581. A man advanced in years, belonging to a cadet branch of the great house of Alba, devoted heart and soul to the royal service, on entering Peru he resolved to make a tour of inspection of all the provinces within his government, to investigate the conditions prevailing throughout the country and the laws and customs of the natives.[15] He did cover most of what are now now the republics of Peru and Bolivia, and on the basis of this experience he issued over the years a series of ordinances for the government of the viceroyalty. These ordinances were received by subsequent viceroys as an authoritative text, and became in large measure the basis of later royal legislation; so that Toledo has often been referred to as the 'Peruvian Solon.' In so far as they dealt with the management of the Indians, they were to some extent based on traditional native practice, regulating land tenure in the native villages, judicial procedure, tribute, the position of the hereditary chiefs, labor on the cocoa plantations, the organization of the *mita*, and the reduction of the Indians to village life. Toledo's legislation also defined the functions of the Spanish *cabildos*, of the *corregidores*, and of the officers of the exchequer, and included a complete mining code for the viceroyalty. His municipal ordinances for the city of Cuzco were of especial importance and influence. He also made the university of Lima independent of the Dominican monastery where it had vegetated for twenty-five years, and endowed it with chairs in Latin, Philosophy, Theology, and Law.

Among the best of the viceroys were some of those appointed toward the close of the eighteenth century, notably Antonio María Bucareli and the second Count of Revillagigedo in New Spain, men who were really great administrators and left a permanent impress upon the life and prosperity of the regions they governed. Revillagigedo (1789-94) was a remarkable, if somewhat eccentric, character, and a prodigy of energy and ability. He improved the administration of justice and finance, encouraged agriculture, mining, and industry, promoted schools and roads, reorganized the militia, established weekly posts between the capital and the northern military stations, and advanced exploration of the Pacific coast to the Bering Straits. That no matter needing redress might escape attention, he placed a locked box in a public place into which petitions and other communications might be dropped. Before his time, in spite of the efforts of his predecessors, Mexico City was filthy beyond description. The great central plaza was given over to vendors of *tamales* and fruits, most of the streets were unpaved, unlighted at night, and infested with thieves. Under Revillagigedo the city began to wear the aspect of a modern metropolis, the central streets were paved and lighted, and the policing improved. The plaza was cleared and new markets were estab-

---

15 Fortunately assisted by men of ability and experience, especially Polo de Ondegardo and Juan Matienzo, who had filled important administrative posts in Peru and to whom we owe much of our knowledge of the political and social organization of the Incas.

lished in several quarters of the city.[16] The lengthy memorial or *Instrucción* which the viceroy left for the guidance of his successor, a document of 353 printed pages, is one of the most noteworthy state papers that have come down to us from colonial times.

The principal check upon the arbitrary exercise of power by a viceroy or captain-general lay in the royal *audiencias,* one of which was located in the principal city of each of the important provinces. These American *audiencias,* like many other institutions in the Spanish Indies, were a faithful reflection of a similar institution in the peninsula. The *audiencias* and chancelleries of Spain, however, were purely judicial tribunals. In America they performed a twofold function, judicial, and political or administrative. In their corporate capacity they shared in large measure with the viceroy, captain-general, or president, the functions of government, and were even empowered to review the acts of these high officials. Over the *audiencia* in his own capital the viceroy or captain-general presided *ex-officio.* Such *audiencias* were called *pretorial.* As already explained, the subordinate *audiencias* had presidents of their own, but the ultimate governing power was vested in the viceroy.

The size of the tribunal depended, quite naturally, upon its location and importance, it increased with the growth of the colony and the expansion of business. In Mexico City, for example, the *audiencia* originally consisted of four judges (*oidores*) and a president. In the seventeenth century there were twelve judges divided into two chambers, a civil chamber of eight *oidores,* and a criminal chamber of four *alcaldes del crimen;* also two *fiscales* or attorneys for the crown,[17] one for civil, the other for criminal cases. There was likewise a host of lesser officials: a chancellor, high sheriff, and chaplain, besides reporters, notaries, custodians of funds, attorneys' assistants and a lawyer and a solicitor for poor suitors. At the end of the eighteenth century the number of *oidores* had increased to ten, divided into two chambers, *alcaldes del crimen* to five, and *fiscales* to three, the third *fiscal* devoting himself exclusively to exchequer cases.[18] In the other viceregal *audiencia,* at Lima, the organization was much the same.[19] The *audiencias* of lesser importance had by law from three to five *oidores,* who served in both civil and criminal suits, and one or two *fiscales,* besides the minor officials indicated. But the number in residence was often below the legal assignment, owing to

16 Revillagigedo, *Instrucción,* par. 244-6; 273-97; 300-303.

17 The *fiscal* was a sort of royal watchdog who defended the king's interests wherever they might appear, but especially in cases affecting the exchequer, the Church, and the rights of the Indians. He also tendered legal advice to the viceroy or governor in matters of administration.

18 Revillagigedo, *Instrucción,* par. 66; Alamán, op. cit., 1, 86.

19 A separate criminal chamber was established in the Lima *audiencia* by the viceroy Toledo in accordance with his original instructions of December 1568. Schäfer, *El Consejo real y supremo de las Indias,* 167.

illness, death, or absence on special missions, or to the neglect of the crown to fill vacancies; and the colonists frequently complained of the failure to supply a sufficient number of judges to cope with the press of legal business.

As a court of law, the *audiencia* heard and decided appeals from inferior tribunals in the colony, i.e., from the *corregidores* and other local governors, and from the numerous administrative courts such as those of the *mesta* or sheep-raisers' guild, the *consulado* or guild merchant, the mint, the custom house, the Tribunal of Accounts (after 1605), and in the eighteenth century the *protomedicato,* and the *cuerpo de la mineria* or miners' guild. In criminal cases the decision of the *audiencia* was final—there was no reappeal to Spain. But important civil suits might be reappealed to the Council of the Indies. In the beginning this right was reserved to cases involving a minimum of 600 pesos de oro (about 1,000 silver pesos of eight reales) . By the New Laws of 1542 the minimum was raised to 10,000 pesos, and remained so into the eighteenth century. In order to free the Council from an accumulation of inactive appeals, the appellant was required to follow up the case in Spain, either personally or through an attorney, within one year.

The protection of the interests of the aborigines was presumed to be one of the *audiencia's* most important functions, and generally two days a week was reserved for suits between Indians, or between Indians and Spaniards. The natives were relieved of legal costs in lawsuits, and had attorneys designated by law to defend them. In the 1570's in New Spain, and thirty years later in Peru, this role of the *audiencia* was taken over by a special court, the *juzgado de indios.*[20] *Recurso de fuerza* was also made to the *audiencia;* that is, appeal to secular justice against abuse of authority by an ecclesiastical judge, as when he claimed jurisdiction not belonging to him, or tried to prevent lawful appeals. The *audiencia* likewise, in the event of complaints, might sit in judgment on acts of the viceroy or president, and in such cases the latter was required to absent himself from the session.

The *audiencia* also possessed original jurisdiction. It served as a tribunal of first instance in *casos de corte,* i.e., criminal cases that arose within the city in which the *audiencia* resided and within a distance of five leagues round about, and all cases in which the interests of the crown or its officials were directly involved. Such were of course all exchequer cases, and also after 1609 suits relating to *encomiendas* of Indians. Before that date all matters relating to the *encomiendas* had been especially reserved to the Council of the Indies. The *audiencia* likewise decided in first instance ecclesiastical cases of a secular character, such as disputes between the religious orders, or cases affecting the disposition

---

20 Cf. *ante,* p. 61.

of tithes or church lands or vacant benefices. Within its competence were also crimes committed by the clergy under the civil law. In all such cases of original jurisdiction, appeals might be carried to the council in Spain. But under no circumstances were appeals possible from one *audiencia* to another. One temporary exception is found in the history of New Spain, where for a few years it was permitted to carry appeals from Guadalajara to Mexico City. But this was only in the very beginning, before administrative practice in the New World had been clearly formulated. The distinction therefore between a *pretorial* and a subordinate *audiencia,* between that of a viceroy and of a presidency, rested solely upon its political or administrative capacity. All of the *audiencias* as judicial tribunals were of equal or coordinate authority.

The viceroy or captain-general, as president of the *audiencia,* unless he was trained as a lawyer had no voice or vote in the determination of judicial decisions, and he was by law expressly forbidden to meddle in matters concerning the administration of justice. Solórzano tells us that the viceroy might not call up before him suits from the ordinary magistrates, and still less those pending in the *audiencia,* nor embarrass, rescind, or annul judicial sentences. Viceroys, however, had the responsibility of general supervision; as president they allocated the cases among the judges, and kept watch to see that justice was administered with discernment and integrity. They might attend the tribunal at the commencement of suits and at the discussions for their determination, and they had the right of pardon in criminal cases. But as a matter of fact, as time went on they were apparently less and less inclined to appear at the judicial sessions. For one thing their time was fully occupied with problems of political administration, and they were not likely to take much interest in the routine work of the court calendar. On the other hand, the viceroy was empowered to decide whether a case was judicial or administrative in character, the occasion of frequent disputes; and when a case with important political or personal implications was on the docket, the viceroy was just as likely to exercise his right to preside and to bring the weight of his official presence to bear upon it.

In the last quarter of the eighteenth century, in 1776, was created in each *audiencia* the post of regent, an official who ranked next below the viceroy or captain-general, and presided over the chamber of justice in his absence. In Mexico City and Lima where there were two chambers, he might sit as judge in either or both.

The immediate reasons for this innovation are not clearly stated, but one seems to have been the need of cutting short the endless disputes among officials of the tribunal over powers, functions, precedence, the assignment of work, and similar questions. The regent was expected to keep informed of the status of all pending suits and to expedite judicial procedure. It was his special care to see that no obstacles were put in the way of the free exercise of the right of appeal to the *audiencia* against administrative decisions; he settled all questions of conflict or jurisdiction, and he might, if occasion required, form an 'extraordinary chamber of civil or criminal justice.' In event of the death or absence of the viceroy or president, the regent might exercise *ad interim* the powers and prerogatives belonging to that office. In short, he was given general management of all the day-by-day details of the *audiencia's* organization and functions. He served as a buffer between the judges and the president or viceroy, relieved him of the necessity of settling many annoying petty questions, and left him free to devote all of his time to larger problems of government and of policy.[21]

Below the *audiencia* the administration of justice in the Spanish colonies came to be subdivided to an extraordinary degree. The royal exchequer, the tribunal of accounts, the superintendent of the mint, the administrator of the post office, the merchant guild, the miners' guild, the grazers' guild, the *protomedicato* regulating the medical profession, and other similar entities each exercised a separate jurisdiction (*fuero*) in civil suits pertaining to its sphere of administration, or to which its officials or employees were a party. These many special courts, some of them dating from the eighteenth century, led to increasing confusion and frequent conflict, and to great inequalities in the dispensing of justice.

Perhaps the most famous of these special jurisdictions was that of the so-called *Acordada* in eighteenth-century New Spain. A revival of the *Santa hermandad* or rural constabulary first created in the middle of the sixteenth century [22] for the pursuit and summary punishment of brigands in the country districts, it was re-established in its later form by a royal decree of 1710. Under the authority of a supreme judge called the *Juez* or *Capitán de la acordada,* the tribunal employed a force of some 2,500 agents, most of whom rendered service without pay for the honor and privileges it conferred upon them in their own communities, and its jurisdiction extended over virtually the whole of New Spain. Its procedure was prompt and effective, and without the expense connected with other courts; a summary trial before the local judge of the *Acordada* and one or two assessors, and sentence from which in the beginning there was no appeal. Punishments were severe—hanging or shooting with

---

21 Revillagigedo, however, complained that the *decamo* or senior *oidor* had previously exercised most of the functions of the regent with entire satisfaction, and that the new office merely added one more functionary and one more expense for the crown, *Instrucción*, par. 14.

22 By the viceroy Luis de Velasco in 1553. Banditry was very common in most of the colonies, owing chiefly perhaps to the great number of idle, homeless vagabonds issuing from the irregular unions of the three races. In the sixteenth century the *audiencias* were overwhelmed with cases of the sort, and at times local magistrates were given final jurisdiction, even to the death penalty, and without appeal.

arrows. The independence of the *Acordada* roused the jealousy of the *alcaldes del crimen,* who sometimes succeeded in restoring the right of appeal to Mexico City, but never permanently. From the time of the second Revillagigedo, however, its sentences before execution were subject to review by the viceroy assisted by a special judicial committee.

The *audiencia* as a council of state deliberated with its president on certain days of the week in matters of political administration. These administrative sessions were called *acuerdos,* and the decisions arrived at *autos acordados.* When dealing with matters of public finance, the officials of the exchequer were added to the group, and the meeting became a *junta de hacienda.* Through the development of the *acuerdo,* the colonial *audiencia* came to be possessed of legislative and administrative powers that made it for its particular district somewhat analogous to the Council of Castile in Spain.

These political attributes of the *audiencia* were coextensive with those of the executive who presided over it. With its president it saw to the execution of all royal orders and decrees relating to the government of Church and State. It supervised the administration of the property of those who died intestate or without heirs in the Indies. It superintended the inspection and censorship of books, and all matters of ecclesiastical finance, especially the administration of tithes and endowments, vacant benefices, and the construction of churches and monasteries. It reviewed the credentials of newly appointed prelates and other clergy; also all papal letters, bulls, or briefs, forbidding the publication of those which had not received the approval of the Council of the Indies because deemed derogatory of royal rights and privileges. It might correspond directly with the king over the head of the viceroy or captain-general. And as stated before, if a vacancy occurred in the executive due to death or serious illness, the *audiencia* usually governed *ad interim* until the arrival of the successor, the senior judge presiding, at least until after 1776, when the temporary administration was reserved to the regent. In the eighteenth century, however, the viceroy or captain-general was usually provided with a sealed letter, *pliego de mortaja,* addressed to the *audiencia* and to be opened only in case of his death. In it was designated the person who should fill the vacancy until a successor arrived.

The question may well be asked as to where the ultimate authority in the colony rested, in the viceroy or in the *audiencia.* As a court of law, the *audiencia,* it is clear, maintained an unquestioned supremacy, saving only the right of appeal from its decisions to the king and council in Spain. But in the area of executive and administrative affairs, although the Laws of the Indies stated that the *audiencia* must submit to the decisions of the viceroy, in actual practice the case was not always so clear. *Audiencia* and governor were expected to work in harmony, to the glory of God and to the maintenance of the king's interests and the happiness of his subjects. Much depended upon the character and personality of the viceroy or captain-general. If he was weak and irresolute, the *audiencia* was likely to dominate the situation. If he was forceful and energetic, the opposite would be true, although he might find himself in constant conflict with jealous and acrimonious judges.

In the final analysis, however, the viceroy generally wielded the whiphand. He was in a special sense the personal representative of the king, and therefore usually assured of support by the government in Spain. And his position was consolidated by wide powers of appointment to vacancies in the interim until the king's wishes were known. The judges might advise and remonstrate, but in the event of an open breach what the viceroy decided must be carried into execution, and the *audiencia's* only resort was appeal to the Council of the Indies.

The *oidores*, in addition to their regular judicial functions within the *audiencia*, were from time to time invested with duties outside the tribunal, for some of which they received special compensation. One was associated with the Commissary General Subdelegate of the *santa cruzada* [23] as legal counsel and judge in cases arising from the collection of this tax. Another served as probate judge (*juzgado de bienes de defuntos*) appointed for a term of two years. One acted as *visitador* or inspector of fleets and armadas; still another as judge of appeals in commercial disputes arising within the *consulado*. As members of the *audiencia* they also possessed certain semijudicial functions, on the borderline between justice and administration. With the viceroy or governor they had an important part in local *residencias* and *pesquisas*, or judicial investigations into the conduct of political office, the nature of which will be discussed in greater detail later.

There was also by law a triennial *visitación*, or tour of inspection, made by one of the judges chosen by the viceroy or president, usually in turn. This was a searching inquiry throughout the entire province into economic, religious, and judicial conditions, the treatment of the natives, the conduct of the *encomenderos* and of the local magistrates. Everything came within the purview of the *visitador*, even to the inspection of the apothecary shops for bad or deteriorated drugs. He might fine or suspend offending officials, subject to appeal to the *audiencia;* and he was expected in his report to the tribunal to make suggestions for the improvement of conditions in the province.

It is clear that the *oidores*, like the viceroys and captains-general, were men of great prestige and influence in the colonies.[24] In their official acts they were surrounded by a complicated protocol. When on feast days and other public occasions they attended the cathedral in their

---

23 Cf. *post*, pp. 286-7.
24 Their salaries in the seventeenth century ranged from 2,000 to 3,000 pesos, in the sixteenth were somewhat less.

corporate capacity, they were received with the honors due to representatives of the royal person and vice-patrons of the Church, and were assigned special seats near the altar. Indeed frequent disputes over matters of precedence formed some of the most amusing and interesting episodes in the history of the American colonies. On the other hand, the government tried in every way to keep the judges aloof from influences that would attach them to the community, or might prejudice them in the impartial administration of justice. The policy of choosing most of them from among peninsular Spaniards was doubtless due in part to this consideration.[25] And even when Creoles were appointed as *oidores*, it was almost invariably to tribunals in other provinces than that of which they were native. Viceroys, judges, and their children were not allowed to marry in the colony without royal consent. They might not engage in business of any sort, borrow or lend money, and neither they nor their wives or children might own real estate in the cities in which they resided or anywhere else within their jurisdiction. They might not even legally exchange hospitalities, act as godfather in families outside their own official circle, or be present at marriages or funerals.[26] If permitted to marry within the community while they held office, they were generally transferred to another province. Some of these restrictions may seem puerile, and doubtless could not be strictly enforced. Their purpose may easily be appreciated given the distances separating the king from his servants in the New World; but their effect was to widen the gulf of misunderstanding appearing already in the seventeenth century between the Spanish colonials and their somewhat patronizing cousins from the homeland.

The *audiencia* was the most important and interesting institution in the government of the Spanish Indies. It was the center, the core, of the administrative system, and the principal curb upon oppression and illegality by the viceroys and other governors. Viceroys came and went; the *audiencia* was a more permanent and continuous body, which acquired a long line of corporate tradition. And even though it was Spain's policy to keep the office of *oidor* a virtual monopoly of European Spaniards, the institution took root in the colonies and became closely identified with colonial life. Many of the judges ended their days in America and became the founders of important Creole families.

The *audiencias* have been of outstanding significance to American historians and jurists of a later day, for they played an important role in the social and political evolution of the Spanish American nations. They helped to give to the cities in which they resided a cultural, military, and economic pre-eminence which made them the nuclei of larger

---

25 In this connection it might be recalled that most of the governors of British crown colonies today are not colonials but natives of the British Isles.

26 *Recopilación*, lib. ii, tit. 16, leyes 48, 49, 69, 74.

areas bound together by a community of sentiments and interests. They embodied a 'tendency toward jurisdictional autonomy in spite of royal pragmatics and the ill-concealed jealousies of viceroys and governors'; [27] and the regions they administered in most cases foreshadowed the territorial limits of the modern Spanish American republics.

27 Enrique Ruíz Guiñazú, La Magistratura indiana, Buenos Aires, 1916, 37-8.

VIII

❧

*Royal Government
in the Indies*

❧

(a) PROVINCIAL ADMINISTRATION

The impact of viceroys and royal judges upon the development of Spanish society in the New World was often considerable. Coming from old Spain, reflecting the whims and prejudices, or as often a truly social conscience, of king and ministers at court, they might exercise a great influence for good or for evil. But they were nearly all European born, comprising an official aristocracy kept somewhat remote from the Creole society about them. It was in the structure of local government that the Creole element was more conspicuous.

For purposes of local administration the vast areas called captaincies-general or presidencies were for convenience divided into smaller territorial jurisdictions; and these in turn into municipal districts, if there was sufficient population to allow of concentration in urban centers. These local jursdictions, differing greatly in size and importance, were governed from their chief towns by officials called variously *gobernadores, corregidores,* or *alcaldes mayores.* The district administered by a *gobernador* was usually of greater territorial extent than the *corregimiento* or the *alcaldía mayor,* and its territory was less definitely associated with a single town than was generally the case in the other administrative units. An examination of the colonial map reveals that either it was an area originally conquered and settled by an *adelantado* who was rewarded with the title of governor of the pacified region, the same title being continued subsequently in the royal administration of the province; or it was an outlying area, a sparsely settled frontier region, where considerable personal authority and a firm hand were needed to preserve the king's peace.

The *gobernadores, corregidores,* and *alcaldes mayores* possessed both political and judicial authority within their respective districts, but the *gobernador* sometimes combined with his title that of captain-general, which added military powers to the extensive civil authority he already exercised. While the *gobernador,* especially when also captain-general, must therefore be considered as an officer of somewhat higher rank and probably more independent status than the *corregidor* and *alcalde mayor,* the duties of these officials were identical, and for all practical purposes the terms may be taken as synonymous. Hereafter unless otherwise indicated, although in the main only the term *corregidor* will be used, it should be borne in mind that the statements apply equally to the provincial governor and to the *alcalde mayor.*

The geographical distribution of the *gobiernos, alcaldías mayores,* and *corregimientos* throughout the New World demonstrates that no systematic plan was followed or uniformity sought in the nomenclature of local administrative units. All three existed in the viceroyalties of New Spain and Peru, and even appeared within the limits of a single *audiencia.* It is interesting to note, however, that while both *alcaldías mayores* and *corregimientos* were found in the districts of the *audiencias* of Mexico and Guadalajara, *corregimientos* alone existed in the territory under the jurisdiction of the *audiencias* of Lima, Quito, and Charcas.[1]

During the earlier years of the Hapsburg era the viceroys and governing *audiencias* appear to have been in possession of rather wide power in the appointment of local officials. This power was restricted as time went on, and the designation of all the more important provincial officers came to be exercised directly by the crown. The districts not included in the list of royal appointments remained at the disposal of viceroys and presidents in America, subject to the approval of the Council of the Indies. These American authorities were also permitted to make ad interim appointments to posts which lay in the gift of the sovereign, but generally on half-salary.

To check malpractice in government, no individual was permitted to hold the office of *corregidor* in the district in which he had his residence, nor might *encomenderos* or proprietors of lands or mines be appointed to that office within the area in which their property was located. Viceroys or presidents, in appointing to *corregimientos,* were forbidden to name relatives within the fourth degree of any of the more important officials of the province. In Spain the *corregidor* was almost always a civil lawyer *(letrado).* This preference for lawyers in administrative offices was not carried over into the New World. Lawmen *(de capa y espada* was the phrase) were frequently sought for local government posts, and viceroys and presidents were expected to forward to the crown each year a list of such persons believed deserving of royal favor.

The term of office of *corregidores* whose nomination rested with the king was five years if the person chosen was in Spain at the time of

---

1 In the *Ordenanzas para los nuevos descubrimientos, conquistas y pacificaciones* issued by Philip II in 1573 it would appear that the *corregidor* was thought of as administering a smaller area than that of an *alcalde mayor, Col. doc. inéd.,* 1st ser., XVI, 158. The distinction, if it existed, was not borne out in practice.

appointment; if the appointee was in the Indies the period was three years. The term of both began with the possession of office, and continued until a successor appeared. Viceroys and *audiencias* might not remove *corregidores* at the end of their term and replace them with officials of their own choice pending the arrival of a successor; nor might a new incumbent assume office until the term of his predecessor was completed, even though he arrived earlier. Reappointment was permissible, but was generally to another district. In Peru, however, the *corregidores* named by the viceroy were appointed for a single year and, if their administration was satisfactory, the appointment might be extended for a second year.

The *corregidor,* at least from the early years of the seventeenth century, was required before undertaking the duties of his office to present an inventory of his goods and estate. The reasons are not far to seek. If the nominee was in the Indies, this inventory was recorded with the *audiencia* within whose limits his district lay; in Spain it was filed with the Council of the Indies. He also deposited a bond in the chief town of his jurisdiction, the purpose of which was to ensure his remaining there for the period of *residencia* and to guarantee the payment of any fines that might result from that process.

Once during his term of office the *corregidor* was by law required to make a tour of the district, informing himself about local administration of justice and government, hearing cases and taking remedial action when necessary, inspecting inns, hospitals, and markets, and reporting the results of his inspection to the *audiencia*. That such *visitas* might not become an undue expense and burden to the community, he was forbidden to make more than one unless ordered to do so by the viceroy or president, or unless a situation arose which imperatively demanded it.[2] He was also debarred under heavy penalties from engaging in business operations while in office, and from accepting gifts of any nature or personal services from Spaniards or from Indians. Like the judges of the *audiencias,* he might not marry within his district without special license from the crown, and might not choose any of his subordinates from among relatives within the fourth degree. If appointed by the crown he had authority to designate and remove deputies (*tenientes*) at will in the principal towns of his jurisdiction. Interference in these appointments by viceroys and *audiencias* was strictly forbidden except in cases of maladministration. Yet with that cheerful inconsistency frequently encountered in the laws of the Indies, *tenientes* if in the New World when chosen had to be approved by the local *audiencia;* if in Spain, they were examined before the Council of the Indies. They were subject

---

2 In making *visitas* the *corregidor* was forbidden to accept fees or extra salary for services rendered, or to impose himself upon any citizens as a guest against their will—an indication perhaps that such practices were not uncommon.

to the same rules in regard to bonding, participation in business, and marriage as was the *corregidor*.

The multiplicity of regulations, often repeated in royal instructions and decrees, is sufficient evidence that honesty and integrity in provincial government were not easy to maintain. Removed from effective control of the crown by the intervening ocean, protected from interference by viceroy and *audiencia* except for serious cause, *corregidores,* and provincial governors, especially if they owed their appointment to the crown, were in a position to exercise considerable independence and sometimes tyrannical authority. Local justice and the police power were combined in their hands. For an aggrieved person the *audiencia* was likely to be far away, and the journey an intolerable expense, especially as the *audiencia* generally required the plaintiff to appear in person before it. In any case the governor was apt to be fortified with friends at court. The Council of the Indies was still farther away. In important disputes it often solicited information from other parties—bishops, *cabildos,* exchequer officers—and given the notorious sluggishness and deliberation of its procedure, years frequently elapsed before a decision was finally arrived at. Criminals therefore might escape retribution, and injured parties be discouraged, hold their silence in the face of abuses, or resign themselves to complicity with fraud and injustice.[3]

In general the *corregidor* was closely associated with the local *cabildos* or municipal councils, although undoubtedly he was not always an integral member. As early as 1537 he was given authority to intervene in the affairs of the *cabildo* whenever public interest or the service of the crown demanded, and he confirmed the election of *alcaldes* in towns situated more than fifteen leagues from the seat of an *audiencia.* The more important civil and criminal cases went by appeal from the municipal magistrates to the *corregidor,* and from him to the *audiencia. Corregidores,* however, could not ordinarily call before them cases pending before the *alcaldes,* although custom varied in different places; nor could they demand that prisoners detained by local authorities be brought before them for trial. Unless the *corregidor* was trained as a lawyer, he called in an *asesor* or legal counsel to assist in the trial of judicial cases.

The ordinances drawn up by the viceroy Toledo for the *corregidor* of Cuzco throw considerable light upon the latter's relations with the municipality of the old Inca capital.[4] The *corregidor* was there an organic part of the local governing body, meeting with the two *alcaldes* elected by the *cabildo* and the six *regidores* or aldermen to govern the municipality. It is not clear whether the *corregidor* presided over the

---

3 Roberto Levillier, ed. *Correspondencia de los oficiales reales de hacienda del Rio de la Plata con los reyes de España,* vol. 1, 1540-96, Madrid, 1915, x-xii.

4 Roberto Levillier, ed., *Ordenanzas de Don Francisco de Toledo, virrey del Perú,* 1569-1581, Madrid, 1929, 36-142.

body regularly or not, but if he was in the city no meeting could be held without him. If he was absent for good reason his place in the *cabildo* was taken by his chief lieutenant, who succeeded to the powers and authority of his superior. As was the case in Spain, the *corregidor* was required to leave if matters concerning himself were discussed. But during his absence the *cabildo* might bring up no other subject, nor might the session be adjourned until his return to the assembly. When the *cabildo* undertook the election of *alcaldes* and other officials, the *corregidor* apparently always presided and invested with the staff of office those receiving the highest number of votes.

It has already been pointed out that, as part of the Spanish policy of imposing the externals of European civilization upon the aborigines, the natives were generally concentrated, insofar as was possible, in towns and communities organized along Spanish lines. Those towns which paid tribute to the crown were also grouped into *corregimientos,* over which were placed *corregidores de pueblos de Indios.* They were first appointed in New Spain in 1531, in response to orders sent out to the second *audiencia* in the previous year. According to Solórzano, Governor Lope García de Castro in Peru (1564-9) initiated the practice there of placing *corregidores* in the Indian towns; and the policy was extended and developed by his successor, the viceroy Toledo, who laid down ordinances for their regulation and guidance. *Corregidores de indios,* like the magistrates in Spanish districts, exercised both judicial and political authority, but it was their special duty to protect and foster the welfare of the natives.[5] They were permitted to have *tenientes* to aid in administration, but only with the permission of the viceroy when there was demonstrated need for a protector of the Indians in the locality.

This somewhat tedious exposition of the position and functions, within the political hierarchy, of the local governor in the colonies, whatever his title, is perhaps sufficient indication of his importance in the general scheme of Spanish administration, and of the influence he wielded for

---

5 Special attention was to be paid to the manner in which the natives lived, but their customs were not to be disturbed unless in conflict with the tenets of the Catholic faith. In time of famine or shortage a supply of foodstuffs and other provisions must be made available at reasonable prices. The *corregidor* was to take note of the policing of the Indian towns, see that the market place was kept clean, and that streets, bridges, and other public works were maintained in good repair. Reports and suggestions concerning such matters must be forwarded to the local *audiencia*. The extreme paternalism of the Spanish government is reflected in the law requiring the *corregidor* to see that the Indians kept themselves busily occupied upon their farms or in the workshops, utilizing their time and resources to best advantage. On feast days he was expected to enforce attendance at Mass, when the natives were instructed in the beliefs of the Church. Indians, however, might not be required to provide foodstuffs for the *corregidores* or other magistrates, nor were the latter permitted to avail themselves of native labor without giving compensation in return.

good or evil upon the lives and fortunes of those placed under him. He was at once the political leader of the province, its legislator in matters of local policy, generally the commander-in-chief of its military establishment if there was one, and its most important judicial officer. But his salary was small, sometimes a percentage of the local revenues, and he had every temptation to increase his income from extra-legal sources. So much indeed is implied in the requirement in later Hapsburg times that before entering upon the duties of office he present to the Council of the Indies or to the *audiencia* an inventory of his goods and estate.

The easiest and most immediate source of additional income lay in the economic exploitation of the Indians; and in spite of laws and royal injunctions making it the special responsibility of the *corregidores* to defend the lives, property, and general well-being of the natives, this was the very function in which they were most delinquent. The tyranny of the *corregidores* was notorious. They subjected the Indians to all sorts of exactions in the way of unremunerated personal services and illegal and excessive tributes, and generally conspired with the local priest and the native *caciques* to exploit them to the limit of endurance. The Indians were forced to sell their grain and other produce at prices below the market value, or to provide articles of their special skills or handicraft which were resold by the *corregidores* at lucrative prices. The latter were permitted a practice called the *repartimiento* of merchandise, which authorized them to introduce into their district certain goods to be distributed among the natives at reasonable rates. Under cover of this privilege they imposed upon their Indian charges excessive amounts of unwanted articles at arbitrary prices. The Peruvian viceroy, Manuel de Amat y Junient, wrote in the *Relación* for his successor in 1776:

I have already observed to your Excellency that the object of the *corregidores* of the kingdom is not the administration of justice, nor the preservation of peace, nor the safe-guarding of the people in their charge; but rather it is their purpose to trade with and have dealings with them, using for that end the authority inherent in their position which serves them as a guarantee in their undertakings. Because of this it frequently happens that the peace is disturbed, for traffic of such kind cannot fail to make the magistrates depart from the rectitude which should govern their acts.[6]

It was an abuse of power which caused frequent local Indian revolts, and in spite of all efforts by the crown it was never effectively remedied down to the very end of the colonial regime.

Among the outstanding reforms in colonial administration introduced

---

6 Quoted by Philip Ainsworth Means, *Fall of the Inca Empire*, New York, 1932, 197.

by Charles III in the latter part of the eighteenth century were certain changes in local government. The old Hapsburg system of *gobiernos, corregimientos,* and *alcaldías mayores* was supplanted by administrative areas called *intendencias.* The *intendencia* was an institution introduced into Spain by the Bourbon kings from France, and apparently with good results. It was first tried out in America in a limited form in 1764, when an *intendencia* or special office for the closely related services of war and finance was established at Havana. The *intendente's* responsibilities also covered contraband trade, public lands, and fortifications, and his rank was equal to that of the captain-general. Four years later, while José de Gálvez was visitor-general in New Spain, he proposed to the crown the establishment of *intendencias* in that area on a much broader basis of authority. After several other local experiments,[7] Gálvez, now Minister of the Indies, introduced the system entire in 1782 in the viceroyalty of Buenos Aires, in 1784 into that of Peru, and in 1786 into Chile and New Spain. Finally in 1790 the plan was put into general operation throughout the colonies. Four years earlier had been published a comprehensive Ordinance for Intendents in New Spain, consisting of 306 articles covering over 400 printed pages. This epochal document of colonial legislation was soon applied in Peru as well, and it became in fact, with later amendments, the fundamental administrative code for all the empire.[8] In New Spain there had been about 200 *corregidores* and *alcaldes mayores.*[9] In their place were set up 12 *intendencias.*[10] Eight were created in the viceroyalties of Peru and Buenos Aires, respectively, and a lesser number in the other important divisions of the empire. Certain frontier provinces remained under military governors.

The *intendencia* was presided over by a *gobernador intendente* chosen in Spain, and was divided into districts (*partidos*) each in charge of a *subdelegado* nominated by the *intendente* but appointed by the viceroy. The subdelegate served for a term of five years.

The announced purpose of this reorganization of local government was the increase of royal revenues by improving the fiscal administration of the colonies. The outcome of the Seven Years' War, the great colonial struggle between France and England which ended in 1763, had virtually eliminated France as a colonial nation, and left England and Spain face

---

7 In Sonora and Sinaloa in 1768, in Venezuela in 1777, and in the provinces of Tucumán and Córdoba (viceroyalty of Buenos Aires) in 1778.

8 An English translation of the Ordinances may be found in Lilian Estelle Fisher, *The Intendent System in Spanish America,* 97-331. A new code of Ordinances was issued in 1803, but was suspended the following January and never wholly in force.

9 'Informe general que . . . entregó el Exmo. Sr. Marqués de Sonora . . . al Exmo. Sr. Virrey Frey D. Antonio Bucarely y Ursua,' 31 December 1771, in *Instrucciones que los vireyes de Nueva España dejaron a sus sucesores,* 2 vols., Mexico, 1873, 1, 17.

10 New Mexico and Upper and Lower California remained apart as military districts.

to face in the New World as the only two remaining great imperial powers. There was a feeling in many quarters that Spain's turn might come next, that the abounding energy and the indomitable sea power of England might in another war wrest from Spain her empire, as they had already despoiled France. Spain since the acquisition of Louisiana was threatened along the frontier of the Mississippi River by English aggressions from the seaboard colonies and from Canada. In California on the Pacific she was threatened by an English advance from the Hudson Bay country. An eventual conflict seemed inevitable.

Imperial defense, therefore, after 1763 was for Spain a pressing problem, especially in view of the Family Compact with France and its many implications; and a larger program of defense required increased revenues. Although since the coming of the Bourbons, conditions in the monarchy had considerably improved over the material bankruptcy of the seventeenth century, national revenues were still small, the army and navy were weak, colonial trade was hampered by an antiquated system inherited from the Hapsburgs, and colonial administration was very corrupt. To secure revenues for defense, therefore, it was necessary to increase the wealth and prosperity of the empire, and to make more competent its financial administration. The results were the commercial and administrative reforms of Charles III, including the system of *intendencias*.

The fundamental aim of the new system was by centralizing administration to make it more efficient. The *intendentes* and their local subordinates, the *subdelegados,* concentrated in themselves the political, judicial, and military functions of the former *gobernadores, corregidores,* and *alcaldes mayores,* together with the financial jurisdiction of the officials of the exchequer. They were made responsible for an honest, economical, and rapid administration of justice, being expected to visit all parts of their *intendencia* each year for this purpose.[11] They were expected to pay special attention to the promotion of agriculture, industry, and commerce, and in every way to foster the economic prosperity of their districts. They were to develop irrigation, promote cattle raising, and every four months make crop reports to the viceroy. They were expected to improve the administration of municipal finances, look after the cleaning and paving of streets, the water supply, and the proper functioning of public granaries, markets, mints, bridges, and inns. Among their military duties were the pay of troops, the supply of provisions and equipment, the quartering of soldiers, inspection of depots and magazines, and a voice in the councils of the viceroy or captain-general in planning frontier campaigns, or in the movement and dis-

---

11 In this capacity they were assisted by an *asesor* or legal advisor, examined and approved by the *audiencia,* who generally took cognizance of civil and criminal suits within their jurisdiction.

tribution of troops. They also exercised the functions of vice-patron within their respective districts. The *intendentes,* in short, were the head of a complex department of government, with secretaries, fiscal agents, judicial officers, and many subordinates.

The most important services of the *intendentes,* however, were to be in the collection of royal revenues, over which they had exclusive jurisdiction.[12] At first they were entirely divorced in financial matters from the control of the viceroy, and subjected to a *superintendente general* in the capital city. There the latter presided over a *junta superior de real hacienda* or council of finance, consisting of the viceroy, the regent of the *audiencia,* the fiscal of the exchequer, the senior member of the Tribunal of Accounts, and one or two others. Exclusive cognizance of all legal cases relating to the exchequer was vested in the *intendentes,* or in the *partidos* in first instance in the subdelegates, with appeal to the *intendente* and thence to the *junta de hacienda.*[13] Under this arrangement the viceroy and *audiencia* were shorn of virtually all their fiscal attributes. But the division of authority immediately proved to be impracticable, and within a few years the two offices of viceroy and superintendent general were combined in the same person. Exchequer organization at the top, therefore—the viceroy in consultation with a special board of finance—remained very much the same as it had been.

This new system of local government provided for greater centralization of functions in the provinces, and for greater uniformity, if not simplicity, of administration. It also relieved the viceroy of many burdens of office detail. The *intendencias* were much larger in area than the older *corregimientos* and *alcaldías,* and commanded a higher type of official with presumably a greater sense of responsibility. Salaries ranged from 5,000 to 8,000 pesos a year, besides incidental emoluments which made the total much greater. The *corregidores* and *alcaldes mayores* had been appointed for short terms, most of them by the viceroy or president; and they received little if any salary, being attracted chiefly by the perquisites of office, generally at the Indian's expense. Most of them had been Creoles. The *intendentes* were appointed by the king and generally were European Spaniards. Some of them were exceptionally able men. To some extent the abuses of local and provincial government were corrected. Royal revenues apparently increased, and more efficient methods were introduced for collecting taxes and eliminating fraud. Although many less prosperous regions still produced an annual deficit, it was more than compensated for by the surplus from other dominions. New Spain yielded a profit of five to six million pesos, Peru about a

12 Except that *alcabala* and certain monopolies including tobacco, which were separately administered.

13 Lawsuits involving minor treasury officers went directly to the *intendente,* those involving the latter directly to the *junta de hacienda.*

million, Buenos Aires and New Granada each about half that amount. And besides there were the indirect profits through the trade and investment relationships of Spanish subjects with America, which increased with increasing prosperity.

Whether in the long run, however, the system produced any profound change in the methods and spirit of Spanish administration is not at all clear. The question was much debated by viceroys and others in New Spain and Peru; and in the beginning at least some of them indulged in considerable adverse criticism, if only because the amplitude of their own authority was somewhat diminished. Moreover good government, or a stricter administration of public affairs, was not necessarily popular with the wealthier inhabitants who had profited from the laxness in administration which the new system was expected to correct. It is doubtful whether the *intendentes* by and large contributed much to the improvement of agriculture and trade, of industry, and public works. In many cases they were probably hampered by lack of funds, or by indifference and absence of public spirit among the educated, upper-class inhabitants. Their exercise of the function of vice-patron often brought them into serious conflict with the local bishop, who resented the presence near him of an official clothed with so much authority.

The new system certainly removed the Spanish American Creoles still farther from participation in important offices of colonial government, which was an unfortunate and, as later events proved, a fatal policy. And while the *intendentes* as a whole were a somewhat better group of men than their predecessors, the spirit of the lesser officialdom below them, whether Spanish or Creole, could not change overnight, and much of the weakness and venality of the older order continued. The subdelegates, we are told by the viceroy Revillagigedo, were miserably underpaid, receiving only 5 per cent of the Indian tribute they collected, so that it was difficult to find suitable persons for the position. They were often ignorant of the law by which they administered justice, and were dependent upon judicial fees and other perquisities to make a bare living.[14] Some of them continued to trade with the Indians through the *repartimiento*, although this was forbidden by the Ordinance. The *asesores* too were sometimes badly chosen, and were greedy and unprincipled.

Unfortunately Charles III died within a few years of the introduction of the *intendente* system into the American colonies, and his reforms were in large measure neutralized by the reappearance of improbity and incompetence in the reign of his successor. Officials in the Indies promptly reflected the ineffectiveness of the government in Spain, and

---

14 *Instrucción*, par. 122.

gave just cause for the complaints and dissatisfaction of the colonists at
the opening of the nineteenth century.

(b) THE RESIDENCIA AND THE VISITA

The great distances which separated the Castilian sovereign from his
American possessions, the enormous extent of the overseas territories,
and the slowness of communications rendered effective control of royal
officials in the New World a perennial problem. Abuse of power was a
constant temptation to the dishonest or unscruplous, and jealousy and
distrust on the part of the crown were an inevitable consequence. Under
such circumstances it was natural that the Castilian institutions of the
residencia and the *visita,* as means of controlling the actions of distant
officials, should assume great importance among the administrative practices applied in the Indies.

The *residencia,*[15] or judicial review of an official's conduct at the end
of his term of office, first heard of in Castile in the reign of John II, had
been developed and systematically applied by the Catholic kings as a
means of control over the office of *corregidor.* In America it very early
became a cardinal feature of royal government. The first recorded resort
to this device goes back to 1501, when Nicolás de Ovando, appointed
governor of the Indies, was instructed to conduct a *residencia* of his predecessor, Francisco de Bodabilla. And he in turn was subjected to the
same process by his successor Diego Columbus in 1509. Thereafter this
procedure was customary throughout the Spanish American dominions,
every public official being held by law to strict accountability for all acts
during his term of office.

A specially designated commissioner, *juez de residencia,* traveled to
the principal town of the province or district in question, and there
issued a proclamation of the day when the *tribunal de residencia* would
open and the place where it would sit. Anyone was free to come forward
and present accusations or give evidence. Notice of the *residencia* must
be so published that it came to the attention of the Indians and gave
them opportunity to appear with complaints. The judge of residence
was provided with elaborate instructions regarding procedure. He must
not be satisfied with general accusations, but must get specific facts and
spare no pains to learn the truth. And he must inform himself concerning the conduct of subordinate officials and the general state of the district. In the case of a viceroy, if acts called into question resulted from
formal consultation with the *audiencia,* the judges of the latter shared

---

15 See *Recopilación,* lib. v. tit. 15.

the responsibility.[16] If there were charges of fiscal delinquencies, they were transmitted to the exchequer officers of the district who ascertained the shortages and held the bondsmen of the official investigated responsible. After hearing the defense of the *residenciado,* the judge prepared his report, favorable or unfavorable as the case might be, pronounced sentence, and remitted it to the Council of the Indies or to the local *audiencia* as circumstances required. Heavy fines, confiscation of property, imprisonment, or all three, were the usual penalties for malfeasance in office.

The *residencia* of officials appointed by the crown was entrusted to judges nominated in the Council of the Indies, presumably from a list of eligible individuals prepared and forwarded to Spain by the viceroys and presidents. In the case of officials appointed in America the appointing agency named the judge of residence. For those who had acquired proprietary rights to an office for one or more lives, a *residencia* was supposed to be taken every five years, in this case again by a judge designated by the viceroy or president.[17] He might be a reputable lawyer or, if the importance of the case warranted, one of the *oidores.* The latter procedure seems to have been the usual one followed.

The salary of the judge of residence was defrayed from fines and forfeitures imposed on the official under investigation if pecuniary sentence was given. If funds from such sources were insufficient, as was frequently the case, the amount necessary was charged to the *penas de cámara* of the *audiencia* or to its general expense account.[18]

Until near the close of the Hapsburg era no definite time limit was placed on the *residencia* of a viceregal administration. The undue temporizing which resulted led to a decree of 28 December 1667 (according to the *Recopilación*) which required a viceroy's *residencia* to be completed within six months. The time limit for the conclusion of *residencias* of presidents, *oidores, corregidores,* and other minor officers was ordinarily sixty days. If *demandas públicas*—defined by Solórzano as specific public charges brought against the official under review[19]—were presented, sixty days were permitted for the completion of the findings dating from the day on which the accusations were filed.

The Council of the Indies reviewed the *residencias* of all officials appointed by the crown. Appeals from sentences were also carried by the *residenciado* to the Council, except when claims against him amounted to less than 600 pesos de oro, when they went to the local *audiencia.* The decision of the Council was final except for sentences involving corporal

---

16 Ibid. lib. v, tit. 15, ley 2 (7 October 1622).

17 Viceroys were required to consult the *audiencia* before making appointments, but were not bound to follow the advice thus received.

18 *Recopilación,* lib. v, tit. 15, ley 42.

19 Solórzano, *Política indiana,* lib. v, cap. 10, par. 41.

punishment or deprivation of office held in perpetuity, when reappeal was allowed to another panel of judges. Sentences in fact were not infrequently modified or reversed in Spain if they reflected the personal animosities of officials in the Indies, or if the person investigated could command sufficient influence at court. Presumably appeals from sentences pronounced by judges of residence appointed in the Indies were heard by the *audiencia* in whose district the accused official exercised jurisdiction.

The requirement of the *residencia* seems generally to have been rigidly enforced,[20] and, as in the Old World, the substitution of a proxy for the *residenciado* was not allowed except in urgent cases, the official being forced to remain at his post for the full period prescribed by law. Solórzano, quoting Bobadilla, cites the extreme case of an *oidor* who, in order not to lose passage on a fleet due to sail for Spain, left a day before the termination of his period of *residencia,* and upon arrival in Europe was forced by the Council of the Indies to return to America to complete the process.[21] *Residencia* by proxy, however, was sometimes permitted by the judge, at his own discretion, to an official transferred to another post when to remain the full period would materially delay the latter's assumption of his new duties.

It was several times reiterated in royal decrees that governors and other officials in the Indies might not review the administration of their predecessors unless the latter were of proven integrity and efficiency. But this happened in practice rather frequently, even when the safeguards indicated were not present. It was a device that did not have much to recommend it except economy. A new governor, full of zeal to make a good record for himself, often hearing nothing but evil of his predecessor from a host of interested witnesses, was scarcely a fit person to conduct an impartial investigation. On the other hand, to send a judge of residence to the New World every time an important official was replaced would have been an incredibly costly procedure. And even the designation by the Council of the Indies of individuals in America to serve in this capacity was sufficiently expensive in time and money. Yet this, and the principle of the division of authority between several agents in the same jurisdiction, were the only mechanism the crown ever devised to check the independence and usurpation of its representatives in the New World. And probably, given the circumstances, no better mechanism could be evolved.

One might expect that the system of *residencias* would not only be a check on bad government, but would make for good government as

---

20 By a decree of 24 August 1799 the *residencia* thereafter was required only of political officers below the rank of *intendente* if complaints against them had reached the *audiencia* or president.

21 Solórzano, op. cit., lib. v, cap, 10, par. 6.

well. It should have had as its object the revelation of the commendable features of an official's administration as well as its shortcomings. So much indeed is indicated in a decree of Philip III dated 1620, as found in the *Recopilación*.[22] Professor Merriman, however, questions whether the *residencia* as developed by the Catholic kings in Spain was intended primarily to secure the highest standard of conduct and efficiency among the kings officers, or whether the crown was merely attempting to gain for itself a closer hold over agents who represented it at a distance from the seat of royal power. The same doubts may be expressed regarding its operation in the empire overseas.

In any case a conscientious and vigorous administration of public affairs was difficult to achieve. One of the most apparent results of the system in America was to discourage healthy initiative on the part of viceroys and governors, and prevent important political and economic developments in the colonies. Always faced with the likelihood of charges by some malicious foe, conscientious magistrates feared to deviate in the slightest degree from instructions composed, often quite ignorantly, by the Council in Spain. Evils of government of which the authorities at home knew little or nothing were perpetuated, and a sort of creeping paralysis ultimately came to pervade the entire political structure of the Spanish empire in the New World.

Even as a check on bad government the *residencia* was not always effective. It might be dispensed with by royal order, as sometimes happened in the case of high officials with powerful social and family connections at court. Thus one of the last viceroys of New Spain, the Marquis of Branciforte, was excused through the influence of his brother-in-law, the royal favorite Godoy, although many justified complaints were brought against him. The German scientist and traveler, Alexander von Humboldt, wrote at the very end of the colonial regime: 'If a viceroy is rich, clever, and has the backing of a bold adviser in America and of powerful friends in Madrid, he may govern arbitrarily without fear of a *residencia.*' Moreover a dishonest official was generally ready, and with every likelihood of success, to use bribery to overcome the scruples of the visiting commissioner, and so escape serious punishment even if misconduct was revealed in the investigation. Antonio de Ulloa tells us in his *Noticias Secretas* that in Peru it was customary for the *corregidores* to send agents to the court of the viceroy to interview the prospective judge of residence and come to some understanding before the latter departed on his mission.

The *residencia* was also frequently an unsatisfactory device because of the notorious unreliability of many of the witnesses on both sides. As Ernesto Schäfer has remarked, if they were enemies of the official under

---

22 Lib. v, tit. 15, ley 32.

examination he was represented as the greatest criminal and malefactor in the world, while his friends lauded him to the skies as the ideal of a good and faithful servant of the crown. Malice, spite, or disappointed ambition had their field day; and often it is impossible for the modern investigator to sift the grain of truth from the mass of contradictory statements.[23]

In the case of less important officials the *residencia* was probably more effective than for the viceroys. For most of them throughout three centuries of colonial rule the *residencia*, whatever its shortcomings in practice, served as a formidable institution of royal control.

The *visita* was a procedure somewhat different from the *residencia*, although both had the same end in view, namely, the assurance of loyal and efficient administration by government officials in the New World. The *residencia* was public, and occurred at the close of the term of office or upon removal to another post. The procedure in a *visita* was supposed to be secret, and it might come without warning at any time during the period of an official's incumbency. Generally instituted because of a serious emergency or a general condition of mismanagement, it denoted dissatisfaction on the part of superior authorities. It served not only to expose illegal actions of colonial officials, but also at times to prod delinquent officials into unwonted activity.

Visitas were of two sorts, which may be called specific and general. The former applied to a single official or province; the general *visita* was an inspection or investigation of an entire viceroyalty or captaincy-general. Everything came within the purview of the *visitador-general*, from the conduct of viceroys, bishops, and judges to that of the local parish priest; although when a viceroy was included in a *visita*, it was only in his capacity as president of the *audiencia*. Examination of his acts as a political and military officer was left for the *residencia*.

The manner of choosing the *visitador* was much the same as in selecting judges of residence. If he was to investigate officials appointed by the crown, he was commissioned by the Council of the Indies after consultation with the sovereign. In other cases he was chosen by the viceroy or president in consultation with the *audiencia*. The latter determined whether investigation was merited and how it should be conducted; the viceroy or president made out the commission and appointed the judge. The visitors-general were always sent out from the court, men high in the confidence of the king, and frequently members of the Council of the Indies.

The principle of the *visita* may be said to have been first applied in the Indies by the Catholic kings, when Francisco de Bobadilla in 1499

---

23 Ernesto Schäfer, *El Consejo real y supremo de las Indias*, 53, n. 2.

was designated as *juez pesquisidor* to investigate the government of Christopher Columbus and take remedial action. As was shown elsewhere, Bobadilla was evidently also instructed to supplant the Discoverer as governor, so that his inquest in a sense partook of the nature of a *residencia*. In fact this episode may be said to be the germ of both institutions in the New World. The *visita* took definitive form, however, in the later years of Philip II who made wide use of this device. A series of laws promulgated by Philip in 1588, and embodied in the *Recopilación*,[24] may be regarded as the legislation which fixed the permanent character of the institution.

The first serious general investigation of government in America took place in the years 1544-7, when Francisco Tello de Sandoval, a member of the Council of the Indies, was dispatched as visitor-general to New Spain. The occasion for his coming was the enforcement of the New Laws of Charles V; in fact he sailed on the same fleet with Blasco Núñez Vela, first viceroy of Peru, who was sent out to achieve this purpose in South America. This *visita* was of greater importance and extent than was formerly suspected. Recent investigations have shown that it was in large measure the outcome of a well-planned attempt by the *conquistador* Hernando Cortés to oust the viceroy Mendoza from office. Relations between the two men had never been cordial; each was jealous of the other's influence in the colony; and Mendoza had rather effectually cramped Cortés' plans for the exploration and conquest of the northern wilderness, which were ultimately carried out by Vásquez de Coronado under the viceroy's auspices. When Cortés returned to Spain in 1540, therefore, to lay his grievances before the king, he was out to 'get' the viceroy, and the *visita* of Tello de Sandoval was the consequence. But although directed really against Mendoza, the latter emerged unscathed. In this instance the higher officials in the colony stood together, and Sandoval departed leaving the impression that he had proceeded upon a very limited knowledge of the colony's affairs.[25]

During such an investigation the visitor-general had authority to call before him anyone he saw fit, and viceroys and presidents were expected to aid him in all ways possible. They were expressly forbidden to obstruct him by permitting appeal from his decisions. Indeed it was a question whether the authority of the *visitador*, or that of the viceroy, was supreme for the moment. Much depended upon the character and personality of the two individuals involved. When the *visitador* José de Gálvez, for instance, landed in New Spain in July 1765, he found himself immediately in conflict with the viceroy, a situation which ended in the latter's recall. His successor the Marquis of Croix was sent out with strict

---

24 Lib. II, tit. 34.
26 Arthur Scott Aiton, *Antonio de Mendoza, First Viceroy of New Spain*, 158-71.

orders to facilitate the work of Gálvez, and thereafter it moved ahead with an efficiency hitherto unheard of in America.

The *visitador,* in the accomplishment of his task, might sit with the judges of the *audiencia* during public hearings, although he was denied a vote in the determination of cases before that tribunal. The records of the administrative sessions of the *audiencia* (*libros de acuerdo*) were open to his inspection, except correspondence by the judges in regard to his *visita.* The names of those who gave testimony in the general inquest were withheld from colonial officials, so as to prevent tampering with witnesses or threats that might result in the concealment or distortion of evidence. Ministers of justice or officers of the exchequer found to have committed grave offenses against the public weal, might immediately be suspended from office, as well as officials who impeded the *visitador* in the performance of his duties. If it seemed desirable, they might be exiled from the province or sent to Spain. Report in cases where officials were gravely culpable was sent to the Council of the Indies before the results of the *visita* were fully ascertained, so that immediate action might be taken by that tribunal. Affairs of slight moment could be remitted to the viceroy or president, or to other officials of justice and exchequer, freeing the *visitador* for more important duties. All measures taken by him, either against officeholders or in rectification of abuses, were subject to ultimate approval by the crown. The findings and charges developed, as well as a complete report of the procedure, were forwarded to the Council, which reviewed the record and determined the final action to be taken.

If placed in competent hands and authorized upon adequate grounds, the *visita* was an institution capable of making a considerable contribution to good government. Unfortunately the crown usually assigned no definite time limits within which the investigation was to be completed, and the result was often an unwarranted amount of time consumed with little to show in return. Solórzano states that he had seen few *visitas* carried to a successful conclusion, citing as examples the general *visita* of the *Audiencia* of Lima by the *Licenciado* Bonilla, and the *visita* of the Marquis of Villa Manrique, viceroy of New Spain, both of which were undertaken in the closing years of the reign of Philip II. The first of these was begun in 1588 and dragged on for many years, Bonilla finally being named Archbishop of Mexico. He never assumed his new duties, however, for death claimed him in 1596 while he was still engaged in the *visita.*[26] The process, however, was not always interminable in length or barren of results. Solórzano's editor cites the case of the general *visita* of the *Audiencia* of Mexico entrusted to Francisco Garzaron, an *inquisitor* of New Spain during the viceregal adminstration of the Mar-

26 Solórzano, op. cit. lib. v, cap. 10, par. 21.

quis of Valero. This official conducted the *visita* with great dispatch and efficiency, and in reward was elevated to a bishopric in the Indies.

'Specific' *visitas* were generally authorized by the crown upon receipt of complaints against particular officials in the Indies, and Solórzano tells us that the bases of these accusations were not always sufficiently investigated. Consequently an inquest was likely to be ordered for inadequate reasons. The *visitador* was also subject to challenge, and if the Council admitted the objection, an associate accompanied him to scrutinize public charges or private suits in which those who entered the objecton were concerned. In general matters concerning the *visita,* however, he was empowered to proceed with entire independence.

With all the possibilities for good inherent in the *visita* its purpose, as in the analogous process of the *residencia,* was often defeated. Many times efficient and honest officials suffered more severely from the process than those whose acts were censurable; for the latter found means of escaping their deserts, while the former, trusting to their record, took no precautions against the criticism and enmity which a constructive policy frequently incurred. The oft-quoted opinion of the Marquis of Montesclaros, viceroy of Peru in 1607-15, offers perhaps the best contemporary evaluation of the institution. The viceroy compared the *visitas* to gusts of wind which one frequently encounters in streets and public squares and which accomplish nothing but to raise the dust, straw, and other refuse and cause everyone to cover his head.

What amounted to a local *visita* appeared in the practice of dispatching *pesquisidores* or *jueces de comisión* to investigate and report on the administration of a *corregidor* or other minor official. It was supposed to be resorted to only in cases of flagrant scandal, especially in the treatment of the Indians, and the crown was solicitous that it be not abused. These commissioners, appointed by the viceroy or president in consultation with the *audiencia,*[27] generally possessed little power themselves either to punish guilty officials or to remedy unsatisfactory conditions; and they were strictly forbidden to supplant in any way officials whose acts they were sent to examine. Their duties as a rule were purely investigatory. Sometimes they were sent to obtain additional evidence in connection with a case pending before the *audiencia.* If they found the official under surveillance chargeable with malpractice in judicial affairs, however, they might suspend him from office or commit him to prison, and send a full report to the tribunal.[28] That body then called the persons involved before it, heard their case, and passed judgment.

There was no lack of legal machinery, therefore, by which the crown

---

27 Except in certain *casos de gobierno* requiring secrecy, when the viceroy or governor could act alone. *Recopilación,* lib. VII, tit. 1, ley 10.

28 If the *pesquisidor* happened to be a judge of the *audiencia,* he might render a definite sentence, subject to appeal to the tribunal as a whole. Ibid. ley 14.

endeavored to maintain loyal, honest, and efficient government in its American empire. If the machinery did not always function, or if it grated and jarred in operation, this was in large measure due to conditions imposed by the age in which the empire was settled and organized, or over which the crown had no control: the long distances separating the colonies from the home country and the human weaknesses of the agents who represented the sovereign in the New World. Also the inherited principle of royal absolutism, which prevented concentration of authority anywhere except in the king and council in Spain.

The colonial system of Spain did not greatly differ in essentials from that of other colonizing nations of that age. All of them met similar conditions with similar methods. But no European country had ever ruled so great an empire, and none could compare with Spain in the reach and exercise of royal authority. The measures employed seemed to be the only possible ones at that time; they frequently brought good results; and Spain was not to be blamed if she could not forsee the future more clearly than her rivals. What must be remembered is that she maintained her empire undiminished for three centuries; and if she lost it in the end, because unable to adapt herself to new methods and new conditions, it was no more nor less than happened to her great colonial rival, England, in the revolution of the North American colonies. Not only to have conquered such an empire, but to have held it so long, was an extraordinary achievement.

IX

The Cabildo

The local unit of political government in Spanish America as in Spain itself, the lowest stage in the administrative hierarchy, was the municipal corporation or *ayuntamiento*—the *cabildo* as it was generally called in the colonies.[1] And at least from one point of view, this institution in the history of the American empire was of extreme importance. It was the only institution in which the Creole or Spanish American element in society was largely represented. And it was one of the few institutions which retained even a small measure of local autonomy.

As early as 1507 attorneys sent to Spain from Santo Domingo to seek concessions from the crown requested that settlements on the island be granted the powers and privileges ordinarily exercised by municipal councils in Castile. And the *conquistadores* of the sixteenth century generally, on entering a new region to subdue and occupy it, as a first step founded a town, set up some form of municipal organization. Cortés did so at Vera Cruz in 1519, before starting out on his daring march into the heart of the empire of Montezuma. Valdivia did so in 1541, founding Santiago as a shelter and a base for the conquest of that earthly paradise, the central valley of Chile. It was a natural thing to do. The English followed the same procedure when they crossed the Atlantic to the eastern shores of North America, at Jamestown, Boston, and Philadelphia. And it was very necessary, for protection against attacks by the aborigines, and to ensure by cooperative effort in the beginning an adequate supply of food. Moreover, at the outset of Spanish colonization the *cabildo* often served as a kind of general authority for the whole of the newly acquired territory until the establishment of a system of royally appointed officials.

But municipal organization, concentration in an urban community, was much more natural and characteristic in the early history of Spanish colonization in the New World than in that of English America. The urban tradition was much stronger in the history of Spain than in that of England. The Mediterranean institution of the free city state, the *civitas*,

---

1 The word *cabildo* was used to designate not only the municipal council but also other analogous bodies, such as a cathedral chapter. It was also applied to the 'town hall' in which the municipal council held its meetings.

perpetuated in the Roman Empire as the unit of local administration, had been implanted in the Hispanic peninsula during the flourishing days of Roman occupation; and this Roman municipal tradition, acquired with the Latin language and civilization, became so deeply rooted in the mind and habits of the inhabitants of Spain that the Visigothic and Moslem conquests of eight centuries were unable to eradicate it. In early medieval Spain the *municipium* emerges almost intact from the mists of the distant past, and in an age of insecurity somehow survived amid weak kings and quarreling nobles.

Moreover, during the wars of the Reconquest, when territory on the military frontier frequently changed hands in the struggle between the Christian and the Moor, the population naturally concentrated in towns for protection against the invader. And outside the larger towns, the village rather than the isolated homestead was for the same reason the characteristic fixture of the countryside. The sheep industry, whose early development and importance were largely related to the circumstances of the Reconquest, also contributed to the same result. Hostility between Christian and Moslem encouraged grazing rather than agriculture, for if the fortunes of war were adverse and the battle line was pushed back by the foe, you could take your sheep with you, but not your farm. And the predominance of sheep raising at the expense of agriculture meant that fewer people were distributed throughout the country and more concentrated in urban centers.

For these reasons the cities and towns of medieval Castile and Aragon played an unusually important role in the political organization of the state, and many of them, like the free towns of early England, had been granted charters (*fueros*) under which they enjoyed a large measure of autonomy in the management of their internal affairs. Flowing from this tradition, town life was more characteristic of Spanish colonization than of English. The first English settlers in North America concentrated in towns or villages in the beginning, only to scatter soon to individual farmsteads or plantations; and the creation of early English towns was very informal. In Spanish America urban communities remained the dominant type of political and social organization. Full-fledged municipalities were set up from the very first days of the conquest, and owing to the presence of aboriginal labor to exploit in fields and mines, the rural population remained almost entirely Indian.

As Bernard Moses has put it,[2] in the Anglo-American colonies the towns grew up to meet the needs of the inhabitants of the country, in the Spanish colonies the population of the country grew to meet the needs of the towns. The primary object of the English colonist was gen

---

2 Bernard Moses, *The Spanish Dependencies in South America*, 2 vols., New York, 1914, II, 370-71.

erally to live on the land, and derive his support from its cultivation; the primary plan of the Spaniard was to live in the town, and derive his support from the Indians or Negroes at work on plantations or in the mines.

The Spanish colonial town might grow out of an earlier Indian mission, or a mining settlement,[3] or a garrison or *presidio* on the frontier, but as a rule it was created consciously in accord with a predetermined plan of action. It generally had an individual founder who (to follow Moses again) went about his undertaking as one would fix the location of a manufacturing establishment. He selected the town size, indicated the place for the central plaza, the church, and the town hall, marked out the street plan, distributed the lots, and gave the future city a name. All of those present who were to become members of the municipality signed the act of organization and took an oath to support it. The founder then appointed a town council and magistrates, and before this body himself swore to maintain it.

The English colonial town, on the other hand, grew up more or less spontaneously where it was found, by the experience of many persons, that such a community would be of service to a large number of persons or families. Moreover, in English America local political institutions were allowed to rise and develop of their own accord, without much interference from the crown; although they naturally imitated the forms with which Englishmen had been familiar in the old country. In Spanish America, at least after the first few years, this spontaneity and independence were not permitted. The organization and activities, and the physical plan, of Spanish colonial municipalities were regulated in minutest detail by laws framed in the council chambers of the king. As they appear in the *Recopilación*, they follow mainly a royal edict of 1573.[4]

Spanish American cities followed a classical tradition of town planning, the gridiron pattern developed in Greek colonial cities as far back as the fifth century B.C., adopted in the many planned cities of the expanding Roman Empire, and after a temporary eclipse during the Middle Ages, revived in Europe, with the renaissance of art and learning, in the sixteenth and seventeenth centuries. Royal ordinances directed the founders of a Spanish colonial town to take into account climate and the quality of the soil, availability of water, the direction of

---

3 Mining towns, which generally started as haphazard settlements in mountains or desert, often in places quite unsuitable as a town site because of the rugged nature of the terrain, were less likely to conform to the conventional Spanish American pattern. A settlement or municipality in which the chief economic interest was mining was in New Spain called a *real de minas*.

4 *Ordenanzas . . . para los nuevos descubrimientos* etc., 13 July 1573 (*Col. doc. inéd.*, 1st ser., XVI, 142-87). The total number of Spanish settlements in America in 1574 was officially reported as about 200, of which half were in South America (Juan López de Velasco, *Geografía y descripción universal de las Indias*, Madrid, 1894, 2, 337).

sun and winds, ease of communications, and suitability for defense. Legislation fixed the size and shape of a central plaza, the width and orientation of the streets, the location of the public buildings, and the division of the city blocks into town lots.[5] Consequently all Spanish American cities and towns followed the same general urban plan, streets being laid out in a quadrangular pattern developed round the *plaza mayor,* fronting on which were the principal church, the *cabildo,* and the prison. In the center of the square often stood the *árbol de justicia,* a pillar of stone or wood, as a symbol of political authority and the place where executions and other judicial sentences were carried out.

In the beginning at least, the city blocks were often divided into four corner lots with a frontage each way of 150 feet or more, distributed among the principal citizens. On these lots eventually rose large, low flat-roofed houses constructed in the Mediterranean tradition, built flush with one another and with the unpaved street, with a great portal opening upon the interior, and with many rooms grouped about several courtyards or patios; houses built to accommodate several generations of a numerous family together with many Indian or Negro servants. In the rear were generally the corrals for horses and other domestic animals. Such houses still survive in many of the older Spanish American cities as witness to a simpler and more patriarchal age. Needless to add, cramped and unventilated dwellings in the very poor sections of the town possessed none of the spacious advantages enjoyed by the better citizens.

In the Spanish empire as in the Roman, moreover, the town retained something of the character of the ancient *civitas,* or city state. It war more than an urban community; it included a large surrounding district as well, each town in the more settled regions extending to the bounds of its neighbors. In less settled areas, where towns were separated by stretches of wilderness, their jurisdiction might cover a widespread territory. The jurisdiction of Buenos Aires, for example, extended about 300 miles to the limits of that of Córdoba, about 170 miles toward Santa Fe, and southward as far as the pampas Indians could be held in check. The territory of Popayán measured 66 miles to the neighborhood of Cali which bounded it on the north, and 60 miles to Almaguer on the south. The Spanish American provinces, therefore, were in many instances a collection of municipalities, the latter, as someone said, being the bricks of which the whole political structure was compacted.

Towns in the Spanish Indies, as has been noted, were a transplantation in general of the old Castilian municipality of the Middle Ages. But owing to early regulatory legislation from Spain, there was a uniformity in ground plan and in political organization which was not true of Spanish towns. Municipal authority was vested chiefly in two kinds

---

5 *Recopilación,* lib. IV, tit. 5 and 7.

of officers, *regidores* or councilors, and *alcaldes ordinarios* or magistrates. The number of *regidores* varied with the size and importance of the town. In smaller towns, called *villas* or *pueblos,* the number was generally from four to six. In larger communities, *ciudades,* it was usually eight, and in the great capitals like Mexico and Lima it came to twelve or more. The number of *alcaldes* was one in the small towns, elsewhere invariably two.

From time to time a number of other municipal officers were attached *ex-officio* to most Spanish American *cabildos.* They were chiefly the following: *alférez real*[6] (herald or municipal standard bearer), *alguacil mayor* (chief constable), *depositario general* (public trustee), *fiel ejecutor* (inspector of weights and measures, charged with the supply of foodstuffs and the adjustment of market prices), and *receptor de penas* (collector of judicial fines). We find some or all of these officials sitting as *regidores* 'with voice and vote' (*con voz y voto*) in the *cabildos.* On the other hand, the functions of *alférez real* and *fiel ejecutor* were in some cities—Buenos Aires, for example—exercised by one or more of the *regidores* or *alcaldes* in rotation. The practice ceased in Peru when the officers were by royal order put up for sale toward the close of the sixteenth century. They were certain other officials who, although like the *alcaldes* normally chosen by the *regidores,* did not have a seat in the corporation. Among the more important were the *síndico* or *procurador general* (city attorney), the *mayordomo* (custodian of civic property), one or more *alcaldes de la hermandad*[7] (police magistrates for the rural districts) sometimes called *alcaldes de la mesta,* and the *escribano* (notary) who also served as clerk or secretary at the *cabildo* meetings. In later times, if the city was a large one, there were often *alcaldes de barrio* who had general police supervision over the several wards or parishes.[8] In other towns the wards were each under the jurisdiction of one of the *regidores* or *alcaldes.*

Until 1622 the officials of the exchequer (*oficiales reales*) of the kingdom or province, although they were not municipal officers, had the right to sit and vote as *regidores* in the *cabildo* of the capital city, and in some cases—for the terms of their commissions varied—in the *cabildo*

---

6 The *alférez real* occupied the place of honor among the *regidores,* presumably received double their salary, and substituted for the *alcalde* in case of his death or absence.

7 An additional *regidor,* the *alcalde provincial,* was introduced into the *cabildos* of Peru in 1635, and probably in New Spain at about the same time. Theoretically his duties seemed to be the same as those of the *alcalde de la hermandad,* but the crown ordered that the latter should continue to be elected as had been the custom.

8 The judicial organization in Mexico City at the close of the eighteenth century was peculiar to that municipality. The city was divided into eight districts (*cuarteles*) under the jurisdiction respectively of the five *alcaldes de corte,* the *corregidor,* and two *alcaldes ordinarios,* and under them in each ward were four *alcaldes de barrio.*

of any town where they might be within the province, taking rank above the other *regidores*. The governor or *corregidor* possessed the same right, if the town was his official residence; and in such cases he had the privilege of presiding at the sessions. Otherwise his deputy, or the first or second *alcalde*, sat in the *cabildo* and presided over it. A governor usually had the right, not always exercised, of appointing a deputy (sometimes called *justicia mayor*) to preside in the *cabildo* of every town in his province. The governor or his deputy was nominally, it seems, without a vote, but he took a leading, sometimes decisive, part in the discussions and gave the casting vote in case of need.[9]

In the beginning the founder of the town—usually the *adelantado* in a new colony—designated the first *regidores* and *alcaldes*. And sometimes he reserved to himself the right to choose part or all of them thereafter. Royal instructions issued to Columbus for his second voyage empowered him to designate municipal officials, but only in first instance, the appointment of *regidores* thereafter being reserved to the crown on nomination by the Admiral. The letters of Cortés to the emperor reveal that he nominated the first *alcaldes* and *regidores* in all of the several towns which he founded; and when he dispatched Olid to start a settlement in Honduras, he appointed the capitulars of the city-to-be before Olid set out from Mexico. On 1 January 1525, although Cortés had started two months earlier on his own expedition to Honduras, his deputies in Mexico City 'presented an election' signed by Cortés of two *alcaldes*, four *regidores*, and a *procurador general*, which the *cabildo* promptly accepted. Other early *conquistadores* followed the same practice. Some of them, Pizarro and Valdivia, for instance, received from the crown the privilege of appointing three *regidores* with life tenure in every town they established.

It is true that in the first ordinances issued by Charles V in 1523 to regulate the manner of establishing new settlements, it was stated that unless there were specific provisions to the contrary the *regidores* should be elected annually by the *vecinos* or property owners within the town, and be incapable of re-election until after the lapse of a year. Such had been the general custom in the free towns of medieval Spain. The two *alcaldes* were to be chosen annually by the *regidores*, on 1 January, and might not be elected again until after two years.

Spanish colonial towns, however, did not long retain this democratic complexion, if they ever possessed it at all. Indeed, given the situation in

---

9 After the arrival of the first viceroy, Antonio de Mendoza, in Mexico City, he as governor always appointed a judge of the *audiencia* to preside at the election of *alcaldes* and other municipal officials on the first day of the year. The viceroy himself very occasionally presided at the regular *cabildo* session, and the *regidores* were accustomed to repair periodically to his palace to discuss matters of current importance. No act of the *cabildo* had legal force until confirmed by the viceroy.

Spain, it is surprising that the emperor ever made this concession to his subjects in America. In Castile in the fifteenth century the former free communes had entered upon a period of frank decadence. They had changed from elected bodies to close corporations, membership in which was purchased, or inherited, or a gift from the king, or passed around in rotation among the principal families of the town. This was part of the process of centralizing political control in the crown, which was begun by Isabella and Ferdinand, and it was occasioned by the irregularities and disorders in the government of the free towns themselves.

An analogous development took place in America. Whatever the original scope of the *cabildo's* independence and power, these were progressively narrowed and weakened as the early frontier character of the towns was lost, as the Indians were pacified, and royal government was able to entrench itself in a stable colonial society. The members of the town council were nominated by the local governor, often from lists drawn up by the retiring *regidores;* or they were chosen by the outgoing *regidores* subject to approval by the governor (as in Santiago de Chile throughout the sixteenth century) ; or they received their office directly from the king. As early as 1518-19 Charles V nominated two *regidores perpetuos* (designated for life) for each of five Cuban towns; and eight years later he made many additional appointments of the same nature in the seven town councils on the island, so that the annually elected *regidores* seem to have completely disappeared.[10]

In June 1525 Alonso Pérez de Valera presented to the *Cabildo* of Mexico City a provision of his majesty that granted him a *regimiento perpetuo* in that body. A year later two other men appeared with royal appointments as *regidores* 'during the king's pleasure,' and in the last months of 1528 ten additional royal provisions were presented in the same *cabildo*, nominating eight *regidores perpetuos* and authorizing the *alguacil mayor* and the commandant of the arsenal to sit in the council *con voz y voto.* From that time the municipality of Mexico consisted entirely of life members nominated by the crown, many of them new arrivals from Europe 'carrying in their baggage a title of *regidor* signed by the king a year or so earlier in Madrid or Valladolid.'[11] A similar story can be told of the municipalities of Lima and Quito in the southern viceroyalty. In fact it can easily be established that in most of the important cities of America the appointment of *regidores* was from earliest times entirely in the king's hands or in those of his colonial represen-

---

10 Irene A. Wright, *The Early History of Cuba,* 1492-1586, New York, 1916, 62-3, 89-90, 107-13.

11 F. A. Kirkpatrick, *Regidores and Alcaldes Ordinarios* (MS.). The time limit for presenting the royal title to the *cabildo* varied from ten to twenty months, and in some cases to two years or more.

tatives, and that any privilege of election that might be granted to the *cabildo* was a concession from the crown.

By Charles's son and successor, Philip II, the practice was introduced of selling offices to the highest bidder. As León Pinelo tells us in his learned and interesting work, *Tratado de las confirmaciones reales,* Philip on the abdication of his father in 1556 found himself with a virtually bankrupt inheritance, and under the necessity of seeking immediately new sources of revenue, especially in the provinces overseas. Among the devices resorted to was one already familiar in Spain, the sale of public offices, beginning in 1559 with that of notary (*escribano*), both ordinary notaries and those attached to the *cabildos.* Very soon other offices associated with the *cabildo* were put up for sale, that of *alférez real* as early as 1559 in Cuba, and in the towns of Peru in 1565. In Peru the *depositario general* and the *receptor de penas* followed in 1581, and the *alguacil mayor* and the *fiel ejecutor* in 1591. Apparently sale of the office of *regidor* had not been uncommon for some time; but in this same year 1591 a *cédula* ordered the viceroy of Peru 'on account of the necessities of the crown' to sell all vacant life *regimientos* in cities and towns where such existed and to add as many as seemed suitable, to be disposed of 'at the prices which are usually paid and which seem just.' And in places where the *regimientos* were annual, and people were ready to buy them for life, the annual posts were to be abolished and life offices to be sold 'in the number which seem suitable according to the quality of these pueblos and the number of *vecinos.*' [12] The proceeds were to be used to build and maintain the Armada of the Ocean Sea, after the destruction of the Great Armada in 1558.

These orders were duly carried out, and the revenue obtained from this source during the viceroy's term (Marquis of Cañete, 1590-96) was 206,647 ducats. It was always prescribed that in awarding office by public auction consideration be given to men of capacity, and whenever possible to original settlers and their descendants. But there is plenty of evidence that these precautions were not always observed. At first appointments were for one life only; but in 1581, as pressure was brought to bear upon the crown, the office of *escribano* was offered for two lives; and in 1606 all vendable offices were granted in perpetuity, with a right of resale or bequest within the holder's lifetime on condition of paying, the first time a half, and thereafter a third part of their value into the royal exchequer.[13] Every transfer had to receive formal confirmation by the king within three years. The innovation had the effect of increasing

---

12 Kirkpatrick MS.; *Col. doc. inéd.,* 1st ser., XVIII, 217-20. It is not at all unlikely that some of the *regidores perpetuos* nominated by the crown in the previous reign paid for their office in Spain.

13 If the previous occupant died within twenty days of the transfer, the transfer was voided and the post reverted to the crown. Transfer of the office to another person, sometimes for a money payment, had not been infrequent in the sixteenth century, but only by special permission obtained by application to the crown.

the value of the office to the purchaser without, in the long run, serious financial loss to the crown.

Municipal office thus became to all intents and purposes a piece of private property which passed freely by sale from one person to another, or between members of the same family, within the limitations stated. A vacancy might even be purchased for a minor, the post being held by the father or other suitable substitute until the coming-of-age.[14]

Most municipal offices by the beginning of the seventeenth century had become both proprietary and hereditary. The rule, however, was not invariable. In some cities—Santiago de Chile, for example—we find a mixed constitution, part proprietary, and part elective. Frequently the *cabildo* paid for the privilege of election, formally purchasing one or more proprietary *regimientos* from the crown so that it might continue the practice of choosing its members.[15] In some instances *regimientos* were let out by the governor or the *audiencia* at a yearly rental to the crown, the *cabildo* being allowed to choose the paying tenants. In the end, however, the office of *alcalde ordinario* remained everywhere elective, subject to confirmation by the viceroy or president, or by their proxy the local governor.[16] Municipal administration passed into the control of a narrow circle of wealthy and influential families and became an 'oligarchy in which the private interests of the regidores did not always coincide with the general interests of the communty they represented.'[17]

The Mexican historian Lucas Alamán describes the *Cabildo* of Mexico City, just before the wars of independence, as follows: There were fifteen permanent, hereditary *regidores,* men whose ancestors had possessed the office for generations, men who often were of little education or ruined fortune, but descended from families once rich and influential, and therefore still owning this perpetual right to share in the government of the city. These hereditary *regidores* chose each year the two *alcaldes,* and every two years they selected six honorary *regidores* [18] from

14 Transfer of an office to a minor, as distinguished from the purchase of a vacancy from the crown, was forbidden by law (*Recopilación*, lib. VIII, tit. 21, ley 10), but the law was not always strictly observed.

15 Ibid. lib. VIII, tit. 20, ley 19. The *regimiento* had, however, to be tied to the life of one individual so that on his death the crown might be paid its composition for the election of his successor.

16 Exceptional cases occurred in Potosí and Quito early in the seventeenth century where *alcaldes* were ordered to be chosen by lot because of tumults over the elections. F. A. Kirkpatrick, 'Municipal Administration in the Spanish Dominions in America,' *Trans. Royal Hist. Soc.*, 3rd ser., IX, 104.

17 José María Ots Capdequi, *El Estado español in las Indias*, Mexico, 1941, 52.

18 Added to the *cabildo* by ordinances issued for Mexico City by the *visitador* José de Gálvez in 1771. Herbert Ingram Priestley, *José de Gálvez, Visitor-general of New Spain*, 1765-1771, Berkeley, Cal., 1916, 300. At first they were chosen by the viceroy, but later a decree was obtained from the crown permitting their election by the *cabildo* itself.

among the more notable merchants, lawyers, and proprietors of the community. And these honorary officials by their superior ability and intelligence generally exercised a preponderant influence in the municipal corporation. The hereditary *regidores* were of course all Creoles, American-born; but it was the custom to choose the *alcaldes* and honorary *regidores* half from American, half from Spanish residents of the city.

As reported by the French traveler Depons, the *Cabildo* of Caracas at about the same time contained twelve proprietary *regidores,* and four whose office was conferred gratuitously by the king upon Spanish-born residents on the recommendation of the governor. The practice of choosing *alcaldes* equally from European Spaniards and Creoles was also followed in Guatemala City, to avert animosity between the two groups.

In less important towns, remote from the metropolitan centers of authority—Buenos Aires, for instance—posts in the *cabildo* were not in great demand, and many or all frequently remained vacant for lack of a purchaser, or if purchased at a small price were allowed to lapse on the death of the occupant. After various vicissitudes, the *Cabildo* of Buenos Aires in the middle of the eighteenth century received from the king the privilege of annually electing six *regidores* and compelling them to serve. This practice prevailed until the days of independence, the elected members constituting a majority of the corporation. But it was a rare exception to the general rule.

The *cabildos* exercised the normal, routine functions of such an institution; that is, they distributed lands to the citizens, imposed local taxes, provided for local police, levied a militia for defense in time of danger, gave building permits, maintained jails and roads, inspected hosptals, regulated public holidays and processions, supervised local market prices for the protection of the consumer, etc. They met in closed sessions, and the members were bound by oath not to violate the secrecy of their deliberations. By law *regidores* and *alcaldes* might not engage in trade directly or indirectly without royal permission, be associated with municipal contracts, or hold any other city office; and in some places, it seems, they received no salary.

The two *alcaldes* possessed civil and criminal jurisdiction as courts of first instance, even in cases in which judges or *fiscales* of a resident *audiencia* or their immediate relatives were involved.[19] That was their main function. Although elected annually by the *cabildo, alcaldes* might not legally be chosen from among the *regidores* themselves; but the law was not always strictly observed, and some municipalities, like Lima and Potosí, by paying a large sum to the crown obtained the privilege of naming one of their number as *alcalde,* the other being selected from the general body of citizens. In small and unimportant places irregularities

---

19 *Recopilación,* lib. v, tit. 16, ley 42.

were not infrequent, and were probably disregarded by the distant *audiencia* or governor unless they became a scandal. A law of 1573 [20] prescribed that in cities possessing a governor or *corregidor* the *alcaldes ordinarios* were to be excluded from the *cabildo* 'except where custom may have introduced the contrary'; but it is clear that custom had introduced the contrary in most places, and the law was seldom enforced. In most towns the *alcaldes* sat with the *regidores* in the *cabildo* and took their full share in the proceedings.[21]

Viceroys, governors, and judges were forbidden to impede the capitulars in the free election of *alcaldes*.[22] But since the need for confirmation implied the right of rejection, or at least restricted choice to persons likely to merit the governor's approval, an active and officious governor might have a considerable part in the election. There was some reason for control of these elections. It seems strange enough that judges should be chosen annually for a single year by a municipal council, even under the best conditions. But evidence abounds of rivalries, jealousies, disorders, and rancor over these appointments in many places. The choice of these part-time judges by partisan maneuvers or family favor required a check. Manuel Cervera in his *Historia de la ciudad y provincia de Santa Fe* tells us that in 1739 the governor of Buenos Aires recommended the abolition of *alcaldes ordinarios* in Santa Fe, Corrientes, and Montevideo on the ground that they were unnecessary in small towns and were the cause of disturbances and popular passions, all the persons concerned being related to one another, and the *alcaldes* using their staves of office merely as instruments of vengeance. His advice was not taken, but the abuses which he describes are proved by evidence elsewhere.[23]

Appeals from the *alcalde's* court were usually taken to the local governor or his deputy, and finally to the *audiencia* of the region. In Lima and Mexico City they went directly to the *audiencia*. The governors, however, sometimes exercised concurrent jurisdiction as a court of first instance, although we find this practice forbidden by a law inserted in the *Recopilación*.[24] In minor civil cases (involving not more than 60,000 maravedís) appeals might be carried to the *cabildo* and terminated there.

If the local governor died in office without a deputy, the municipal

20 Ibid. lib. v, tit. 3, ley 14.

21 In Mexico City this law of exclusion was enforced except when an *alcalde* was summoned to preside in the absence of the *corregidor*. Solórzano cites a letter from the king to the viceroy Toledo in 1575 ordering that where there was a paid *corregidor* there should be no *alcaldes ordinarios* at all; but he adds that these instructions were not generally enforced, except in some smaller towns to reduce the number of jurisdictions. *Política indiana*, lib. v, cap. 1, par. 25, 26.

22 *Recopilación*, lib. IX, tit. 9, ley 7. Dated May 1625.

23 Cervera, op. cit., 2 vols., Santa Fe, 1907, I, 657. For monopoly of office by a few families in Córdoba (Argentina), see Roberto Levillier, *Antecedentes de política económica en el Río de la Plata*, 2 vols., Madrid, 1915, II, 152-63.

24 *Recopilación*, lib. v, tit. 2, ley 14.

alcalde took over political control in his jurisdiction until a permanent or interim appointment could be made by the viceroy or other appropriate authority. A decree to this effect, however, issued in 1560 in favor of the towns in Venezuela was interpreted as giving them, in case of a vacancy, the right to govern themselves like so many little city republics, to the exclusion of the *Audiencia* of Santo Domingo; and it led to several bitter conflicts of jurisdiction. The settlers in Paraguay, too, received from Charles V as early as 1537 the privilege of choosing their own governor *ad interim* in the event of a vacancy. Doubtless inspired by the remoteness and isolation of that province, it was not forgotten by the colonists. The right was freely exercised, vacancies were even created upon occasion, and not until two centuries later, after the celebrated War of the *Comuneros*, was the decree declared obsolete.

Most of the cities of colonial Spanish America were granted by the crown a coat-of-arms, sometimes in return for a money gift or benevolence, and also the right to be addressed as *muy noble y muy leal*. In 1548 Mexico City received from Charles V the designation, 'la muy noble, insigne, y muy leal e imperial ciudad de México,' and was awarded the privileges and pre-eminences of grandee, as the metropolis of New Spain.

Municipal revenues in America were very meager. In most towns they were derived largely from the common lands with which from earliest times every municipality, whether of Spaniards or of Indians, was by law supposed to be endowed. Part of this land was used as a municipal commons (*ejido*), from which the householders might take firewood, or where in enclosed pastures (*dehesas*) they might turn their cattle to graze; part was distributed as arable fields to the townsmen; and part, the *propios del consejo*, was rented in plots for gardens and country houses, and became thereby a source of income to the municipality.[25]

We also find that to some towns the local judicial fines (*penas de cámara*) were assigned as *propios*, or the income from the sale of certain offices, or perhaps the services of a *repartimiento* of Indians. There was likewise a limited right of local taxation in the way of licenses of wine shops, market dues, and anchorage dues in seaports. Direct taxation for some specific object of general utility, such as a public fountain or bridge, was limited by the *Recopilación* to a maximum of 15,000 maravedís, or about 55 pesos, except by consent of the *audiencia* which might raise it to 200 pesos. Above that sum the approval of the crown was required.[26] Except in the larger cities, therefore, municipal taxes, or *arbitrios*, were of little importance.

---

25 *Recopilación*, lib. IV, tit. 7, leyes 7, 14.

26 *Recopilación*, lib. IV, tit. 15, ley 3. For the budget of the city of Santiago de Chile at the end of the eighteenth century see Julio Alemparte R., *El Cabildo en Chile colonial*, Santiago, 1940, 84-7. For Mexico City, *c.* 1745, see Joseph Antonio de Villa-señor y Sánchez, *Theatro Americano* 2 vols., Mexico, 1746-8, 1, 54-6.

Freedom of expenditure, moreover, was as narrowly restricted by the crown. Without previous consent of the *audiencia* or provincial governor, extraordinary appropriations from general revenues were limited to the ridiculous figure of 3,000 maravedís. The viceroy Revillagigedo near the close of the eighteenth century said that in New Spain municipal funds were generally sufficient if well administered, but the *regidores*, being men who bought their office, rarely were persons of sufficient intelligence or zeal for the public welfare. The irresponsible expenditure of public funds in lawsuits, fiestas, and useless offices, was a perennial source of complaint.[27]

Community spirit, as we interpret the term today, was scarcely to be looked for in a Spanish colonial town. Public works, such as roads, bridges, water supply, were delayed for years and even for centuries, and if achieved at all were allowed to fall in disrepair, because of the unwillingness of the citizens to be taxed. The roof of the *cabildo* might leak, rivers overflow, and bridges fall, the streets be filthy and filled with mudholes, the common resort of cattle and pigs, while lavish sums were expended on civic and religious celebrations, extravagant clothes, and magnificent funerals. The great number of poor in the cities, unemployed and unemployable, was a perennial social problem, and the standard of living of the mass of the population was extremely low. The natural concomitant of undernourishment, then as now, was excessive indulgence in alcohol among the lower classes. Murders in the streets were common, and asylum was still granted by the churches to criminals. Epidemics were frequent due to lack of elementary sanitary precautions. Not until the close of the eighteenth century were there public cemeteries in such important cities as Vera Cruz, Puebla, and Mexico. And it was only under the administration of the second Revillagigedo that streets in Mexico City were lighted at night, at first as a responsibility of the individual householders, later as a public service of the *cabildo*.[28]

For the discussion of matters of grave importance, such as local defense in time of war, there was sometimes called together a wider assembly of the more notable citizens, including the bishop and the principal clergy, to deliberate with the *cabildo* in what is commonly referred to as an 'open *cabildo*' (*cabildo abierto*).[29] Sometimes such an assembly

---

27 *Propios* and *arbitrios* were frequently farmed out to the highest bidder. Each year an accounting of municipal income and expenditure was supposed to be taken by the local exchequer officials and sent for audit to the *audiencia*.

28 Julio Alemparte R., op. cit. chs. 2, 4, 5, *passim;* Revillagigedo, *Instrucción*, par. 227-46.

29 'To say "*the* cabildo abierto" would be an error, for there was no such established institution. I find no mention of it in Solórzano Pereira and only one mention in the Laws of the Indies, lib. IV, tit. 8, ley 8 (dated November 1623) which orders that the election of *procurador* of the city should be "by votes of the *regidores*, as in the case of the other annual posts and not by the cabildo abierto." ' Kirkpatrick MS.

was summoned to make a gift of money to assist the king in his European wars, to receive an important communication from the crown, or to celebrate the birth of an heir to the throne. Customarily the meeting was called by the governor or his deputy, but the *cabildo* might take the initiative by requesting him to issue the summons. Apparently all of those present were privileged to speak and to vote on the matters brought before them, but their proceedings were chiefly of an advisory nature. Decisions were not necessarily binding upon the municipal council, and in any case they rarely impinged upon the powers normally exercised by officials of the crown. It appears from the record that in remote or less important towns of the empire, such as Buenos Aires or Santiago del Estero, where the colonists were fewer and left more to themselves, the citizens or some of them were more frequently called in for assistance or assent.[30] Such occasions, however, did not constitute in a strict sense a *cabildo abierto,* nor did more informal gatherings of the citizens to which this term has sometimes been applied.

The *cabildo abierto* has occasionally been compared with the democratic town meeting of the English colonial towns. The comparison, however, is not exact. All the residents of a town in New England had the right to attend the town meeting, and in this assembly of the citizens were invested all the powers of the local government. It elected the officials and made all the decisions, like the municipal council of a Spanish American town. The *cabildo abierto,* on the contrary, was an extraordinary assembly called together only at long intervals, and only those citizens who were specially invited had the right to attend.

On these wider assemblies, however, rested the strongest case for the *cabildo's* potential democracy. Although they never included all the nominally free members of the municipal population, they were not unlike the variety of democracy practiced in the Greek city-state. And the *cabildos abiertos* were in many instances a vital factor in the outbreaks that inaugurated the wars of independence in the nineteenth century. For these Spanish American revolutions, like most great revolutions of the world's history, were essentially urban movements; and as it was in the *cabildos* alone that the Creoles played any prominent political role, they were usually the nuclei of revolutionary agitation. In them the popular will first found self-consciousness, and in the *cabildos abiertos* the people made their first attempts at self-government.

It is interesting to note in the Spanish American colonies in the sixteenth century the beginnings of a course of development which, under different auspices, might have evolved a species of colonial assembly. From time to time delegates from the principal towns in an island or mainland province met together to discuss and take action in matters of

---

30 See also recorded instances in the early records of the *Cabildo* of Santiago de Chile (*Colección de historiadores de Chile,* I, 450, 464).

common importance. Sometimes they joined together in petitioning the crown for concessions of one kind or another, or in defense of their rights against the encroachments of royal officials.

In the first half of the sixteenth century we find assemblies of this sort on the islands of Cuba and Hispaniola, and later on the mainland in New Spain and Peru. Altogether, we are told, there is record surviving of about forty such meetings during the first hundred years of the colonial era. But we know little of their history or effectiveness. They seem to have remained simply means of communication between the towns or of petition to the king. The whole trend of Spanish political development was against the rise of provincial autonomy or legislative freedom, and toward ever increasing autocracy and centralization. As early as 1530 Charles V, when conferring upon Mexico City the privilege of first place among the municipalities of New Spain in any such assemblies, at the same time announced that 'without our command it is not our intention or will that the cities or towns of the Indies meet in convention'; [31] and even though this injunction was not obeyed to the letter, it was impossible that anything like a colonial *Cortes* should ever arise or survive in America. Local gatherings of this sort, however, did occur from time to time. As late as 1739, for instance, an assembly referred to as a *cabildo provincial* met in the province of Tucumán, consisting of delegates from all the 'cities and *cabildos*' of the province and recommended a tax for the support of two hundred men to protect the region from Indian incursions.[32]

Throughout the colonial era from earliest times the municipal *cabildos,* like most other political entities in America, possessed the privilege of communicating directly with the king in Spain. Instances are very frequent, either by petition in writing, or by instructions to an agent or proctor.[33] Some of the cities kept attorneys permanently resident in Spain to represent their particular interests before the authorities there, just as the English colonies in more recent times have kept agents resident in London. And it is this institution of the colonial agent in the peninsula that may have suggested to Spanish liberals in 1812 the idea of inviting the principal cities of Spanish America to send delegates to the first modern Spanish *Cortes.*

In an earlier chapter reference was made to the constant concern of the Spanish government that Indians scattered and dispersed throughout the country abandon their nomad habits and be concentrated in towns and villages of their own, like their European neighbors. Official regulations regarding these Indian pueblos were as meticulous as those relating to the towns and cities of the Spaniards. Each Indian commu-

---

31 *Recopilación,* lib. IV, tit. 8, ley 2.

32 Levillier, op. cit. II, 131.

33 The city attorney (*procurador general*) might be sent to Spain in special cases only, presumably with the consent of the viceroy or *audiencia* of the district.

nity must be provided with a church, and with a priest (*cura doctrinero*) paid out of the tribute, as well as with a sacristan to take charge of the church fabric and its ornaments. Every pueblo of a hundred or more Indians was to have two or three chanters (*cantores*), besides two *fiscales* who were to be old men over fifty years of age charged with the duty of calling the Indians to religious service and instruction. The sites of the newly created Indian towns must be carefully selected as to accessibility, water supply, arable land and woodland available, and must be provided with a commons (*ejido*) at least a league in extent for the pasturage of cattle. From one to four Indian *regidores* and one or two Indian *alcaldes*, depending upon the size of the pueblo, were to be chosen each year in the presence of the priest and the local *corregidor* (later the subdelegate) and relieved during their term of office of tribute and personal services. The *alcaldes* shared jurisdiction with the hereditary native chief or *cacique*,[34] were aided by one or more Indian *alguaciles*, sometimes collected the local tribute, and had authority to make arrests and to punish minor offenses such as drunkenness and failure to attend Mass. More serious offenses were referred to the *corregidor* or other local Spanish official.

Each Indian village was also possessed of a community fund (*caja de comunidad*), accumulated from the produce of certain common lands or labor of the village, or derived from quit-rents of communal lands let out to Spanish or Indian farmers. The income was used to defray municipal expenses such as legal services, support of a hospital, aid to widows and orphans, repair of roads and bridges, or to pay the tribute of members who were ill or absent. The *caja de comunidad* was an adaptation at least in Peru, of primitive aboriginal customs to the social policies of the Spanish crown. Its funds, administered by the local officials of the exchequer or more generally by the *corregidor*, were a constant temptation to the Spaniards entrusted with them. The *corregidores* were in the habit of using these funds as private capital for business enterprises in their respective districts, sometimes on a gigantic scale; and there are many recorded instances of suits arising from their loss due to speculation or actual theft. Toward the end of the eighteenth century, when the *corregidores* had been supplanted by the *intendencia* system, apparently these irregularities somewhat abated, and on occasion the surplus from such funds was appropriated by the viceroy and sent to the crown in Spain.[35]

---

34 In the pueblos of Yucatan there was also a native 'governor' chosen by the town but receiving his appointment from the Spanish authorities, who might or might not be the *cacique;* also sometimes a steward or mayordomo and a town clerk. Ralph L. Roys, *The Indian Background of Colonial Yucatan*, Washington, 1943, 134-41.

35 For these paragraphs see *Recopilación*, lib. VI, tit. 3, based largely upon royal ordinances of 1619 and 1639. For the organization of Indian pueblos in Peru in the time of the viceroy Toledo see *Ordenanzas de Don Francisco de Toledo, virrey del Peru,* 1569-1581, Madrid, 1929, 305-22. For Yucatan, see Roys, op. cit. 129-74.

The Spanish municipalities in America very early lost their popular character. They also more and more lost their autonomy, due to interference in their affairs by the provincial governor or *corregidor,* or in Mexico City and Lima by the viceroy. One condition in fact must have helped to bring about the other; for with the loss of popular interest and support the *cabildo* was less able to withstand the encroachments of the governor, who as the direct representative of the crown could impose his will on the town corporation. If need be, he might modify or ignore with impunity the *cabildo's* program or orders, for appeal to the *audiencia* was a slow and expensive process. And where any vestige of election remained in the choice of the personnel of the *cabildo,* such elections were generally subject to the approval of the governor or of the viceroy. The latter could fine the capitulars for failing to elect their nominees and frequently did so, in spite of the law which forbade viceroys, presidents, and *oidores* to interfere with the free choice of persons for public office.

And so, as the *cabildos* were gradually deprived of whatever initiative and independence they may have possessed in the beginning, the office of *regidor* became politically of less and less consequence. Yet it was greatly sought after by the Creoles. Municipal posts were almost the only positions in the political hierarchy to which they might aspire, almost the only sphere of action in which they could distingush themselves above ther fellow subjects. They gained therefrom little or nothing in political authority, but great prestige in colonial society. *Regidores* were regarded as of the higher ranks of the untitled aristocracy and the natural leaders of public opinion in the community. To that extent the *cabildos* continued to represent local interests and remained in some slight measure responsive to local sentiment. They also retained some memory of their former autonomy, though thwarted and crossed in their normal development by the increasing centralization of the crown. And it is not surprising that it was usually in the *cabildos* in the early nineteenth century that the first sparks of revolution were kindled.

It was doubtless owing to these circumstances that the last century of the colonial regime saw a notable decay in many of the Spanish American municipalities. This seems to have been especially true in New Spain, although travelers report much the same situation in other parts of the empire. When the great *visitador* José de Gálvez was in New Spain in the years 1765-71, he found the *cabildo* of the important city of Guadalajara, the second in the kingdom, entirely moribund. San Luis Potosí had only two *regidores,* and these were deputies acting for nonresident proprietors, and one of them was also *alcalde.* In some of the delinquent municipalities the *visitador* himself created new *regidores,* to be elected annually as had been the primitive practice in America.

In all the cities of the viceroyalty municipal finances were in a state of incredible disorder and confusion. In many towns no books at all were kept of simplest receipts and expenditures. Corruption in public administration was universal. The situation was so bad that a general accounting office (*contaduría general*) was established in Mexico City to which all municipalities had to send their ledgers for audit. No expenditure of city funds might be made by the *regidores* without prior consent of the *contador general*.[36]

It was this total want of efficiency and order in local government that was largely the excuse for the reforms in colonial administration after 1780, especially the ordinances creating the system of *intendencias*. *Intendentes* and their subordinates, the subdelegates in the local districts, took over virtually complete control of municipal affairs—budgeting of town funds, street cleaning, water supply, regulation of hospitals and jails, markets and bakeries, etc.—subject to review by the special committee of finance (*Junta superior de real hacienda*) in the capital of the viceroyalty or captaincy-general. To the *cabildos* was left only the routine drudgery. The subdelegates frequently supplanted the *alcaldes* in the administration of municipal justice, and the *regidores*, with few functions and no independence of action, were reduced to a level of complete irresponsibility.

These reforms—this extreme centralization of authority—did lead to valuable municipal improvements which under other circumstances might have materialized much more slowly.[37] Certainly at the close of the eighteenth century most of the important cities of Mexico and South America began to experience an outward transformation that for the first time gave them the appearance of modern cities. Streets in the center of the city were paved for the first time, and lighted at night; the plaza was cleaned and beautified—cleared of fruit and vegetable vendors and other hucksters who were relegated to markets on the outskirts; and *paseos* and *alamedas* were laid out for the delight of later generations. But on the other hand these improvements served only to emphasize a trend referred to in discussing the *intendencia*, the trend of the native Spanish American to remove himself still farther from opportunity for education in self-government, and from interest in matters of local public welfare. For this he was partly himself to blame. It stands in curious contradiction to other tendencies of that time, the increasing dissatisfaction of the colonials with Spanish administration as it stood and the demand for a larger measure of political and economic liberty.

It also serves to correct a view of the *cabildo* which appears in many conventional texts. Municipal government as a sphere in which the

36 Herbert Ingram Priestley, 'Spanish Colonial Municipalities,' *California Law Review*, September 1919, 411.

37 The viceroy Revillagigedo, however, reported in 1794 that mismanagement of municipal funds in New Spain was as prevalent as ever. *Instrucción*, par. 154-63.

creole preserved a strong tradition of freedom, has frequently been ex-aggerated. As already pointed out, in some cities the *cabildo* had vir-tually disappeared at the end of the colonial era. In other places its per-sonnel was only in part Creole; peninsular Spaniards were also admitted. Everywhere in Spanish America, except on the frontier and in the remoter agricultural areas, the activities of the *cabildo* were absorbed or completely dominated by a royal representative, the provincial gover-nor, or his deputy, or in capital cities the viceroy or captain-general. The municipal councils were little aristocracies, consisting mainly of per-manent officials who had purchased or inherited their posts, and who seemed to have little concern for their role as representatives of the people. As a repository of the people's liberty, a training school for the democratic system to be set up after independence, the *cabildo* possessed no potency at all. It had little or no freedom in action or responsibility in government. Its weakness was not a recent development at the turn of the nineteenth century. On the contrary, the institution had been in a state of collapse for generations. If it became in some places the instru-ment by which revolutionary tendencies in 1810 made themselves felt and heard, it was often due to pressure from outside brought to bear by the more radically minded members of the community.

Nevertheless the *cabildo* had a decisive role to play in spite of itself! The important facts about it are two, already adumbrated: that it was the one self-perpetuating local institution in the colonies, and not a mere administrative appendage of the mother country; and that it was the sole agency of government wherein the Creoles retained a large for-mal participation. When therefore royal government collapsed in Spain with the captivity of Charles IV and his son Ferdinand and the seizure of Madrid by the usurper Joseph Bonaparte, and the American colonists did not know whom to obey, the *cabildo* became in many places the only political center about which the Creoles might rally. Through the tra-ditional medium of the *cabildo abierto,* it was the only agency capable of taking the initial steps to construct a provisional government.

X

The Church in America

'Spain was impelled to two kinds of militant action at that momentous period of her history: the one militarist the other spiritual, both combative and eager to conquer; in the former the purposes to conquer power, territory, and riches prevailed; in the latter the prime aim was to win adherance to Christianity. There was an interweaving between the two, a mutual aid that engendered phenomena of social symbiosis of great juridical and political importance. A realization of that permanent interrelation between two organisms, each of which depended for its existence on absorbing a part of the vital juice of the other, is quite fundamental for the understanding of Spanish colonization. The will to power and the will to imperium, in the double dimension so loved by the Renaissance, material and spiritual, reached through Spain to its apex.[1]

These words of Fernando de los Rios supply the theme of the chapter which follows. Spain transmitted to America her culture, and in large measure her political ascendency, through the instrumentality of the Church. Whether or not 'the guiding idea of the Spanish state during the conquest and colonization was a religious one'—and the question admits of debate—without doubt the dominant note in Spanish society in those days was religion. Ferdinand and Isabella by their policy of religious and racial unification had greatly accentuated the religiosity of the Spanish people, and in the sixteenth and seventeenth centuries the clergy in Spain increased tremendously in numbers, in political power, in social and spiritual influence, and in accumulated wealth. They became the dominating class in Spanish society. And Spain in America reflected the indissoluble union of the altar and the throne. They mutually supported one another. The Church defended the divine sanctity of kings; the crown upheld the ecumenical authority of the Roman Catholic Church.[2]

---

1 Fernando de los Rios, 'The Action of Spain in America,' *Concerning Latin American Culture*, 53.

2 'Las Leyes de Indias . . . pueden resumirse en la fórmula de ortodoxia religiosa y omnipotencia politica para el Estado, que en su compenetración insuperablemente estrecha con la Iglesia, protege a ésta pero obtiene de ella medios de suprema eficacia.' Niceto Zamora, *Impresión general acerca de las leyes de Indias*, Buenos Aires, 1942, 22-3.

The Church in America was under the direct and immediate control of the crown in all matters except doctrine and religious discipline. And this control was much closer, much stricter, than in any Catholic monarchy of Europe. The patronage of the Church was regarded as the most honorable and valuable of the crown's attributes, 'the richest stone, the most precious pearl, in the royal diadem.' Ferdinand and Isabella, in spite of their staunch Catholicism, were always very jealous of papal and other foreign influences in the government of the Church in Spain. And soon after the discovery of America they solicited and obtained from Pope Alexander VI the grant of the ecclesiastical tithes in all the new-found regions. The bull was issued on 16 November 1501, with the condition that the Spanish sovereigns made themselves responsible for the introduction and maintenance of the Church and for the instruction and conversion of the Indians. In short, the tithes were to be used for ecclesiastical purposes but under the control of the crown.[3] A few years later, in July 1508, Pope Julius II by another bull conferred on Ferdinand and his successors the exclusive right of patronage in the New World, i.e., control over the founding or construction of all churches and monasteries, and the disposal of all ecclesiastical benefices. As the popes had adjudicated the newly discovered lands to the Catholic kings in order that they might preach and spread the Christian religion, a task manifestly beyond the material resources of the Papacy alone, as a corollary ample powers were granted to the sovereigns in matters of ecclesiastical government and financial aid.

It might conceivably be argued that these duties and privileges were implicit in the bulls of Alexander VI of 4 May 1493.[4] It was the papal concessions of 1501 and 1508, however, and the rights and duties flowing therefrom, which made the king in a very real sense the secular head of the Church in the Spanish Indies. He not only controlled the administration of ecclesiastical taxation, but nominated all the higher church dignitaries and in theory the parish clergy as well; although this last function was generally left to the viceroys and governors in America in their capacity as vice-patrons. Archbishops, bishops, and abbots were nominated by the king directly to the pope. Canons and other members of cathedral chapters were nominated by the king or his council to the American prelates. Curates and *doctrineros* (priests in Indian parishes) were nominated to the prelates by the viceroy or governor. In the case of both cathedral and parish clergy the bishop presented a list of three candidates from which the king or his deputy chose one.[5] Private indi-

---

3 Cf. *post*, pp. 283-6.

4 Faustino J. Legón, *Doctrina y ejercicio del patronato nacional*, Buenos Aires, 1920, 181-3.

5 The *terna* or list of three candidates became a source of conflict between the bishops and the civil power, the former endeavoring to establish the rule that the vice-

viduals who with royal permission founded churches, hospitals, monasteries, or other pious works might exercise the patronage under the jurisdiction of the bishop.

The independence of the crown in elections to episcopal office in fact extended even farther. The king not infrequently chose an ecclesiastic as bishop-elect and sent him as governor of the diocese *en vacante,* with instructions to the cathedral chapter to appoint him as such as canonically as it was empowered to do, until the bulls arrived. Sometimes the bulls never arrived, or the bishop-elect died or was transferred before they appeared. In practice in such cases the king was really usurping the Pope's prerogatives.

The juridical doctrine of the *Patronato Real,* the body of rights and privileges involved in the papal concession, was a development by the Spanish crown and the legal commentators during the course of the sixteenth century. And given the absolutist tendencies of the government, the result was an extraordinary accretion of faculties of every sort, not only in the matter of presentation of the clergy but in everything relating to ecclesiastical government.[6] By law no cleric might go to the Indies without special license from the crown. Monasteries, churches, and hospitals, were erected in America only in accordance with royal ordinances.[7] Revenues of vacant benefices, from archbishopric to lowest prebendary, accrued to the use of the king. He had the right to fix the limits of new dioceses and to change them as he saw fit. Bishops might not remove an ecclesiastic from his benefice without previous satisfactory explanation to the king or his deputy. Any bull, brief, or other communication emanating from the Holy See or its delegates might be published or enforced in the colonies only after preliminary examination and approval by the Council of the Indies. The same rule applied to the decisions of diocesan and provincial councils in the New World. And throughout the colonial period we find reiterated orders from Spain directing *audiencias* and governors to send back to the Council of the Indies all documents of this nature which had not received its exequatur. Although the Spanish monarchy was too steeped in Catholicism

---

roy or governor should choose the first on the list, leaving the nomination therefore really to the bishop.

The Council of Trent had prescribed that candidates for parish benefices be selected by the bishops by public competition, and this appears in the *Recopilación* (lib. I, tit. 6, ley 24). The bishops apparently tried to enforce this rule in the Indies, but with indifferent success. It was observed in form, but selection too often depended upon the favoritism or private interests of the examiners. G. Desdevises du Dezert, 'L'église espagnole des Indes a la fin du XVIII siecle,' *Revue Hisp.,* XXXIX, 173-4.

6 Legón, op. cit. 187-90.

7 Apparently in the beginning the crown undertook the construction of churches and monasteries entirely at its own expense. As the colonists increased in numbers and wealth, it shared the cost with the local community, Indians and landowners both contributing.

ever to endanger the Church's orthodoxy, even matters of ecclesiastical reform were subject ultimately to the authority of the crown. The Spanish Bourbons, under the influence of French Gallicanism, went a step farther, and claimed the right of the *Patronato* not by virtue of a papal concession but as a direct consequence of their own sovereignty. And during the course of the eighteenth century the royalist sentiment in the government of the Church steadily increased. The ancient right of asylum was restricted; the jurisdiction of the civil courts over the clergy was enlarged to include all crimes under the common law and cases involving pious funds and foundations; and the royal exequatur was extended even to questions of dogma. The trend may be said to have culminated in the summary and unheralded expulsion of the Jesuit Order from Spain and its colonies by Charles III in 1767.[8]

The power exercised by the crown under the *Patronato Real* made the Church in a very real sense another branch of royal government, another means of political control over the colonists. As Desdevises du Dezert has remarked, here was a remarkable example of a civil constitution of the clergy accepted by the Holy See. The American Church became in fact a national church, living within the orbit not of the Roman Papacy but of the Council of the Indies, and attached to Rome by very tenuous bonds.[9] The American episcopate was always notable for its staunch royalism, and the Church became through its spiritual and moral influence the most powerful agency for maintaining the dominion of the Spanish kings over their distant and far-flung trans-Atlantic possessions.

Whether a priest accompanied Columbus on his first voyage to the Indies has often been debated. There is no contemporary evidence to show that there was one,[10] although this may seem surprising in view of the deeply religious nature of the Discoverer. With Columbus on his second voyage was sent Friar Bernal Boyl as first vicar apostolic of the New World, together with about a dozen other religious to begin missionary work in the new lands. Among them was the Franciscan, Juan Pérez de Marchena of the convent of La Rábida, who had helped persuade the queen to support Columbus's enterprise. Father Boyl, evidently a man of spirituality and intelligence, had been acting superior of the Benedictine monastery of Montserrat near Barcelona, and stood high in the service and regard of the king. But his sojourn on Hispaniola was

---

8 Ibid. 215; Jorge Basadre, *Historia del derecho peruano*, Lima, 1937, 256. A decree of June 1789 ruled that in criminal cases the ecclesiastical judge had only disciplinary power, the judicial process to be conducted by a civil magistrate in the presence of the ecclesiastical judge, and the final decision to be reserved to the Council of the Indies.

9 Desdevises du Dezert, op. cit. 171-2.

10 Elizabeth Ward Loughran, 'Did a Priest Accompany Columbus in 1492?' *Cath. Hist. Rev.*, XVI, 164-74.

not a happy one. Quarreling with Columbus over the latter's harsh methods of discipline, and discouraged by the grim realities of pioneering in the tropics, he returned to Spain at the end of a year; and there is no record of the immediate appointment of a successor to his episcopal faculties,[11] although calls for additional priests were issued from time to time.

Father Boyl was the first prelate in the Indies. Ten years elapsed before another effort was made to set up a separate ecclesiastical juris- diction overseas. In November 1504, after the great colonizing expedi- tion of Governor Ovando to Hispaniola, the crown obtained bulls creating an archbishopric and two bishoprics on the island, and ap- pointing three incumbents. But these topheavy arrangements were never carried out. Ferdinand held back the bulls of appointment until he had secured from Rome the right of patronage over the new churches, and when this concession was obtained in 1508, centers of population had so shifted in the West Indies that the king petitioned the Pope to substi- tute new sees for those created in 1504. Finally in 1511 the latter were annulled, and three new ones were set up according as Ferdinand re- quested, at Santo Domingo and Concepción de la Vega on Hispaniola, and at San Juan on Puerto Rico. All three were suffragan to Seville. The same clergymen were named for the new bishoprics, and two of them within a year or so actually took possession; but Bishop Padilla of Santo Domingo never reached his see, leaving its administration to a vicar-general until his death in 1515.[12]

Thus an ecclesiastical hierarchy was set up very early in America, on the same footing as in Spain. And thereafter the crown generally fol- loed the policy of having a bishopric erected immediately upon the colonization of any new region. The first bishopric established on the American mainland was at Darien in 1513, removed in 1524 to the City of Panama. For the Mexican area, Clement VII as early as January 1519 created the diocese Carolense associated vaguely in the beginning with Cozumel and Yucatan, but later (1525) translated to Tlaxcala, and finally moved to Puebla de los Angeles. Within the next forty years there were no less than 7 bishoprics erected in New Spain,[13] 6 on the Caribbean mainland,[14] and 3 in Peru.[15] Until 1545 all the American

11 Elizabeth Ward Loughran, 'The First Vicar-apostolic of the New World,' *Eccles, Review*, 9th ser., II, 1-14.
12 Elizabeth Ward Loughran, 'The First Episcopal Sees in Spanish America,' *Hisp. Amer. Hist. Rev.*, x, 167-87. The first diocese on the island of Cuba was erected at Baracoa in 1518, and removed to Santiago in 1522.
13 Mexico 1530, Oaxaca 1535, Michoacán 1536, Chiapas 1538, Guadalajara 1548, Yucatan 1561.
14 Comayagua (Hond.) 1531, León (Nic.) 1531, Coro (Venez.) 1531, Sántiago (Guat.) 1534, Cartagena 1534, Santa Marta 1535 (removed to Santa Fe de Bogóta in 1553).
15 Túmbez 1529, Cuzco 1536, Lima 1539.

dioceses were subject to the archbishop of Seville, but in that year 3 provinces were created independent of Spanish ecclesiastical jurisdiction, centered in Mexico City, Lima, and Santo Domingo. By the end of the colonial period there were 10 archepiscopal provinces and 38 dioceses in Spanish America,

Meantime, at the request of the crown the dignity of Patriarch of the Indies had been created in Spain itself, possibly in imitation of Portugal which had its Patriarchate of the East Indies. Apparently the first to be elevated to this high office was Ferdinand's minister for the colonies, Juan Rodríguez de Fonseca, then Bishop of Palencia, in 1513.[16] On his death in 1524 Antonio de Rojas, Archbishop of Granada and president of the Council of Castile, was appointed, followed in 1533 by Gabriel de Guiena, Bishop of Bari, and in 1546 by another archbishop of Granada, Fernando Niño. After the latter's death the office long remained vacant, owing it seems to the misgivings of the Papacy over the growing independence of the American Church under the royal *Patronato;* and the crown did not succeed in having a successor installed in office until 1602.[17]

The Patriarch of the Indies as vicar-general was presumed to have general superintendence of all ecclesiastical matters in the New World, and to reside at the court so that he might be in immediate contact with the Council of the Indies. He generally bore the title and honors belonging to the cardinalate, and served at the same time as chief chaplain of the royal palace. But his functions appear to have remained largely honorary, and to have had little part in the government of the Church in America.[18]

The most numerous clergy in the Indies in the beginning were the friars, who came out very early. The first Franciscans arrived at Santo Domingo before 1500, and the first Dominicans appeared in 1510. And they were followed by Mercedarians and members of other Orders, so that in a short time small monasteries were very numerous.[19]

The chief motive of the coming of the friars in the beginning was missionary work. In the sixteenth century Spain had before it the stupendous task of Christianizing and civilizing the natives, a task soon made more difficult by the enormous extent of territory to be covered,

16 Ernesto Schäfer, *El Consejo real y supremo de las Indias,* 167, n. 2, Mariona Cuevas, however, states that the office was created by Clement VII in 1524 at the request of Charles V, *Historia de la iglesia en Mejico,* 1, 304.

17 Schäfer, op. cit. 167, 191; Cuevas, op. cit. 1, 304-06.

18 The office was supported out of funds from vacant benefices in the New World.

19 The first Franciscans were sent to New Spain on the mainland in 1523, 3 Flemings who came with Charles V from the Low Countries in that year. In 1525, arrived 12 more Franciscans, sometimes called the Twelve Apostles of Mexico. In 1526 came the first Dominicans, also 12 in number. In 1533 arrived the first Augustinians, 7 in number. The first Jesuits came to New Spain in 1572.

and achieved only to a limited degree. A large part of the instructions to virtually every explorer and governor is occupied with exhortations and commands to treat the natives kindly and justly, and to bring them as soon as possible into the Christian faith. The early bishops were concerned chiefly with superintending this work of conversion, and with efforts to protect the natives from their despoilers. But the earliest and most active agency was that of the friars. At first the Dominicans stood out as the foremost champions of the rights and the conversion of the Indians. In later times the Franciscans and the Jesuits came to be the most active missionary Orders.

The friars therefore in the beginning were much needed, and every effort was made to encourage them to emigrate. They were sent to the Indies by the crown free of expense,[20] and were transported there by viceroys and bishops. On their arrival in America they were assisted and provided for, until the Orders were able to establish houses and communities of their own. The king also contributed from the royal exchequer in the colonies to the construction of monasteries, and to the poorer establishments gave presents of silver services, candles, wine, and oil. Indeed provision of wine, wax, and oil for the monasteries continued to be a regular part of the cargo of outgoing fleets to the end of the seventeenth century. Gil González Dávila reports that Philip IV in 1633, when the Spanish crown was bankrupt, assigned out of the royal revenues 300,000 ducats a year for wine and oil used in the monasteries of New Spain and Peru.[21]

The Papacy also made concessions to the friars in the Indies, following the custom already established for Orders which labored among the infidels in heathen countries. As the secular clergy in the beginning were too few in number to perform the rites of the Church throughout the length and breadth of a rapidly expanding empire, papal bulls permitted the friars to administer the sacraments and perform other duties of a parish priest in places where no secular clergyman was available, without express authorization by the bishop.[22]

These concessions were desirable in the early years when the colonies were new and the need for priests and missionaries was very great. Not all of the early friars who came out to the New World were worthy of their high calling; but the vast majority meant to do their duty, even if

---

20 Friars selected by the Orders for missionary work in the colonies were recommended by them to the Council of the Indies, which issued passports to the *Casa de Contratación*. Travel expense from the monasteries to Seville was furnished by the crown, the cost of clothing and food for the voyage by the *Casa*, and the passage money by the royal treasury in the Indies after safe arrival. *Recopilación*, lib. 1, tit. 14, leyes 4, 6.

21 *Teatro eclesiástico de la primitiva iglesia de las Indias occidentales*, 2 vols., Madrid, 1649-55, 1, 17.

22 Bull of Adrian VI, 9 May 1522, confirmed by a bull of Pius V in 1567. Robert Ricard, *La Conquete spirituelle du Mexique*, Paris, 1933, 133-4.

their missionary achievements were not always commensurate with their intentions. Given the primitive mentality of many of the Indians, and their limited capacity for comprehending the spiritual doctrines of Christianity, in the early 'rage of conversion' the natives without doubt were often taken into the Church without sufficient preparation or instruction. Zumárraga wrote in 1531 that the Franciscans since 1524 had had baptized more than a million Indians.[23] Toribio de Motolinia tells us that some of the early Franciscan friars in New Spain baptized as many as 1,500 Indians, children and adults, in one day. He goes on to say that several of them baptized each over 100,000 during their sojourn there, and that altogether the friars baptized over four million Indians during the first fifteen years after the conquest.[24] Peter of Ghent in a letter of June 1529 speaks of 14,000 as being baptized in one day. Indians proselytized in this fashion mingled the old with the new, their inherited superstitions with the splendid formalism of the Catholic Church. The bishops themselves sometimes reported that the Indians understood little of the religion that was preached to them.[25] Moreover, severe physical punishment was often resorted to by the clergy in an endeavor to eliminate 'heathen' practices among these baptized but scarcely converted natives, as witness Bishop Landa in Yucatan in the early 1560's. To the same end temples everywhere were torn down and idols burned or smashed, although the accusation that the clergy destroyed wholesale the manuscripts and picture writings of the Indians of New Spain is in most cases without foundation.

By the time of Philip II monasteries had increased with extraordinary rapidity in numbers and wealth. In 1574 there were over two hundred religious houses reported in New Spain, most of them with two or three inmates located in Indian towns where they supervised the spiritual and to some extent the social and economic welfare of the natives. Many of the friars, however, lost the early apostolic fervor and humility of a Zumárraga or a Quiroga, had now only monotonous, routine tasks to fulfil. In the principal cities there were great establishments with costly buildings and possessing extensive estates. Monastic simplicity gave way to luxury and relaxation of discipline. And the feeling grew in many quarters that the monasteries served chiefly to increase the number of idle, unproductive, and often licentious members of the community.[26]

---

23 Ricard, op. cit. 112.

24 *Historia de los indios de la Nueva España*, Mexico, 1941, pt. II, cap. 2-4, 7 It has been denied that the Indians were baptized by aspersion, but if the figures of contemporary missionaries are to be believed, it could scarcely have been otherwise.

25 On the wholesale or premature conversion of the Indians in Peru, see the Memorial of Francisco de Toledo in *Relaciones de los vireyes y audiencia que han gobernado el Perú*, 3 vols., Lima, 1867-72, I, 5-7.

26 The regular clergy, however, were always less numerous in the colonies than in Spain.

Moreover, when the secular church came to be fully established and bishoprics covered the land, and when it became possible to appoint secular priests in parishes more and more remote from the population centers, the usefulness of the friars in parish work was more limited. There was bound to be a collision of interests between regular and secular clergy, between the provincial and the bishop. And the result was a long and bitter struggle over ecclesiastical jurisdiction and sacramental privilege. The secular clergy felt competent to administer the rites of the Church without further aid, and were jealous of sharing their authority, while the Orders were as determined to retain their privileges intact. Where they had sown, others now came to reap. So they disputed every point with the priest and the bishop, and the antagonism in some areas lasted down to the nineteenth century.

In reality two issues were involved: tenure of benefices by the friars, and their regulation by the bishop. Among the reforms issuing from the Council of Trent was the reiteration of the principle that no clergyman might have jurisdiction over secular persons with cure of souls unless he was subject to the episcopal authority. The rule was immediately enforced in Peru, some of the friars being displaced and those who retained their benefices submitting to examination, visitation, and correction by the bishop. In New Spain the rule was stubbornly resisted, perhaps because of the number of Indian missions scattered over the wide empty spaces of the north. In some areas there were no secular priests at all, and in others the *doctrinas* were too poor to support a priest. In 1567 Pius V issued a brief suspending the rule of the Tridentine Council in New Spain. A series of contradictory papal pronouncements and royal orders followed, and practice in America varied greatly. One of the most celebrated episodes was the bitter quarrel between the Jesuits of Puebla in New Spain and the bishop, Juan de Palafox, who for a few months held concurrently the offices of viceroy, visitor-general, and inquisitor-general, and was even offered the archbishopric of Mexico. The procedure seems to have been gradually established, however, that the friars should continue in possession of Indian parishes only where no secular priests were available.[27]

The Orders therefore always lost ground, for the government encouraged the secular clergy to assert their rights. The special privileges of the friars were gradually annulled, and the Orders were restricted to their normal functions. But the movement was a slow one, extending into the eighteenth century. It culminated so far as legislation could affect it in a decree of Ferdinand VI of June 1757 which forbade the members of any Order thereafter to take charge of a parish with cure

---

27 Pedro Joseph Parras, *Gobierno de los regulares de la América*, 2 vols., Madrid, 1783, pt. III, cap. 1-3.

of souls, and declared that on the death of existing incumbents none but secular priests might be presented to vacant benefices.

An intense rivalry also grew up between the clergy who came from Europe and those born in America.[28] In the very beginning few Creoles were admitted to Holy orders, and for obvious reasons. The early period of conquest and adventure brought out few laymen with the training or aptitude for the religious life, and educational facilities in the colonies were scant. Mestizos were especially suspect, because most of them were of illegitimate birth and grew up as vagabonds or under the care of their ignorant Indian mothers. Later, as colonial society became more stabilized, the bars were let down both among the secular clergy and in the religious Orders. Most of the prelates, however, were European born, and were naturally inclined to favor their compatriots from overseas. The viceroys and governors who acted for the crown as vice-patrons also were peninsular Spaniards. In the religious Orders the feeling was often intense, the Spaniards excelling in influence, the Creoles in numbers. In the Franciscan Order in New Spain the rule was established in 1618 that in the admission of new members and the distribution of offices peninsulars and Creoles be accepted alternately; and the practice spread gradually to other Orders and to other provinces of America. It as finally introduced into Peru in 1664.[29] But the prelates found ways of circumventing this rule, and complaints and quarrels persisted.

That the increase of the monasteries in wealth and numbers tended to be out of all proportion to the needs of the new American settlements, and was inconsistent with conditions of life in pioneer, New World communities, was early sensed by Spaniards both in Europe and in America. As early as 1535 the crown decreed that lands in New Spain might be bestowed on *conquistadores* and other worthy settlers only on condition that they were never alienated to an ecclesiastic, a church, or a monastery.[30] In 1559 it was decreed that monasteries outside the cities must be at least 6 leagues apart. As many of the establishments had only a few inmates although possessing considerable revenues, and as these were increasing in number, Pope Paul V in 1611 issued a bull suppressing all not occupied by at least 8 resident friars.[31] At this time, according to the ecclesiastical writer Gerónimo de Mendieta, the Franciscans alone in New Spain had 166 religious houses. And besides these

28 See Luis de Betancourt i Figueroa, *Derecho de las iglesias metropolitanas i catedrales de las Indias, sobre que sus prelacias sean proveidas en las capitulares dellas, i naturales de sus provincias,* Madrid, 1637, *passim.*

29 Parras, op. cit. pt. II, cap. 26-8.

30 *Recopilación,* lib. IV, tit. 12, ley 10.

31 *Conventillos,* or small houses illegally constituted and containing less than 8 friars, electing their prior and seeking representation in the provincial council, continued to be an abuse till the end of the eighteenth contury. Desdevises du Dezert, op. cit. 223-4.

there were the houses of the Dominicans, Augustinians, and other Orders. In Lima at the same time, a city of some 26,500 inhabitants, with 19 churches and monasteries, a census revealed that 10 per cent of the population were priests, canons, friars, or nuns. Moreover, the erection of these countless churches and monasteries, their upkeep, and the maintenance of so numerous a clergy, rested chiefly if not wholly upon the labor of the Indians. The clergy shared in the use of forced labor in the form of the *mita* or the *repartimiento* as did other Spaniards, and often only served to increase the heavy burdens upon the miserable aborigines.

The colonists themselves felt the inconveniences of this state of affairs, as when in 1578 the *cabildo* of Mexico City urged the viceroy to limit the acquisition of land by the Church. Again in 1644 the *cabildo* of the same city petitioned the king to this effect, and also requested that no more convents or monasteries be founded, that no more friars be sent to New Spain, and that the bishops be restricted in the number of clergy they might ordain.[32]

Not until the eighteenth century, under the new Bourbon dynasty, was any real effort made by the Spanish government to remedy this situation.[33] A decree of 15 March 1717 declared that the number of friars was a burden upon the land, hindered the cultivation of the fields and the increase of public wealth, and that thereafter no conventual establishments were to be created in the Indies. In 1734 the crown ordered, with the approval of Rome, that for ten years no one in New Spain be admitted under any pretext to a religious Order. Twenty years later, in 1754, the king expressly forbade any member of a religious Order to interfere in the drawing up of wills. The extensive domains of the monasteries were generally acquired by bequest, for, as the Chilean historian Barros Arana remarked, 'a will which did not include some legacy in favor of the monasteries passed for an act against religion.' But although in 1775 a decree was again issued forbidding confessors or their convents to be heirs or legatees, the policy of the crown was not always consistent, nor were its decrees enforced. When the great German scientist Baron von Humboldt visited New Spain in the opening years of the nineteenth century, he found in Mexico City 23 monasteries and 15 nunneries with over 3,300 inmates in a population of perhaps 100,000.[34]

Whatever may have been the services of the Church in maintaining and spreading the Christian religion and in gradually weaning the Indians from barbarism, there can be little doubt that in certain respects

---

32 González Dávila, op. cit. I, 16-17.

33 See the remarks of Campillo regarding the excessive numbers and wealth of the clergy, *Nuevo sistema de gobierno económico para la América*, 46-7.

34 Villa-señor y Sánchez (*Theatro americano*, 1746, 34) lists 36 monasteries and 19 convents of nuns.

the ecclesiastical establishment, as the royal decree of 1717 declared, was an economic burden upon the colonies. These were chiefly two: the acquisition of so much of the best agricultural land by way of benefactions, purchase, or mortgage, and the system of ecclesiastical taxation, especially the tithe. The tithe amounted to a ten per cent income tax collected at the source on agricultural and pastoral industries. While this assessment was common throughout European Christendom, its effect must have been prejudicial to the progress and prosperity of a young, frontier, agricultural society. The gross amount of tithes collected in New Spain in the decade 1769-79 was nearly thirteen and a half million pesos. In the following decade, it rose to nearly eighteen and a half million.[35]

The engrossing of much of the best land by the Church was unfortunate for the colonies in that it aggravated the evils of the system of large estates. The Church was not responsible for the *latifundia*, nor were all the *latifundia* in the hands of the Church. But the concentration of so much land in the control of one great corporation, or group of allied corporations, intensified the drawbacks of the system in the American colonies. For in most pioneering countries relatively small landed holdings and the stimulus of private ownership by many individuals are generally needed to encourage immigration and secure the most profitable and economical use of the soil. In the case of ecclesiastical lands the outlook was the more hopeless because the 'dead hand' of the Church prevented properties from changing owners or being redivided and distributed.

The amount of ecclesiastical property in the Spanish American colonies controlled by the secular Church or by the Orders, in estates and in mortgages, has been variously estimated. Humboldt wrote, in his description of New Spain at the beginning of the nineteenth century, that in some of the provinces four-fifths of the land was held in mortmain. The estimate must have included lands on which ecclesiastical societies held heavy mortgages, for the Mexican historian Alamán, a not unfriendly writer, tells us that there was scarcely an estate in New Spain that was not so encumbered, and that at least half of the landed wealth was controlled by the Church.[36] At the end of the colonial period the aggregate value of agricultural property belonging to the Church and to pious endowments in what is now the Republic of Mexico was probably in the neighborhood of fifty million pesos. Indeed the property and wealth of the Church, and the political influence which such wealth enabled it to exercise, constituted one of the most troublesome

---

35 Alexander von Humboldt, *Political Essay on the Kindgom of New Spain*, 4 vols., London, 1811, III, 96.

36 Lucas Alamán, *Historia de México*, I, 99, 100 n. 46.

problems bequeathed to the nascent republics of the nineteenth century.

The prevalence of ecclesiastical mortgages arose from two circumstances typical of Spanish colonial society. Agriculture was not a capitalistic enterprise that endeavored to produce a surplus of liquid capital for investment. In fact there was little opportunity for investment except in land or mines, and of land the great proprietors already had a great sufficiently. The colonies were not industrialized communities. On the other hand, the Spanish American landed aristocracy in general inherited a tradition of prodigality and extravagance that may be said to have come down to them from the feudal society of medieval times.

As there was little surplus liquid capital, there was little need of organized banking until near the close of the colonial era. In 1716 the viceroy Linares reported that there were only two banks in Mexico City, one under control of the Tagle family, the other belonging to Isidro Rodríguez.[37] It was not until the time of Matías de Gálvez (viceroy, 1783-4) that the celebrated Bank of San Carlos was founded. Consequently, when the improvident landowner needed to borrow, he applied to the monasteries. For they alone, generally less prodigal and extravagant than the private landowners, had an accumulated surplus to invest. They were in a sense the banks of Spanish colonial America.

There is, however, another side to the picture. Virtually all of the social services of the community in colonial days were the peculiar and exclusive domain of the clergy. They created and managed the schools, hospitals, and asylums. They administered the numerous pious funds established by devout laymen or ecclesiastics. Private philanthropy was as common in Spanish colonial society as it is in these more modern times, perhaps more so than has been customary in the Spanish republics of today. But in a society so completely suffused with ecclesiasticism, in which education, science, and letters were largely dominated by the clergy, and charitable activities were entirely in their hands, private beneficence was canalized in the direction of the Church. A repentant millionaire, instead of endowing private colleges, laboratories, or museums, built a chapel or a monastery or gave money to the Church to be administered for the poor and infirm. This not only brought great wealth to the Church, but also imposed vast responsibilities upon it. Consequently its social and charitable contributions to society in the colonies were quite as important as its religious ministrations.

A notable example of the millionaire philanthropist of those days was Alonso de Villaseca, who came out from Spain to Mexico City around 1540 and shortly after married a Creole heiress. He became possessed of rich silver mines in Pachuca and elsewhere, and of vast

---

87 Lillian Estelle Fisher, *Viceregal Administration in the Spanish-American Colonies*, Berkeley, 1926, 103.

cattle ranches. An austere, rigid, somewhat intractable man who preferred to live in retirement on his estates, he yet became a leading figure in the capital because of his wealth and numerous charities. He gave some 300,000 pesos to various benefactions in Europe. He was a liberal patron of the Franciscan missions on the savage frontiers, endowed the chair of Scripture in the new university, and gave furnishings and ornaments to the Church of Our Lady of Guadaloupe. But he was especially generous to the Jesuits, the first of whom came out to New Spain in his time and largely with his assistance. Altogether he gave over 140,000 pesos to further their educational work, and endowed their celebrated school in Mexico City, the College of St. Peter and St. Paul.[38]

Another notable early figure in the history of Mexican philanthropy was Vasco de Quiroga, Bishop of Michoacán. Quiroga came to New Spain in 1530 as an *oidor* of the second *audiencia* appointed to repair the evil done by its predecessor and undertake the organization of the country. Educated as a lawyer, he was a man of great piety and erudition, and left a library of over six hundred volumes. He was profoundly influenced by the *Utopia* of Sir Thomas More, and inspired by the innocence and simplicity which he believed he found in the Indians, he conceived the project of adjusting their lives to the ideals set forth in More's famous book. He would organize the natives in village communities holding all land in common, but with each household assigned its own cabin and garden. Giving a moderate amount of labor on the common fields (six hours a day) or on the cattle ranches, the Indians would be self-supporting; at the same time they would be instructed 'en toda buena orden de policía y con santas y buenas y católicas ordenanzas,' under the patient and sympathetic guidance of three or four friars. So he would elevate the life of the aborigines to a degree of virtue and humanity impossible amid the ambition, pride, and malice of society in Europe.

Embarking immediately upon his experiment, in 1531 or 1532 he purchased at considerable personal sacrifice certain lands near Mexico City, and founded his first so-called 'hospital-pueblo' or experimental town which he called Santa Fe. In 1533 he organized another with the same name on the shores of Lake Pátzcuaro in Michoacán. In 1537 he was chosen the first bishop of Michoacán, although up to then he had received only the tonsure. In this capacity he continued his organizing activities, creating other communities and undertaking to instruct his pueblos in different industries so as to bind them together by trade between them. Late in life he drew up his famous Ordinances of the

---

38 Elizabeth Ward Loughran, 'A Mexican Millionaire Philanthropist,' *Thought*, VII, 262-78.

Hospitals of Santa Fe whose model and spiritual ancestry were avowedly found in More's *Utopia*.[39] These social experiments by Quiroga were so successful that their characteristic arrangements were taken over by the religious Orders in the missions they established among the Indians.

The Spaniards who came out to the New World, nurtured in the medieval Catholic tradition, took it for granted that they must care for the sick and the needy in almshouses and hospitals. Governor Ovando as early as 1503 was instructed to 'build hospitals to care for the poor, both Spaniards and Indians,' and the first was established in the same year at Santo Domingo. Commissioners from the island in 1508 petitioned for more generous endowment for hospitals. Perhaps the earliest pious foundation in Mexico City was the Hospital of the Immaculate Conception established almost immediately after the conquest. Another hospital, *del Amor de Dios,* was built between 1535 and 1540 by Bishop Zumárraga for contagious diseases, open to Spaniards and Indians—the famous 'hospital de las bubas.' At Zumárraga's request it was placed under the patronage of the crown, and it remained one of the best equipped and managed of the hospitals in the Mexican capital.[40] Several years earlier the Bishop had written to the Council of the Indies urging that three hospitals be established along the road from Vera Cruz to Mexico City to take care of travelers from the seacoast, one in the port, one in Puebla, and another halfway between.[41] He reported that hundreds of those arriving on ships from Spain died of fevers at Vera Cruz or on their way to the capital. Hospitals were all the more necessary because of the terrible epidemics which periodically swept over the country—in New Spain three great epidemics between 1520 and 1576, besides smaller, local outbreaks. In towns and cities disease probably took the heaviest toll, especially among natives unaccustomed to the crowded conditions of an urban community. In Mexico City a hospital exclusively for Indians, called *de Señor San José,* started about 1530 by Peter of Ghent, in 1554 also became a 'royal hospital' under the crown's patronage, although it apparently received no material support from royal funds. Just a decade later the *Hospital de San Lázaro* for lepers was founded privately by a philanthropic physician, Dr. Pedro López, who also established a general hospital for Negroes, mulattoes, and mestizos called *Nuestra Señora de los Desamparados.*[42]

In Lima there were eight hospitals founded during the course of the sixteenth century. As early as 1538 the municipal *cabildo* had set aside ground for a hospital, but none was established till 1545, with funds

---

39 Silvio Zavala, *Ideario de Vasco de Quiroga,* Mexico, 1941, *passim.*

40 Cuevas, op. cit. I, 407-09.

41 Ibid. I, 126-7. As a matter of fact, two hospitals were very soon founded for this purpose, at Petrote by Bishop Julián Garcés of Tlaxcala, and at Jalapa.

42 Ibid. I, 410-11.

supplied mostly by the municipality. This was the Hospital of *San Andrés*, which became the largest and most important for Spaniards in the city. Shortly thereafter the Archbishop Gerónimo de Loayza founded a hospital solely for Indians, called *Santa Ana*. It came to be the richest in Peru, with an endowment of 30,000 pesos. *San Andrés*, with expenses of between 25,000 and 30,000 pesos a year, had an endowment of only 14,000 pesos, the deficit being made up by alms and bequests. Both hospitals early came under royal patronage, and both were rebuilt on a larger and more durable scale in the first quarter of the following century.

The other hospitals, all of them established by private initiative, were less pretentious: *San Cosme y San Damián* (1549) for women, white and colored; *del Espíritu Santo* (1573) for mariners, supported by an assessment on the wages of sailors on ships leaving Callao; *San Lázaro* (c. 1573), a small hospital for lepers; *San Diego* for convalescents, resulting from a bequest of Cristóbal Sánchez Bilbao and his wife in 1594; *San Pedro* (1599) for poor clergy; and *Nuestra Señora de Atocha* for abandoned infants.[43]

In those days a Spanish American hospital not only provided treatment for the sick, but was frequently a kind of poorhouse as well, where the aged, the halt, and the blind were cared for and where alms were dispensed to the indigent.[44] By tradition there was generally one near the cathedral under the supervision of the bishop, and others attached to important parish churches and to monasteries. Among the religious Orders, the most active in the founding of hospitals were the Franciscans and the Augustinians. Frequently a hospital was supported, and sometimes managed as well, by a *cofradía* or confraternity, a voluntary association of members pledged to work in the hospital without pay, taking turns as nurses and contributing according to their means and generosity.

The Hospital of the Immaculate Conception in Mexico City, since the seventeenth century generally known as the *Jesús Nazareno* because of a much-venerated image in the church, was founded by the Confraternity of Our Lady, of which Cortés was a leading member. In 1529 Pope Clement VII granted to Cortés the patronage of the hospital in perpetuity, and because of this grant and Cortés's liberality toward the institution, it came to be known also as the Marquis's Hospital. A two-story building about three hundred feet long erected before 1535 was divided into two wards, one for men, the other for women. Cortés supplied a large part of the funds for its construction, and a thousand ducats

---

43 Bernabé Cobo, *Historia de la fundación de Limas*, Lima, 1882; III, cap. 25-33; Antonio Vázquez de Espinosa, *Compendium and Description of the West Indies*, Washington, 1942, 443-4.

44 Elizabeth Ward Loughran, 'The Marquis's Hospital,' *Mid-America*, XIV, 41-2.

a year in rents and mortgages for running expenses. In his will he added an additional income from his estates of about two thousand pesos. Many of the early *mayordomos*, who had the management of the hospital, were wealthy *conquistadores*. Part of the original building is still standing, but the institution was a few years ago expropriated by the State, and the *Jesús Nazareno* now functions as a government institution.

In the course of time, we are told, nearly every Indian town had a small hospital, served generally by native herb doctors and maintained by the voluntary offerings and services of the natives. The Indians, too, had their *cofradías* whose members in weekly relays ministered to the sick. Cuevas says that these small native hospitals were sometimes better tended and provided for than were the larger institutions in the Spanish cities. They also served to provide food and lodging for passing travelers, and as a house of retreat for the Indian attendants.[45]

By and large, however, the Spanish colonies were never adequately supplied with hospitals, even in the cities. At the beginning of the nineteenth century there were only six in the whole province of Guadalajara, one of the most populous in New Spain, and physicians could be had only in two or three important towns.[46] Periodic epidemics still carried off large numbers of people. The resources of some of the dioceses were not very great, and gifts and pious bequests went more often into endowments for Masses, the erection of chapels, and the like, rather than into public charities. Even in Lima the resources of the hospitals were very inadequate. In the letters of viceroys and bishops we often find complaints of ignorant attendants, and wretched management or embezzlement of funds by the *mayordomos*. The poorest and worst served, as might be expected perhaps, were generally those intended for the Indians. We hear of hospitals falling in ruins, badly infected, with shattered roofs, lacking mattresses for the beds and even medicaments. Leprosy hospitals were often so ill-provided that the inmates were allowed to roam the streets to beg for food. Royal legislation on hospitals and their management was generally excellent, but rivalries between the civil and ecclesiastical powers, and the incompetence or dishonesty of those in charge, often made enforcement a remote possibility.

It was in the missions among the barbarous tribes on the Spanish frontier that the clergy displayed their greatest energy and zeal. They made their way boldly into the forests and deserts, studied the language and customs of the natives, endured great hardships, hunger, mosquitoes, and disease, and often won the halo of martyrdom. Indeed the role of the missionary martyrs is one of the finest pages in the history of

45 Cuevas, op. cit. I, 409, 413-14; Ricard, op. cit. 188, 190, 194.

46 Desdevises du Dezert, op. cit. 229. In British America the Pennsylvania Hospital, founded in Philadelphia in 1751, was before the Revolution the only general institution of its kind.

the Spaniards in America. If the friars succeeded in 'reducing' a group of Indians, they united them in a village or mission in an endeavor to teach them the elements of civil and religious life. Often the mission was a kind of agricultural and industrial school, for its essence was discipline: training in Christian doctrine, but also in agriculture and handicrafts, and sometimes in arts and letters. In time the mission might be converted into a *doctrina* or Indian parish, conducted by a priest and under the administration of a *corregidor*. Spanish settlers came in to occupy the lands, and the missionary moved on to fresh fields of endeavor.

The conversion of these savages was not easy, especially among the more refractory tribes. The Indians, we are told, were sometimes five, six, or seven years in a mission before they were ready for baptism. Meantime it was difficult to hold them if they objected to a sedentary life, and there were often repeated attempts at escape. Occasionally the entire mission population decamped. The missionaries themselves would then go in pursuit, with one or two soldiers perhaps and a few 'trusties,' and sometimes they covered long distances before the fugitives, or some of them, were caught and persuaded or forced to return.

In Spanish America from California and Texas to Paraguay and Chile these frontier missions multiplied—advance posts of the empire in which lived thousands of Indians in a sort of intermediate state between primitive barbarism and European civilization. Explorations by the missionaries contributed to contemporary knowledge of geography, botany, and zoology, and in the diaries, grammars, dictionaries, and other works which they have left us we have priceless information regarding aboriginal languages and customs.[47] In spite of handicaps of climate and geography, some of the missions became very productive. Depending on their location and the nature of the soil, they promoted cattle ranches or sugar plantations, produced cotton cloth, hammocks, and leather goods, developed fruit culture, raised tobacco and cacao. But they also frequently aroused the jealousy of their Spanish neighbors. The missionaries were accused of exploiting the Indians, a privilege which the civilian population would have preferred to reserve to itself, and the more evident their prosperity, the greater the envy and resentment.

The Orders most closely identified with missionary endeavor were the Franciscans and the Jesuits, although the Capuchins and the Mercedarians were also active. The Franciscans had labored chiefly in the cities and in Indian parishes until the establishment of their Missionary Colleges, the first of which was founded at Querétaro in New Spain in

---

47 For an appreciation of the scientific work of the Jesuit missionaries, see Alfred Metraux, 'The Contribution of the Jesuits to the Exploration and Annthropology of South America,' *Mid-America*, XXVI, 183-91.

1683, and followed by a long series throughout America in the course of the following century. They became centers for the intensive training of missionaries, as well as retreats for those who returned for rest and recuperation from the strenuous labors in the field.[48]

Perhaps the most celebrated missions were those founded in the seventeenth and eighteenth centuries by the Jesuits, especially the missions of Paraguay. They resembled in some ways the 'hospitals' of Bishop Quiroga, and became a model of this type of semipolitical, semitheocratic regime. The first Jesuits arrived at Asunción from Peru in 1605, and two years later founded the Jesuit Province of Paraguay.[49] About 1610 they began to establish their missions, among the Guaraní Indians in the valleys of the upper Paraná and Uruguay Rivers, and among the Tapes in a region called Guayrá northeast of Asunción and east of the Paraná. The missions in Guayrá were soon attacked and ruined by slave raiders from the Portuguese province of São Paulo. In four years, we are told, between 1627 and 1631 the Paulistas destroyed 9 mission pueblos and carried away 60,000 Indians. And in 1631 the Jesuits began moving their pueblos farther south to the neighborhood of the Guaraní missions. In 1652 it was reported that the Jesuits had established in all 48 missions, of which 26 had been destroyed by the Paulistas, leaving 22 with a population of 40,000 Indians.[50] The missions, however, increased in number and size, and by the middle of the eighteenth century there were 30 harboring over 100,000 neophytes.

The Jesuits were said to have borrowed their theocratic system from the Incas of Peru, with the Christian religion substituted for pagan rites. But the derivation is unnecessary, for it was a natural and logical development out of the circumstances of the case. Their missions differed little in basic organization from those of the Franciscans, Capuchins, and other Orders scattered from California to Venezuela and the Gran Chaco. It was an organization in conformity with general Spanish colonial legislation, but in the case of Paraguay perfectly adapted, in the beginning at least, to the psychology of the natives. The missions were pastoral and agrarian communities in which the Indians, ruled in every detail by the priests, enjoyed in peace and quiet the amount of civilization compatible with their primitive intelligence. The degree

---

48 Francis Borgia Steck, *Ensayos históricos hispanoamericanos*, Mexico, 1940, 57-73. The missionary colleges were independent of the Provincial and were limited to a maximum of thirty residents. It is interesting to note that virtually all of the friars trained in these colleges were recruited in Spain, while the majority of those under the jurisdiction of the Provincial were Creoles. Consequently there was often considerable feeling between the two groups within the Order.

49 Guillermo Furlong Cardiff, 'Las misiones jesuíticas,' *Historia de la nación Argentina*, III, 596.

50 Ibid. 601.

of culture they absorbed depended on the character and docility of the tribes reduced.

Organization was as rigid as in a schoolroom. The day's work began and ended with catechism and prayer in Guaraní, for Castilian was not generally taught. In the beginning all the lands of the mission were held and worked in common; but in the eighteenth century each Indian family was given its little cottage and garden as private property to cultivate and to bequeath as it pleased.[51] The herds of cattle and the *yerba* plantations were always the common property of the mission. The Indians were called from their slumbers an hour before sunrise, at sunrise listened to Mass in the church, and after receiving a ration of *yerba*, set out to work on the common land or farm of the mission. In order that labor on the farm might not appear a task, the Jesuit fathers transformed it into the semblance of a festival, to which the Indians marched out in procession, to the sound of music and carrying before them the image of a saint. Craftsmen were not subject to labor on the common lands. The workday was from four to six hours.

The proceeds of both common and family labors were gathered into storehouses, from which each drew in proportion to his contribution, and from which were supported the widows and orphans. The surplus —cotton, *yerba*, tobacco, hides—was sent in boats downriver to Corrientes and Buenos Aires to be exchanged for church ornaments, hardware, etc., needed in the reductions, to pay the royal tribute,[52] or to be sold for the general benefit of the Order. All trading with the outside world was managed by the Jesuits, although the Indians might trade among themselves with their own limited possessions.

Every detail of work or play was controlled by the missionaries, even to the quality and kind of clothes the natives wore and to the choice of their brides. Over each mission were placed two or more clergy depending upon the size of the community, one charged with the spiritual, the others with the civil, government of the mission. Each pueblo was organized politically like Spanish or Indian towns elsewhere, with *alcaldes, regidores, alférez real, alguacil mayor,* and *escribano*; but these officials, as might be expected, were the instruments of the presiding fathers. The judicial and disciplinary power was reserved in practice to the latter, and corporal punishment was the usual penalty imposed.

The Jesuits as a general rule endeavored to separate their Indian charges from all contact with Europeans save themselves. The bishop and the governor of the province visited them from time to time, and occasionally other well-disposed Spaniards were welcomed by the missionaries. A belated traveler was entertained in the guest house for three days only, and then sent forward on his journey. After 1644 the

51 Ibid. 611.
52 After 1649 eight silver pesos per capita.

mission Indians were provided with arms against their Paulista enemies and given a military organization. And thereafter they were frequently employed in the defense of the Argentine provinces, especially in the successive attacks upon the Portuguese at Colonia del Sacramento and elsewhere in the Banda Oriental.

Under Jesuit instruction the natives made remarkable progress in the graphic arts, in sculpture, painting, architecture, and music. Workshops were established in nearly every mission pueblo, and the product of their handicraft was sought after by Spanish settlements in the Argentine provinces. Eloquent testimony remains in the ruins today of the size and profuse decoration of their churches. Illustrated books in Guaraní were printed on mission presses in the early years of the eighteenth century, the presses, type, and ink being manufactured by the natives. Other lesser works were published, such as calendars, astronomical tables, and pious manuals. One Indian, Nicolás Yapuguay, wrote two religious works which merited printing,[53] and the histories of at least two of the missions were written by Guaraní residents.

These missions were prosperous and the Indians apparently led happy, contented lives. They certainly stirred up the persistent jealousy of the governors and planters of Paraguay, who repeatedly intrigued to have the villages delivered to the civil authorities so that forced labor on the plantations might be exacted from them; so much so that in 1726 civil jurisdiction over the mission area was transferred by the crown to Buenos Aires. But from a larger viewpoint the Jesuit regime was in many respects a failure. The Indians were never really taught to be much more than helpless, dependent children. They lived in a perpetual minority. Isolated from Spaniards and from their own kind, they were never trained to govern themselves or to take their place ultimately in the civilized society about them. And after the expulsion of the Jesuit Order from Spanish America in 1767, when the neophytes lost their guides and mentors, it was discovered how little progress they had actually made. Friars of other Orders and civil administrators sent to replace the Jesuits lacked the will or the aptitude to maintain the system intact. Many of the Indians were quite unable to continue it themselves alone. Under the rule of ignorant or rapacious officials, often in conflict with the clergy, the missions gradually disintegrated, the ranches and cotton fields disappeared, the *yerbales* decayed, and many of the natives returned to their former barbarism. Yet that the Guaraní Indians were capable of a deeper intellectual and moral culture is attested by the achievements of their descendants in the Paraguayan nation today.[54]

The missions in colonial Spanish America have been the occasion for a considerable polemic literature. By some writers, chiefly ecclesiastics, they

---

[53] Ibid. 615.

[54] The mission communities were finally abolished altogether by royal decree in May 1803.

have been lauded to the skies. By others they have been sharply criti-cized.[55] That some of the missions prospered is certainly true, and that they often saved the Indians from heartless exploitation by the civil population cannot be denied. Yet it has been questioned whether the cultural progress of the mission Indians was much greater than that of the 'free,' independent Indians, or whether in agricultural and pastoral pursuits they achieved more than did those submitted to the secular arm. On the northern frontier of New Spain among less submissive tribes, enemies of the missionaries accused them of overworking and underfeeding their charges, and of disciplining them by flogging. Evi-dence shows that on some of the missions the death rate was very high, especially among children—whether due to overwork, or to crowding in confined, unsanitary quarters to which the Indian was unaccustomed, it would be difficult to establish. At any rate, in many cases the mission Indians declined steadily in numbers.

Moreover a better understanding today of so-called primitive man tells us that the radical change implanted in the lives of the natives at virtually every point was in many cases disastrous. The Indians had been conquered not only in a military way but in spirit as well. Their own religious life had been suppressed, their gods defeated; their social mores were disorganized, their priests and leaders often killed. Alexander von Humboldt observed as much in his celebrated travels in Spanish America in the first decade of the nineteenth century.

The effects of this insulated system have been such, that the Indians have remained in a state little different from that in which they existed, when their scattered dwellings were not yet collected round the habita-tion of a missionary. Their number has considerably augmented, but the sphere of their ideas is not enlarged. They have progressively lost that vigour of character, and that natural vivacity, which in every state of society are the noble fruits of independence. By subjecting to invariable rules even the slightest actions of their domestic life, they have been rendered stupid, by the effort to render them obedient. Their subsistence is in general more certain, and their habits more pacific; but subject to the constraint and the dull monotony of the government of the missions, they [reveal] by their gloomy and reserved looks, that they have not sacrificed their liberty to their repose without regret.[56]

That the Indians in many cases were really Christianized may also be doubted. Under the cloak of Christian rites they retained their old religious concepts—the cult of Nature and its forces—and even wor-

---

55 For a friendly but objective criticism of the village mission system see Robert Ricard, *La Conquête spirituelle du Mexique,* 183-5.

56 Alexander von Humboldt and Aimé Bonpland, *Personal Narrative of Travels to the Equinotical Regions of the New Continent, during the Years* 1799-1804, 7 vols., London, 1814-29, III, 4-5.

shipped their ancient gods in secret. The Church had to be content with conformity with externals.

The mission in Spanish America was not only a religious, proselytizing institution. It was also one of the most conspicuous pioneering devices of the Spanish government, a military and political agency designed to push back and defend the frontiers, pacify the natives, and open the country to European occupation. As Professor Bolton has reminded us,[57] each colonizing nation in America had its peculiar frontier institutions and classes of men. In the French mainland colonies it was the fur trader and the individual missionary preacher. They together brought the savages into friendly relations with the government and into profitable relations with the French outpost settlements. In the English colonies, too, the fur trader led the way. But it was especially the backwoods settler who subdued the forest and pushed back the Indian.

In the Spanish colonies in the beginning the military explorer or *conquistador* and the accompanying friar laid the groundwork, but as time went on especially the missionary. As the semicivilized, sedentary Indians were all subdued and reduced to a virtual servitude, and as the frontiers were pushed beyond into the areas of the nomad savages, there on the frontier the mission played its great political role. Its function was to civilize the savage frontier, press it farther and farther into the interior, or away from the established European centers, and so prepare the way for further colonization. It also served to maintain the borders against foreign encroachment, as in Texas and California, in Guayana south and east of the Orinoco, and on the eastern margins of Upper Peru and Paraguay.

The mission therefore was an agent of the State as well as of the Church, a vital part of Spain's pioneering system. And in many cases it was largely supported by the State, receiving an annual stipend of several hundred pesos. The more obvious the political and material ends to be served, the more liberal was the royal subsidy. If necessary, military protection was also supplied, a *presidio* or garrison of half a dozen armed soldiers. On the exposed borders of New Spain the mission plants themselves were often built to serve as fortresses, with great compounds or patios enclosing the church, granaries, dormitories, and other buildings, and protected by walls eight feet thick.

The Inquisition was established in the Indies by Philip II. Till then inquisitorial powers had been exercised by the bishops.[58] By a decree

---

57 In this and succeeding paragraphs I am following Bolton, 'The Mission as a Frontier Institution in the Spanish American Colonies,' *Am. Hist. Rev.*, XXIII, 42-61.

58 Inquisitorial powers were first extended to bishops in the Indies by Cardinal Jiménez de Cisneros, the Inquisitor-General of Spain, in 1517. In 1519 Bishop Manso of Puerto Rico and the Dominican, Pedro de Córdova, were appointed inquisitors for all the Indies. After the first Dominicans arrived in New Spain they apparently exercised general inquisitorial authority on the mainland. Cuevas, op. cit. I, 220-23.

of 25 January 1569 two tribunals were created subject to the Council of the Suprema in Madrid; one in Lima for the southern viceroyalty, erected in 1570, the other in Mexico City for the northern viceroyalty and the Philippine Islands, set up in 1571. Later, in 1610, a third was established in Cartagena with jurisdiction over the archepiscopal provinces of Santa Fe and Santo Domingo. The purpose of the Inquisition in America, as in Spain, was to maintain the purity of the Faith, protect Spanish subjects from contamination by heretics, Jews, and Moslems. There were few Protestant heretics in the colonies—Protestants were by law jealously excluded. The few were mostly captured corsairs and foreign merchants. As far back as 1501 Governor Ovando when preparing to go to Hispaniola had been instructed that no Jews, Moors, reconciled heretics, or recent converts from Islam be allowed in the colony. And later decrees had excluded their sons and grandsons, as well as gypsies and their families. But these laws were difficult or impossible to enforce, especially as the *conversos* or New Christians comprised the class most likely to possess the aptitude and capital needed to develop colonial trade and industry. Moreover there were always ways of reaching America, clandestinely or for a price to the crown. In spite of prohibitive laws, therefore, Jews and New Christians, both Spanish and Portuguese, were found in the Indies in increasing numbers. And it was against them that the Inquisition was mainly directed. Still, its chief occupation proved to be of a minor, disciplinary character, the punishment of bigamy, blasphemy, witchcraft, adultery, and immorality among the clergy. Its function was chiefly that of moral censorship. Indians, being regarded as in a state of tutelage, were not under its jurisdiction. They were, however, subject to disciplinary action by the bishop.

The judicial processes and the penalties employed by the Inquisition, the use of torture and the *autos da fe*, need not be discussed here. They reflected the standards of a more callous age, and the clergy like other classes of society were the product of their environment. Much depended upon the temperament and the character of the individual members of the tribunal. Things happened which shock us today as evidence of cruelty, injustice, stupidity. On the other hand, at a time when people generally regarded heresy as a crime against society, the inquisitors as often displayed a fairness, a reasonableness, and a quality of mercy which command our admiration.[59] On the whole the institution was not as active in America as it was in Spain. Burnings at the stake were much less frequent—Lima over a period of 250 years saw about 30. Only on scattered occasions were there outbreaks of intense popular fanaticism, usually directed, as in the Middle Ages, against the Jews

[59] See documents in *La Inquisición de México, sus origines, jurisdicción, competencia* . . . (Doc. inédit. o muy raros para la hist. de Mexico, vol.v, Mexico, 1906).

because of their economic activity and success. Such an outbreak occurred in the years 1634-9 in Peru, to which many individuals of Jewish descent had come by way of Brazil and the Rio de la Plata, and in the following decade in New Spain.

The Inquisition served not only a religious and moral purpose, to suppress heresy and punish public or private scandal. It had also a political function. It was a defensive mechanism of the state. By its censorship of books it not only prevented the reading and circulation of works containing propositions offensive to Roman Catholic dogma, it made the entertainment of foreign political and philosophical ideas difficult or dangerous. In the sixteenth and seventeenth centuries censorship was directed especially against heretical religious works; in later times it was directed against books which expressed the political and philosophical concepts of eighteenth century rationalism. Its officers possessed a jurisdiction independent of the ordinary courts, and in search of prohibited books might enter the domiciles of suspected persons by day or night. They were required by law to board every incoming ship before passengers and freight were discharged, question crew and passengers, and examine the cargo. And the Inquisition was one of the chief means used to suppress revolutionary stirrings in Spanish America in the eighteenth and nineteenth centuries, till in the end treason came to be identified with heresy.

In America as in Spain the Inquisition did serve to keep the people loyal and orthodox. As a check upon intellectual progress and freedom of opinion, its influence was obvious. On the other hand, in this as in so many other aspects of colonial administration, the spread between theory and fact, between law and practice, was often considerable. In spite of the vigilance of the local Spanish authorities, writings of the eighteenth century political philosophers were smuggled into the colonies in appreciable numbers, and found their way even into the private libraries of ecclesiastics. In the West Indies books and newspapers from the English and French islands were introduced under the very noses of the inquisitors. French translations of the Declaration of Independence of the United States in this fashion found their way into the Spanish colonies, and copies of the 'Declaration of the Rights of Man.'

The Inquisition, it should be added, while from its inception an arm of royal government, also at times impeded the efficacy of the civil power, by obstructing the action of the secular judicial courts, and by insistence upon its extensive powers and privileges. Its familiars invaded every sphere of life and administration, and at times confounded secular and religious matters as personal or private interests dictated. It has often been accused of accumulating great wealth by means of its fines and sequestrations, and of retarding economic progress by its attacks directed against foreigners and Jews, often the most

enterprising elements in the community. These charges it would probably be difficult to sustain. Such capital funds as the Inquisition controlled seem to have been largely employed in pious works and charitable foundations. There is certainly no clear evidence that the economic backwardness of the colonies can be ascribed to the Inquisition

There were many complaints in the colonial era of corruption, worldliness, moral disorders, among the clergy both secular and regular in
Spanish America. The evidence is abundant in the accounts of travelers,
in the reports of bishops and viceroys, in edicts of the Inquisition, and
in royal decrees and papal bulls. These complaints go back as far as the
time of Hernando Cortés, in his letters to Charles V. In part this simply
reflected conditions found in some regions of Southern Europe itself.
In part it was due to the weakening of social restraints and inhibitions
not uncommon on the peripheries of civilization. And of course charges
against the clergy in Spanish America must be weighed with caution.
It is the infraction of social laws that attracts attention, while the
thousands who live within the law pass unnoticed.

Many of the bishops and cathedral clergy were men of learning and
high character. Many were noted for their humility, charity, and austerity
of life, men who befriended the Indians and endeavored to protect them
from their oppressors. We read of prelates disposing during their lifetime of over a million pesos in alms and pious endowments, prelates
whose clothing, food, and furniture were of the meanest, and who in
some cases were themselves buried by charity. Toribio de Mogrobejo,
Archbishop of Lima near the end of the sixteenth century, and later
canonized, was such a person.

Against the Jesuits, among the religious Orders, few charges were
ever made, except perhaps of overweening ambition for the ascendency
of their Society. More carefully selected as novices, trained under a
discipline more complete, distinguished among ecclesiastics in the New
World for their literary accomplishments—most of the accounts of civil
and natural history of these regions written by ecclesiastics have come
from their pens, whether in Spanish, Portuguese, or French—the Jesuits
in both North and South America seem to have maintained a very high
standard of conduct. Their activities in school and college were outstanding. And when they were expelled by royal order in 1767, the same year
in which they were expelled from Spain, some of the colonies could ill
afford to lose them. In New Spain there were several small outbreaks of
popular protest which had to be suppressed by force.[60]

However, there were religious as well as military adventurers who
flocked to the New World, men who looked on an ecclesiastical career

60 The Jesuits also incurred the jealousy ot the other clergy, who did not raise a
voice against their expulsion. Indeed royal magistrates and prelates seemed to vie with
one another in carrying out the royal orders.

THE SPANISH EMPIRE IN AMERICA

in America merely as an opportunity to gratify the desire for a life of ease and self-indulgence. Priests and friars, men of mediocre lights who had little prospect of success or distinction in the old country, came out to the colonies to seek their fortune. The circumstance was not absent from the history of the Church in some of the more backward Spanish American republics in the nineteenth century.

Mention has been made of the great number of idle, wordly religious in the monasteries, especially in the large cities.[61] Concubinage, fraud, speculation, riotous living, engaging in trade, were common charges. From time to time the Council of the Indies sent over an ecclesiastical visitor to inspect the overseas monasteries and correct the more crying abuses; but his measures were generally without much effect, for he found all factions united against him in passive or open resistance. In the cathedral chapters the prebends were too often sinecures for indolent or factious ecclesiastics.[62] Bishops of the poorer dioceses complained of the lack of proper educational facilities to train up an intelligent clergy. Parish priests extorted excessive fees for marriages, funerals, Masses, and other services of the Church. The crown frequently legislated against the abuse, ordering the clergy to collect no fees beyond the limits established by provincial councils, or by the canons of the Council of Trent,[63] but apparently with little effect.

Opportunity for exploitation was especially abundant in the more remote Indian parishes, to which the more worthless friars were frequently sent. There the clergy enjoyed an immense personal influence and prestige because of their religious office and the depth of popular superstition. Piety to the primitive native mind consisted in the pomp and ritual of religious observance rather than in character and morality. And this security of the clergy was one of the chief causes of its ignorance and corruption. Priests in parishes or *doctrinas* far removed from inspection by their superiors frequently imposed upon the simple Indians, and indulged in all the pleasures and luxuries of the laity and in some of its vices. *Cofradías* or religious, philanthropic guilds, which appeared in great numbers in the colonies in the seventeenth and eighteenth centuries, in the Indian villages seemed to exist chiefly to contri-

---

61 Jorge Juan and Antonio de Ulloa, *Noticias secretas de América,* London, 1826, pt. II, chs. 4, 8.

62 Desdevises du Dezert, op. cit. 157-67; 207. In 1790 the archbishop of Mexico declared the tonsure obligatory for priests, and forbade their wearing a queue or curling their hair or binding it with a ribbon or a ring. He called upon ecclesiastics to wear long clothes, a cassock and mantle, and a clerical hat. He forbade their wearing the Spanish cape, or a white beret, or clothes made of leather, and found it indecent that priests were permitted to smoke or take snuff in the sacristies, or to gamble, dance, or go to cock fights. Ibid. 179.

63 *Col. doc. inéd.,* 1st ser., XIX, 44; 2nd ser., X, 409. *Recopilación,* lib. I, tit. 7, leyes 15, 43; tit. 13, ley 13; tit. 18, ley 10.

[192]

bute in their festivals to the perquisities of the local priest. Their members were frequently required to give extralegal personal services to the priest, in the fields or in his household. Legislation forbade the clergy to require the Indians to work for them against their will and without wages, to dispose of useless articles to the Indians or take anything from them without just payment, or to punish them by imprisonment or flogging; but these admonitions were frequently ignored in practice.[64] As the priests were subject only to the bishop and his ecclesiastical court, or to the provincial of the Order, it was not easy for the civil power to reach them in disciplinary matters. As late as the last decade of the eighteenth century the viceroy Revillagigedo in New Spain felt obliged to order that the Indians be not compelled to perform personal services for the priests or to pay them any form of tribute.

One might close with the observation of Desdevises du Dezert that the moral worth of the clergy is always proportional to the moral worth of the people in whose midst it lives. The civilization of the Spanish Indies, 'very much on the surface, without marked progressive tendencies, asleep in a sanctimonious quietude . . .,' yet at times very materialistic and very violent, could create in its image only a clergy inferior to its task and indifferently edifying. If we wish to judge the clergy fairly we cannot separate it from its environment. Given the men with whom it had to deal, it perhaps did its best to prevent them from being worse and did all that could reasonably be demanded of it.[65]

---

64 *Recopilación,* lib. I, tit. 13, leyes 7-12; VI, tit. 12, ley 43. Leslie Byrd Simpson, *The Repartimiento System of Native Labor in New Spain and Guatemala,* 84-6.

In the report of the Marquis of Montesclaros to the crown, August 1607, we read: 'Es el color que se da á todo lo que religiosos en causas de los naturales de estos reinos, su defensa amparo; pero la verdad, Señor, es que cuantos tienen la cosa presente, juzgan por tan otros los motivos de lo que ellos parecen, que se tiene por cietro ser la mas pesado opresión de los indios que sufren de los frailes, así en el trabajo personal como en los tributos é impusciones, si bien es de la que menos quejas forman por tenerlos impuestos en que solo juzguen por su bien ó mal aquellos que el ministro pusiere nombre de tal; esto se verifica en que cada pueblo emplea mas indios en servicio del convento que en todos los otros ministerios del reino proprios y comunes, y no contribuyen viente indios tanto á V. M. como un solo tributa al ministro de doctrina; y baste por muestra en materia que se podria decir mucho proponer á V. M. que cuando un religioso va a decir misa á cualquier pueblo, demás de la limosna que por ella se le da y de lo que come y bebe, que todo es sin moreración, y de las obvenciones que para multiplicarlas les basta multiplicarles los nombres, les obliga á que den doce reales para herrar su caballo; y como se han calzado con el nombre de sus protectores, en esta fe quieren que so se dé nombre de agravio á las exorbitancias que por su mano se ejecutan contra ellos.' *Instrucciones que los virreyes de Nueva España dejaron a sus sucesores,* Mexico, 1876, 251-2.

66 Op. cit. 167-8.

XI

※§ஜ※

School and Society

※§ஜ※

One of the most constant features of Spanish colonial policy during the three centuries under review was fear and distrust of the colonists, and of the officials sent to rule over them, by the home government. It was very marked under the Hapsburg kings, apparent to the very end under the Bourbons, and was manifested in many ways. It was perhaps justified by the distance of the American provinces from Madrid, the slowness of communications in those days, and by the spirit of independence and the individualistic tendencies which generally characterize a frontier, colonial community.

Viceroys and other high officials were by law separated as much as possible from the body of the people they governed, and to the close of the colonial era most of them were European Spaniards. Officials in the upper categories were frequently changed, sometimes too frequently to permit of an energetic and lasting impulse to the direction of affairs. Divisions of class, of social caste and racial discrimination, were rather encouraged than otherwise by law.

It was the aristocracy and the gentry in Spain who profited most from the lucrative posts in the Indies. Creoles were generally excluded from places of responsibility and authority. They were represented in the *cabildos,* to a slight extent in the ecclesiastical hierarchy, and more frequently in minor administrative posts such as that of *corregidor.* Very occasionally a Creole rose to the rank of *oidor* in one of the colonial *audiencias,* or was appointed to a post in the royal exchequer. But in such cases the appointment was made in a colony other than that of which the Creole official was native.

The Mexican historian Alamán tells us that of all the viceroys who ruled in Spanish America up to 1813 only 4 were American born; and this circumstance was quite accidental since they were the sons of Spanish officials. He adds that of the 602 captains-general, governors, and presidents, only 14 were Creoles, and that of 706 bishops and archbishops 601 came from Spain.[1] During the first two centuries of Spanish rule an ecclesiastical career was apparently more accessible to the colonists, and

---

1 *Historia de México,* I, 57 n., 58 n. His figures, if not strictly accurate, are approximately so.

there were numerous instances of distinguished clerics of American birth. But under the Bourbons, perhaps as a consequence of increasing centralization of control in Spain and a latent fear of colonial independence, the opportunities were greatly circumscribed. A traveler in Chile in the eighteenth century reports that not only the bishop but every member of the cathedral chapter came from Europe. And Alamán states that in New Spain in 1808 all of the bishoprics save one, and most of the canonries and wealthier parishes, were in the hands of European clergy.[2]

The law made no distinction between Spaniard and Creole. Indeed the crown repeatedly instructed viceroys and presidents that in filling vacancies preference be given to properly qualified men born in the Indies, especially to descendants of the *conquistadores* and other early settlers.[3] But appointments made in Spain almost invariably went to peninsular Spaniards, if only because they were closer to the fountainhead of all honors. The practice was also largely a matter of deliberate policy, based upon the principle that no official should exercise authority in a district to which he was bound by ties of kinship or economic interest. The policy seemed especially necessary in distant possessions where sentiments of loyalty to the crown were apt to be weaker than in the older communities in Europe. It was likewise a form of exploitation of the colonies. The Indies constituted a rich source of patronage for the crown, and for impoverished or ambitious Spaniards the American Church and civil service provided a golden opportunity.[4]

The consequences were in every way unfortunate for the colonists. The Creoles could aspire to little but wealth in mines or plantations, and to empty titles and decorations with which the government in Madrid was as a rule very generous. Indeed some wealthy American families kept attorneys permanently resident in Spain to pick up whatever appeared in the way of such distinctions.[5]

The Creoles in general suffered other disadvantages. They were not only excluded from high public employment; they were also practically excluded from large commercial enterprise. The great import and export houses were Spanish, with headquarters at Seville or Cadiz, and their American agents or correspondents were generally peninsular Spaniards. Sometimes Creoles in Lima or Mexico City sent consignments of bullion or goods to Spain with instructions to remit their value in

---

2 Ibid. 58.

3 See, for instance, *Recopilación*, lib. III, tit. 2, ley 14.

4 In New Spain European-born Spaniards were called *gachupines*, apparently a word of Aztec origin meaning 'man who wears spurs.' In the South American provinces the nickname was *chapetón*, meaning a tenderfoot.

5 See the remarks of Campillo regarding the lack of careers for Creoles in America and in Spain, *Nuevo Sistema de gobierno económico para la América*, 48-9.

European textiles or other exports. But in the eighteenth century Spanish mercantile interests made strenuous efforts to eliminate this competition altogether.

The virtual exclusion of Creoles from important business activities in America was said to be due to certain idiosyncrasies which they had inherited or acquired in America. They were accused of being indolent, superficial, given to extravagant display and legal wranglings, lacking in sustained energy—characteristics which put them at a disadvantage in competition with enterprising immigrants from Spain.[6] In the eighteenth century these immigrants came more and more from the north of Spain, Catalonia, and the Basque provinces, or from the Canary Islands. They were young, poor, but frugal and industrious, superior in character and energy to the average Creole. The great commercial houses found it to their interest to employ them, as being more efficient and reliable. And so wholesale trade, overseas commerce, came to be almost entirely in their hands. They saved money, associated themselves with other Spanish residents, the judges and high civil officials, watched their opportunities and became owners of lands and mines, and married Creole heiresses. As they rose in wealth, in acquired social amenities and in the favor of Creole women, these intruders were regarded by the colonists with increasing hostility and jealousy. And the Spaniards returned their enmity with a supreme contempt.[7]

The shortcomings attributed to the Creoles were sometimes said to be due to the climate, in an empire that lay mostly in the tropical zone. It should be remembered, however, that most of the European population in tropical America lived on the plateaus where the climate was cool and salubrious. The hot coastal lowlands about the Mexican Gulf and the Caribbean Sea, and on the shores of the Pacific, were peopled mostly by Negroes, Indians, or mulattoes. With few exceptions the important colonial cities were in the highlands of the continent. Caracas lay over three thousand feet above the sea, Mexico over seven thousand feet, Bogotá over eight thousand feet, Quito over nine thousand feet, Cuzco over eleven thousand feet, and La Paz over twelve thousand feet. Lima lies almost at sea level, only a few miles from the Pacific, but owing to the moderating influence of the cold Humboldt Current the climate of the Peruvian coast is far from enervating.

The faults ascribed to American Spaniards were due in large measure

---

6 Alamán, who secretly regretted the passing of the Spanish regime, describes the Creoles in colonial times as "generalmente desidiosos y descuidados; de ingenio agudo, pero al que pocas veces acompañaba el juicio y la reflexión; prontos para emprender y poco prevenidos en los medios de ejecutar; entregandose con ardor á lo presente y atendiendo poco á lo venidero; pródigos en la buena fortuna y pacientes y sufridos en la adversa. Op. cit. I, 56-7.

7 See Jorge Juan and Antonio de Ulloa, *Noticias secretas de América*, pt. II, ch. 6.

to the very limitations imposed upon them by lack of opportunity and of effective education. Young Creoles were born into a society in which all the labor was performed by 'inferior,' servile races. As sons of the well-to-do belonging to a superior race, surrounded by Indian and mulatto servants, their upbringing was apt to be trivial and superficial. They might study law or theology in the universities, but with pretentions above those of the mere toiler after fortune, they found no sphere in which to give healthy rein to their energies and ambitions.

Pride of birth, class distinctions, always jealously guarded in Spain as in other countries of semifeudal Europe, were intensified in America by the number and the mixture of diverse races. The primary races were the white, the 'red,' and the black, and on the Pacific side of the continent a few Malays and Mongolians brought over on ships from the Philippine Islands. Mexico City had its Chinatown even in the sixteenth century. As women always formed a small proportion of the immigrants from Europe—near the close of the colonial era only about ten per cent—race mixtures soon abounded: mestizos, mulattoes, zambos (part Indian, part Negro), and endless subdivisions. Of course education, wealth, and honors were concentrated almost exclusively in the whites whether Spaniards or Creoles. Between them and the castes lay socially an immense gulf, and the distinction was recognized by law. On the one hand was discrimination in order to maintain purity of blood, limpieza de sangre, a phrase writ large in the social and religious history of Spain. On the other hand was the striving of the half-caste mixtures to enroll themselves among the whites.[8]

The Spanish government from the beginning tried to build up a numerous white, Spanish population in the Indies by promoting the emigration of Spanish families, and by forbidding married men to sail for the New World without their wives except by express royal dispensation. Spaniards found in the colonies with wives in Spain were by law required to return immediately, or post a bond that they would send for them within two years. However, as the law was consistently evaded, offenders were allowed to compound with the government, and in the ledgers of colonial treasurers we find penas de casados a fairly regular item of income. In 1539 it was also decreed that encomiendas might be held only by married men or women, and possession of a wife and family became a qualification for appointment as corregidor.[9]

The few descendants of the conquistadores, others who were related to distinguished families in Spain, higher civil officials, and wealthy

---

8 Gil Fortoul suggests that dislike by the Creoles for European-born officials was due in part to the latter's more even justice dealt out to the castes and other inferior people. Historia constitucional de Venezuela, 2nd ed., I, 72.

9 C. E. Marshall, 'The Birth of the Mestizo in New Spain,' Hisp. Amer. Hist. Rev., XIX, 167.

Creoles who had obtained a title or decoration or acquired some perpetual office, formed a colonial aristocracy based chiefly upon wealth.[10] The possessed a virtual monopoly of access to the legal profession, to militia commands, and to the higher clergy. They were the *gente decente,* and were distinguished from other subjects by their finer apparel. Nobles and even ordinary citizens of Lima, said Father Cobo in 1629, wore clothes only of silk. Since 1503 Castilian law allowed any subject above the rank of peasant to erect his property, real or personal, into a *mayorazgo* or entail, and thus acquire the privileges of *hidalguia* with the title of *don,* which forbade his entering any profession attached to commerce or industry on pain of loss of status. The privilege of *hidalguia,* however, could always be obtained from the crown for a price, often with dispensation (*gracias a sacar*) from the quality of mestizo. In 1557 Philip II, to meet his pressing financial necessities, ordered one thousand *hidalguias* sold to persons of all classes without question of defect of lineage, and later sovereigns followed the same practice.[11] Every Creole therefore who acquired a fortune sought to buy a title or decoration and to create a *mayorazgo.* In Lima in the eighteenth century there were over forty families of counts and marquises. Those not very sure of their *limpieza de sangre* drew up long and minute *informaciones* as proof of their *hidalguia,* although many of them were really mestizos.[12]

Below the colonial aristocratic class were always a number of small Spanish proprietors living in towns and villages and dedicated to agriculture or grazing; while in the principal cities groups of artisans were organized in guilds for the pursuit of their respective professions. Toward the close of the colonial era a tendency to a slight leveling off of the social classes was also observed. Increasing freedom of trade made for a subdivision of fortunes in America. With the rise in the amount and frequency of shipping came also an increase of Spanish immigration. The newcomers because of their numbers were forced into trades and occupations formerly left to mestizos and mulattoes, and even into domestic service. It was the beginning of a social readjustment that was essential to any approach to democracy in the later republics, a process by no means yet complete.

From the discovery of America the right to emigrate to the New World was reserved, except for a short interval under the emperor Charles V, to peninsular Spaniards. In theory no foreigners were tol-

---

10 Alamán, op. cit. I, 60-61.

11 Gil Fortoul, op. cit. 75.

12 Application was made to the crown directly or through the viceroy, and evidence of the nature and value of the property involved was presented to the local *audiencia* which made its recommendation in turn to the Council in Spain. José María Ots Capdequi, *Instituciones sociales de la América española en el periodo colonial,* La Plata, 1934, 202-03.

erated, even Flemings, Sicilians, or Milanese who might be under the political sovereignty of the Spanish kings. It was also a stringent rule that every passenger to America, whatever his profession or purpose, must obtain a royal license and be registered at the *Casa de Contratación*. This supervision was the more necessary as the government endeavored to confine emigration to persons of unquestioned orthodoxy.[13] The king, however, could always grant special dispensations or letters of naturalization,[14] and foreigners appeared in the Spanish settlements very early. It is also evident from the many laws in the *Recopilación* that they became increasingly numerous, both in the seaports and in towns of the interior. Some were naturalized, others were there by special royal favor, but many had found their way into the Spanish colonies without authorization. The preparation of forged licenses became a profession in itself, and when punishment was made more severe the principal effect was to increase the price of these papers and develop the ingenuity of brokers and buyers. Unlicensed Spaniards as well as foreigners got over secretly as sailors, soldiers, stowaways, would-be merchants, or from foreign ships professing to be driven by storm into American ports. Before the close of Philip II's reign the government was acquiescing in an irretrievable situation, and contented itself with exacting a composition from unlicensed persons in proportion to their property and income. While never admitted to public office, foreign residents sometimes did obtain *encomiendas* of Indians, although such royal favors were by law reserved for deserving Spanish colonists.[15]

Indians and mestizos in general were considered to be on a higher plane socially than Negroes and mulattoes. The Indians, as has been made abundantly clear in earlier pages, lived as a nation apart. A few individuals or groups of individuals, trained in the colleges founded by Spaniards, succeeded in associating themselves with the European culture about them, but they were soon more or less assimilated with the conquerors and their descendants. The hereditary Indian chiefs were exempt from the payment of tribute and other exactions endured by ordinary Indians, and were by law if not in society virtually identified with the whites. Even in the Laws of Burgos they had been treated with

---

13 The second Revillagigedo remarked that Spain limited the immigration of Europeans into the colonies, but encouraged the introduction of Negroes. *Instrucción reservada . . . a su sucesor en el mando, Marqués de Branciforte,* par. 145.

14 For the naturalization of foreigners see Haring, *Trade and Navigation between Spain and the Indies,* Cambridge, Mass., 1918, 108-09. Miners or skilled craftsmen or mechanics of foreign birth were sometimes permitted by special royal license to establish themselves in the colonies, under bond to continue employing their special skills there. And dispensation was occasionally granted to a foreigner who offered to introduce an invention useful in mining or some other industry.

15 Solórzano, *Política indiana,* lib. III, cap. 6, par. 37, 39; *Recopilación,* lib. IX, tit. 27, ley 22.

special consideration. They were to be better clothed, owe no tribute, and have the right to servants. Where on the continent the Spaniards found a genuine native nobility, they did not try to abolish it as might have been expected, but rather encouraged its survival. Chiefs might receive the privilege of riding a horse, or bearing arms, or being addressed as *don*. In the course of time some of them became men of wealth and education, and even acquired titles in the colonial nobility; *vide* José Gabriel Condorcanqui, *curaca* of Tungasuca and Marquis of Oropesa, who under the name Tupac Amaru II led the great Indian rebellion of 1780-81 in Peru. Many of the Indian chiefs, however, served chiefly as the accomplices of the Spanish *corregidores* in their exploitation of the Indians under their charge.

Most of the Indians lived in their own villages, either aboriginal settlements or reductions made by the Spaniards, separate from the Europeanized population. There they governed themselves, forming municipalities in which they preserved their language, dress, and social customs. In many regions they continued from early times their clan or tribal organization intact. Although by law held to be minors in a perpetual state of tutelage, and protected by a vast legislation against exploitation by their betters, most of them were in a condition of semi-serfdom, subject to unlimited exactions in labor and produce by the *corregidor*, the *cacique*, and the priest. Kept to a very low standard of living, wretchedly housed, and generally undernourished, they found solace in alcohol,[16] as happens among the wretchedly poor today. And drunkenness among the Indians was assumed by the Spaniards to be a congenital vice. Their miserable condition led to innumerable servile revolts that only occasionally assumed serious proportions, but that were severely repressed. The Mixton War in New Spain in the sixteenth century and the rebellion of Tupac Amaru mentioned above, are too well-known to merit recital here. Others are less frequently referred to by historians. Around 1740 in Peru, for instance, appeared a subversive movement under an astute Indian leader who assumed the name Juan Santos Atahualpa, claiming, like Tupac Amaru II, to be a descendant of the last Inca rulers. He apparently had received some education in Spain, and returned to Peru imbued with ideas which he tried to apply for the freedom of his own people. Establishing himself in the *montaña*, in the inaccessible interior where the viceregal forces could not reach him, for thirteen years he kept the authorities at bay by his guerrila tactics. He raided the *haciendas* and Indian pueblos of the *montaña*, defeated the meager forces sent out to catch him, and forced many

---

16 'Instrucción del Conde de Revillagigedo al Marqués de Amarillas,' 1754, *Instrucciones . . . vireyes de Nueva España*, I, 8-10.

of the landowners to flee to the sierras or to the seacoast. And the movement collapsed only with the death of its leader in 1755.[17]

The question whether Indians should be admitted to the clergy was
much debated. An ecclesiastical junta in Mexico in 1539 decided to admit a few carefully chosen Indians and mestizos to minor orders, as
an aid to the priests in parish work. But the Mexican church council
of 1555 denied Holy Orders to mestizos, Indians, and Negroes, and a
similar stand was taken later by church councils in Peru. By 1570 or
earlier the Franciscans in New Spain had formally closed their ranks
to Indians on the ground that they were lacking in the necessary apti-
tudes, and the Dominicans followed suit in 1576.[18] There were always
exceptions, however, in special cases, and in later generations, as the
racial situation became more stabilized, friars of mixed blood, Indian
or Negro, were not uncommon. Occasionally in some of the dioceses
a few Indians were admitted to Holy Orders, and therefore into the
seminaries and *colegios,* but they were generally confined to the rural
parishes, and had little hope of advancement. Much depended upon the
nature of the local population. If it was predominantly European, the
clergy were also Spanish or Creole. Where the population consisted
chiefly of people of color, parish clergy of Indian or even Negro ante-
cedents were not uncommon.

In a strictly legal capacity mestizos were the equal of Creoles and
peninsular Spaniards, although socially inferior. They were permitted
to dress as whites and were recognized as *gente de razón,* rational folk,
as Indians, Negroes, and mulattoes were not. They also secured admittance to minor offices in Church and State. The mestizos generally
comprised a lower middle class—farmers, stewards, shopkeepers—although
unquestionably many of the wealthy, aristocratic families had traces of
Indian blood in their ancestry. The English friar Thomas Gage reported many well-to-do mestizo farmers in the regions he visited in
Mexico and Guatemala. Mestizos also formed the majority of the population of the large cities and towns, if only because of the concentration
there of charities and wealth. Often with an admixture of Negro blood,
they came to form a special ethnic type represented today by the middle
and lower classes of many of the Spanish republics. Because of the irregular origin of many of the mestizos and their upbringing in utter
ignorance and neglect, they also contributed most to the criminal and
vagabond class.

Although the small number of Spanish women in the early years of
colonization was an important factor in encouraging the fusion of races

17 Francisco A. Loayza, ed., *Juan Santos, el invencible. Manuscritos del año de 1742
al año de 1755,* Lima. 1942.
18 Robert Ricard, *La Conquête spirituelle du Mexique,* 275-6.

by intermarriage, there is little evidence that this circumstance long continued, for it appears that the number of colonial-born white women rapidly increased. Illegitimacy, however, was always a prolific source of the mestizo class, and concubinage became and continued to be a widespread custom. It is significant that in the sixteenth century 'mestizo' and 'illegitimate' were often used as synonymous terms.

The mestizos were often disparaged by whites as unstable and licentious, inheriting the bad qualities of both races, but the charge has never really been substantiated. The whole question of heredity in the blending of dissimilar races has yet to be studied in a detached and scientific manner. There is nothing in Spanish American history to prove the congenital inferiority of the mestizo. Whatever inconstancy of character or temperament he may have displayed can easily be accounted for by conditions of social inheritance and environment. In colonial times much depended on color of skin, features, and economic status. If an individual was poor, uneducated, or a 'bad actor,' he was a mestizo. If rich, educated, and a good citizen, he might easily be counted among the whites. The mestizos in reality came to constitute.

a separate race, although always added to by recent crossings; pretty thoroughly amalgamated, marrying within its own class, perpetuating and stabilizing itself as a new and different race, a race to which some believe the future of many parts of Latin America belongs.[19]

Negroes, mulattoes, and *zambos* were on the lowest rungs of the social ladder, whether slaves or freedmen. If free, they paid tribute and had by law to reside with recognized employers, under penalty of being consigned to the mines or to labor contractors. In early days in the colonies when fear of servile insurrection was widespread, some of the local legislation regarding Negro slaves was very barbarous. But in later times it was the general consensus among travelers that Negro slaves in Spanish America were better treated than were those in the English or French colonies. Spanish law with respect to slavery was comparatively humane. There were many protective regulations regarding food, shelter, clothing, labor, and punishments. A slave might marry the wife of his choice, and buy his freedom at the lowest market rate, as well as that of his wife and children. If ill treated, he might choose a new master provided he could induce one to purchase him; or he could appeal to the courts and possibly be declared free. Slaves sometimes were permitted to work for themselves and so accumulate a purchase price. Consequently the number of freedmen in Spanish American communities was consider-

19 C. H. Haring, *South American Progress*, Cambridge, Mass., 1934, 21.

able, and at the close of the eighteenth century tended to equal or surpass that of the slaves.[20]

Free mulattoes and *zambos* were regarded as peculiarly inferior. They might not appear on the streets after dark, carry arms, or have Indians as servants. Freedmen were excluded from public office, although they were accepted in the militia. They were not admitted to the craft guilds, and their women were forbidden by law to possess or wear luxurious clothes, silk, gold, and pearls. Altogether there was a deep prejudice against them. Yet Alamán tells us that they were the most useful part of the population, employed not only in the mines and in the army, but in the mechanical trades and as confidential servants in town and country. Although generally uneducated, and subject to many vices and other defects, they possessed great possibilities for good or for evil.[21]

It was on the West Indian islands, in the hot coastal regions about the Caribbean Sea and Gulf of Mexico, and on the Pacific coasts of New Granada and Peru, that the Negroes were most numerous. There the aboriginal population had soon disappeared, and its place was taken by importations from Africa. While the initial cost of Negroes was greater, in hot tropical areas they also proved to be more efficient and therefore more economical as workers. In the highland areas on the continent there were few Negroes, and Indians continued to constitute the great bulk of the laboring population. Negroes appeared chiefly as household servants in the large towns, and they were probably fewest in the provinces of the Rio de la Plata and Chile.

The first official recognition of the institution of Negro slavery in America appears to have been in 1501, when Governor Ovando was authorized to take over Christianized slaves born in the peninsula. The permission was withdrawn by Isabella two years later at Ovando's request, for he reported that the Negroes fled and corrupted the Indians. But Isabella died in 1504 and Ferdinand, less scrupulous about human slavery, occasionally sent out a few to labor in the mines. In 1510 he gave permission to ship slaves from Seville to a maximum of two hundred, for sale to the settlers or for work on the royal properties. After Ferdinand's death, the Cardinal-Regent Jiménez suspended the traffic altogether. But soon recommendations came from Las Casas, from the commission of the Hieronymite friars, and from the clergy at Santo Domingo, that the Indians be spared by a more general substitution of Negro labor. Moreover with the rapid spread of sugar cane culture in the Antilles came an insistent demand by the colonists for more workers,

---

20 The total number of Negroes in New Spain at the close of the eighteenth century was probably about 20,000, in Peru about 82,000, and in Venezuela about 500,000. E. G. Bourne, *Spain and America*, New York, 1904, 278-81 and sources cited there.
21 Op. cit. I, 67-8.

and in the decade 1520-30 the supply of Negroes greatly increased. Eight thousand or more were sent out during that period alone. After the middle of the sixteenth century territorial expansion on the mainland and the official ban against the enslaving of Indians still further augmented the traffic, either directly with Africa or by way of the slave mart in Lisbon.

In 1518 the first license to transport Negroes in quantity directly from Africa to America was granted by the young king Charles to a Flemish favorite, Laurent de Gouvenot, Master of the Royal Household. It involved the sole privilege for eight years of introducing blacks into the Indies, to a maximum of 4,000, free of all fiscal obligations.[22] Gouvenot immediately sold the privilege to some Genoese in Andalusia for 25,000 ducats. The first *asiento,* or formal contract with an individual or company for the exclusive right of furnishing Negroes to the colonies overseas, was concluded with two Germans connected with the Spanish court in 1528. They were obligated to ship 4,000 to America, to be sold at not more than 45 ducats apiece. They were to pay immediately into the royal treasury 20,000 ducats, in return for which the crown promised to issue no more licenses for four years.[23]

The system of monopoly was soon abandoned as unsatisfactory to both colonists and metropolis, and until 1580 the supply of Negroes to America was administered directly by the government. Licenses were issued to individuals, at first mostly to Castilians, then to other subjects of the crown such as Germans, Flemings, and Italians, and finally more and more to the Portuguese because of their 'factories' on the African coast and practical monopoly of supply. During the union of the Spanish and Portuguese crowns between 1580 and 1640 the earlier system of *asientos* was revived and extended. The number of *piezas de Indias* [24] contracted for per year steadily increased, as well as the duty on each Negro and the bonus paid to the crown. So also increased the prices demanded for slaves in the colonies. Thereafter the *asiento* remained the settled policy of the Spanish government for controlling and profiting from the slave trade. In the second half of the seventeenth century Dutch capitalists became involved in the traffic; during the War of the Spanish Succession the *asiento* was granted to a French Royal Guinea Company; and by the Treaty of Utrecht it passed as one of the spoils of war to the South Sea Company in England. Each of Spain's more aggressive or

---

22 Georges Scelle, *La traite négrière aux Indes de Castille,* 2 vols., Paris, 1906, I, 139 ff.

23 Ibid. 169 ff.

24 *Pieza de Indias,* 'a prime slave, sound in wind and limb, usually between the ages of eighteen and thirty, and seven Spanish *palmos* tall.' James F. King, 'Evolution of the Free Slave Trade Principle in Spanish Colonial Administration,' *Hisp. Amer. Hist. Rev.,* XXII, 36.

more mercantilely minded neighbors in succession turned its hand to this miserable business.

When the rights of the South Sea Company were extinguished through purchase by Spain in 1750, the crown momentarily reverted to its early policy of giving individual licenses to Spanish subjects to supply local areas in the Indies. But these small *asentistas,* dependent upon English slave marts in Jamaica and other West Indian islands, became but another vehicle for contraband trade in manufactures. The crown therefore after the Seven Years' War made one more effort to control the Negro traffic by means of a single slave-trading company centered in Spain.[25] Its egregious failure, and the need of an adequate slave supply at reasonable prices to meet the growing demand in the Indies, led to a gradual liberalization of Negro traffic in 1773 and following years. The export of specie or colonial produce to foreign ports to pay for Negroes was permitted, the centuries-long expedient of extracting a royal revenue from the trade was abandoned, and the crown shifted to a policy of encouraging free importation of Negroes by Spaniards and foreigners alike. The basic decree was issued on 28 February 1789, conceding free trade provisionally to Cuba, Santo Domingo, Puerto Rico, and the province of Caracas. In 1791 it was extended to the viceroyalties of New Granada and Buenos Aires, and four years later to the seaports of Peru. In 1793 Spanish subjects were permitted to carry colonial products, except gold and silver, received in exchange for Negroes to foreign countries of Europe and America; and by successive extensions of time the new freedom was continued to the outbreak of the independence movements in 1810.[26]

Although the number of Negroes was never sufficient for the needs of the colonists, they were early a source of public insecurity. As early as 1514 the increase of African slaves on Hispaniola was becoming a matter of concern to the Spanish settlers, and the royal treasurer Pasamonte wrote requesting that as few as possible be sent out from Spain. By 1560 the natural increase of this prolific race, together with the constant inflow from Lisbon and West Africa, had created an alarming preponderance of their number over that of the whites. Menéndez de Avilés, in a letter of this period to the king, says that in Puerto Rico there were 15,000 Negroes and less than 500 Spaniards, on the island of Hispaniola over 30,000 Negroes and probably 2,000 Spaniards, and that the same general situation prevailed in Cuba and on the coastal mainland from Vera Cruz round to Cartagena and the shores of Venezuela.

25 Ibid. 36-44.

26 Diego Luis Molinari, *La trata de negros. Datos para su studio en el Rio de la Plata* (Prologo al tomo VII de *Los documentos para la historia argentina*), Buenos Aires, 1916, 61-6, 72 n. 5; King, op. cit. 50-55.

The first Negro uprising occurred on Hispaniola in 1522, when about forty fled to the hills and committed some murders. Another outbreak took place on Puerto Rico five years later, and in 1531 a general uprising in Panama that was repressed with great difficulty. There was constant danger that fugitive slaves would join hands with rebellious Indians, as happened in the uprising on Hispaniola in 1533 led by the *cacique* Henríquez, which it took ten years to suppress. A Negro conspiracy in New Spain in 1537 caused such alarm that the viceroy Mendoza requested the suspension of new importations from Africa. 'Wild' Negroes (*cimarrones*) who fled to the inaccessible hills and forests of the interior and there organized independent communities, were a permanent source of insecurity in tropical America throughout the colonial period, especially on the Isthmus of Panama where travel off the main highways was exceedingly dangerous. The preponderance of Negro slaves in the community became a matter of even graver concern to the Spaniards when French Protestant privateers were preying upon towns and shipping in the West Indies and attempting to establish colonies in Hispanic America from the Carolinas to Brazil. For the French, among whom slavery was not recognized by law, by freeing Negroes and Indians might conceivably with their assistance seize the islands and mainland settlements. This was illustrated with startling suddenness when in 1538 Negroes in league with French corsairs put the town of Havana to sack.[27] Although these dangers were plainly evident to the colonists, and local slave insurrections continued to be a frequent occurrence, there was always an insistent demand from the Indies for more manpower; and the crown itself, in its efforts to defend the aborigines, more and more urged the substitution of Negroes in the mines and on the plantations.

The belief that Spanish colonization in the beginning was almost entirely military in spirit and personnel is far from the truth. Farmers and artisans came out very early, both under official auspices and on their own initiative. Among the hundreds of persons Columbus was authorized to take to the New World on government stipend on his second and third expeditions, a considerable number, it was specified, were to be farm laborers, gardeners, and artisans of all sorts. And as these colonists of the laboring class were inclined to desert their trades and secure an allotment of Indians, the crown in 1508 ordered that they be compelled to work at their accustomed occupations.[28] In 1511 the king was urging the *Casa de Contratación* to send out as many farm laborers as possible, to simplify the formalities at Seville, and to advertise

27 Scelle, op. cit. I, 165-7; Woodbury Lowery, *The Spanish Settlements Within the Present Limits of the United States*, 2 vols., New York, 1901-05, II, 14-15.

28 Silvio Zavala, 'Los trabajadores antillanos en el siglo XVI,' *Rev. Hist. Amer.*, no. 3, 74-5.

throughout the poorer regions of Castile the richness of the islands and the opportunities for improving one's lot by emigration.[29] In September of that year permission was temporarily extended to all the inhabitants of the kingdom to go to the Indies on the sole condition that they register at the *Casa,* and a number of fiscal inducements were offered.[30] In 1518, in response to representations by Las Casas, farmers who would go to Hispaniola or Tierra firme were promised passage and maintenance from the day they arrived in Seville until they disembarked in America, besides lands, implements, seeds, livestock, and living for a year, the services of a physician and an apothecary, relief from taxes. and premiums for the best husbandry.[31] Concessions such as these were repeated in later years.

As the West Indies became progressively depopulated, in competition with the richer allurements of the mainland,[32] the crown authorized various Spaniards to recruit married farm laborers for the islands. In 1533 sixty farmers and their families arrived at Santo Domingo. At the same time permission was even being given to take over Portuguese laborers, and as late as 1565 Philip II authorized the introduction of one hundred and fifty Portuguese, at least one-third of whom were to be married and to take their families.[33] Efforts were consistently made throughout to attract married colonists, although mixed marriages were permitted in the Indies.

There were also numerous examples of emigrants who found their way to America on the same basis as the indentured servants of the early English colonies or the *engagés* of the French islands. Finding no opportunity to join a military expedition, they contracted with another Spaniard in return for transportation to give their services in the colony for two or three years, with or without pay. There is also some early

---

29 In 1509 and 1510 Ferdinand, moved by petitions from the colonists, wrote to the officers of the *Casa* to make haste to send master stoneworkers and materials for the building of churches, and two architects, Juan de Herrera and Orduño de Bretendón, with workmen under pay for three years, sailed in June of the latter year. Elizabeth Ward Loughran, 'The First Episcopal Sees in Spanish America,' *Hisp. Amer. Hist. Rev.,* x 176, and sources indicated there.

30 *Col. doc. inéd.,* 2nd ser., v, 331-6.

31 Ibid. IX, 77.

32 According to the report of the *oidores* Espinosa and Zuazo at Santo Domingo, 30 March 1528, Hispaniola in 1513 had about 17 towns and villages. Now nearly all were in decay or had completely disappeared. La Concepción which formerly had 200 householders now had only 20; Santiago and Puerto Real each of which formerly had about a hundred households, now had only 8 and 15 respectively. Cuba at one time possessed 7 towns. Now only Santiago was of any importance, with 50 householders. The same general situation existed in Jamaica and Puerto Rico. (Ibid. 1st ser., XI, 343 ff.) In 1526 the crown went so far as to forbid migration from the Antilles to the mainland on pain of death and confiscation of property.

33 Zavala, op. cit. 75-6.

documentary evidence of permission to individual Spaniards to take white, Christian slaves to the Indies, but of this we know little or nothing.[34]

The crown was equally preoccupied at times with the maintenance of a stable agriculture in the colonies. Royal orders of 1533 and later years required *encomenderos* to invest each year at least one-tenth of the income they derived from the Indians in buildings and other permanent improvements, or in the cultivation of their properties. And in the *Recopilación* are numerous instructions to viceroys and governors to see to the planting of trees, or the cultivation of hemp, flax, or other products, and to encourage husbandry in general.[35]

It is true, as Zavala reminds us, that 'peaceful colonization by farmers and artisans did not become the normal and general pattern of the emigration of Spaniards to America during the first decades of the colonial period.'[36] Soldiers who had taken part in the conquest of Granada, officers returned from the campaigns in France and Italy, younger sons of the nobility disinherited by entails, formed the nucleus of the earlier expeditions. But even before the military conquest was achieved, the crown made consistent efforts to promote a steadier, more industrious type of emigration. That some difficulty was encountered in establishing a considerable number of farmers in the Indies is evident from the record. The cost of transportation was doubtless high. Aristocratic landlords in Spain did not contemplate with equanimity the loss of laborers from their manorial estates. But perhaps a greater obstacle lay in the fact that agricultural labor in the colonies was altogether servile. The Spanish immigrant refused to be identified with the Indian farm worker, and aspired to become himself an exploiter of native labor.

There were numerous schools and colleges scattered throughout the Spanish American world, most of them conducted by the religious Orders, but also a few founded by the crown or by private benefactors. Education, however, reflecting the society to which it ministered, remained essentially aristocratic, confined to a select class, to Creoles, Spaniards, and upper-class mestizos. The first schools were in the monasteries of the Mendicant friars, and, as in the early Middle Ages, it was generally out of monastic or church schools that developed the universities. Most of the larger towns came to be provided with *colegios* which supplied secondary education under ecclesiastical auspices, the most celebrated being those of the Dominicans and the Jesuits. In towns where

---

34 Scelle would interpret it as an incipient 'white slave' traffic in the modern sense. Op. cit. I, 218-21.

35 José María Ots Capdequi, *El estado español en las Indias*, 127-9; *Col. doc. inéd.*, 2nd ser., X, 155.

36 *New Viewpoints on the Spanish Colonization of America*, Philadelphia, 1943, 112.

there was a university the *colegios* were frequently affiliated with it. Many of the *colegios*, however, depending upon an uncertain income from gifts and bequests, were very deficient in both books and teachers. The Council of Trent had decreed the establishment of a residential seminary (*seminario convictorio*) in every diocese for the training of candidates for the priesthood, but the ordinance was not everywhere obeyed, and even in the eighteenth century many of the poorer American dioceses were without such an institute. Nevertheless in New Spain alone at the close of the colonial era there were some forty colleges and seminaries, nineteen of which prepared students to take degrees.[37]

Creole children received their primary instruction in a monastery, or in a school maintained by the secular clergy, or from private tutors. In theory every municipality was to support one or more primary schools, but municipal revenues were generally meager and to the end of the colonial regime the number of public schools was small. On the other hand, it should be remembered that popular education on the continent of Europe was scarcely thought of before the second half of the eighteenth century, and that there were no public primary schools in France before 1789.[38] Spain gave to the colonies what it had. Whatever shortcomings there were, existed also in the mother country.

The crown very early required that a school for teaching the elements of Spanish be maintained in every Indian *pueblo*, and the rule was reiterated in royal decrees throughout the colonial era, but it was honored more in the breach than in the observance. In the remoter Indian villages only the chiefs or *principales* understood Castilian or could read or write, and the same may be said of many Indian communities in the Spanish American republics of today. In the earliest years in New Spain Indian children were gathered together by the hundreds in the porches and patios of the churches and monasteries—sometimes eight hundred or a thousand, we are told—chiefly for religious instruction, but also to learn to read and write! In a few of the larger towns important foundations were soon established for the education of the natives, both boys and girls, chiefly in the industrial arts, but sometimes also in higher branches. Indeed in the beginning there were more schools for Indians than for the sons of Spaniards. The first two in Mexico were established by Franciscans, one in Tezcoco in 1523 by a lay brother, Peter of Ghent, the other in Mexico two years later by Friar Martín de Valencia. Peter of Ghent (1480-1572), a near relative of Charles V, was outstanding among these early missionary educators.

---

37 John Tate Lanning, *Academic Culture in the Spanish Colonies*, New York, 1940, 26.

38 In the English colonies, outside New England, primary education was until the Revolution considered primarily the duty of the family or the church. Everts Boutell Greene, *The Revolutionary Generation*, 1763-1790, New York, 1943, 117 ff.

Arriving in Mexico in 1523, he remained there until his death at an extreme old age without ever revisiting Europe. Famed for his humility and self-effacement, he never took Holy Orders but devoted himself heart and soul to the education of the natives. And in the great school of San Francisco in the Indian quarter of Mexico City, which he directed for over forty years, generations of Indians were taught to read and write, received instruction in various trades, or were trained as painters, sculptors, and silversmiths to adorn the churches arising on every side.

Some of the early foundations in Lima and Mexico City for the education of Indian youth were intended to be real colleges, where would be trained the leaders of the American race as teachers and missionaries of civilization and religion among their own people. It was a time, immediately after the conquest, when the Church contemplated a vast program of raising the entire Indian population in a generation or two to a European level of culture, a program which soon proved to be impossible of achievement. But an excellent start was made, especially in New Spain. Perhaps the most famous of these early colleges was Santa Cruz in Tlaltelolco, the Indian quarter of Mexico City. It was attached to the Franciscan convent of Santiago,[39] and apparently preceded similar educational facilities for Spanish children, although the Dominicans did open a college in Mexico City in 1537 for Spaniards and Indians. Owing its origin really to Bishop Ramírez de Fuenleal, president of the second *audiencia*,[40] it was opened by the viceroy Mendoza in January 1536, soon after his arrival from Spain, and was later in part supported by Mendoza and his successors. It started with sixty students, carefully selected from families of Indian chiefs, who were taught Latin, rhetoric, logic, philosophy, music, and Mexican medicine. The Indian boys led an almost monastic life, eating together in the refectory and sleeping in an open dormitory. The school had eminent teachers, Spaniards and Frenchmen, such as the great antiquarian, Bernardino de Sahagún, and Juan Focher and Juan de Gaona from the University of Paris. Within a few decades, however, it began to decline. For one thing, the Franciscans about 1548 turned the college over to its Indian graduates, who thereafter chose the rector, councilors, and professors from among their own number. This optimistic experiment lasted about twenty years, and was not an unqualified success. The fabric of the school fell into complete ruin, and although eventually the Franciscans took charge again, Santa Cruz never recovered its former eminence. But there were also other obstacles: the jealous opposition of the Dominicans and other Orders, and the growing prejudice among many laymen and ecclesiastics against higher education for the Indians.

---

39 Founded by Bishop Zumárraga in 1534.
40 Mariano Cuevas, *Historia de la iglesia en Méjico* I, 386; Ricard, op. cit. 266.

The scholars apparently displayed extraordinary aptness in acquiring the new disciplines, and many of them became excellent Latinists, surpassing the Latinity of some of the clergy from Europe. But they were accused of superficiality, lack of real understanding of Christian doctrine, or of sufficient facility and dignity in expounding it to their people; not to be trusted therefore as teachers or preachers, and a source of confusion in the deep and holy mysteries of the Faith. Viceroys after Velasco withdrew their support, the school was allowed to decay from lack of revenues, and although similar schools were early established in other centers, notably in Michoacán, further experiments along these lines were not encouraged. The college of Tlaltelolco was converted in the middle of the seventeenth century into a *casa de estudios* for Franciscan friars. In some cases the foundations were diverted to the education of Creole children.[41]

Schools were also opened for Indian girls, the future mothers of families, eight of them by 1534 we are told, in various towns of New Spain. There they were probably taught, not reading and writing, but Christian living and the domestic arts, the catechism, sewing, and embroidery. The girls were kept in these schools from the age of five or six until puberty, when they were married to the boy pupils of the missionaries, thus creating a sound basis, it was hoped, for the Christianization of Indian society. But this system, too, lasted for only a generation. Lay women teachers brought out from Spain especially for this purpose were not an unqualified success, and the schools faded out for lack of continued official support.[42]

As already remarked, mixed marriages and irregular unions with Indian women produced a large class of mestizo children, who were mostly thrown upon the care and support of their Indian mothers. Great numbers of these children grew up with no home training or influence, and constituted an outcast, vagabond class that overran the cities and towns. Perpetuating themselves in the same irregular way, they were an ever increasing source of potential criminals and prostitutes, who corrupted the Indians and remained a running sore in Spanish

---

41 Ricard, op. cit. 262-76.

Harvard also had an Indian College for the training of natives for the Christian ministry. It was built in the Harvard Yard in 1654-6 to accommodate twenty students, and was financed from England by the Society for the Propagation of the Gospel in New England. But 'by reason of the death and failing' of the few Indians sent there, it was soon used mostly for English scholars, fell into decay, and was pulled down in 1698. In this Indian College building was issued, from the college press in 1663, John Eliot's great Algonkian Bible, the first Bible printed in the New World. An Indian college had also been planned for the Virginia colony in 1617-22, but never materialized. Samuel Eliot Morison, *Harvard College in the Seventeenth Century*, 2 vols., Cambridge, Mass., 1936, I, 341-60.

42 Ricard, op. cit. 252-5.

colonial society. Numerous schools and asylums were founded for the rescue of these unfortunates, but not enough to make a serious impression upon the general problem.

As early as 1533 the authorities in Mexico City felt the need of providing a refuge and school for founding mestizo boys, and another for mestiza girls: and similar institutions were erected in Lima and other large colonial towns. The girls were sometimes provided with dowries, in the form of money from the royal coffers, or *corregimientos* or other offices, in order to encourage their marriage by Spanish colonists.[43] Such a school was *San Juan de Letrán* founded by the viceroy Mendoza and Bishop Zumárraga in 1547, devoted to homeless mestizos and directed by the Franciscans. Teaching the elements of language and religion as well as the handicrafts, it was supported by charity and a subsidy of 2,000 ducats a year from the crown. But it was carelessly or dishonestly managed. The number of children dropped from about 200 in the 1550's to 60 or 80 in 1579, and these were wretchedly housed, fed, and clothed.[44] The school lasted, however, into the nineteenth century. *Nuestra Señora de la Caridad,* established at about the same time for mestiza girls—and to which some Spanish girls were also later admitted for lack of a school for them—had a similar history.[45]

Many appeals were sent from both New Spain and Peru to the Jesuits to come out and establish colleges for which they were already celebrated in Europe. These Jesuit colleges were boarding schools in which were taught Latin, Greek, scriptures, logic, and often theology and philosophy as well. In their famous pedagogical system, the *ratio studiorum,* the emphasis was upon moral and intellectual training, discipline, and loyalty. The first Jesuits arrived in New Spain in 1572, and two years later were able to open a school that was to become their *Colegio Máximo* of St. Peter and St. Paul. Within twenty years they had established other student residences in Mexico City (in 1588 combined in the *Colegio de San Ildefonso*) and five colleges in other cities of New Spain.[46] The first members of the Society in Peru came out in 1569. Ultimately there was a Jesuit college in nearly every important city in the Indies.

The first university in America in the sense of an institution empowered to grant higher degrees was that of Santo Domingo. By virtue of a papal bull of 28 October 1538 the school maintained in the Dominican convent was raised to university rank with the powers and privileges possessed by the celebrated Alcalá de Henares in Spain founded just forty years earlier by Cardinal Jiménez de Cisneros. But there is no

43 Marshall, op. cit. 169-173.
44 Cuevas, op. cit. I, 392-6.
45 Ibid. 400-402.
46 Ibid. II, 321 ff. Paula Alegría, *La educación en México,* Mexico, 1936, 226 ff.

evidence that the bull received before the eighteenth century the requisite exequatur of the Council of the Indies, or indeed that the institution really functioned as a university for many years. At most it seems to have been a school of theology. The bull, however, survives as evidence of the university's pontifical origin.[47]

The two earliest major universities in America, which were both 'royal' and 'pontifical,' were those of Mexico City and Lima, established by imperial decrees in 1551. Both were created in response to appeals from laymen and ecclesiastics in the colonies, who urged that young Creoles be spared the perils and expense of travel to the universities of Spain. The first to be formally opened with endowments and professorships was the University of Mexico, which was installed with great pomp and ceremony by the viceroy and *audiencia* in January 1553.[48] It received an annual subsidy from the royal treasury of 1,000 pesos de oro, and started out with academic chairs in Latin, rhetoric, philosophy, civil and canon law, scriptures, and theology. The first rector and two professors were judges of the *audiencia;* the rest of the faculty were ecclesiastics. Later on the rectorship alternated between ecclesiastics and laymen. Among the distinguished early professors were Juan Negrete (theology), Alonso de la Vera Cruz (scriptures), and Dr. Cervantes Salazar (rhetoric). Ultimately there were 24 chairs in all, including 2 in medicine and after 1640 2 in Indian languages, Aztec and Otomí.

The university at Lima was less fortunate in its beginning. Housed in the Dominican monastery, with virtually no endowment, it languished until the days of the viceroy Toledo. In 1571 the crown separated it from its Dominican connections, Toledo provided it with ample funds from the income of several *encomiendas,* and by 1578 the University of San Marcos was operating with a dozen or more chairs, including 2 in native languages and one in medicine.[49] The first 2 rectors, it is interesting to note, were medical doctors. Mexico and Lima became

---

47 *La Bula In Apostolatus Culmine del Papa Paulo III* (Publ. Univ. Sto. Dom., vol. xxvii, Ciudad Trujillo, 1944), 7 ff.; Lanning, op. cit. 12-13. A secular college at Santo Domingo endowed by Hernando de Gorgon was converted into a *stadium generale* by royal decree of 23 February 1558. But again there is little evidence that it functioned as a university in the sixteenth century, and in 1603 it was made a diocesan seminary.

48 Classes began in June, each holding its first session on a different day so that the viceroy and *audiencia* might honor it with their presence.

49 Bernabé Cobo, *Historia de la fundación de Lima,* Lima, 1882, 231-52; Jose Dávila Condemarin, *Bosquejo histórico de la fundación de la insigne universidad mayor de San Marcos de Lima, de sus progresos y actual estado,* Lima, 1912, 7-13. Classes began in May 1577. The chair in medicine soon lapsed, but 2 were established by the viceroy Chinchón in 1634, and a third (without salary) on method in 1690. Cobo, op. cit. 249; Antonio de la Calancha, *Crónica moralizada de la provincia del Peru,* Barcelona, 1639, 17, 29; Luis Antonio Eguiguren, *Católogo histórico del claustro de la universidad de San Marcos,* 1576-1800, Lima, 1912, 53-60.

the models for many other universities in colonial America, and ultimately 6 institutions were ranked with them as major universities in
the New World. There was also a category of minor universities. These
were colleges, most of them conducted by the Jesuit and Dominican
Orders, in provinces more than two hundred miles distant from a
general university, which by royal or pontifical favor obtained the
right to award higher academic degrees.[50] There were 2 in Cuzco, Jesuit
and Dominican, 2 in Bogotá, and 3 in Quito, all of them established in
the seventeenth century, and several dating from the eighteenth century in the Caribbean area. Altogether about 15 of the minor sort appeared in the colonial period, 8 of them established by the Jesuits. By
the time of the outbreak of the wars for independence, Spanish America
possessed between 20 and 25 institutions (depending on the criterion
used) in some 18 cities and towns claiming to offer instruction and
degrees above that of bachelor.[51] After Mexico and Lima the most distinguished were perhaps the University of La Plata in Upper Peru, and
that of Guatemala. Some of the others, as has happened elsewhere in
the world, seem to have been universities in name only. In general the
royal government was very niggardly, and endowments even of the
major universities were extremely meager.

The constitutions of most of the Spanish American universities were
modeled directly or indirectly upon that of Salamanca in Spain. Government was in the hands of a 'cloister' composed of the faculties and
the doctors and masters residing in or near the university city. Over
it presided a rector elected from among the doctors in the community
each year. Although there were often complaints of viceregal interference in the choice of rectors and professors, or in the recommendation of candidates for degrees, the university was one of the few corporations in America that retained any degree of autonomy. As in
Oxford and other medieval universities, the rector possessed police
jurisdiction over members of the cloister, officials, and students, and
regulated the students' residences and their mode of dress. Student garb,
reflecting the ecclesiastic origins of the universities, generally consisted
of a cassock, a long cloak, and a brimless cap. Matriculation fees were
very small, but degree fees were apt to be high. Investiture as a doctor
in Mexico or Lima in the eighteenth century might cost anywhere from
2,000 to 10,000 pesos, for ceremonies were very elaborate and apparently
all members of the cloister expected to receive gratuities of one kind
or another. An impecunious candidate sought a patron to bear the
expense and share the honors of the occasion. Grants-in-aid, or exemption from fees, however, were frequently extended to able students

50 By royal decrees of 1622 and 1624. Lanning, op. cit. 25, 27-8 and n. 49.
51 Lanning, op. cit. 21-33.

of poor family, and most of the colleges and universities maintained scholarships supported by royal funds or private endowment.

University instruction was in theory open to Indians, especially to the sons of Indian chiefs, and in Hapsburg times apparently even to free mulattoes. But in the eighteenth century there was a growing prejudice against the admission of any mixed bloods, doubtless because they were appearing in increasing numbers in the professions. The viceroy Count of Monclova in Peru (1689-1705) forbade the admission of Negroes, mulattoes, and quadroons, and the Count of Superunda (1745-61) added mestizos and *zambos* to the list. A certificate of legitimacy and purity of race (*limpieza de sangre*) including freedom from the taint of heresy was required in order to matriculate or to proceed to a degree. This discrimination was confirmed by royal decree in 1752, and was not rescinded until the first decade of the nineteenth century.[52] All persons possessing Negro blood were also by statute excluded from the colonial university of Mexico, but in the smaller, provincial institutions social and racial prejudices seem to have been less evident. There must have been many exceptional cases in the larger universities as well.

Professorships were of two kinds, temporary and proprietary. Temporary chairs were filled for a term of three or four years, proprietary chairs were held for life. Both were secured by competition before a board of judges. The latter in Mexico in the beginning included all members of the cloister as well as all matriculated students, but later a smaller and more select committee awarded the professorships.[53] The religious Orders sometimes endowed chairs in theology or the arts, to be filled by a member of their own society, and occasionally a chair was founded by a private benefactor. Cobo says that in his time (1639) all the professorships at San Marcos were held by Creoles, most of whom were graduates of the university.

Professors had to take an oath to defend the doctrine of the Immaculate Conception, observe a modest conduct, and keep away from theatres, dances, and other unseemly diversions.[54] Salaries ranged generally from one hundred to seven hundred pesos, with little change upward in the course of two and a half centuries.[55] In short, teaching in

52 Lanning, op. cit. 39-40, 42; Roberto MacLean y Estenós, 'Escuelas, colegios, seminarios y universidades en el virreynato del Peru,' 1er cuatrim, 1943, 31-3.

53 Herbert Ingram Priestley, 'The Old University of Mexico,' *Univ. Calif. Chronicle,* XXI, no. 4, 9.

54 Ibid. 8; Dávila Condemarin, op. cit. 14.

55 Professorial salaries were somewhat higher in the University of San Marcos in Lima, ranging from approximately four hundred and fifty to fifteen hundred pesos (Calancha, op. cit. 12; Cobo, op. cit. 250.) Proprietary professors continued to draw their stipend after retirement, and usually employed a substitute to deliver their lectures.

a university was an avocation rather than a profession. Professors were usually churchmen, judges, or government officials, and a university chair was often sought for the social prestige it carried with it. This tradition has persisted in most colleges and universities throughout the Spanish American republics today.

Following the Continental tradition, the university was primarily a group of professional schools. But instruction in the liberal arts in a *colegio* or preparatory school, leading to the bachelor's degree, was a necessary preliminary to professional studies. The preparatory disciplines were Latin grammar and rhetoric, philosophy (the *Ethics, Metaphysics,* and *Logic of* Aristotle) , and mathematics, including the geometry of Euclid. Sometimes the *Physics* of Aristotle was included, for science before the eighteenth century was a branch of philosophy taught in medieval Latin.

Then came the professional schools: theology, law, and medicine. The premier studies were theology and law. Representing the two great powers of Church and State, they were the pillars of a Christian society. Moral and dogmatic theology consisted of the subtleties and abstractions of the medieval schoolmen, of whom St. Thomas Aquinas and Duns Scotus were the accepted masters. Law was Roman law and Canon law and the decretals of the popes, often explained by obsolete commentators. At least until the eighteenth century, methods of study, as in the universities of Spain, remained deductive, syllogistic, in contrast with the inductive, experimental approach of a later day.

In ordinary circumstances the regimen produced men of stupendous rote memory, along with imposing but inappropriate and artificial allusions to the ancients and to the myths. These had long been the symbol of the 'compleat' intellectual, the proudest result of education and the surest mark of the colonial scholar.[56]

University libraries were small and poor. As late as 1803 the viceroy Marquina in New Spain reported to his successor that the University of Mexico 'no tiene gabinete y su biblioteca está escasa de buenas obras modernas.' [57]

Medical science in the colonies before the eighteenth century, as in Spain itself, lagged behind that of contemporary Europe, and often included a goodly mixture of astrology and superstition. As late as 1723 in Lima there were found some to debate the evidence of the circulation of the blood.[58] Few physicians appear in the colonial record

---

56 Lanning, op. cit. 64.

57 'Instrucción del Señor Marquina al Señor Iturrigaray,' 1 January 1803, *Instrucciones que los vireyes de Nueva España dejaron a sus sucesores,* II, 629.

58 Lanning, op. cit. 104.

in the sixteenth century. As late as 1573 the important city of Quito had neither physician nor apothecary. Perhaps the best known in Mexico was Dr. García Farfan, a graduate of the university who left a treatise on surgery and two on medicine, one for Indians who had no physician available, and who later became an Augustinian friar. There was also the Friar Lucas de Almodovar who cured the viceroy Mendoza of a serious illness.[59] But the list is a short one. In fact native medicine among the Indians of Mexico and Peru at the time of the conquest was probably as efficacious as that which prevailed among the Spaniards, and the latter held it in considerable respect. Owing to the lack of physicians, medical practice in the hospitals of the Indian pueblos frequently was of the native variety, and many Indian drugs and herbs picked up by the missionaries were accorded a high place in the Spanish pharmacopoeia.

As early as 1535 royal decrees were issued against quackery and dishonesty in the practice of medicine and the dispensing of drugs in America,[60] and in some of the more important colonial cities a *protomédico* was appointed by the *cabildo*. The *protomédico* examined and licensed physicians, surgeons, and druggists, inspected apothecary shops, and through the local magistrates enforced compliance with the criteria established by law. Philip II gave form and substance to this office by sending out a number of physicians from Spain, for whom he issued detailed instructions in 1570.[61] They were to take up residence in the capital cities of their selection, and were apparently expected to raise the standards of the profession throughout the colonies. But above all it was their function to collect all available information about medicinal plants and their use in America, and send specimens and reports back to Spain. Out of the office of *protomédico* eventually developed, in the principal centers of authority, a board of examiners or *tribunal del protomedicato general* whose members were usually appointed by the viceroy.

Medical education in the colonies, however, even in early Bourbon times had advanced little beyond the concepts of Hippocrates, Galen, and Avicenna, and remained almost wholly innocent of any real knowledge of anatomy. In the course of the eighteenth century the necessity of anatomical studies came to be more widely recognized, and toward

---

59 Ricard, op. cit. 186-7.

60 *Recopilación*, lib. v, tit. 6, leyes 5, 7.

61 Ibid. ley I, The first *protomédico* sent out by Philip II was Dr. Francisco Hernández who was in New Spain from 1571 to 1577, and returned, it is said, with some fifteen or more volumes of studies of natural history and Indian 'antiguedades.' All were deposited in the library of the Escorial and were burned in the fire there in 1671. Portions of his work, however, had meantime been published in Spain and in Italy. Joaquin García Icazbalceta, *Los médicos de Méjico en el siglo XVI*, Mexico, 1896.

its close there were significant reforms in medical instruction in both Peru and New Spain.[62] The great advances in medical theory and practice in Europe spread to the New World, and under the influence of such men as Dr. Hipólito Unánue [63] in Lima, Dr. Luis Montaña in Mexico, and Dr. Narciso Esparragosa in Guatemala, modern medical books became known and modern techniques were introduced. More attention was paid to clinical surgery, obstetrics, and pharmacy, and to the allied fields of chemistry, physics, and botany. Inoculation against smallpox was practiced at least after the middle of the century, and vaccination was made compulsory soon after its introduction into Europe. Indeed the Spanish government, under what is commonly regarded as the inept rule of Charles IV, displayed a remarkable sense of responsibility for public health, not only in the distribution of smallpox virus in America, but in circulating information about any new remedies or techniques evolved abroad.

62 It is well to remember that in the English North American colonies there was no formal instruction at all in medicine until 1765, and no licensing of physicians till 1760 (New York) and 1772 (New Jersey). Greene, op. cit. 87-93.

63 Hipólito Unánue (1755-1833), colonial Peru's most distinguished physician, professor of anatomy at San Marcos, established the first anatomical theatre in Lima in 1792, and was chiefly instrumental in founding the medical school of San Fernando in 1811, today the medical faculty of the university.

XII

❧❧

Literature, Scholarship and the Fine Arts

❧❧

Given the lag in literary and intellectual activities that always exists between a colonial people and an older, more mature society, Spanish America produced a notable assortment of scholars, both American born and men born in Spain who wrote in America. In the sixteenth and seventeenth centuries important works were produced in geography, natural history, bibliography, law, and the languages and customs of the natives. Some of our richest sources of knowledge of Mexican anthropolgy and Aztec culture are in the books of scholars associated with the old university of Mexico, such as Sahagún, Motolinia, and Torquemada. For information about the ancient Peruvian Indians we turn back to sixteenth century writers such as Cieza de León, Garcilasso de la Vega (El Inca), Francisco de Avila, Blas Valera, and Polo de Ondegardo. Distinguished works on the physical geography and the flora and fauna of the Indies were written by José de Acosta and Bernabé Cobo, and on colonial political institutions by Juan de Matinzo, Escalona Agüero, the erudite bibliographer León Pinelo,[1] and the great jurist Solórzano Pereira. Francisco de Avila and Garcilasso de la Vega were born in Cuzco, Escalona Agüero and the Augustinian antiquary, Antonio de la Calancha, in Chuquisaca, the racy chronicler of New Granada, Rodríguez Fresle, and the historian, Lucas Fernández Piedrahita, in Bogotá where they also received their education. León Pinelo and Escalona Agüero were fellow law students in Lima at the university of San Marcos.

One of the most learned and versatile scholars in the history of colonial America was the celebrated Carlos de Sigüenza y Góngora,

---

1 Antonio León Pinelo was the son of a Christianized Portuguese Jew, Diego Lopes de Lisboa, who came to Buenos Aires via Brazil in 1594 to escape persecution by the Inquisition. Diego Lopes engaged in trade in Buenos Aires and Córdoba, served as *regidor* in the latter city, later studied theology in Chuquisaca, and was appointed chaplain to Archbishop Fernando Arias de Ugarte who was to be constant friend and protector. Antonio's brother, Diego, was at one time rector of the University of San Marcos.

who was born in Mexico City of Spanish and Creole parentage in 1645. Mathematician and astronomer, historian and antiquarian, poet and critic, chronicler of events at the court of the viceroy, in nearly every activity he excelled among the men of his time. He was Royal Cosmographer to the king, corresponded with learned men in Europe, and apparently was invited by Louis XIV to become a pensioner at his court. He occupied the chair of mathematics in the university, was consulted in engineering and other scientific problems such as the drainage of the Valley of Mexico, and was associated with the Spanish exploration and occupation of Pensacola Bay at the time of La Salle's expedition to the Gulf of Mexico. Scholar and practical man of affairs, in the words of Menéndez y Pelayo, he was 'one of the most illustrious men that Mexico has produced.'[2]

Another scholar who made all fields of human knowledge his province was Pedro de Peralta Barnuevo, a contemporary of Sigüenza in Peru. He was born in Lima in 1663, and during his entire life of eighty years 'apparently never traveled beyond the limits of his birthplace.' He too was a mathematician and chief cosmographer and engineer of the viceroyalty, who built a breakwater at Callao and improved methods of extracting and assaying silver ores. He was likewise a doctor of Roman and Canon law, practiced before the *audiencia,* and held offices in that and other tribunals. Professor of mathematics at the University of San Marcos for 34 years, he was its rector for 3 years and its historian. He made investigations in botany, chemistry, and medicine, such as they were in those days; and like Sigüenza he determined more accurately the latitude of the capital city, and prepared a series of almanacs. But he was also a prolific man of letters, and a remarkable linguist. He wrote verse with facility in Greek, Latin, French, Portuguese, and Italian, composed neo-classical dramas in imitation of the French theatre (among the earliest on the Spanish stage), and wrote a not unworthy *História de España vindicada.* His most ambitious literary effort was a ponderous epic poem, *Lima Fundada,* in ten cantos and some nine thousand lines, which, although admired by his contemporaries, like most colonial poetry of that time is scarcely readable today.[3]

In view of the vast influence exercised by the Church in both the temporal and the intellectual life of the colonies, it is not surprising that the bulk of the literary output, especially in the two earlier centuries, should have been of a religious or theological nature: missionary

2 For the life and works of Dr. Sigüenza see Irving A. Leonard, *Don Carlos de Sigüenza y Góngora. A Mexican savant of the seventeenth century* (Univ. Calif. Publ. Hist., vol. 18), Berkeley, 1929.

3 Irving A. Leonard, 'A Great Savant of Colonial Peru: Don Pedro de Peralta,' *Philolog. Rev.,* xii, no. 1, 54-72.

chronicles, sermons, works of religious mysticism or asceticism, and the like. But there also appeared a considerable secular literature apart from the works of scholars. The spectacular exploration and conquest of a strange New World called forth a number of vivid and circumstantial historical chronicles, some of which possessed considerable literary merit as well; such as those of Bernal Díaz del Castillo, and Cieza de León, or the *relaciones* of Cortés, Valdivia, and Jiménez de Quesada. Colonial literature, reflecting as a rule the same influences that were operative in the mother country, was essentially imitative, looking for pattern and inspiration in the books that came out of Spain. As in Spain epic verse was widely cultivated, to record the great exploits of the *conquistadores*. The celebrated *La Araucana* of Alonso de Ercilla set the mode, which was followed by a whole school of lesser poets in the sixteenth and seventeenth centuries. A Dominican friar, Diego de Hojeda (1571?-1615) also wrote in a Lima convent the best sacred epic in the Spanish language, *La Cristiada*, which has been likened to *Paradise Lost*. And there was much writing of other verse, most of it in the highly artificial and self-conscious Gongoristic style then fashionable in the peninsula. On every public occasion and important religious festival, the birth of an heir to the throne, or the entry into the capital of a new viceroy, there was a flood of more or less poetic verse, in Latin and in Spanish, or the celebration of a poetical contest.

An exception to the poetasters of the period was Sor Juana Inés de la Cruz, the first and greatest lyric poet of colonial Spanish America, contemporary and friend of Sigüenza y Góngora. Born in New Spain in 1651, learning to read at three and write at five, consumed throughout her lifetime by a boundless intellectual curiosity, craving to attend the university in male attire to learn all that it had to teach, noted alike for her beauty and for her erudition, maid-of-honor to the vicereine but entering a convent at sixteen to be free to pursue her studies, she wrote much poetry and some plays, both sacred and profane, and her fame extented far beyond the borders of Mexico to Spain itself. She died during an epidemic in Mexico City in 1695.

In the eighteenth century the infiuence of French thought and French letters penetrated into the colonies almost as soon as into Spain, and set a new fashion in literary taste. But while French plays,[4] essays, and philosophical writings were read openly or in secret—a knowledge of French and the use of French books became increasingly common among the educated class—literary production in the colonies seems to

---

4 Perhaps the earliest adaptation of one of Corneille's tragedies for the Spanish stage was written and presented in Lima c. 1724, *La Rodoguna*, by Pedro de Peralta Barnuevo. Irving A. Leonard, 'An Early Peruvian Adaptation of Corneille's *Rodogune*,' *Hisp. Rev.*, v, 172-6.

have suffered a decline. The impact of foreign ideas was more discernible in the realms of philosophy and science. The advances in medicine to which reference has already been made, were only one facet of a change in intellectual and scientific outlook generally. A notable scientific revival was beginning in Spain, receiving its inspiration from France, Germany, and England, and through Spanish authors and European travelers its influence soon spread to the colonies. It is said that as early as 1736 Descartes, Leibnitz, and Newton were taught in Quito, chiefly by Jesuits.[5] And even before Newton's death his system had been propounded to the cloister of San Marcos. In the second half of the century the authority of Aristotle, and the pedantries and abstractions of the schoolmen, began to be attacked by bold spirits even in the provincial universities. In the sixteenth and seventeenth centuries Mexico had been the most distinguished of the American centers of learning. San Marcos in Peru by the end of this period had fallen into a notable state of decay. But in the later age of the Enlightenment, the schools and universities of Lima and Chuquisaca set the pace in liberalism in higher education. The Peruvian, José Eusebio Llano Zapata, who had traveled in Europe and America took the lead in scientific innovation. The viceroy Amat (1761-76) insisted that at least one modern philosopher be taught at San Marcos, and urged that students be permitted to accept any system of philosophy that appealed to them. Father Isidoro Celis, who published in Madrid in 1787 a well-known compendium of the mathematics and physics of Sir Isaac Newton, was a lecturer in philosophy at Lima.[6] The Convictorio of San Carlos, established by Amat in 1770 by the amalgamation of three earlier *colegios* and supported by endowments of the exiled Jesuits, was especially distinguished. Under its energetic rector Toribio Rodríguez Mendoza, and with the aid of the educational reformer Mariano Rivero and the humanist Ignacio Moreno, a revised curriculum stressed Cartesianism and the Newtonian system at the expense of the prevailing scholastic routine.

The decline of the schoolmen was also reflected in students' theses which Professor Lanning has collected and studied to such excellent purpose. Although often embedded in scholastic formulae, their propositions reveal a remarkable speculative activity and a constant preoccupation with the philosophies current in contemporary Europe. The crumbling of the medieval scholastic tradition was mirrored in the organization of numerous societies for the promotion of useful knowledge—*Sociedades económicas de amigos del país* as they were generally called. One of the more original creations of the eighteenth-

---

5 John Tate Lanning, *Academic Culture in the Spanish Colonies*, 65, 69.
6 Lanning, op. cit. 69-70.

century Enlightenment in Spain, they spread toward the end of the century to the colonies. They devoted themselves to such subjects as agriculture, popular education, political and social problems, and the development of the physical and natural sciences. In the spreading interest in experimental investigation, science emancipated from theology began to be cultivated in an independent manner.

In New Spain José Antonio Alzate, a contemporary of Benjamin Franklin and sometimes called 'Mexico's first experimental scientist,' shared the same interests in physics and natural history, and published several short-lived journals of preponderantly scientific import. He was familiar with the *Transactions* of the American Philosophical Society in Philadelphia, and translated some of Franklin's scientific papers. Among his Mexican contemporaries, Antonio de León y Gama was a very competent geographer and astronomer, as was Joaquín Velázquez y León who first measured accurately the latitude and longitude of Mexico City. To Mexico also belongs the distinction of producing America's first medical journal, the *Mercurio Volante* in 1772, and the first engineering school in its celebrated School of Mines twenty years later.

Intellectual circles in New Granada were stirred out of a medieval somnolence by the presence there of a distinguished scientist, José Celestino Mutis. A Spanish physician born in Cadiz in 1732, passionately interested in mathematics and the natural sciences, he came out to Bogotá in the train of the viceroy Messia de la Cerda. There he taught mathematics and astronomy in the Colegio del Rosario (1762), introducing his pupils to the Copernican system, an innovation that created a considerable ferment and for which he was roundly denounced by the Dominicans. In New Granada he began the study of botany, corresponded with Linnaeus, and his fame extended to the scientific academies of Europe. In 1783, at the instance of the Spanish government and with a subsidy provided by the viceroy-archbishop, Caballero y Góngora, he undertook a vast botanical project, the so-called *Expedición botánica*. Its purpose was to make a systematic collection of specimens and drawings of all the South American flora north of the Equator, a program which was continued until after his death in Bogotá in 1808, but never completed.[7] He had several distinguished young Creole pupils, notably Francisco Antonio Zea, later director of the Botanical Garden in Madrid, and the better known Francisco José de Caldas. At the instigation of Mutis, there was built in 1802 in the Botanical Garden at Bogotá an astronomical observatory

---

7 The program in its inception included also astronomical and geographical observations, and the preparation of a map based upon them. But this part of the plan was never carried out. Later a zoological section was added, under the direction of Jorge Tadéo Lozano.

of which Caldas for a time was director. It remained in active service throughout the nineteenth century, and still stands in the center of Bogotá as a revered monument of a former day.[8]

Another center of traditional culture in Spanish America, the city of Quito, produced toward the end of the colonial era a brilliant scientific intellect in Francisco Javier Eugenio de Santa Cruz y Espejo (1747-95). Of very humble origin—his father was Indian, his mother mulatto—but of vast talent and enormous industry, he became the most learned man in the colony and wrote abundantly on literary criticism, law, medicine, philosophy, social questions, public hygiene. In *El Nuevo Luciano de Quito* and other writings he mordantly criticized education, government, and society of his day, indulging dangerously in personalities, and creating many enemies. He was the founder of the *Sociedad patriótica de amigos del país*, principal editor of *Las Primicias de la cultura*, Quito's first periodical (1792), and director of Quito's first public library.[9] But he was also a precursor of independence, disseminating ideas of democracy and liberty. For this he was several times imprisoned by the authorities, and died as a result of the physical privations thus endured in 1795.

The ideals of the Enlightenment were transmitted to the Spanish colonies in many ways. Spanish Americans who traveled or studied in Europe, and officials and merchants who came out from Spain, brought with them the progressive ideas current abroad, and often scientific apparatus and books, many of the latter on the prohibited lists. English, French, and Dutch contrabandists who were active on all the American coasts introduced at the same time the revolutionary literature of France.

The enfranchisement of natural science was fostered by numerous expeditions of European savants to Spanish America in the eighteenth century, under official auspices—another testimony to the increasing enlightenment of the Spanish government under the Bourbon monarchy. The Laws of the Indies since the time of Philip II had strictly barred foreigners from the American colonies except by special royal license. But although the law remained unchanged, in practice it was greatly relaxed, and distinguished foreign scientists were sometimes invited to the Indies by the crown—Frenchmen, Italians, Germans—as explorers, naturalists, mining experts. The expedition that was sent to Quito by the Academy of Sciences in Paris in 1735 to

---

8 For Mutis see A. Federico Gredilla, *Biografía de José Celestino Mutis con la relación de su viaje y estudios prácticos en el Nuevo Reino de Granada*, Madrid, 1911; Federico González Suárez, *Memoria histórico sobre Mutis y la expedición botánica de Bogotá en el siglo Décimo octavo* (1782-1808), Quito, 1888.

9 Created out of the libraries of the Jesuits after their expulsion, as was also the first public library in Bogotá.

measure an arc of the meridian at the Equator, and that spent nine years in America, is perhaps the best known. But equally important were German mining experts dispatched by the government to New Spain, Peru, and New Granada in the latter part of the century. Botanical expeditions sponsored by the crown were extraordinarily numerous.[10] Spanish scientists such as Antonio de Ulloa and Félix de Azara left behind important writings of their investigations in the New World. The most distinguished of these visitors was the great German scholar, Baron Alexander von Humboldt, who in the years 1799-1804, in company with the French naturalist, Aimé Bonpland, made a scientific journey through Mexico and northern South America. The results were published in a long series of works under the general title, *Voyage aux régions équinoxiales du nouveau continent,* the most important scientific contribution on Spanish America before the days of independence.

These European visitors exerted a substantial influence upon the intellectual movement in Spanish America itself. Everywhere they were received in the best social circles, everywhere they conversed with the leaders of educated opinion in the colonies, and they helped greatly to spread abroad the intellectual and scientific concepts prevailing in Europe. It is true that the revolution against the tradition of medieval scholasticism was far from complete. Although some of the universities modernized their curricula, theological influence continued to the end to be strongly marked. Most of the clergy were unaffected by the new current of ideas, and disputes between Thomists and Scotists in ecclesiastical circles persisted. Yet it was in an atmosphere of intellectual renovation that the younger generation of revolutionary leaders was

---

10 A Dutch physican and botanist, Nikolaus von Jaequin (1727-1817) made extensive scientific explorations in the West Indies and on the Venezuelan coast in 1755-9. At the same time a young Swedish botanist, Peter Loefling, on a parallel venture sponsored by the Spanish crown, spent two years in Cumaná and Guayana and died at a mission station in that area in 1756. Botanical expeditions under the Spanish naturalists, Hipólito Ruiz, José Pavón, and Joseph Dombey, spent a decade traversing the interior of Peru and Chile (1777-88). The physician, Dr. Martin Sessé, head of an analogous mission dispatched to New Spain in 1787 to study its natural history, established the Botanical Garden in Mexico City in the following year and was its first director. Accompanied by the Mexican naturalist, José Mariano Mociño, he explored parts of California, New Spain, and Guatemala in the years 1791 and 1795-1804. The celebrated politico-scientific expedition which sailed (1789-94) under the leadership of the Italian Alejandro Malaspina, on its way to the Orient made botanical excursions on the coasts of Uruguay, Patagonia, the Falkland Islands, Chile, Peru, and New Spain. It included several European naturalists, among them the Bohemian Thaddeus Haenke, who later settled for sixteen years as a physician in Cochabamba in Upper Peru. The imposing collections and reports emerging from these many expeditions came most of them to repose in the Botanical Garden of Madrid where they remain today. In some cases the botanists themselves succeeded in publishing works generally regarded as among the most important of their time.

trained. Intelligent, thoughtful, avid of ideas, yet remaining within the bounds set by the traditional Church, they were prepared to lead the more or less inert masses to secession. Simón Bolívar received a very irregular and informal education, but by his own testimony he read Locke, Condillac, Buffon, Lalande, d'Alembert, Montesquieu, Voltaire, Rousseau, and Helvetius,[11] besides the classics of antiquity and of Spain, Italy, and France.

The oft-quoted royal decree of 4 April 1531, addressed to the *Casa de Contratación,* strictly prohibited the shipment to the Indies of 'libros de romance, de historias vanas y de profanidad como son el Amadís y otros desta calidad . . . salvo tocante a la religón cristiana é de virtud,' because their reading would be harmful to the Indians. The prohibition was repeated in decrees of 1543 and 1575, and in instructions to the authorities of New Spain and Peru [12]—a clear indication of lax enforcement—and it was incorporated in the *Recopilación* of 1680. It was even retained, curiously enough, in the projected recodification of the Laws of the Indies under Charles IV at the close of the eighteenth century.[13] Yet we know today that it was quite without effect. Works of fiction and whatever else was printed in Spain passed freely to America unless they were on political or religious grounds specifically banned. Spaniards and Creoles in America had access to the same current literature as had their contemporaries in Spain. The officials of the *Casa de Contratación* and the Inquisitors of Seville, charged with the censorship of books shipped to the Indies, both were extremely liberal, and rarely interfered with the shipment of imaginative literature to the colonies. Vigilance by delegates of the Inquisition in American ports seems generally to have been more strict than at Seville. Yet heretical and other forbidden books slipped through *sub rosa,* circulated among the intellectuals, and were found in private libraries, even in those of ecclesiastics.[14] This was to be especially true of the writings of the French and English philosophers of the eighteenth century, and of books and pamphlets relating to the French Revolution and to the independence of the United States.

Books might be printed in Spain only after prior examination and license by the highest judicial tribunal of the district. By a royal decree of September 1556 works relating to America were placed under the

---

11 Of this list, Condillac, Montesquieu, Voltaire, Rousseau, and Helvetius were on the *Index* of prohibited books of 1790.

12 Irving A. Leonard, *Romances of Chivalry in the Spanish Indies,* Berkeley, 1933, 3-6; José Torre Revello, *El libro, la imprenta y el periodismo en America durante la dominación española,* Buenos Aires, 1940, appendix, i-vi, xxiv.

13 Torre Revello, op. cit. 38 n.

14 Many of the best libraries in America belonged to the clergy or to the religious Orders, and if they included prohibited works it was often by special permission of the Inquisition.

exclusive jurisdiction of the Council of the Indies; and four years later it was expressly stated that no such book might be printed or circulated in the colonies without the license of the Council. Even the decisions of diocesan synods might be published only after they had been remitted to the Council for examination and approval.[15] There is plenty of evidence that the rule was frequently ignored both in Spain and in America; nevertheless many authors in America sent their manuscripts to the Council for approval, in spite of the risks of the long sea voyage and of neglect or dishonesty on the part of attorneys in Spain. Frequently the official license carried with it the sole right to print and distribute the book for a term of years.

Religious works formed a large majority of the imports from Spain —theology, liturgy, catechisms, lives of the saints—perhaps from 75 to 80 per cent. But in early American libraries also appeared Greek and Latin classics in the original and in translation, history, jurisprudence, architecture, poetry, and the romances of chivalry so popular in sixteenth-century Spain. Latin and Spanish grammar were sent out in large quantities, especially the grammar of the great Spanish humanist Antonio de Nebrija. The mines and *haciendas* of Peru and New Spain produced ample fortunes and a leisure class that constituted a profitable market for the book business. Many of the clergy also were important customers. And men and women in the colonies had plenty of opportunity to purchase and read the works of Spain's great writers almost as soon as they were published in the peninsula. In the second half of the sixteenth century, consignments of 20, 30, or 40 cases to a single correspondent in America were not uncommon, each case containing form 20 to 100 books. There is record of one book dealer who in January 1601 made a single shipment of 80 cases containing some 10,000 volumes.[16] It is generally believed that most of the first edition of *Don Quijote* found its way to the New World in 1605.[17] A picaresque novel of equal if not greater popularity, *Vida del pícaro Guzmán de Alfarache* by Matéo Alamán, appears to have reached America in even greater numbers. In 1606, 490 copies of *El Pícaro* alone were sent to New Spain.[18]

If in the sixteenth century Spanish taste ran to romances of chivalry and to picaresque and pastoral novels, after 1600 the trend was away

15 Torre Revello, op. cit. 39-44. Books exported to the colonies were exempt from all taxes except the *avería* or convoy tax until 1766, when protectionist duties were imposed at Cadiz and in American ports on books printed abroad. In 1780 an export duty of 3 per cent was levied on Spanish books as well. Ibid. 48-50.

16 Irving A. Leonard, op. cit. 14.

17 Irving A. Leonard, 'Don Quijote and the Book Trade in Lima, 1606,' *Hisp. Rev.*, VIII, 93-112.

18 Irving A. Leonard, ' "Guzmán de Alfarache" in the Lima book trade, 1613,' *Hisp. Rev.*, XI, 210-20.

from the prose novel to the metrical drama, both as read and as enacted. The *comedias* of Lope de Vega and those of his imitators and successors, both Spanish and Creole, found a large and appreciative audience in the colonies. An examination of such ship manifests as survive shows that a flood of dramatic works—those of Tirso de Molina, Calderón, Moreto—poured into the Indies in the seventeenth and eighteenth centuries and far exceeded any other class of secular literature.[19] *Corrales* or *casas de comedias* appeared in Mexico City and Lima almost as soon as in Madrid and Seville, actors from Spain organized a theatrical company in Lima as early as 1599,[20] and the development of the colonial theatre closely paralleled that of the peninsula. The *casa de comedias* was the popular center of amusement, frequented by all classes of colonial society. Convents and universities erected private theatres for special performances, and viceroys offered plays to a select audience of guests in the patio or in the grand salon of the palace. So great was the popular passion for the theatre that the clergy often felt called upon to denounce it from the pulpit, but without real effect. Plays received careful inspection by officers of the Inquisition, and were subject to emendation or expurgation of licentious lines or offensive situations. Although the later years of the seventeenth century saw a notable decline and loss of inspiration in the theatre, in the colonies as in Spain, the popularity of dramatic literature was unabated and continued far into the age of the Bourbons.

A majority of the more important works written in or about the Indies were printed in Spain. A printing press, however, appeared early in the New World, first in Mexico City and later in Lima. It is generally believed that the first press was brought to Mexico through the efforts of Bishop Zumárraga in 1533 or 1534 for the production of religious works, that the printer was a certain Esteban Martín, and that in the following year was issued the first printed book, *Escala espiritual para illegar al cielo,* Spanish translation of a sixth-century Latin book of devotions.[21] But it is significant that no copy of this

---

19 Irving A. Leonard, 'A Shipment of *Comedias* to the Indies,' *Hisp. Rev.*, II, 39-50.

20 Guillermo Lohman Villena, *Historia del arte dramático en Lima durante el virreinato. Vol. I, Siglos XVI y XVII,* Lima, 1941, 51. The first 'theatres' in the colonies had been very primitive, generally an open air stage for the crude representation of *autos sacramentales* on Corpus Christi Day. Lima and Mexico City each possessed two public theatres as early as the first years of the seventeenth century, and possibly earlier. In Lima in 1662 was erected the *Coliseo,* somewhat more substantial than the earlier, ruder structures; and after the great earthquake of 1746 a still more imposing *Coliseo,* the first theatre that really merited the name by modern standards. It was in this *Coliseo* that appeared the famous Creole actress, La Perricholi, mistress of the viceroy Amat, in the 1760's (Ibid. 194-5; Leonard, 'El teatro en Lima, 1790-1793,' *Hisp. Rev.,* VIII, 96-97). The first theatre in Bogotá, also called the *Coliseo,* was not erected till 1793, on the site of the present Teatro de Colón.

21 The first book printed in the English colonies, the Bay Psalm Book, was produced in Cambridge, Massachusetts, in 1640.

book has been found, or of any other product of this press before 1539
It was in the latter year that a public press was established with official
sanction, and that a book appeared of which at least one copy survives.
In June 1539 Juan Cromberger, German master printer of Seville, concluded a contract with an Italian, Juan Pablos of Brescia, to set up a
branch establishment in Mexico City. Before the end of the year the
latter had reached Mexico and published his first book, a small catechism in gothic type, *Breve . . . doctrina christiana en lengua mexicana y castellana.* At the same time Cromberger obtained a monopoly
for ten years of both the printing and the importing of books in New
Spain.[22] The monopoly was retained till 1559 by Juan Pablos who in
the meantime had purchased the press from Cromberger's heirs. During this period he had published at least 34 works, including 13 catechisms, 4 philosophical or theological books by the eminent Augustinian friar, Alonso de la Veracruz, several religious works by the
learned and devout Franciscan of Michoacán, Matarino Gilberti, 3
vocabularies of Indian languages, and at least one collection of laws
and one book of commercial lore. Between 1539 and 1600, 174 works
are known to have been printed in the capital of New Spain, besides
some 58 of doubtful authenticity.[23]

Most of the books printed in Spanish America in the sixteenth century were either of a religious nature, especially books of Christian
instruction for the natives, or were grammars and vocabularies of native languages. But this perhaps was only to be expected, for in those
formative years the demand was greatest from the clergy and from
the missionaries engaged in the gigantic task of Christianizing and
civilizing the Indians. In the following century, with the emergence
of a stabilized and cultivated colonial society, production was more
varied, and included many works on geography and history, law, mathematics, and medicine.

The first book printed in Peru appeared nearly fifty years after the
inauguration of the press in New Spain, a catechism for the instruction of the Indians in Quechua and Aymara. Antonio Ricardo of
Turin, who had been a printer in Mexico since 1577, three years later
left for Lima, and in 1584 obtained royal permission and the sole right
to establish a press there. But the press in Lima was never so active
as that of Mexico, and typographically its productions were generally
inferior. The extension of the press to other parts of Spanish America
was very slow, and was largely the work of the Jesuit Order. One was

---

22 Torre Revello, op. cit. 99-100.

23 Ibid. 138-43; José Toribio Medina, *La Imprenta en Mexico,* 1539-1821 (8 vols.,
Santiago, 1907-11), I xlvii-lxxv; Emilio Valton, *Impresores mexicanos del siglo* XVI,
Mexico, 1935, 6-18, 37-62; Juan B. Iguíniz, *La Imprenta en la Nueva España,* Mexico,
1938, 7-13.

set up in Puebla de los Angeles in New Spain in 1640, and another began to function regularly in Guatemala after 1660, through the efforts of the bishop, Enríquez de Rivera. All other presses date from the eighteenth century.[24] Between 1700 and 1747 books and tracts were printed in the Paraguayan mission stations, with press, type, and ink manufactured by the Indians, and illustrations made with woodcut blocks—an 'all American' production except for the paper, which was imported. Nearly all the items were in Guaraní.

The first extant newssheet printed in Spanish America came off the Lima press in 1594. It describes the capture of the English privateer Richard Hawkins. Although not a regular periodical, such sheets usually retailing news of events in Europe or of extraordinary occurrences at home, appeared with fair regularity about once a month until 1720, when there is a gap of a quarter century till 1744. They were generally a single-fold sheet of four pages, crudely printed. In Mexico it was only from 1620 that such occasional newssheets were issued.

The first periodical in the colonies appeared in Mexico City on 1 January 1722, the semiofficial *Graceta de México, y noticias de Nueva España*.[25] It was a monthly of eight pages, and ran through six issues. A second *Gazeta de México* was more successful, lasting from 1728 to 1742.[26] In the second half of the century appeared a number of short-lived periodicals, beginning with the *Diario literario de México* published by the Mexican scientist, Antonio de Alzate, which ran through eight months and in 1768 was suppressed by the government. Mexico was remarkable for a number of scientific periodicals at this time, notably the *Mercurio volante* edited by the physician, José Ignacio Bartolache, from October 1772 to February 1773; two equally short-lived scientific journals initiated by Alzate in 1772 and 1787; and a third by Alzate, the important *Gazeta de literatura de México*, a monthly of from 6 to 18 pages which lasted from 1788 to 1794.

The second city in Spanish America to earn the distinction of pro-

---

24 Torre Revello, op. cit. 148-50, and authorities cited there. According to evidence so far available, a printing press appeared in the principal cities of Spanish America in the following order, although in some cases the press functioned for only a few years and only one or two items are known:

Havana, 1707 or 1724	Cartagena, 1769-76
Oaxaca, 1720	Santiago (Chile), 1776?
Bogotá, 1738-42, 1777	Buenos Aires, 1780
Ambato, 1754	Santo Domingo, 1782?
Quito, 1760	Guadalajara, 1793
Valencia (Venez), 1764	Vera Cruz, 1794
Córdoba (Arg.), 1766-7	Santiago (Cuba), 1796

25 Preceded in the English colonies by the *Boston News Letter*, 1704.
26 A third gazette with the same name began in 1784 and lasted until 1810.

ducing a periodical was Guatemala. In November 1729 was published the *Gazeta de Goathemala,* which continued for about two years. It was revived in 1794, when as a weekly it succeeded in carrying on for 22 years. Lima came third, with a *Gazeta* in 1743. A bi-monthly of 16 pages, it survived until the middle of 1767.[27] But to Lima also belongs the credit of producing the first daily newspaper in America, the *Diario de Lima, curioso, erudito, económico y comercial,* four quarto pages which appeared for exactly three years, from October 1790 to September 1793, when it closed for lack of a sufficient number of subscribers.[28] And in January 1791 appeared the more celebrated *Mercurio peruano.* Published by the *Sociedad de amantes del país,* which represented most of the intellectual and literary talent of the viceregal capital, it exerted a profound influence upon the cultural and political development of Peruvian society. Appearing every three days, half newspaper and half review, it yet was chiefly a literary, scientific, and historical journal, including the ablest minds of the Creole community among its contributors, reflecting the intellectual curiosity of the time, the mouthpiece of a nascent Peruvian nationality. It survived till 1795.[29]

The first periodical in Havana appeared in 1764, in Bogotá in 1785, in other cities not until the eve of independence. Most of them were of brief duration. The most distinguished among the many Cuban publications was perhaps the *Regañón de la Habana* (1800-02), a journal of literary criticism that Medina regarded as the best periodical published in the colonial era. In Bogotá one of the most important was the *Semanario del nuevo reyno de Granada,* edited by the distinguished scientist, Francisco José de Caldas between 1808 and 1811, a journal remarkable for the number and high quality of its scientific contributors.[30]

Except for the *Diario de Lima,* daily newspapers date from the first decade of the nineteenth century. The earliest was the *Diario de México,* which began on 1 October 1805, continued for twelve years, and played an important role in both the stimulation of Mexican letters and in the crystallization of the political conscience of the Creoles.

---

27 It was revived in 1793-5, and again in 1798-1804.

28 The founder and first director was a young Spaniard, Jaime Bausate y Mesa, 25 years of age, who had arrived only a few months earlier from Europe.

29 Curiously enough, in the same year 1791, appeared in Lima a weekly of quite a different stamp, *El Seminario crítico,* published by a young Franciscan just arrived from Spain, Juan Antonio Olavarrieta. Patronizing, jejune, representing the ultra-conservative, pro-Spanish party, it was soon at open war with the *Mercurio* and lasted three and a half months. Ella Dunbar Temple, 'Periodismo peruano del siglo XVIII. El Semanario crítico,' *Mercurio peruano,* xxv, no. 198.

30 For the best general survey of colonial periodicals see Torre Revello, op. cit. 160-205.

These colonial periodicals and early newspapers were usually more important for their articles of general interest than as purveyors of current news. They carried reports of government activities, and such foreign news (generally months in arrears) as was available to them. But they also printed numerous essays on literature, geography, history, agriculture, trade, public improvements, and similiar topics, contributed by the ablest men of their generation. That most of them survived but a short time, a few months or years, is not surprising, for the colonial reading public was very small and in some instances strangely indifferent or hostile to these manifestations of cultural progress. Paper, which was generally imported, was often scarce whether for books or for periodicals, and in any case its cost was very high. And there was always the official censorship, sometimes dilatory or merely stupid, and the misgivings of the Church and the Inquisition. In 1805 reading of the *Diario de México* by the nuns was forbidden by the archbishop.

When Peter of Ghent established in Mexico his famous school for Indian boys in the 1530's, he included instruction in music and drawing. This has sometimes been referred to as the first art school in America. One would not expect, however, the appearance of a significant artistic culture in the first few generations of the colonial era. Times were precarious, the savage frontier was immediately present or just over the horizon, and for most of the settlers material considerations of daily living were uppermost. Churches and public buildings were simple and utilitarian, severe in outline and decoration, sometimes almost fortress-like. In some instances we find plateresque decorative details concentrated about portals and windows. What works of art appeared, images or paintings, were mostly imported from Spain. Only in the second half of the sixteenth century did a few artists come over from the mother country. Such little local art as there was, was mediocre, limited in range and outlook, but no less interesting and important as a reflection of the preoccupations and sensibilities of the society which produced it. Much of it was the work of artisans, ofttimes Indian, rather than of artists. Aesthetic considerations may not have been absent, but originality and technical skills—knowledge of composition, drawing, anatomy—were generally lacking. The principal if not the sole clients of artistic endeavor were the churches and monasteries. And in any case religion alone furnished the motive and inspiration of painters and sculptors, religion which was 'the center of all activities and the immediate determinant of every opinion,' and which penetrated every nook and cranny of colonial life and sentiment.

In the seventeenth century the number of painters in the colonies, Spanish and Creole with a sprinkling of artists of Indian extraction, was considerable. And canvases by Murillo, Zurbarán, and other distinguished contemporaries, or copies of the originals, were imported from Spain to decorate the churches of the wealthier cities. Artists came from the peninsula attracted by the propitious environment of luxury and wealth in the American communities, bringing to colonial painters a technical equipment hitherto lacking, and initiating a colonial art which reached its highest expression in the Schools of Cuzco and Quito. Occasionally an isolated artist, virtually self-taught, struggling against a hostile or unsympathetic milieu, achieved genuine distinction. Such was the prolific Gregorio Vásquez de Arce y Ceballos (1638-1711) in Bogotá. In New Spain Baltásar de Echave the elder (fl. 1590-1630) from Guipuzcoa, and the Sevillian Sebastián de Arteaga (1610-?), were the foremost in a considerable group of artists from the Old World, some of whom painted colonial portraits as well as religious themes. In general, however, colonial painting was a faithful imitation of Spanish masters.

In architecture the fortress-like buildings of early times were succeeded by churches and monasteries in the severely classical style associated in Spain with Juan de Herrera, architect of the Escorial—edifices much enlarged in form and size, better proportioned with predominantly rectilinear lines. The cathedral at Puebla de los Angeles in New Spain, finished in 1649, is the finest example. But the Herrerian influence was soon supplanted by the highly ornamented Spanish American baroque, which prevailed throughout the seventeenth century, and which in the eighteenth developed into the exuberant and sometimes tortured, but often charming, churrigueresque. Sculptured ornament often revealed the hand of the Indian worker, both in form and in execution, especially in Cuzco, Potosí, and other interior cities of the Andes; and here and there a sculptor of religious images in wood achieved real distinction. Altars, pulpits, and choir stalls, and in private houses carved beams and latticed balconies, tables, chairs, and marquetry chests, attested the skill and beauty of colonial woodwork.

As in Spain, painting in the Spanish colonies attained its apogee in the seventeenth century. The following century was very prolific in the number and size of paintings executed, but they were generally of inferior merit. The age of the Bourbons produced little of distinction in the fine arts except in the realm of architecture. The baroque of Mexico represents perhaps the finest achievement in the history of the arts in the American colonies. It surpassed that of all other regions in the number of examples and in the variety and excellence of design. But toward the close of the century there was a movement in Spain to put an end to baroque extravagance and complexity of form, and return to the more sober classical tradition. This was promptly reflected in the New World. Two architects in Mexico, one a Creole, the other a native of Spain—Francisco Eduardo Tresguerras (1745-1833) and Manuel Tolsá (1767-1825)—toward the end of the colonial era was outstanding. Tresguerras is remembered especially for his superb church of the Carmelites in Celaya, Tolsá for the exterior of the cathedral in Mexico City and for the School of Mines.

Mexico City enjoyed the distinction of having the first school of fine arts in the New World. An academy of painting is supposed to have been projected there as far back as 1753, but it never materialized.[31] The later Academy of San Carlos may be said to have had its first modest beginnings in a school for engravers inaugurated in the Mint in May 1779 under the direction of Jerónimo Antonio Gil. The superintendent of the Mint, Fernando José Mangino, then proposed to the viceroy Mayorga the foundation of an academy 'of the three noble arts.' Classes began before the end of 1781 in the Mint under Gil as director general. The *Cabildo* agreed to contribute annually 1,000 pesos for its support, the *Consulado* 3,000, the *Cuerpo de minería* 5,000; and several thousand more were obtained from provincial cities and by private gift. In December 1783 it was received under royal patronage as the *Academia de las nobles artes de San Carlos de la Nueva España* affiliated with the Academy of San Fernando in Madrid, and as such it was formally inaugurated two years later. The crown endowed it with an additional subsidy of 13,000 pesos, 9,000 from the exchequer and 4,000 from the temporalities of the Jesuits.[32] Chairs of architecture, sculpture, painting, and engraving were filled by men selected in Spain; and in 1791 classes were transferred from the Mint to the building formerly occupied by the *Hospital del amor de Dios,* still so used today. In the same year arrived the architect Manuel Tolsá and the painter Rafael Jimeno as head of their respective departments. Tolsá brought with him the famous collection of plaster casts of classical statuary, books, and prints costing 40,000 pesos, the gift of the king. By statute sixteen scholarships were established in the Academy, of which four were reserved to Indians; and in 1792 or 1793 about a half dozen scholarships were created for study in Madrid, which still existed in 1807.[33] The Academy decayed after the beginning of the struggle for independence, and for several years was closed altogether; but it survives today in the Faculty of Fine Arts of the National University of Mexico.

---

31 Luis González Obregón, *México viejo*, 1521-1821, Paris, 1900, 519.

32 The second Revillagigedo reported that it had an income of 26,580 pesos. *Instrucción,* par. 342-5. ?

33 González Obregón, op. cit. 517-23; Diego Angulo Iñiguez, 'La academia de bellas artes de Méjico y sus pinturas españolas,' *Arte en America y Filipinas,* cuaderno I, Sevilla, 1935, 50-51.

XIII

❧§❧

Agriculture and Industry

❧§❧

Colonists from the time of Columbus carried out to the New World the plants and domestic animals of Spain. Of useful domestic animals the Indians had almost none, and those introduced from Europe— horses, cattle, sheep, swine, and goats—were extraordinarily prolific in America. Within a generation or two cattle were running wild over the grassy plains of the Rio de la Plata and the Orinoco, and on the savannahs of the West Indian islands. But Isabella and her immediate successors were also greatly interested in the agricultural development of the new lands. Repeated attempts were made to acclimatize wheat in the West Indies. In 1512 the *Casa de Contratación* was ordered to send rice to Hispaniola for planting, accompained by elaborate instructions for its cultivation. In the following year Ferdinand instructed Pedrarias Dávila to recruit farmers for his colony on the Isthmus of Darién who would try and raise wheat, barley, and other grains, and to offer rewards for anyone who succeeded.[1] A decade later his grandson Charles V wrote to Cortés in New Spain promising to send him trees, plants, and seeds, and issued such orders to the *Casa de Contratación*. The early records of the *Casa* are full of references to the shipping of supplies of this nature, as well as of farming implements. Not only cereals, vegetables, garden herbs, and fruits of the temperate zone, but the orange, olive, sugar cane, and other subtropical plants were thus for the first time introduced into America, and added vastly to the agricultural possibilities of the young colonies.

Las Casas tells us that sugar cane was carried to the West Indies by Columbus from the Canary Islands on his second voyage. The first plantings on Hispaniola apparently were not successful, and it was only in or about 1515 that Fernández de Oviedo took the first samples of American sugar to Spain. Herrera says that the Hieronymite governors lent 500 pesos de oro for every sugar mill set up on the island. Soon Canary Islanders were sent out to construct sugar mills, the materials needed were excused from custom duties, and Negroes were in-

---

1 Success was not achieved until the Spaniards reached the highlands of New Spain and Peru. In each case, we are told, the first wheat was grown from grains found in shipments of rice.

troduced in increasing numbers to work the plantations. Sugar before long was being exported commercially to Europe, and it became ultimately the principal economic mainstay of the island.[2]

From Hispaniola cane cultivation was carried to Cuba and Puerto Rico, and ultimately to New Spain and Peru. In 1523 the king ordered the *Casa de Contratración* to lend 4,000 pesos de oro to responsible settlers in Cuba to help finance the building of sugar mills. In later years the crown made similar advances to the Cuban planters, but a century elapsed before the industry assumed any importance. The production of sugar on the Peruvian coast, especially in the district of Trujillo, also goes as far back as the sixteenth century, although it was not until recent times that sugar has become an important article of export. The enormous quantities of sweetmeats and conserves consumed by the colonial population, and the production of rum, more than accounted for the local supply. As for New Spain, López de Gómara wrote in the middle of the sixteenth century that it was already growing so much cane that sugar was shipped from Vera Cruz and Acapulco to Spain and Peru. Humboldt reports that at the end of the eighteenth century New Spain was producing nearly 25,000 tons of sugar, and exporting two-thirds of it.

Colonial Peru produced little agricultural surplus except wine and olives. Both Chile and Peru produced excellent wines, at half the price of those imported from Spain. Although the wine industry was one of the most important of the mother country, the *Casa de Contratación* had in 1519 been instructed to send with every ship sailing to the islands a number of vines to be planted there. And in 1531 a special effort was made to send seeds and shoots of the vine and the olive to New Spain. The experiments there were not a success,[3] but in Peru with the establishment of peace and order after the long civil wars, grapes began to be cultivated intensively, and for many years without official interference. The first crop, we are told, was picked in 1551. Toward the close of Philip's reign Spain became more concerned over competition with the home product, and various proposals were put forward for the restriction or elimination of the Peruvian vineyards. In the seventeenth century further plantings were forbidden, and the export of wine to Central America, New Spain, or any other region that could easily be supplied from Europe, was strictly prohibited. Enforcement, however, was spasmodic, and clandestine exports were common. At the close of the eighteenth century the wine industry still flourished in colonial areas such as Chile and Mendoza whose

---

2 Manuel de la Puente y Olea, *Los trabajos geográficos de la Casa de Contratación,* Sevilla, 1900, 400-410.

3 New Spain produced grapes, but never succeeded in creating a wine industry.

climate and soil were propitious, despite the subborn policy of the Cadiz monopoly, and finally even the pretense of enforcement was given up.

The history of olive culture runs parallel with that of the grape. Olive shoots sent out early to the Antilles and New Spain did not flourish, but introduced about 1560 into the irrigated coastal valleys of Peru, especially near Lima, they rapidly became the progenitors of extensive groves. In this dry coastal area, entirely devoid of forests, olive wood was also in demand for construction and fuel. In the beginning it was more profitable to pickle the olives for sale in Peru and abroad, and only in the seventeenth century did the production of oil begin. Later the planting of new olive groves and the export of oil were also forbidden, without notable success, until in late Bourbon times the industry was allowed to expand with the knowledge and even the encouragement of the viceregal government.

Silk raising became one of the principal occupations of New Spain in the sixteenth century. As early as 1503 Governor Ovando had been instructed to promote the growing of mulberry trees so that a silk culture might be developed on Hispaniola. But it was on the continent that the industry took root. From small beginnings around 1530, fostered especially by the Dominican friars, silk cultivation spread with great rapidity throughout central and southern New Spain, with its center in the Mixtecan region of Oaxaca. In 1537 Martin Cortés, son of Hernando, entered into an agreement with the viceroy in return for certain privileges to plant within fifteen years 100,000 mulberry trees for the production of silk, and soon a speculative boom ensued. *Encomenderos,* small farmers, native chiefs, and Indian communities rushed into silk raising. Motolinía reports that in 1541 the crop in New Spain amounted to over 15,000 pounds, said to surpass in quality that of Granada, and numerous establishments sprang up in the principal cities for the manufacture of taffetas and velvets. Henry Hawkes, an Englishman who lived several years in New Spain, reported that the country manufactured silks of all sorts—satins velvets, taffetas—as good in quality as those imported except that the colors were less perfect. But this prosperity was short-lived. The boom in the marginal areas subsided, and after 1580 silk production suffered a general decline, until by the middle of the following century it remained only a petty industry among the Indians. A major cause was the importation of cheaper Chinese silk by way of the Philippine Islands, but other reasons are found in the competition of more profitable forms of agriculture in the warmer regions of the south, and possibly in a decline in numbers of the Indian laboring population. After 1596 silk raising in the colonies was officially discouraged, as interfering with textile imports from Spain, but the industry was already decaying. Attempts of the later Bourbons to revive it had no success.[4]

So far mention has been made only of plants imported into the New World from Europe. America's contribution of plants to the colonial economy of the Spaniards and to the world at large, was also a notable one. Virtually all of them came from what is now 'Latin' America: the potato, tomato, maize, yam, peanut; tobacco, coca, cinchona, sarsaparilla; pineapple, guava, cacao; rubber, dyewoods, and many vegetable fibers. Some of these plants were cultivated for the first time by Spaniards on a capitalistic, plantation basis, notably tobacco and cacao. As we all know, Columbus saw Indians smoking tobacco when he first touched on the islands, and Spaniards later found the same practice prevailing in Yucatan and New Spain, although not in South America. The first propagandist of its virtues in Europe was the physician Nicolás Monrades who recommended it for his medicinal properties, but it was not smoked there until the seventeenth century. Cacao was in common use as a beverage among the Mexican Indians, and also as a medium of exchange. Dissolved in water and flavored with sugar and spices after the Indian fashion it became chocolate, one of the most prized foods of the Spanish colonists. Cacao was not imported into Spain, however, until about 1580. It appeared in Italy twenty-five years later, and its use in other European countries spread slowly during the course of the following century.

The crown in its colonial legislation paid no less attention to stock raising than to agriculture. From the time of the first settlements it ordained that there be woods and grasslands for the common use of all the colonists, so that they might freely pasture their cattle; and this rule was applied even to land use on the great estates conceded to the leaders of the *conquistadores*. Legislation also attempted to regulate the size of the lands distributed to grazers, and provided for careful separation of private grazing lands (*hatos*) from the lands of their agricultural neighbors. The unit was by law an area one league in diameter, which was to accommodate no less than 2,000 head of cattle and have on it at least one building of stone. For 6,000 head or more, two units were to be assigned, and for 10,000 head three units. Any concession of more than three units must be by special royal license.[5]

---

4 Woodrow Borah, *Silk Raising in Colonial Mexico* (Ibero-Americana no. 20), Berkeley, Cal., 1943.

A royal decree of 1545 directed colonial governors to encourage the natives to raise hemp and flax. Later their cultivation in certain areas was forbidden. Again under the later Bourbons efforts were made to revive cultivation, in order to supply the textile industry of Spain and provide sailcloth and rigging for the navy.

5 José María Ots Capdequi, *Manual de historia del derecho español en las Indias y del derecho propiamente indiano*, 2 vols., Buenos Aires, 1943, II, 48-50; *Recopilación*, lib. IV, tit. 17, leyes 5, 6, 7, 11, 14.

The sheep raisers guild, or *Real corporación de la mesta*, which played so important a role in the history of medieval Spain, and with such unfortunate effects there upon the development of agriculture, was also introduced into the colonies. Its beginnings on the continent of America may be found in resolutions taken by the *cabildo* of Mexico City in June 1529 requiring every grazer to have a private brand or mark for his cattle registered with the *cabildo*.[6] A set of 17 ordinances issued by the municipality 8 years later and confirmed by the crown in 1542, gave the institution a more formal and legal existence. Every stock raiser possessing 300 or more sheep, swine, or goats, or 20 or more head of cattle, was required to join. A much more elaborate group of ordinances was issued in 1574, regulations which came to be applied in other parts of the Indies and were incorporated in part in the *Recopilación* of 1680. The guild was now much more plutocratic in membership. It was confined to those possessing *haciendas* with at least 1,000 head of cattle or 3,000 sheep.[7] The *mesta*, however, never seems to have acquired in America the economic and political importance it enjoyed in Spain, and conflicts between grazing and agricultural interests were less frequent or serious; perhaps because of the greater extent of available lands in proportion to the population, the existence of vast *haciendas*, and the circumstance that it was generally less necessary to move the stock over long distances from one season to another. The chief sufferers were probably the lands belonging to the Indians.

From the above it is abundantly clear that the commodities supplied by the colonies to Spain were by no means confined, as is the popular impression, to gold and silver, pearls and emeralds. After the middle of the sixteenth century agricultural and forest products held an increasingly important place in the trans-Atlantic trade: sugar, cotton, hides, dyewoods, sarsaparilla, and cochineal. With the expansion of colonial agriculture in the seventeenth and eighteenth centuries, also indigo, tobacco, cacao, as well as vanilla, cinchona, and cabinet woods. Tropical America for the first time was furnishing opportunity for the large-scale production of 'colonial staples,' whether indigenous or acquired from the Old World, which were increasingly demanded by an expanding economy in Europe. The inauguration of a freer commerce by the Bourbon kings had a happy effect upon the prosperity of both agriculture and stock raising, and by the close of the eighteenth century the annual value of the agricultural produce in New Spain was greater than that of the precious metals.

---

6 José Miranda, 'Notas sobre la introducción de la Mesta en la Nueva España,' *Rev. Hist. Amer.*, no. 17, 14-15.

7 Ibid. 23-6.

As stated in an earlier chapter, the ultimate proprietorship of all lands in the Indies was held to belong, in theory and by right of conquest, to the Castilian crown. Only by royal grace or concession might title be acquired by private individuals. Thus permission was granted to the leader of every early pioneering expedition to distribute lands of specified extent to himself and to his followers. And in the beginning the municipal *cabildos* were given, or they assumed, the right to assign lands and town lots to members of the community. Later similar authority was extended to viceroys and governors, in municipal areas by agreement with the *cabildos*. It early became the rule, recognized in the *Recopilación*, that settlers receiving lands must ordinarily take effective possession, i.e., construct a house and begin cultivation, within three months, and maintain continuous occupancy for a specified number of years, generally from four to eight.

The concept of private ownership of land in the Spanish or European sense probably did not exist among most of the Indians whom the Spaniards conquered. But however this may be, and although the crown repeatedly ordered that the allotment of lands to the *conquistadores* and later settlers should not impair those possessed by the natives, the early colonists distributed lands among themselves in utter disregard of any claims or needs of the Indians about them. And in later times, when the Indians' proprietorship over their lands was clearly established and protected by law, there is plenty of evidence that ways could always be found, by pressure or deceit of one kind or another, to deprive the natives of their rights. The consequence was unending complaints, petitions, lawsuits by Indian communities against their Spanish neighbors, sometimes continuing generation after generation.

From the time of Philip II, with the increase of population in the colonies, rising land values, and the mounting necessities of the crown, public lands were more generally put up for sale by the royal exchequer. It is also clear that squatting on public lands, ill-defined property lines, and encroachment upon neighboring areas were extremely common, as is not surprising in a large and sparsely settled continent. Before the end of Philip's reign it was enacted that occupiers without title or with defective title, if of ten years' standing or more, must clear by means of a money composition, based upon area and value, paid to the crown; otherwise the property reverted to the State to be sold to the highest bidder. Although it seems that a general review of land titles was occasionally undertaken, confusion and irregularities evidently continued. By a decree of November 1735 viceroys and governors were deprived of the right to dispose of vacant lands. Twenty years later, however, in October 1754, the *audiencias* were authorized to concede lands and to decide all questions relating to their ownership. Lands occupied since before 1700 were to be considered as held by prescription, but on condition that they were cultivated; title to all royal lands acquired since then must be cleared and confirmed by the designated authorities in the Indies, but again on condition of effective use.[8] The extensive instructions issued at that time prevailed to the end of the colonial era.

Of the various moral and material factors that contributed to create and maintain an aristocracy in the Spanish American colonies—differences of race, economic legislation, religion, land tenure—the last was probably the most important, and was the nucleus of most fortunes, land whose value was created by those who did not own it, by Indians and Negroes. Land was the principal source of riches and prestige in a society which disdained trade and industrial pursuits, and the successful miner invested his income in farms and haciendas. Landed property was also an indispensable requisite for the exercise of the few political rights which the colonists enjoyed. A minority of fortunate landowning Creoles lived much like their Spanish ancestors, imbued with similar aristocratic prejudices, and with similar improvidence and lack of foresight.

From the beginning the Spanish crown permitted, if it did not encourage, the large estate as the prevailing form of land tenure in the colonies. The manorial concept of landholding—large areas cultivated by an ignorant, depressed peasantry, typical of Spain as of other European countries in the sixteenth century—was transferred to America intact. And it was perpetuated by the legal device of entailing estates, i.e., preventing the disintegration of landed properties by limiting succession to the eldest son or nearest kinsman under the rule of primogeniture as an inalienable inheritance.

The system was in some respects inimical to colonial progress. For, as remarked in an earlier chapter, in a relatively unoccupied pioneer country where lands are to be reduced to cultivation, it is usually the promise of private ownership which promotes immigration and assures the most profitable use of the soil. A country of vast estates could offer few inducements to attract farmers from Europe. Prospective colonists generally want to become proprietors. It is the proprietary instinct, the desire to possess land, which has instigated most men to settle in new and undeveloped countries. What was more, agricultural labor on the large estates remained the labor of the Negro and the Indian, had a servile quality with which the small free farmer did not care to be identified. And lastly, if estates were very extensive, the proprietor could obtain ample returns from the careful tillage of a relatively small part of the land, or from the primitive cultivation of larger areas. There was little incentive to till all the land, or to

8 Manuel Fabila, ed., *Cinco siglos de legislación agraria en Mexico* (1493-1940), vol. I, Mexico, 1940, 34-8.

till it all in an effective manner. Improvements in agriculture were slow and much of the land remained untouched, land that in many instances might have been cultivated by the small independent farmer had it been available.

It is true that the presence of the Indians, and the opportunity afforded to exploit their labor, probably served to encourage the creation of *latifundia*. And in the hot tropics, where was evolved the large-scale production of such staples as sugar and tobacco, concentration of ownership, and an abundant supply of cheap (in this case generally Negro) labor such as European immigration in those days could scarcely provide, seemed a natural and inevitable development. Nevertheless in the areas where climatic conditions were attractive to the European, it is probable that the monopoy of land in large estates discouraged immigration and retarded the progress of the colonies in wealth and population.

Such were the conditions in most parts of Spanish America, and in many of the republics after independence. Land belonged mostly to wealthy families or to ecclesiastical corporations, was tilled by servile or semiservile labor, and by primitiive methods. Consequently both agriculture and population suffered. It is true that in royal legislation there were always stressed, or implied, the social objectives of a land policy: effective use, increase of wealth and of population, and protection of the defenseless Indians. Nevertheless usurpation of Indian lands was not uncommon, *latifundia* only partially cultivated became a characteristic feature of rural economy, and defective titles and uncertain boundaries of rural properties were an inheritance of nearly every Spanish American republic in the nineteenth century.[9]

Agriculture or mining, or both, were the basic industries of all the Spanish colonies in America, as they have continued to be in the Spanish republics since. Manufacturing industries had no extensive development in the colonies, in part because the Spanish government after the period of the conquest was inclined to discourage or forbid industries which competed with the manufacturers and trade of the mother country; but more fundamentally perhaps because, as today, natural conditions were conducive to the production and export of raw materials to the exclusion of most everything else. Colonial industries could hardly have competed, in many lines, with those of Europe.

Interference by the metropolis with colonial industry, however, was never very systematic. The objects of the crown were clearly to reserve the profits of American commerce to its Spanish subjects, and above all to prevent the leakage of American gold and silver into for-

---

9 León Pinelo, *Tratado de confirmaciones reales*, pt. ii, cap. 2, 23; *Recopilación*, lib. iv, tit. 12; Ots Capdequi, op. cit. ii, 12-41.

eign countries. Spain consistently maintained its privilege of alone supplying the colonies with European commodities, but it did not uniformly require the colonists to take these commodities in preference to products of their own manufacture. Occasionally attempts were made to suppress a colonial industry, either in the interests of peninsular trade or to protect native labor from exploitation, but it was rarely possible to enforce the decrees in their entirety. Under the more generous rule of the Emperor, the colonists were encouraged to raise silk, hemp, and flax, and the manufacture of wine and textiles was permitted wherever circumstances warranted. From the time of his son, Philip II, the tendency to paternalistic interference and control was much more apparent. In later Bourbon times controls were relaxed. But even among the more enlightened ministers of the Bourbon regime thought was divided regarding manufactures in the Indies, whether to discourage competing industries, or to promote every form of economic activity in order to increase population, income and the demand for Spanish goods.

The manufacturing industry more widely developed than any other in the colonies was that of textiles. Something has already been said about the early growth of silk manufactures in New Spain. Woolen and cotton cloths were also produced, and factories (*obrajes*) soon appeared both in the Indian pueblos and in the Spanish cities. Only the upper classes wore the finer fabrics imported from Spain; the common people—Indians, mestizos, mulattoes—were clothed in the coarser domestic materials. Woolens were the more common in the highlands of New Spain and Peru, and of wool there was an abundant supply from the merino sheep extensively raised throughout the colonies. The colonial cloth industry was officially recognized in early royal decrees, and *obrajes* were found everywhere from Guadalajara in the north to Tucumán in the south. The exploitation of Indian labor in the *obrajes* was notorious, both by the native *cacique* and by the Spanish entrepreneur, and from the time of Francisco de Toledo in Peru and Martín Enríquez in New Spain efforts were made to regulate the conditions of work and spare the natives, even to the extent of trying to prohibit Indian labor altogether.[10] Instructions were issued in 1609 and later years limiting the number of *obrajes,* and forbidding the opening of new ones or the enlarging of those already existing without permission from the crown. But the viceroys hesitated to interfere in so important and well entrenched an industry. And while textile manufactures were palpably decaying in Spain, the number of establishments

10 See *ante,* p. 66 and **n.**

in the colonies continued to keep pace with the growth of population.[11]

In mines lay the origin of many great private fortunes in America, and the principal source of the revenues derived by the crown from the Indies. Their number and productiveness steadily increased with the expansion of the frontier into the mountain areas and with improvements in methods of exploitation. Prosperity of the miners was in turn reflected in the activity of other industries. With the increase of money in circulation came an enlarged demand for goods, a rise of land values in a society in which land was the only form of investment, and a spur to the construction of churches, hospitals, and other buildings both public and private.

The earliest remittances of treasure to Spain consisted almost exclusively of objects of gold. Silver found among the Indians on the continent was generally of low grade mixed with copper. But sources of gold were soon discovered to be relatively few, the store found among the Indians being due to slow accumulations over the years, while silver mines soon proved to be plentiful. The first silver mines were discovered by Spaniards in New Spain in 1531 or 1532, in the general area of Michoacán west of Mexico City; [12] and toward the end of the latter year the *audiencia* issued the first mining ordinances in the history of America, although no known copy is extant.[13] About four years later, it seems, some Germans arrived skilled in mining technique and bringing with them apparatus for smelting silver ores. It was only then that the shipment of mined silver to Spain began to assume importance. In 1548 were discovered the great mines of Zacatecas, destined with those of Guanajauto to be the richest in New Spain, and in 1552 the famous Real del Monte mines at Pachuca. By the middle of the century the industry had reached such proportions that the viceroy Mendoza in January 1550 issued a comprehensive mining code that was to remain in force in New Spain for several decades in spite of regulations issued from the metropolis. Meantime similar developments were

---

11 Humbodlt as late as the first decade of the nineteenth century testified that 'Free men, Indians, and people of colour, are confounded with the criminals distributed by justice among the manufactories, in order to be compelled to work. All appear half-naked, covered with rags, meagre, and deformed. Every workshop resembles a dark prison. The doors which are double remain constantly shut, and the workmen are not permitted to quit the house. Those who are married are only allowed to see their families on Sundays. All are unmercifully flogged if they commit the smallest trespass, on the order established in the manufactory.' And Humboldt adds that the practice of peonage was universal. *Political Essay on the Kingdom of New Spain*, III, 463-4.

12 Henry R. Wagner, 'Early Silver Mining in New Spain,' *Rev. Hist. Amer.*, no. 14, 56-7.

13 Arthur S. Aiton, 'Ordenancas hechas por el Sr. Visorrey don Antonio de Mendoca sobre las minas de la Nueva España, Ano de MDL,' *Rev. Hist. Amer.*, no. 14, 77. They were superseded in 1539 by a series of ordinances touching various aspects and problems of the mining industry, issued by the viceroy Mendoza.

taking place in the viceroyalty of Peru.[14] According to the early chroniclers, silver mines at Porco, a few miles southwest of Potosí, were exploited by Spaniards before 1540. In 1545 was discovered the famous Cerro de Potosí, perhaps the most celebrated in history, and in the same decade rich gold placers were developed in central Chile and in the interior of New Granada to the north.

In Mendoza's time silver was extracted from the ore only by smelting, a process probably brought over by the Germans in 1536 and satisfactory only for rich ores. The introduction of the patio process of amalgamation with quicksilver by Bartolomé de Medina at the Pachuca mines in 1556 [15] permitted the exploitation of lower grade ores, since the percentage of mineral obtained was much greater. The process, carried from New Spain to Peru, was introduced by the viceroy Toledo into Potosí in the 1570's, and was responsible for most of the silver production of America until far into the nineteenth century. As stated elsewhere mercury, thereafter of the utmost importance for the maintenance of the silver mining industry, became immediately a crown monopoly, the government assay offices generally serving as distributing agencies.

Mendoza's mining code of 1550, and the more famous ordinances issued by Toledo for Peru in 1574,[16] prescribed the conditions under which one might discover, claim, acquire proprietorship, and operate a mine, including security for the health and remuneration of the Indian laborers. Indians as free vassals of the crown received equal right with Spaniards to discover and work mines, although it is doubtful if they were allowed to enjoy the privilege. The ordinances of Toledo were formally approved by Philip II in 1589, and in time were applied to all parts of Spanish South America. They became the basis for later legislation,[17] and for many of the laws on the subject gathered together

14 Ibid. 79. Pedro de la Gasca had issued the first mining ordinances in Peru during his short sojourn there as president of the *audiencia.*

15 Medina is usually given credit for this invention, although the origin of the process and its introduction into New Spain remain somewhat in doubt. In a letter of the Mexican *audiencia* to the crown in December 1554, it appears that Medina did not discover the method but learned about it from a German in Europe. If he did not invent it, he apparently developed its practical application to silver mining in New Spain, although several other Spaniards also appeared to claim that distinction. In 1555 the viceroy Velasco granted him exclusive rights for six years, any miner using the process being required to pay him a fee of from 60 to 300 pesos de minas depending upon the number of slaves employed (Francisco Fernández del Castillo, *Algunos documentos nuevos sobre Bartolomé de Medina,* Mexico, 1927, 231 ff.). The amalgamating properties of quicksilver were well-known in Europe, and had already been used in extracting gold from auriferous earths and ores.

16 *Odenanzas de Don Francisco de Toledo, virrey del Peru,* 1569-1581, Madrid, 1929, 143-240.

17 Ordinances issued by viceroy García Hurtado de Mendoza in 1593, and by viceroy Luis de Velasco in 1598, and 1602, together with later editions, brought together in the compilation published by Tomás de Ballesteros in Lima in 1685.

in the *Recopilación*. In New Spain the Mendoza legislation was eventually superseded by the Ordinances of San Lorenzo, a new code framed by Philip II for Spain in 1584 and applied with various adaptations to the colonies.

Mining was as great a gamble in those distant times as today. A few bonanzas created magnates of great wealth; most of the miners were generally in a precarious situation. The Conde Valenciana in New Spain in the latter part of the eighteenth century sometimes netted over a million pesos a year, and accumulated millions in agricultural properties; and there were a number of other titled families with great fortunes acquired in mining. But thousands of impresarios, because of ill luck, or lack of capital or of technical assistance, exhausted energy and resources with little profit, or ended in bankruptcy. And the few old and celebrated mines, such as those of Zacatecas, Guanajuato, and Catorce, required large outlays in capital and labor to meet the technical problems created by increasing depth, flooding, or other factors. Humboldt reported that the Valenciana mine contributed nearly a quarter of all the silver produced in New Spain, and that ninety-five per cent of the mines operated produced less than one-tenth of the total output.[18]

That mining was subject repeatedly to disaster was due in large measure to technological backwardness, empiricism in the direction of work, and absolute lack of economic planning of production.[19] Miners, even the wealthy proprietors, paid little attention to recent scientific improvements in mining or in metallurgy, and efficiency of operation was far behind that of Europe. The industry as a whole also suffered from lack of capital to finance important changes. In the middle of the eighteenth century there were three *bancos de plata,* private banks that specialized in loans to miners, operating in Mexico City, that had over two million pesos invested, and merchants and other individual capitalists, *aviadores,* accounted for as much again.[20] But the fluid capital available was far from sufficient, and after 1750 the number of banks for one reason or another declined.

The need for capital and for technological improvement was generally recognized. José de Gálvez in 1771 in the General Report of his visitation of New Spain recommended a variety of reforms, including a new mining code and the organization of a miners' guild, along the lines of the *consulado* or merchant guild, for the protection and promotion of

---

18 Op. cit. III, 138, 193-4, 199.

19 Miguel O. de Mendizábal, 'Los minerales de Pachuca y Real del Monte en la época colonial,' *Trimestre Econ.,* VIII, 305-6; Arthur P. Whitaker, *The Huancavelica Mercury Mines,* Cambridge, Mass., 1941, 89.

20 Gamboa, *Comentarios,* 146, and 149, quoted by Mendizábal, op. cit. 285. Credit was generally extended in the form of partnerships or mortgage loans.

the industry; [21] and his influence doubtless played an important role in the events which followed. In November 1773 the crown ordered the viceroy Bucareli to call a junta of experts to follow up these suggestions, and nine months later this junta drew up its celebrated *Representación* to the king. The *Representación* received royal approval in a decree of 1 July 1776, and in 1777 the guild or *Real cuerpo de minería* was formally constituted. The new ordinances, completed by the guild and sent to Spain for approval two years later, were redrafted there and promulgated by Charles III in May 1783. This famous code was in the next few years extended to Venezuela, Guatemala, New Granada, Peru, and Chile. It went through many editions both official and private, and served as a basis for the mining laws of most of the Spanish American republics until the latter part of the nineteenth century.

The *Cuerpo de minería* consisted of a central tribunal in Mexico City, and a provincial court of delegation (*diputación territorial*) in each mining district (*real de minas*) composed of elected representatives of the mine owners and operators. The central tribunal was composed of a Director-general, an Administrator-general, and three Deputies-general. The latter were elected for nine years, one every three years by a general court (*junta general*) composed of delegates from all the *reales de minas*. The Director and the Administrator were chosen from among the Deputies-general for nine and six years, respectively.

The Tribunal was the executive organ for the entire industry, a court of appeals (after 1793) in mining cases from the *diputaciones*,[22] and a board of directors of a mining bank (*banco de avíos*). The bank was to raise a capital of two million pesos, interest on which was guaranteed by two-thirds of a real on every mark of silver from the seigniorage duty collected by the crown. From this capital the bank was to make loans to miners for developmental purposes after investigation by competent engineers. The *Cuerpo* also established a School of Mines to provide thorough training in the theory and practice of mining and metallurgy, and twenty-five free scholarships were created open to Spaniards and the sons of Indian chiefs. Members of the guild enjoyed the privileges of nobles, including immunity from arrest for debt, and exemption of certain items of personal property from seizure in satisfaction of judgments. Deserving members of the profession, and their sons and grandsons, were to be preferred in appointments to political, military, and ecclesiastical offices. They were guaranteed a supply of provisions, timber, and other necessities for their mines at minimum prices, and might draft as laborers idle persons or vagabonds except

---

21 Walter Howe, *The Mining Guild of New Spain and its Tribunal General,* 1770-1821 (Ph.D. thesis, Harvard University, 1938), 45-6.

22 It possessed original jurisdiction over cases in the vicinity of the capital.

Spaniards and mestizos reputed to be white. As far as possible Negroes, lower class mestizos, and criminals were to be employed so as to spare the Indians.

The *Ordenanzas de minería* of 1783 (some 314 in number), described by Alamán as a 'model of prudence and intelligence,' were extraordinarily comprehensive in scope. They covered not only the procedure to be followed in the adjudication and operation of mines, and the fiscal and juridical organization of the industry, but also the constitution of the guild, the regulation of labor, trade in the precious metals, banking and credits, technical training for mining engineers, and the privileges conceded to the mining fraternity. Their practical enforcement and whatever success the guild achieved are associated chiefly with the name of Fausto de Elhuyar, a Spanish engineer trained in Germany and Scandinavia, who was appointed Director-general by Gálvez in 1786 and arrived at Vera Cruz two years later. With him came four technicians and seven skilled workmen from Germany, sent over at the crown's expense.[23] At the same time a mission of thirteen German experts, headed by Baron Thaddeus von Nordenflicht, was dispatched by the Spanish government to Peru to improve mining methods there, and remained some twenty years in the colony.

In New Spain the *Cuerpo* had been bitterly opposed by the *audiencia* and by some of the more conservative Mexicans, and Elhuyar was disliked in the beginning, perhaps because of his obviously superior talents. But his industry, honesty, and public spirit soon gained their respect and good will, and in 1796 members of the Tribunal, believing him irreplaceable, successfully petitioned the king that his appointment to Mexico be made for life. He did not retire to Spain until after Mexico gained its independence.[24]

The *Cuerpo de minería,* given the major importance of the mining industry, became one of the most influential institutions in the last years of New Spain; and with the extension of the ordinances to the other colonies, similar guilds were created there. It failed, however, to achieve the high hopes held for it at its inception. Apparently there was little improvement in the administration of justice. Because of financial mismanagement of the General Fund, combined with gifts

---

23 A brother, Juan José de Elhupar had been sent by Gálvez to New Granada, on the viceroy's appeal for mining experts, in 1784. He married in the colony and remained there until his death in Bogotá in 1796. His mission did not have the success hoped for, whether for lack of energy on his part or failure of later viceroys to give him adequate support, is not clear. Vicente Restrepo, *Estudio sobre las minas de oro y plata de Colombia,* 2nd ed., Bogotá, 1888, 230-46.

24 In Spain he continued his distinguished career, drafted a new mining code for the kingdom, and at the time of his death in 1833 was Director-general of Mines (Whitaker, op. cit. 68).

and forced loans to the crown, the supply of capital for developmental purposes failed to be fully realized,[25] and the bank eventually went into bankruptcy for four million pesos. Although the production of silver steadily increased, the guild seems to have made little contribution to the improvement of mining practice. The German experts who came over with Elhuyar visited during several years most of the important mines of the country in an endeavor to modernize mining procedure, but with no great result because of the reluctance of the operators, and even of some of the owners, to depart from established custom.[26] The provincial *diputaciones,* due to lack of character or administrative experience in the majority of those eligible for election as local deputies, were too often guilty of favoritism, corruption, and inefficiency. Standards of conduct among minor government officials were not high, and their example was no inspiration to high ideals of public service.

The School of Mines, established by Elhuyar in 1792, had able professors and modern equipment, and a course combining theoretical instruction with practical experience and research.[27] But its graduates had to contend with tradition and the ingrained prejudice of the miners against book learning or theoretical training. Nevertheless the school was the pioneer in engineering education in America, and from it came many political and intellectual leaders of the republic, including the historian and statesman, Lucas Alamán.

It was in the late years of Charles V that gold and silver from the extraordinarily rich mines of New Spain, New Granada, and Peru began to flow to Spain in quanities till then undreamed of. This increasing production of American bullion was the principal cause of the price revolution in Europe in the sixteenth and seventeenth centuries, which in turn was one of the most vital factors in the rise of modern capitalism.[28] Until 1520 the remittances were entirely in gold from the West Indian islands, but after the conquest of Mexico and Peru and the discovery of vast silver deposits on the mainland, the production of silver rapidly increased until by the middle of the century it constituted perhaps 85 per cent of the bullion shipped to Spain. After the discovery of the fantastically rich ores at Potosí in Upper Peru and at Zacatecas and Guanajuato in New Spain, and the introduction of the amalgamation process of extracting silver from the ore, the pro-

---

25 Howe, op. cit. ch. IV.

26 The Nordenflicht mission in Peru had a similar experience: conflicts with the colonial authorities and vain efforts to combat the innate conservatism of the miners (*Whitaker,* op. cit. 67-71). The experiment cost the crown over 400,000 pesos in New Spain, and probably more in Peru.

27 The building constructed for it, not finished till 1813, is today one of the notable architectural survivals of colonial Mexico.

28 Earl J. Hamilton, 'American Treasure and the Rise of Capitalism, 1500-1700,' *Economica,* no. 27, 338-57.

portion rose in the 1560's to about 97 per cent, and in the seventeenth century to over 99 per cent.[29] The enormous volume of silver from the Indies also had the effect of increasing the relative value of gold, and the official ratio in Spain, fairly stable before the sixteenth century, rose from 1-10.11 *c.* 1500 to 1-12.12 in 1566 and to 1-14.84 in 1643.[30] The average annual imports of the precious metals in pesos de minas of 450 maravedís, by ten-year periods, have been reckoned by a modern scholar as follows: [31]

1503-1510	143 466,3	1581-1590	5 320 724,3
1511-1520	218 875,0	1591-1600	6 961 336,3
1521-1530	117 260,6	1601-1610	5 580 853,5
1531-1540	558 812,5	1611-1620	5 464 058,1
1541-1550	1 046 271,6	1621-1630	5 196 520,5
1551-1560	1 786 453,0	1631-1640	3 342 545,6
1561-1570	2 534 875,1	1641-1650	2 553 435,0
1571-1580	2 915 855,0	1651-1660	1 065 488,3

The above figures are based upon the receipts of registered bullion and specie by the *Casa de Contratación* at Seville. After 1600 there appears a decline, which becomes very sharp from 1630 onwards. This seems to have been due chiefly to a decrease in the fertility of American mines, especially at Potosí, accompanied by a rise in the expense of exploitation. But as is well known, considerable amounts of the precious metals managed to enter Spain unregistered, and increased resort to smuggling, inspired by heavy taxes and frequent sequestrations by the crown, may account for some of the decline of the registered receipts. Illegal extraction of the precious metals through the port of Buenos Aires, and contraband trade with the Orient by way of Acapulco and the Philippines, may also have been a contributing factor.

As the balance of trade of Spain with the rest of Europe was always unfavorable, especially with increasing demands of the colonies for goods, Spain became the distributor of the precious metals to the outside world, in the form of Castilian escudos and reals. Her manufactures, even her grain, came to her from France, England, Italy, Germany, and the Netherlands, and thither went her gold and silver in exchange. In spite of laws prohibiting the export of specie, money filtered out of the country, often with the connivance of the crown itself, and much of the treasure from the New World was probably diverted immediately to the north of Europe.

It was American bullion also which in large measure financed the foreign wars of the early Hapsburgs. Spanish troops and foreign mer-

---

29 Earl J. Hamilton, *La Monnaie en Castille,* 1501-1650, Paris, 1932, 22.
30 Ibid. 23.
31 Ibid. 20.

cenaries in Italy or the Netherlands were fed and clothed by means of the gold and silver on the annual fleets—whether on the account of the crown, or as private remittances requisitioned for its pressing needs —transmitted through the agency of the great foreign merchant bankers. Hapsburg imperialism was undoubtedly stimulated by this stream of treasure from the New World. On the other hand, its importance for the royal exchequer has at times been exaggerated. The chief value to the crown of American remittances was as a supply of ready cash for immediate use. The total revenues from America were far below the gross revenues from sources in Europe. In the final analysis they proved to be more a liability than an asset. Spain fell back exhausted by an imperial effort too vast for her moral and material resources. Rising prices—by the end of the sixteenth century they had already reached a level that they were to hold for the most part until well into the nineteenth—together with increased taxation in a nonindustrial country, handicapped what industry there was and prostrated noble and peasant alike. The lag of wages behind prices served especially to impoverish the laboring classes; and the only beneficiaries were the small group of merchant adventurers in Andalusia.

In the eighteenth century the receipts of the precious metals again took an upward turn, owing to the increasing production from Mexican mines. Between 1700 and 1770 the amount of silver coined at the Mexican mint doubled, from about five million pesos a year to ten or eleven million. In the following thirty years it again doubled, to over twenty million pesos. Over one and a half billion pesos in silver were minted in Mexico between 1690 and 1822, and some sixty million in gold. During the reign of Charles III (1759-88) nearly five hundred million pesos in coin and bullion were imported from the American colonies into Spain. Mexican productivity reached its peak in the last two decades of the colonial era. In the confusion resulting from the secessionist wars after 1810, the output of the precious metals sharply declined.[32]

Although the manufacturing industries, for reasons suggested above, were never of great importance in the Spanish colonies as compared with agriculture and mining, certain products such as silver, leather goods, textiles, and hardware attained to a considerable development; not because they were better than those of Europe, but because importing interests kept the prices of European goods too high, or because raw materials in the colonies were cheaper. And from the larger cities there was always a substantial trade in such colonial goods with the rural towns and districts.

Craft guilds (*gremios de artes y oficios*), very similar to those which

---

[32] J. M. Zamora y Coronado, *Registro de legislación ultramarina*, 3 vols., Habana, 1839, II, 439 ff.; M. D. Nifo, *Noticia de los caudales . . . que han entrado en España . . . Carlos III*, Madrid, 1788, 18.

had prevailed in western Europe since the late Middle Ages, were established in America soon after the conquest. Great numbers were organized in the sixteenth and seventeenth centuries, until in Mexico City there were said to be about a hundred, with others in the more populous provincial towns. Among the more important were those of the silversmiths, goldbeaters, harness and saddle makers, potters, weavers, hatters, and candle makers. Following the custom of the time, each guild was organized for religious and philanthropic purposes as a confraternity (*cofradía*), which with its chaplain and elected officers took care of the spiritual interests of the member. In fact, in point of time the *cofradía* frequently preceded the organization of the guild or business corporation. The *cofradía* observed with splendid ceremonies the feast day of its patron saint, collected alms for the support of its charities, and sometimes maintained a home or hospital where its poor could be cared for and fed. Some of the craft guilds also furnished military companies for the defense of the municipality.

The earliest guilds in America were organized in Mexico City, and some achieved great wealth and prestige, notably that of the silversmiths which was already in existence in 1537.[33] This guild played a principal role in public celebrations, especially in the processions of Corpus Christi and Holy Thursday. In 1685 there were 71 silversmith shops in the capital of New Spain, nearly all of them on a single street, the Calle San Francisco or 'de los Plateros' as it came to be called, today the Avenida Francisco Madero.[34] This guild was the first, and perhaps the only, craft to establish a *montepío* (1777) for the benefit of its members.[35] The corporation of silversmiths in Lima was equally wealthy and influential, and in the beginning of the seventeenth century had 80 shops in the viceregal capital.

The organization and activities of most of the guilds were governed by elaborate ordinances issued by the municipal *cabildos* with the confirmation of the viceroy or the king; ordinances which endeavored to establish an equilibrium between the conditions of labor, the interests of the consumer, and the claims of the royal exchequer. There was a graduated system of instruction from the rank of apprentice through that of journeyman to the rank of master or employer-entrepreneur.

---

33 A royal decree of 1526 forbade silversmiths to exercise their profession in the colonies because silver taken to them for refinement escaped payment of the king's royalty. Within a few years the decree was revoked for all the colonies except New Spain, where it was not rescinded till 1559, and apparently there it was never observed. Torre Revello, *El gremio de plateros en las Indias Occidentales* (Publ. Instit. invest. hist., LXI), Buenos Aires, 1932, 11-12, 14.

34 Ibid. appendix, xxviii-xxix; Manuel Romero de Terreros, *Artes industriales de la Nueva España*, Mexico, 1923, 17-39.

35 The *montepío* served much the same benevolent purposes as the earlier *cofradías*, including assistance to the sick, aged, and infirm.

Admittance to the highest grade depended upon the production of a 'masterpiece,' and membership in the guilds was jealously limited in much the same way as it was in Europe. Indians, Negroes, mulattoes, and in some of the guilds mestizos were debarred from aspiring to the rank of master, and therefore from lucrative participation in the technical trades, although they constituted the bulk of the journeyman workers. Inspectors (*veedores*), elected annually by the guilds but under strict municipal supervision, insured the quality of the product by periodical inspection of shops and workrooms, assisted at examinations, and issued licenses. The ordinances also frequently included the rudiments of a labor code, regulating hours of work, holidays, and other interests of the workmen.

Indians of the more advanced cultures in Mexico, Guatemala, and the Andes possessed considerable natural talent in the arts and crafts, as is attested by the textiles, ceramics, and gold work remaining to us from pre-Columbian times. Many Spanish observers in the sixteenth century remarked upon the imitative abilities of the natives, and the cleverness with which they copied the handicrafts of the conquerors.[36] And without doubt one of the reasons for the exclusion of Indians from membership in the guilds, except as journeymen, was fear of native competition, both in skills and in prices in an open market.

The second Revillagigedo near the close of the eighteenth century reported that the arts and crafts in New Spain were in frank decadence, due to lack of adequate facilities for training workmen. The guild ordinances, most of them dating from the sixteenth and seventeenth centuries, were wholly antiquated and full of requirements that retarded rather than encouraged the development of the industry.[37] The system of masters, journeymen, and apprentices, useful perhaps in the beginning for maintaining standards of workmanship, and the minute regulation of techniques and character of output, had become an anachronism, and led only to monopoly in the hands of a few and to complete stagnation. The craft guilds were not abolished in Mexico, however, until 1861.

Perhaps the most powerful nonpolitical corporations in New Spain and Peru were the *consulados,* or guilds of merchant importers. As the craft guilds represented the Spanish American and mestizo elements in the population, the influence of the European residents was anchored in the merchant guild. As a kind of chamber of commerce it possessed administrative authority in matters concerning trade and communications. It served as a judicial tribunal in disputes over contracts, bank-

---

36 Alonzo de Zorita, *Historia de la Nueva España*, Madrid, 1909, cap. 23, 24; Gerónimo de Mendieta, *Historia eclesiástica indiana*, Mexico, 1870, lib. IV, cap. 13.

37 Revillagigedo, *Instrucción*, par. 337-41.

ruptcy, freights, and similar questions. It kept deputies resident in all the towns subject to its jurisdiction. Commanding vast funds from endowments, and from the administration of the *alcabala* and other taxes, it also contributed much to the public welfare, by financing roads and canals, and constructing handsome edifices such as the Custom House in Mexico City and the Bethlehemite Hospital.[38] A center of wealth and conservatism, it served with the rich miners and the Church as the principal source of fluid funds in the community; and in fact, after the abolition of the Cadiz commercial monopoly by the Bourbons, its members were more and more inclined to employ their surplus capital in financing the mining industry. For a long time limited to the metropolitan cities of Lima and Mexico, in the last decades of the eighteenth century *consulados* were also created in eight other principal cities throughout the American empire.

Many ordinances were promulgated from time to time by the municipal or viceregal authorities governing such matters as the price of bread and other foodstuffs, the supply of meat, the regulation of wine shops, protection of labor in the textile factories, etc. In the retail trade of a colonial city almost every article was carefully controlled as to price, weight, and quality. A member of the *cabildo*, the *fiel ejecutor*, sometimes accompanied by an *alcalde*, inspected the markets, held hearings on the price of articles, and fixed a scale which was set up in a public place where all might see. The object was to protect both the consuming public and the trader by preventing speculation and monopolies while insuring a moderate profit, and by securing an equitable distribution of the raw materials of industry. Foodstuffs especially were watched, for an attempted corner in grain in a year of bad harvests sometimes resulted in mob violence. Such an outbreak occurred in Mexico City in January 1624, complicated by a bitter conflict between the viceroy and the archbishop over questions of jurisdiction and ecclesiastical privilege. The viceroy's palace was partially destroyed by the rioters, and the viceroy forced to flee for refuge to the Franciscan monastery, where he remained for nine months until a successor arrived from Spain. Scarcity of grain caused an equally famous and sanguinary outbreak in Mexico in June 1692, and great apprehension for weeks until new crops brought relief.[39]

To insure to the public an adequate supply of bread at reasonable prices, near the close of the sixteenth century public granaries (*alhóndigas*) began to be built in the principal towns, where farmers had to bring their grain for sale and the bakers obtained supplies. Grain received as tribute from the crown Indians was also stored and distrib-

38 Alamán, *Historia de México*, I, 94.

39 Carlos de Sigüenza y Góngora, *Alboroto y motin de los Indios de México*, transl. in Leonard, *Don Carlos de Sigüenza y Góngora*, 210-77.

uted there. Sales were made both by private individuals and on government account, but at a maximum price or under, depending upon the market supply. In time of emergency the government sometimes stepped into the market as an active trader, buying and selling maize in order to keep the price down to the official figure. A perennial difficulty was the cost of transportation of grain brought from more distant areas, which was always excessively high owing to the primitiveness of communications. Market crises, therefore, were not infrequent and often a cause of concern to the government.[40]

Special efforts were also made to control the public meat markets, but usually on the basis of a contract with one or two individuals who were bound to supply the demand at prices fixed by the *cabildo*. And other fundamental necessities were likewise kept under close supervision. Human ingenuity, however, was as devious then as now, fraud was as common among both officials and merchants, and the enforcement of the regulations often left much to be desired.

---

[40] The difficulties in the way of maintaining an adequate grain supply for Mexico City at reasonable prices are discussed by the viceroy Revillagigedo in his *Instrucción,* par. 308-21.

XIV

The Royal Exchequer

(I)

Whether the vast colonial lands delivered to Spain by the happy accident of the patronage of Columbus were in the ultimate analysis a blessing or a curse to the monarchy is still a debatable question. Castilian writers in the sixteenth and seventeenth centuries loved to dilate upon the territorial extent, the diversity of climate, of flora and fauna, and the unexampled mineral riches of the empire beyond the seas. Catalogues of bishoprics, archbishoprics, and patriarches, of hospitals, convents, and colleges, served to illustrate the great missionary achievements of the race; while the splendor of viceregal courts and the lavishness of public celebrations reflected the wealth and elegance of Spanish colonial society. But already by the time of Philip III a few farseeing Spaniards must have been conscious that this was perhaps only one-half of the story. The mother country, with her immense American resources, was yet growing steadily weaker, declining in both wealth and population. This may have been in part the consequence of Hapsburg imperialism, of a religious and political foreign policy out of all proportion to the needs and the powers of the nation. But may not the Indies themselves, by their very wealth and potential resources, have contributed to the same result?

That the colonies drew from the peninsula many of its most enterprising and adventurous sons could admit of no doubt. But was not this emigration an important cause of the relative depopulation of Spain in the sixteenth and seventeenth centuries? It is a thesis which has yet to be proved. On the other hand, it is clear enough today that the revenues from American mines proved to be one of the nation's greatest misfortunes. Spaniards, consistently with the bullionist theories then current, thought of securing the precious metals to the exclusion of all else; yet complained of the rise in prices which decay of industry coupled with the increase of money brought in their train. The prejudice against manual labor and the mechanic arts, inherited from the military age of crusade against the Moors, was only accentuated, and idleness and an impractical vanity became in the eyes of visiting foreigners the distinctive traits of the Spanish people.

In the sixteenth century, however, as the Hapsburgs accepted more and more seriously the role of champions of Roman Catholicism, with the fatal financial burden it involved, the income from the Indies seemed to be the hope, and indeed the salvation, of Hapsburg policy. Under Charles V this revenue was comparatively small and increased only by slow degrees. In 1516, the year of accession to his Spanish inheritance, it amounted to about 35,000 ducats. In 1518 it was 122,000, but dropped as low as 6,000 in 1521, when the emperor was entering upon his interminable wars with France. In 1538, an unusual year owing to the return of the first of the great treasure-fleets, the receipts of the *Casa de Contratación* rose to 980,000 ducats; but the average during this decade and the following was about 165,000. Only after 1550, when the emperor's career was approaching its melancholy twilight, did this average income swell to a million ducats, i.e., to a sum equal to that which he drew annually from his possessions in the Low Countries. During the next fifty years, in the long and disastrous reign of his son Philip, it increased gradually to between two and three million. In the seventeenth century it somewhat declined, but with growing prosperity under the Bourbons it rose before 1800 to be between five and six million.

Of the vast territories of Spain in America, only New Spain and Peru continuously produced a substantial revenue for the crown. On the larger West Indian islands considerable gold was extracted during the first two decades of the sixteenth century, but thereafter the output rapidly diminished. By 1550 placer mining in the West Indies had virtually ceased, and as the aboriginal population had died out or been killed off, there was soon no such thing as Indian tribute. Receipts failed to meet the ordinary expenses of government, and the islands became dependent on subsidies from the treasury in Mexico City.

The proportion of the treasury receipts in America which was shipped to Spain was greater in the first quarter of the sixteenth century than later. In the beginning, when colonization was centered in the islands and organized government was relatively simple, by far the greater part of the exchequer income seems to have reached the king. But after the creation of the viceroyalties on the mainland, the expenses of colonial administration became much heavier, and in spite of the discovery of rich mineral deposits, in the sixteenth century they probably consumed 50 per cent of the revenues. Toward the close of the following century, when the military expenditures of the viceroyalties were high, expenses accounted for 80 per cent or more of the receipts.

From the first, taxation in the Indies was not light, although always mild compared with that endured by the inhabitants of the Spanish peninsula. New settlements were generally exempted for a period of years, frequently twenty, from the more usual Castilian taxes, except the ecclesiastical tithe. Queen Isabella, in secret instructions to the governor of Hispaniola in March 1503, inquired whether it would be feasible to put a tax on gold bullion, on sales, tillage, grazing, and fishing, or port dues on the lading and unlading of ships. So far as we know, none of these expedients was resorted to. The supply of salt, however, was already farmed out as a monopoly; and from the lifetime of Columbus the colonists were made to pay a duty (*almojarifazgo*) of 7½ per cent on the gross valuation of goods imported from Europe, while the authorities were sometimes permitted to levy a temporary excise on foodstuffs (the *sisa*) to meet the expense of Indian wars or other special local needs. All treasure-trove, jewels, and ornaments from native graves and shrines, belonged in theory to the king; but in America the crown chose to forego this right in consideration of a faithful registry of the treasure discovered and the payment of a half into the royal exchequer.[1] Of the slaves and booty captured in war, no contemptible item in the conquest of Mexico and Peru, a fifth also went to the crown. On some of the West Indian islands, as also in New Spain, the crown seems to have exploited cattle ranches till well into the second half of the sixteenth century, and the profits from them form a regular item in the annual receipts of the local treasury; but they probably never exceeded a few thousand pesos a year, and are negligible as a contribution to the king's revenues.

By law all mines within the territories of the crown were part of the royal patrimony. In 1501 Ferdinand and Isabella forbade anyone to seek or exploit mines in the New World without their express permission. Within three years this permission had been extended generally to all colonists except royal officials, provided they first registered their claims before the governor and the officers of the exchequer, began operations within a stated period, and swore to bring all their bullion to the royal smeltery (*casa de fundición*) to be assayed and taxed.[2] On the other hand, the crown had always required large royalties for the privilege of developing mines, and these royalties continued to be exacted to the end of Spanish domination in America.

In spite of the liberality of the decree of 1504, the search for mines in America continued to be regarded as a royal concession, sometimes for a limited period; and very rich mines, it seems, were reserved to the crown, although their exploitation was frequently given to private indi-

1 Solórzano, however, says that in practice generally only a fifth was claimed by the crown (lib. VI, cap. 5, par. 17). According to the *Recopilación*, the king's share was the *quinto* and one-half of the remainder (lib. VIII, tit. 12, ley 2). Search for treasure might also be undertaken by individual agreements with the colonial authorities which stipulated the share reserved for the impresario, payment of damages to property involved, etc. (ibid. ley 1).

2 *Col. doc. inéd.*, 1st ser., XXXI, 214; Solórzano, lib. VI, cap. I, par. 21.

viduals for a short time, as for one or two years.[3] If an individual discovered a mine on land belonging to another, part of the mine was by
law given to the owner of the property. So too, after the early period
of conquest and settlement, when the distinction between public and
private lands came to be more clearly conceived, of new mines found on
public lands a certain number of square yards were reserved to the
crown.[4] But there seems never to have been any general attempt on the
American mainland to work these claims in the interest of the government. The element of risk was always considerable, the operation of
mines often complex, the yield uncertain, and the temptation to dishonesty by royal administrators very great. Such mines were therefore
almost invariably rented entire, or disposed of by sale or gift to the
discoverers or other private individuals. The only notable exceptions
were mercury mines, especially the famous quicksilver deposit of Huancavelica in Peru expropriated by the viceroy Toledo in 1570, and the
emerald mines of New Granada, which were by a system of leases subordinated to official control.

In Castile during the Middle Ages the royalty on bullion had been
two-thirds; but to hasten the exploitation of the mineral resources of
the new lands, this percentage was quickly reduced. Between 1500 and
1504, in response to petitions from the settlers in Hispaniola, it was
lowered successively to a half, a third, and a fifth.[5] This royal fifth, the
quinto of Spanish American treasury records, was established for ten
years by a decree of 5 February 1504, and remained until the eighteenth
century the general law for all the Indies. Further reductions, to an
eighth, a tenth, or even a twelfth, were made from time to time as an
inducement to prospecting in new districts, or in regions like Central
America and the West Indian islands where the mines or gold washings
were poor or the operating costs very high. From 1548 onwards the
royalty in New Spain was a tenth on silver bullion delivered by the

3 José María Ots Capdequi, *Manual de historia del derecho español en las Indias*, II,
57-60.

4 In the mining laws promulgated in Peru by the viceroy Francisco de Toledo, it
was stated that the first 80 yards (*varas*), i.e., 80 long by 40 wide, of the claim as selected by the discoverer belonged to him; the next 60 in the direction of the vein as
attested under oath by the discoverer went to the king if on public lands, or to the
owner of the land on which the mine was found; and another 60 to the discoverer if
he owned no other mine within a league of the spot. If he possessed such other mines,
the rest went to those who first staked their claims. In the case of gold mines the areas
reserved covered 50 yards. Apparently this legislation reserving mines for the crown
was still in effect in the time of Escalona Agüero (1647), but when the *Recopilación*
was published in 1681 it had disappeared from the statute books. *Ordenanzas de Don
Francisco de Toledo*, Madrid, 1929, 143-240; Escalona y Agüero, *Gazophilatium regium
perubicum*, lib. II, pt. 2, cap. I; León Pinelo, *Tratado de confirmaciones*, pt. II, cap. 23,
par. 31 ff.

5 *Col. doc inéd.*, 1st ser., XXXI, 13, 216; 2nd ser., V, 43.

miners themselves to the assay office, but a fifth when brought by the bullion merchants.[6] This apparently remained the practice till 1723 when the *quinto* became a *diezmo* for all minerals. Finally in 1777 the royalty on gold was further reduced to a flat 3 per cent including all other charges, with 2 per cent added if and when the bullion was introduced into Spain.[7] In Peru the royalty on silver was not reduced to a tenth till 1735, although gold bullion was then paying only 5 per cent.[8]

All bullion had to be delivered to the government smeltery to be assayed, cast in bars, and stamped with its weight and fineness. There 1 per cent (after 1552 1½ per cent) was first deducted as *derecho de fundidor, ensayador y marcador,* and afterwards the *quinto*.[9] The silver or gold bars were then stamped with the royal arms, and were free to go into ordinary circulation. Unstamped bullion was everywhere subject to confiscation, and its coinage in colonial mints (but not in Spain) was punishable by death and the loss of the culprit's property. In the course of time there arose a complex schedule of charges upon gold and silver bullion delivered to the assay office or to the mint, and also additional imposts on the precious metals manufactured into jewelry or plate.[10]

The royal *quinto* was the most lucrative source of the monies drawn annually by the Spanish kings from their American possessions. In theory applicable to all minerals, it was rarely collected on any but gold, silver, mercury, and precious stones.[11] Pearls gathered in the fisheries on the southern coasts of the Caribbean Sea and about the islands near the city of Panama also paid the required fifth to the crown.

The important duty of 7½ per cent in American ports continued to be levied till 1543, when the rate was reduced to five per cent. At the same time, however, the duties customarily collected on maritime trade in Andalusia were extended to goods sent to and from the New World. Till then the American trade at Seville had been free. Thereafter *almojarifazgo* was collected of two and one-half percent on exports, and 5

---

6 F. Fonseca y C. de Urritia, *Historia general de real hacienda,* 6 vols., Mexico, 1845-53, I, 15-16. Bullion merchants were middlemen who made the rounds of the mines to buy up bullion and send it to the assay offices. Moving over regular routes, they could transport and protect the bullion more economically than could the small producers. Earl J. Hamilton, 'Imports of American Gold and Silver into Spain,' 1503-1660,' *Quart. Journ. Econ.,* XLIII, 443.

7 Fonseca y Urritia, op. cit. I, 32, 39.

8 Rafael Antúnez y Acevedo, *Memorias históricas sobre la legislación, y gobierno del comercio de los españoles con sus colonias en las Indias Occidentales,* Madrid, 1797, appendix lxxxvi.

9 Gold found in its pure state had to pay besides the *quinto* an additional ninth or tenth. Escalona y Agüero, op. cit. lib. II, pt. 2, cap. I; *Col. doc. inéd.,* 2nd ser., v, 269, 334.

10 Revillagigedo, *Instrucción,* par. 1229-37.

11 Mines of alum, copper, tin, and lead were generally leased by the crown for a term of years.

per cent on imports plus an *alcabala* or sales tax of 10 per cent whether the goods were actually sold or not. This involved a new burden of 15 per cent on American commodities, while the charge on European goods remained the same, or 7½ per cent.[12] Intercolonial maritime trade in local products also paid customs at the Sevillan rates, and European articles reshipped from one colonial port to another were assessed upon any increase in value accruing thereby.[13]

In 1566 the exigencies of royal finance were the excuse for another change in colonial customs. Duties on European articles were doubled (to five and ten per cent), to equal the tax on American products, but an additional export duty of 2½ per cent was levied in American ports upon articles shipped to Spain. The assessment on imports in the Indies was based, not on the schedule of values employed at Seville, but upon prices in the American market at the time when payment was made. These were generally very much higher, sometimes by several hundred per cent. Both in Spain and in America, however, appraisal was made without opening or unpacking goods for examination, the officials trusting to a general statement by the merchant under oath of the nature and quality of the articles shipped. On this basis *almojarifazgo* continued to be collected till the second quarter of the seventeenth century, except for the Venezuelan coast and the poverty-stricken West Indian islands, for which it was reduced under Philip II by a half.[14]

A radical change in the methods of appraisal was introduced in 1624. Articles for export were divided into a few comprehensive classes, and a uniform valuation for each class was imposed on boxes and bales according to weight, and on rougher cases according to bulk. On that basis *almojarifazgo* and other dues were assessed until 1660. In that year, owing to the tremendous losses of the crown through fraud, *ad valorem* duties on commodities from America were replaced by a fixed sum or composition of 790,000 ducats paid annually by the merchants of Spain and the Indies engaged in the trade. After 1680 the assessment of goods exported to America was frequently on the basis of volume alone rather than of weight, and in 1695 this became the rule. Three years later it was based on the number of pieces regardless of measurement or value; in 1707 the method of cubic measurement was re-established; and the

---

12 No duties were levied on the personal effects of emigrants to America if not intended for sale.

13 Apparently not enforced in Lima till 1566. Manuel Moreyra Paz Soldán, 'El Comercio de exportación en Pacifico a   principios del siglo XVIII,' *Cuadernos de Estudios* (Univ. Catól. Peru, Instit. de Invest. Hist.), II, no. 5, 248-85.

14 Haring, *Trade and Navigation between Spain and the Indies*, 84-5. The addition of a variety of other, minor, imposts in the seventeenth century, however, raised the export taxes considerably above the rate of the *almojarifazgo de Indias*.

system was given permanent form by the well-known Ordinances of 5 April 1720.[15]

Duties thereafter were based upon bulk, weight, or the number of articles shipped. Goods on leaving Spain paid five and one-half silver reals per cubic *palmeo* (21 cm.) if in bales or boxes adapted to outside measurement, regardless of content. But on a list of specified articles there was a schedule of rates according to kind, by number, weight, or liquid content. A similar schedule applied to imports from America.[16] Gold from the Indies paid 2 per cent, silver 5 per cent. These payments now embraced all other imposts formerly levied on the overseas trade except tonnage dues and inspection fees. *Almojarifazgo* in American ports on European commerce was abolished altogether. Customs were now payable only in Spain, on traffic both ways, and taxation was considerably simplified. In intercolonial trade, however, the general rule established in the sixteenth century still prevailed, 5 per cent on imported articles and 2½ per cent on exports. This system continued until the time of Charles III, whose liberal reforms instituted a new era of commercial freedom in the relations between the Indies and the seaports of the peninsula.

The Philippine Islands trade between Manila and Acapulco in New Spain was always treated as a special case. From the time this traffic was confined to the so-called Manila Galleon, 'China goods' entering Acapulco had paid an *almojarifazgo* of 10 per cent. In the eighteenth century the duty rose to as high as 33 per cent. On the few articles shipped to the Philippines (the chief remittance was in silver) there was an export duty of 3 per cent.[17]

The *palmeo*, based on bulk without reference to quality or value, was at best a crude device. Cheap goods paid as much as expensive, and the system bore down with especial weight on trade with the poorer colonies. Consequently in the concessions extended by the crown between 1765 and 1776 to the backward areas of the West Indian islands and the mainland coasts of the Caribbean the *palmeo* of 1720 was replaced by an *ad valorem* duty of 6 per cent on Spanish goods and 7 per cent on those of foreign origin.[18] Re-export of the produce of these areas from Spain to other countries was declared free. A variety of tonnage dues which

---

15 Antúnez y Acevedo, op. cit. 246-7; Albert Girard, *La Rivalité commerciale et maritime entre Séville et Cadix jusqu' à la fin du XVIII* siecle*, Paris, 1932, 72 ff.

16 For the schedule of rates, see Antúnez y Acevedo, appendix, lviii-lxiii. During the War of the Spanish Succession the few fleets dispatched to America had sailed under special concession by the terms of which the duties collected on exports to the Indies were raised to 25 and sometimes to as high as 40 per cent. Ibid. 222.

17 Fonseca y Urritia, op. cit. v, 50.

18 Articles not subject to the *palmeo* continued to pay the rates established in 1720. Louisiana was a special case. Exports to the new colony were duty free; imports from it paid 4 per cent.

had grown up during the previous century and a half—one for the support of the mariners' guild at Seville (1608), another for the privilege of sailing to minor Caribbean seaports (1642), a special tax on foreign-built vessels (1681), a tax to establish and maintain the *Seminario de San Telmo* or school for navigators at Seville (1681), and an admiralty tax (1737)—these also were abrogated, together with inspection and license fees.[19] At the same time, by decrees of 1772 and later years, duties on a considerable number of articles manufactured or produced in Spain or in America were reduced or abolished altogether. These concessions were extended to all the American provinces by the celebrated *Reglamento* of 12 October 1778.

The new rules called for an over-all payment of 3 per cent in both Spanish and American ports on goods originating in Spain or produced in the Indies, and the number of articles on the free list was largely increased. The duty was reckoned on a schedule of prices in Spain plus 12 per cent.[20] On goods of foreign origin the *almojarifazgo* remained 7 per cent. For trade with minor seaports of the Caribbean, the tariff was once more reduced, to 1½ per cent and 4 per cent, respectively.[21] These ordinances remained in force to the outbreak of the wars of independence, although there were some temporary increases in the *almojarifazgo* during the international conflicts following the Revolution in France.

A source of royal income peculiar to the Indies was the tribute of the natives, an annual payment to the king in token of his overlordship, or to *encomenderos* to whom the crown granted the privilege of enjoying this revenue. It was in the form of a personal or capitation tax, i.e., a fixed amount paid by every adult male Indian regardless of his property or other resources. It was analogous to the *moneda forera* and similar medieval dues paid by peasants in Castile.

Such a capitation tax, first mentioned in the early instructions to Governor Ovando in 1501, appears more concretely in those issued to the Hieronymite friars and to Rodrigo de Figueroa in 1516-18 for set-

---

19 A number of similar exactions had accumulated in American ports, and continued to be collected to the close of the colonial era. For the situation in New Spain, see Revillagigedo, op. cit. par. 1329 ff.; R. S. Smith, 'Shipping in the Port of Vera Cruz, 1790-1821,' *Hisp. Amer. Hist. Rev.*, XXIII, 5-20; Pons, François Joseph de, *Travels in South America during the Years* 1801 . . . 1804, ch. VIII.

20 There were various deductions: on certain depreciated goods 10 per cent of the duty; on goods delayed over six months in transit 15 per cent; if a vessel of Spanish construction carried only goods of Spanish origin, one-third of the duty; if two-thirds of the cargo were of Spanish origin, one-fifth of the duty. Fonseca y Urritia, op. cit. v, 53-6.

21 In 1784 Spanish goods exported to this area were declared free of duty, foreign goods subject to a 2 per cent tax. Five years later all trade with the islands was made absolutely free of contributions, including even the *alcabala*. Antúnez y Acevedo, op. cit. 228 n.

tling the natives in free villages. On the continent Indian tribute was universal, and the amount varied according to the custom of the province. Instructions to Cortés and to later authorities in New Spain provided that it was to be approximately the same as that formerly paid by the Indians to their native chiefs or lords.[22] This was largely accomplished during the administration of Bishop Ramírez de Fuenleal, president of the *audiencia* in 1531-5, and his successor the first viceroy, Antonio de Mendoza. Indian tribute was first reduced to a regular schedule in Peru by the viceroy Francisco de Toledo (1569-81), who to this end visited personally many parts of his government and whose *Libro de tasas* became the model for later colonial legislation on the subject.

The tribute seems to have ranged from five to eight pesos a year. It was sometimes exacted entirely in silver, but more generally in money and such produce as the region most readily afforded. In Mexico all married males paid, including the sons of Negro fathers and Indian mothers, and unmarried after the age of 25. In some provinces women and young unmarried men were also subject to the tax, at least to half the amount owed by the adult male. Men ceased to be liable at the age of 55, women at the age of 50. The tributary age began in Peru at 18 and ended at 50, but all women, in theory at least, were exempt.[23] Immunity was also everywhere enjoyed by the native chieftains or *caciques*, in their quality as nobles, by their eldest sons, and by the *alcaldes* of Indian towns during their tenure of office.[24]

In the sixteenth century, when great numbers of tributary Indians were granted in *encomienda* to the colonists, the income of the royal exchequer from this source was relatively small. As the *encomiendas* more and more escheated to the crown, Indian tribute became an item of considerable importance. In 1550 the amount collected annually in New Spain was about 100,000 pesos; by the close of the eighteenth century it had risen to well over a million pesos. When *encomiendas* reverted to the crown, colonists thus deprived of an important source of income were often regarded as possessing a peculiar claim upon the liberality of the government, which came to their rescue with annuities charged upon the tributes gathered into the royal treasury. We find such items in the exchequer accounts long after the *encomienda* as an institution had been abolished.

---

22 As the Indians continued to pay tribute and services to their chiefs, the burden was doubly onerous.

23 The *Recopilación* (lib. VI, tit. 5, ley 19) declares that no women were to pay tribute (decree of 1618), but apparently the custom of the region prevailed in most cases.

24 In 1574 a tribute of two pesos was imposed on free Negroes and mulattoes, raised to three pesos in the eighteenth century. The law in the *Recopilación* (lib. VII, tit. 5, ley 1) set a maximum of a marc of silver, or 8 pesos 3 reals, which might be abated in accord with the ability to pay.

A schedule of what was due from each Indian *pueblo* was supposed to be kept in a book apart, one copy of which was preserved in the archives of the *audiencia,* another in a coffer which held the king's monies, and a third in possession of the native officials of the pueblo. The tribute was collected several times a year by the *corregidores* and *alcaldes mayores,* the produce sold at public auction by the royal factor of the local exchequer office, and the proceeds deposited with the colonial treasurer. That the *corregidores* generally made collection a source of illicit gains at the Indians' expense was a common complaint. After the establishment of the *intendencias* in the last quarter of the eighteenth century, tribute was gathered by the *alcaldes ordinarios* and by the sub-delegates, who received 5 per cent of the proceeds.

Pope Alexander VI, moved by petitions from the Catholic kings to contribute to the cost of secular and religious conquest, granted to them and their successors, by a bull of 16 December 1501, all the ecclesiastical tithes in the Indies; but at the same time he imposed on the Spanish crown the responsibility for preaching and propagating the Christian faith among the Indians, founding and endowing churches, and supplying them with a competent ministry. As in other Christian lands, the tithe was gathered on all fruits of the earth, grain, cotton, sugar, silk, flax, garden-truck, etc., as well as on livestock and dairy products. Even the properties of the crown paid the tithe. Gold, silver, other metals, pearls, and precious stones, of which the *quinto* went to the king, were never subject to this second tax; [25] nor was a personal tithe exacted, i.e., from the fruits of man's industry and labor, although the clergy in some regions tried hard to introduce it.

Whether the natives ought to pay tithes or not, in addition to their tribute, was a burning question among ecclesiastical and civil lawyers throughout the sixteenth century. It was also the occasion for long disputes between the secular clergy and the friars. The former would have the Indians pay this additional tax; the friars, for a variety of reasons not always unselfish, strove to have them exempted. The attitude of the crown seems to have been a variable one, although evidently it was the early intention to collect from the natives. Ferdinand and Isabella in 1501, immediately after receiving the papal concession, directed Ovando, the new governor of Hispaniola, to have both Indians and Spaniards pay, but that tithes were collected from the Indians on the islands is doubtful. On the continent, too, the crown revealed the same general intent, as appeared in its instructions to the second *audiencia* of New Spain. Temporarily, and until the Indians were converted and legally subject to tithing, a contribution sufficient for the building of churches

25 They were specifically exempted in papal bulls of 1510 and 1511. *Col doc. inéd.,* 1st ser., XXXIV, 25-35; 2nd ser., V, 205-9.

and the support of the clergy was to be included in the assessment of tribute, but not in excess of 25 per cent of the whole.[26] It appears also in instructions of 1535, and 1536 to the viceroy, and in the decision of 1543-4, on the viceroy's suggestion, that the Indians pay tithes at least of wheat, silk, and cattle, the production of which had been introduced to them by the Spaniards.[27] These rules became the general practice and were extended to Guatemala and Peru, although in those countries supposedly the amount of direct tithe thus collected was subtracted from that included in the tribute. In general it may be said, therefore, that the natives on the continent were exempt from most of the tithe, a sufficient amount for the support of the local church and clergy being deducted from the tribute paid to the king, to the *cacique,* or to the *encomendero.*[28]

Although by the concession of Alexander VI ecclesiastical tithes in America were given to the crown to levy and collect, the greater part of this income was devoted to the Church for its extension and maintenance. It was the rule from the time of Charles V (1541) that the tithes be divided into two equal parts. Of one part, half went to the bishop of the diocese, half to the dean and chapter of the cathedral. The other was in turn divided into nine parts, of which two were set aside for the royal exchequer; of the remaining seven, four were applied to the parish clergy,[29] three to the construction and repair of churches and hospitals. Thus in reality only one-ninth of the proceeds of the tithes accrued to the crown, and that was generally expended in pious works and the support of schools and universities. The tithes therefore can scarcely be regarded as a source of royal income. On the contrary, they might even be a source of expense to the crown. For if they were insufficient to meet the fixed charges of the diocese, the deficit was made up out of the royal treasury.[30] Although the tithes had belonged to the crown since 1501, it is doubtful that they were systematically levied before 1508 or 1509.

---

26 Vasco de Puga, *Cedulario,* fol. 88, 91 vo. (*cédula* of 2 August 1533).

27 *Col. doc. inéd.,* 2nd ser., X, 256-7, 341; Diego Encinas, *Provisiones cédulas,* etc., 4 vols., Madrid, 1596, I, 181, 183.

28 Solózarno op. cit. lib. II, cap. 22, par. 18-22, 37-9, 45; Encinas, op. cit. I, 181, 186, 201; *Recopilación,* lib. I, tit. 16, ley 12.

29 Later only two-ninths were reserved for the parish clergy, the other two being added to the income of the cathedral chapter. From the gross proceeds of the tithes the *excusado* (tithe of a principal house in each parish of certain dioceses for the support of the cathedral church) was first deducted, and thereafter 3 per cent for support of the diocesan seminary, before the above division was made (Escalona y Agüero, op. cit. lib. II, pt. 2, ch. 32; R. B. Merriman, *Rise of the Spanish Empire,* IV, 443, n. 2; Fonseca y Urritia, op. cit. III, 172). Decrees of 1620 and 1651 incorporated in the *Recopilación* directed that the royal ninth be first deducted from the gross, before the 3 per cent and other charges (lib. I, tit. 16, leyes 25, 26).

30 In the *Recopilación,* the minimum salary guaranteed to the bishop was 500,000 maravedís. Lib. I, tit. 16, ley 22 (*cédula* of 6 July 1540).

At first collection was in the hands of the treasury officials, and as a rule it continued so in the situation just cited; but if the tithes were sufficient to cover all charges, collection was given over to the prelate and cathedral chapter, and was generally farmed out.[31]

The Ordinance of Intendants (1786) directed that a *junta de diezmos* be appointed in the more important cities under the supervision of the *intendentes*. The junta was to make all arrangements for the collection of the tax within the district, generally farming it out to individuals who might not be ecclesiastics. Apparently, in the face of the stubborn opposition of the clergy, the viceroys were unable to enforce compliance.[32]

Probably one of the first Spanish imposts, apart from tithes and customs duties, to be collected in the New World was the queerest of all taxes, the *cruzada*. Bulls of crusade (*bulas de la santa cruzada*), i.e., indulgences sold to provide funds for the wars against the infidel, are believed to date from the twelfth and thirteenth centuries, when they were granted by the Pope to the Christians of Spain in their struggle against the Moors. In the sixteenth century, after the last Moorish stronghold, Granada, had fallen, the proceeds of such indulgences continued to be conceded by various popes to the Spanish kings, generally for periods of six years. The stipulation was always retained that the tax, for such in effect it became, must be employed in the exaltation and extension of the Holy Catholic Faith, a pretext that might find some justification in the Hapsburg wars against heretics and Turks.

Just how early the *cruzada* came to be preached in the colonies is not clear. It is commonly said that the papal concession was extended from Spain to the Indies by Gregory XIII in 1573. However, there exist in the archives at Simancas records of the collection of this tax in South America and the West Indies extending back as far as 1535. A *comisario general subdelegado* was appointed for New Spain in 1537,[33] and in the ledgers of the Mexican treasurers preserved in the *Archivo de Indias* receipts from this source date from about the same time. Probably before 1573 the bulls were preached under the general concession extended to the dominions of the Spanish crown, and only after that date did the Pope specify in particular the American colonies.

The cost of the indulgences varied from time to time and from prov-

---

31 The nomination of the collector general of the diocese, however, and of subordinate officials who had supervision of the collecting of the tithes, was reserved to the crown. For an excellent discussion of the ecclesiastical tithe, see Woodrow Borah, 'The Collection of Tithes in the Bishopric of Oaxaca during the Sixteenth Century,' *Hisp. Amer. Hist. Rev.*, XXI, 386-409.

32 *Real Ordenanza para . . . intendentes . . . de Nueva España,* art 165 ff.; Revillagigedo, op. cit. par. 1245-50.

33 Juan Diéz de la Calle, *Memorial y noticias sacras y reales del imperio de las Indias occidentales,* Madrid, 1646, 49. In 1611 the commissary general was given a seat 'with voice and vote' in the *cabildo* of Mexico City like the officials of the royal exchequer.

ince to province. It also depended upon the kind of indulgence granted, although the scale was determined not by the service rendered but by the capacity of the individual to pay. As a rule, at least, toward the end of the sixteenth century, Negroes, Indians, and others of the humbler sort paid two silver reals, although the law (1543) forbade the bulls to be preached in Indian pueblos or forcibly imposed on the natives. Other Spanish subjects paid eight reals, while royal and ecclesiastical officials and those who possessed *encomiendas* were assessed from two to four pesos. In the eighteenth century the price ranged from two reals to ten pesos depending upon the social class or public office of the purchaser. The bulls were published in America every other year, brought in a considerable revenue,[34] and continued to be imposed until the separation of the colonies from the mother country in the nineteenth century.

The *cruzada,* although its proceeds went into the royal treasury, was always regarded as an ecclesiastical tax and was collected and administered by churchmen. In charge was a Commissary General in Madrid who appointed deputies to the principal cities of the Indies. These in turn chose subdelegates to each of the smaller towns and districts, and treasurers to receive the proceeds of the indulgences and remit them each year to the central authorities. Collection was farmed out on a percentage basis. The subdelegates were usually members of the cathedral clergy, had supervision of the preaching of the bulls, and possessed judicial cognizance in first instance of all matters touching the business. In the middle of the eighteenth century the methods of collection were somewhat altered, and in 1767 administration of the *cruzada* was transferred to the officials of the royal exchequer. Thereafter the indulgences were disposed of by the parish priests who received five per cent of the proceeds.

The *alcabala,* another characteristic Castilian tax (in Spain 10 per cent or more of the value of all sales and exchanges) , was not introduced into the Indies till near the close of the sixteenth century. The crown in March 1503 had ordered Governor Ovando to report on the ability of the settlers to pay such a tax, but so far as we know no further action was then taken. And invariably freedom for a term of years from the *alcabala* was included among the priviliges conceded to newly established colonies. Such an exemption was enjoyed by New Spain immediately after its conquest, and when the first viceroy, Mendoza, went out there in 1535, he was instructed to negotiate with the colonists for the collection of an *alcabala* to aid the emperor in his wars against the Turks. Extension of the tax to New Spain was actually decreed in 1558, but presumably the ordinance was not enforced. Ten years later, when

---

34 About 300,000 pesos annually in New Spain toward the close of the eighteenth century.

Francisco de Toledo was preparing to go to Peru, a junta at Madrid decided that he should make efforts to collect it there. In every instance the colonial authorities were induced by the strength of the local opposition to postpone the execution of the king's commands. The tax was finally introduced into New Spain in 1575, and into Guatemala a year later.[35] It was not established in Peru till 1591, when in the province of Quito it almost caused a revolution.

The rate of the *alcabala* in the colonies was fixed at 2 per cent and remained at that figure till 1636, when it was doubled in the northern viceroyalty to provide 200,000 pesos a year for the maintenance of an *Armada de barlovento* to pursue and destroy 'pirates' from the Windward Islands. As in Spain, the *alcabala* in the principal cities was usually compounded for a lump sum by the municipality or by the *consulado;* and, paid in this fashion, it generally amounted to less than would have been represented by the full legal rate, although probably to more than the net return under royal administration. In the seventeenth century (1627) there was an additional tax on sales of 2 per cent, called the *derecho de unión de armas,* intended to furnish 600,000 ducats a year, 350,000 in Peru and 250,000 in New Spain, for the support of a fleet of galleons to protect the trans-Atlantic trade route. Although limited to a period of fifteen years, as in so many similar cases it continued to be levied until the end of the colonial era.[36] At the same time there arose the practice of imposing by special decree another 2 per cent in time of war, a device often resorted to and sometimes continued long after peace was restored.

The *alcabala* was levied on most saleable articles, at both first and later sales. On goods imported into Spanish or American ports, it was collected immediately at the custom house, whether the goods were sold or not. Laws in the *Recopilación* governing the administration of the *alcabala* were many in number and minute in detail. *Encomenderos,* planters, and ranchers sent every four months to the collector a sworn statement of the nature and value of the product they had disposed of by sale or barter, for cash or credit, within that time; and in the towns and cities wholesale merchants, and retailers with a fixed place of business, did the same. On the basis of these figures the collector issued warrants for the payment of the tax. Itinerant merchants had to report every sale and pay 2 per cent on the same or the following day, and the

---

35 Owing to the inaction or passive resistance of the local authorities, it was not collected in Guatemala till 1602. José Milla, *Historia de la América Central,* 2 vols., Guatemala, 1879-82, II, 228.

36 The combined *alcabalas* of 6 per cent were compounded by the City of Mexico in the seventeenth and eighteenth centuries, at first by the *cabildo,* after 1647 by the *consulado,* for about 280,000 pesos a year. Collection was in turn farmed out to individuals. Fonseca y Urrutia, op. cit. II, 11 ff.

buyers were likewise expected to give word to the collector. This rule of notification within twenty-four hours applied also to brokers through whose hands passed any taxable transaction, and to town criers, who must report every public sale they were called upon to announce. Apothecaries, wine sellers, and saddlers made their payments each week. The collectors submitted their books annually to the royal treasury officials, and if, as sometimes happened, they were not actually in residence in the town to which they were appointed, settled their accounts every four months.[37]

Many articles, however, were exempt from the *alcabala*. Among them were bread, coin, bullion disposed of by the miners at the mint, books, paintings, manuscripts, horses, arms, and falcons. Inheritances and bequests, goods bought or sold on account of the *cruzada,* or by churches, monasteries, prelates, or lesser clerics not for gain, articles sold retail in the streets and markets to the poor and wayfaring, and grains sold from the public granaries, were also exempt. Indians were likewise free of this exaction on the sale of their own produce.[38]

One of the most questionable of the financial expedients adopted by the Hapsburgs in America was the sale of public offices referred to in an earlier chapter.[39] Frowned upon in Spain by the Catholic kings, the practice developed under Charles V toward the middle of the century, and it was immediately resorted to by Philip II. In a vain effort to lift his kingdom out of the financial demoralization in which it had been left by his father, he soon extended it to the colonies. At first the office of notary (*escribano*) was sold, not only of notary public but of notaries attached to various government councils and tribunals. Before the end of the century the system was applied to most municipal offices, and to numerous posts connected with the royal mints, the exchequer, and the courts of law, although by law judicial office was excluded.[40] We find it repeated in numerous decrees that government posts need not necessarily go to the highest bidder, but that the fitness of the would-be purchaser be taken into account as well as the interests of the exchequer. But as minor offices in the colonies were sold under the direction of the

---

37 *Recopilación*, lib. VIII, tit. 13.

38 Escalona y Agüero, op. cit. lib. II, pt. 2, cap. 9. Apparently the tax was sometimes reduced in distant, sparsely settled regions where transportation and other costs were high.

39 See *ante*, pp. 165-6.

40 In the seventeenth century the sale of offices extended even to the personnel of the Council of the Indies. From 1604 the post of notary of the Chamber of Justice was vendable, bringing in that year 13,000 ducats. In 1636 the position of *portero* was put up for sale, and other minor offices followed. In the reign of Charles II even the dignity of Councilor was occasionally sold, in one instance in return for a *servicio* to the crown of 145,000 ducats. Schäfer, *El Consejo real y supremo de las Indias*, 201-02, 263-4, 270-71.

viceroys or governors, this furnished a loophole by which unscrupulous officials might provide comfortable berths for their friends and dependents.

Of course when offices were bought and sold as private property, the price rose and fell with the chances of squeezing an income out of them, and in any case varied with the wealth of the community. In hard times prices generally declined. Some men bought office merely as a speculation, and often tendered other offices in part payment. Many, however, invested in this way to obtain social position or privileges, or to secure an income for themselves or their heirs, reckoning it as a fair percentage on the money invested.

In 1548 the post of treasurer of the mint in Mexico was sold for 130,-000 pesos, 60,000 down and two equal annual installments of 35,000.[41] The same post at Potosí in 1656 brought 124,000 pesos, one-half spot cash, the rest in three annual installments. In Lima the same office was disposed of in 1581 for 20,000 pesos,[42] in 1702 for 80,000 pesos.[43] Another lucrative post aparently was that of *alguacil mayor* of the *audiencia,* which in Mexico in 1611 was purchased for 115,000 pesos. The office of *escribano,* whether of the *cabildo* or of the *audiencia,* was commanding in the same period from 50,000 to 60,000 pesos.[44]

Apparently the position of *regidor* was first put up for sale in Mexico City in 1573 (there were doubtless earlier purchases in Spain), when it brought 41,000 pesos. Five years later the same office seems to have sold for 6,000 pesos.[45] In the early years of the seventeenth century the price ranged from 6,000 to 10,000 pesos.[46] In Santiago, Chile, in the first half of the seventeenth century it fluctuated between 5,000 and 3,000 pesos, in the second half of the century between 8,900 and 2,500 pesos.[47] In 1591 the office of *regidor* brought 1,000 pesos in Arequipa, 2,000 in La Plata (Chuquisaca), and 10,000 in the wealthy mining community of Potosí.[48] A decade later in Havana the office commanded between 1,000 and 2,300 ducats. In the small, frontier town of Buenos Aires, on the other hand, seats in the *cabildo* in the seventeenth and eighteenth centuries sold for anywhere between 250 and 1,250 pesos, and in Santiago del Estero for 200 pesos if a buyer could be found.[49] Some of the ex-

41 F. A. Kirkpatrick, *Regidores and alcaldes ordinarios* (MS.).

42 Manuel Moreyra Paz Soldán, 'La Tesoreria y la estadistica de acuñación colonial, etc.,' *Cuadernos de estudios,* tomo II, no. 4, 10.

43 Moreyra Paz Soldán, 'La Tesoreria de la casa de moneda de Lima, etc.,' *Rev. Hist.,* Lima, XV, 111-12, 140.

44 Diez de la Calle, op. cit. 49-50.

45 Kirkpatrick, MS.

46 Diez de la Calle, op. cit. 50.

47 Kirkpatrick MS. Figures gleaned from the *cabildo* records are as follows: 8,900 (1654), 5,500 (1657), 7,500 (1664), 3,500 (1665), 4,000 (1674), 2,500 (1684).

48 Ibid.

49 Ibid.

officio posts in the *cabildo* were apparently more profitable and commanded a higher figure. The office of *alférez real* in Santiago, for instance, was auctioned in the first decade of the seventeenth century for 9,500 pesos, that of *depositario general* for 12,500 pesos. In Mexico City in 1609 this latter post sold for 44 to 46 thousand pesos. At the same time in Buenos Aires it brought 2,000 pesos, or about three times as much as the seat of a *regidor*. The position of *alcalde provincial* in Santiago in 1648, at a time when prices seemed to be running low, sold for 13,200 pesos.[50]

Some writers have contended that the system—in vogue in France as well as in Spain under the Old Regime—did not result in any apparent lowering of the caliber of the official class as a whole. In America, however, it was open to grave objections. Officials who came out from Spain often had no interest in the colony except to make money, and the price paid was frequently so high that the monetary return was not adequate as salary and interest on the sum invested. The result was corrup-

[50] 'The form of sale or auction of a regimiento perpetuo, or of a post conferring the rights of a regidor, was elaborate. The pregonero, generally a colored man, porter and messenger of the audiencia where that tribunal existed, announced the sale in the public plaza in a loud voice thirty times, usually on successive days for a month. At any time during these pregones, and for a reasonable time afterwards, an applicant could send his offer in writing to the treasury officials, stating the amount, the dates and amounts of instalments (the usual form of payment) and the names of substantial people standing surety for these payments and for the fulfillment of the duties of the office. If another person sent in a better offer in the same elaborate form, the officials made it known to the first applicant, in case he should make a higher bid, and every higher bid was made known to other applicants; until the officials, after satisfying themselves about the character of the man and the reality of his offer, accepted that offer, not necessarily the highest bid, although it would be difficult to find any other conclusion. There was then a form of public auction, the pregonero thrice loudly announcing the price bid and inviting any higher offer. None came—the matter being in fact already settled; and the vacant place was declared to be sold. The purchaser then received from the audiencia a written title, which he presented in the cabildo; and, after due examination, he was admitted and took the oath that he would duly serve the King in the performance of his office and would observe secrecy about the proceedings of the cabildo. The purchaser—or in the case of renuncia, the renunciatario—was required to produce royal confirmation of his title within a specified time. The cédula of 1606 fixed the limit at four years, but it was soon extended to five years for the provinces nearer to Spain and to six years for those more distant, among these latter being Chile and the River Plate. The purchaser or renunciatario was obliged to find, at his own expense, means of sending a petition to Spain, presenting it to the Council of the Indies and getting back the reply. He was also obliged to make provision for any legal expenses which might be incurred in proceedings before the Council of the Indies and to empower an agent in Spain to act on his behalf in any legal business. If he failed to get confirmation within the time limit, the post was to be declared vacant and sold by auction. One-third of the price realized was to go to the treasury and two-thirds to the unconfirmed and dispossessed holder of the post (*Recopilación*, lib. VIII, tit. 22, ley 7). Thus the penalty for failure to obtain confirmation was deprivation and loss of one-third of the value—probably about one-third of the price which the dispossessed holder had paid.' Kirkpatrick MS.

tion in high places. Officials expected to recover at least a part of the initial outlay and perhaps amass a small fortune as well. The colonists therefore suffered from bad government, and the crown from diminished revenues. The viceroy Revillagigedo at the end of the eighteenth century expressed his strong disapproval of the practice, maintaining that the greater efficiency of appointed officials would more than compensate for the loss to the royal exchequer. The system was abolished by the Spanish *Cortes* in 1812, but in some of the colonies it continued for several years thereafter.

In the seventeenth century, as the monarchy became progressively more impoverished, two other methods were adopted for extracting money from public officeholders both in Spain and in the colonies. These were the *mesada* and the *media anata,* both doubtless suggested by the medieval papal annates. The *mesada* was a payment representing a month's income of every newly appointed official secular or ecclesiastical in the colonies. It was first required of all secular officers in 1625, and by papal concession was later extended to churchmen as well. Every newly presented ecclesiastical officer from the archbishop to the simple curate who received an income of 100 ducats or more, paid a *mesada* calculated on the basis of the average annual yield of the benefice during the five years preceding.[51] In 1631 it was replaced for secular officials by the *media anata,* or half the first year's salary and a third of all other emoluments of the recipient of a public office, favor, or concession, whether permanent or temporary, including the inheritor of an *encomienda.*[52] If an official was advanced to a higher post, he paid on the increase of income involved. After 1754 the crown was permitted by

[51] Granted to Philip IV by Pope Urban VIII in 1625 for a period of fifteen years, it was renewed by Innocent X in 1644 and continued to be renewed at intervals thereafter. According to Fonseca y Urrutia it was not actually collected in New Spain till 1637.

In *doctrinas* conducted by the religious Orders, the *mesada* might not be exacted more than once in five years, even though in the meantime the missionaries were replaced.

[52] There were, however, many exceptions, including military officers in active service, judges of residence, employees of the postal, gunpowder and lottery services, recipients of university scholarships, and after Gálvez's *visita* in the eighteenth century *alcaldes mayores* and officials of the tobacco monopoly. For offices without emolument purchased in America the tax was computed at about 5 per cent of the purchase price. *Alcaldes ordinarios* and others on annual appointment paid one-tenth of their salary, those on biennial appointment one-eighth, minor government employees from one to six ducats. The tax was normally due in two payments, one-half in advance of taking office, the other a year or a year and a half later.

An analogous tax imposed at the same time as the *media anata,* the *lanzas,* was an annual payment to the crown by those who held Castilian titles of nobility, as composition for an old requirement that they furnish twenty lancers to the king's armies. In New Spain in the seventeenth century it was fixed at 450 pesos, later dropped to 350 pesos or less, and at best brought in only a small revenue.

Pope Benedict XIV to require the *media anata* of the higher clergy as well (i.e., those receiving an annual salary of 300 pesos or more), lesser clerics continuing to pay only the *mesada;* but it was not actually collected in the colonies till many years later.

The net proceeds from these sources were reserved to the use of the crown, and in New Spain at the close of the eighteenth century amounted to over 125,000 pesos. They were sent to Spain under separate account at the cost and risk of the official who paid the tax. This varied from time to time, but was fixed in the eighteenth century at a flat charge of 18 per cent to cover the cost of shipment, *averia,* and other imposts.[53]

Numerous other sources of revenue, most of them tapped before the close of the seventeenth century, call for but brief mention. Among such were the monopolies of quicksilver (1559), playing cards (1572),[54] gunpowder, salt, pepper (1631), snow,[55] and in the eighteenth century cock fighting and tobacco; stamped paper (1638) required for all legal documents; the income of vacant ecclesiastical benefices; a head tax on Negro slaves imported from Africa; a payment in the form of a composition from *pulperías* over and above the number officially assigned for the supply of each district; [56] judicial fines and confiscations; and various duties and excise taxes on wines and spiritous liquors.

Monopolies were usually operated under license from the crown, or in the case of certain minerals such as salt under a system of contracts or leases, the *concessionaire* having the sole privilege of manufacture and sale within the district. During the course of the eighteenth century the treasury in many cases took over the administration of the monopoly, purchasing the product from the contractor and selling it to the public. Some of the monopolies were more an annoyance to the consumer than

---

53 For the most extended discussion of these taxes, see Joseph de Rezabal y Ugarte, *Tratado del real derecho de las medias-anatas seculares y del servicio de lanzas á que están obligados los titulos de Castilla,* Madrid, 1792. For New Spain, see Fonseca y Urrutia, vol. III. The confusion and arrears in the administration of these taxes in Peru, and the efforts of the Spanish government under Philip V over many years to restore order and a modicum of efficiency, are detailed in Rezabal, 11-20.

54 In 1582, acording to García y Icazbalceta, 9,000 dozen playing cards were manufactured in Mexico 'more esteemed than those brought from Spain.'

55 The exclusive privilege of supplying the inhabitants of a city with snow from neighboring mountains packed hard like ice and used for cooling drinks. It was introduced into Lima in 1634 (Escalona y Agüero, lib. II, pt. 2, cap. 20), into New Spain in 1719. In Mexico City it was farmed out at 10,000 pesos per year, and provided a revenue from the entire viceroyalty of from 25,000 to 28,000 pesos.

In Peru the proceeds from the monopoly of corrosive sublimate (*solimán*) were used in Escalona's time to pay the salaries of the two professors of medicine in the University of San Marcos.

56 Imposed in 1623, but never collected consistently in New Spain, *Pulperías* were shops which sold both alcoholic beverages and provisions.

of profit to the exchequer.[57] Salt, for example, like other minerals, was commonly included among the regalia of the crown, and apparently its sale was farmed out as a monopoly on the island of Hispaniola as early as 1511.[58] Presumably the practice fell into disuse, but according to Solórzano [59] about 1575 the crown decided to take over the exploitation of salt mines and salt pans in New Spain and Peru. The scheme received a fair trial in the northern viceroyalty, where the supplying of salt was ordinarily farmed at a considerable figure; but in the south it was declared to be impracticable, and early in the following century was definitely abandoned. Even in Mexico there were many complaints. If the monopoly was administered by a farmer, the supply was scant and the price high; if by public officials, the costs of operation were greater than the profits. At the same time the natives were deprived of what had been one of their means of livelihood, while the silver miners, who used salt in the process of extracting silver from the ore, found themselves handicapped under the new arrangement.[60]

The monopolies, besides salt, which produced the largest receipts in New Spain were quicksilver, playing cards, gunpowder needed for the mines, and tobacco. In the time of the younger Revillagigedo, playing cards produced annually about 70,000 pesos net, salt 100,000 pesos, and gunpowder 200,000 pesos. Since 1556, when the amalgamation of silver ores was introduced into the New World, the crown had reserved to itself the export and sale of quicksilver, and although it was supposed to reach the miners practically at cost, the hidden profits of the crown were considerable. For the mercury from Huancavelica, which monopolized the Peruvian market, the crown was also after 1570 the sole distributor, buying it under contract from the lessees of the mine, selling it in the great silver area of Potosí, and sometimes exporting it to New Spain.[61]

Of all the monopolies, that of the manufacture and sale of tobacco proved to be the most lucrative. The crown and its advisers, we are told, had long contemplated this fiscal device, but hesitated for fear of vested interests and of the public. The monopoly was first established in the several provinces of Peru in 1752 and succeeding years. In New Spain

---

57 The viceroy Revillagigedo remarked that there were very few monopolies from which the individuals interested did not draw much greater profits than were obtained by the king (*Instrucción*, par. 1374).

58 *Col. doc. inéd.*, 2nd ser., v, 280 (*cédula* of 25 July 1511).

59 Op. cit. lib. vi, cap. 3, par. 8, 9.

60 The government also from time to time exploited salt deposits on the coast of Venezuela for the supply of the salt beef (*tasajo*) industry.

61 To guard against tax evasion by the silver miners, the crown in the Peruvian viceroyalty introduced the practice of computing the *quinto*, not on the basis of the silver reported to the assay offices, but on the amount of mercury purchased from the administration for amalgamation purposes.

the first steps were taken by the viceroy Cruillas in 1764, but the chief impulse to its effective organization came from the *visitador* José de Gálvez. In the early 'seventies the revenue from this source amounted to nearly a million and a half pesos; two decades later, in the time of the viceroy Revillagigedo, to three times as much. Introduced into Venezuela in 1777, the monopoly produced there at the end of the century about 700,000 pesos. The entire net proceeds were reserved for disposition by the crown, and the monopoly continued to be one of the richest sources of public income in America.

There was an extraordinary expedient to which the king might resort in time of great financial need, in the shape of what in English history were called 'benevolences.' As no legislative assemblies resembling the Castilian *Cortes* were permitted to develop in the colonies, there was no machinery for obtaining a money grant or subsidy. But the crown found means of bringing pressure to bear upon individuals to contribute to its necessities. As early as 1501, Ferdinand directed Governor Ovando when he arrived at Hispaniola to secure from the inhabitants of the struggling, nine-year-old colony, a voluntary gift of this sort, and the demand was repeated with increasing frequency in later reigns, if not for a gift, at least for a loan. In 1509 Gil González Dávila, sent out to Hispaniola to audit the accounts of the colonial officials, was instructed also to raise a loan for the king, and Diego Columbus, then governor, was ordered to do all in his power to make the effort a success. As the islands declined in population and wealth, in competition with the more alluring prospects on the mainland, they became less and less able to meet requests of this nature. In 1530 Manuel de Rojas wrote to the emperor from Cuba, excusing himself from sending the thousand pesos which had been required of him, but remitting 400, which he himself had had to borrow. Other letters of a similar tenor flowed into the Spanish court. Juan Barba wrote to the queen regretting that he could not lend the 300 pesos asked for, and complaining that, although he was one of the original *conquistadores*, he had no *encomienda* of Indians and the governor treated him with neglect. The treasurer of the colony wrote in the same strain, while the governor, Gonzalo de Guzmán, to whom fell the responsibility and the odium of enforcing the loan, regretted that for his part he was not in a position to remit more than 500 pesos. But in the island as a whole, he concluded, there was 'great zeal for spending and little diligence in saving.'

To the richer provinces on the continent the crown was much more importunate, and from them expected a more liberal response. Philip II, immediately after his elevation to the throne, lost no time in summoning his American viceroys to find a subsidy in recognition of the auspicious event. In 1574 he ordered the royal authorities in Peru to negotiate for a gift to the crown, or if his loyal and faithful subjects and vassals showed a disinclination to give, which he believed impossible, at least a loan of money and plate would not be unacceptable. But after 1598 the king's tone became truly abject. Instead of demand or regal request, there was apology and even supplication. Philip III needed a 'donativo y emprestido' to assist him out of his financial straits and obligations, enable him to retain control of the seas, and maintain the peace, security, and prosperity of his colonies. He began with the president and judges of the *audiencias*, urging them to set a good example of liberality, and ended with the *pueblos* of the Indians. Indeed, the natives were perhaps more apt to be mulcted, directly or indirectly, than the king's white subjects. In 1591, after the disaster of the Great Armada, the Spanish government, in seeking resources with which to rebuild the Atlantic fleet, exacted from every Indian in its dominions an annual *servicio* in addition to the tribute: in New Spain and Guatemala four reals, in Peru, New Granada, and Tierra firme an amount equal to one-fifth of the tribute, or if the Indian did not belong to a tributary community, one peso. It was intended to be a temporary expedient, was presumably withdrawn in Peru in 1598 and in the lowlands of New Granada in 1614, but according to the Laws of the Indies it was still collected in 1681.[62] Possibly it was for this reason, the loss of the Armada, that in 1591 the crown insisted upon the collection of the *alcabala* in the southern viceroyalty.

As examples of such gifts or benevolences may be mentioned the donation of over 400,000 pesos collected for the king in 1624 by the Marquis of Cerralvo, viceroy in New Spain. Five years later he sent another contribution of 1,100,000 pesos to help replace the losses incurred in the destruction of the silver fleet by the Dutch admiral Piet Heyn off the Cuban coast in the previous year. In 1640 the viceroy of Peru gathered 350,000 pesos as a 'voluntary' donation toward the expenditures caused by the revolt of Portugal under the Duke of Braganza. The viceroy Albuquerque of New Spain transmitted to the crown some two million pesos as a gift from its loyal colonists during the long struggle of the War of the Spanish Succession.

The Spanish crown unfortunately did not stop at requests for gifts and loans. It acquired the insidious habit, initiated by Charles V, of seizing the gold and silver bullion remitted from the colonies to Spain by merchants and other private individuals, giving in exchange annuities (*juros*) bearing from 3 to 6 per cent interest and generally charged upon some one or other of the regular sources of revenue. This practice reached gigantic proportions. Already in 1523, 300,000 ducats were sequestered, all the gold and silver that came on five vessels from the Indies; and in 1535, 800,000 out of the private treasure sent from Peru,

---

62 *Recopilación*, lib. VI, tit. 5, ley 16.

most of it, doubtless, remittances from the followers of Pizarro. Six hundred thousand ducats were seized in 1553, and in the winter of 1556-7, just at the outset of Philip II's reign, the unprecedented sum of 1,800,000, bringing disaster to the merchant houses interested in the American trade. In the seventeenth century such forced loans continued to be frequent, amounting in 1629 and again in 1649 to a million ducats.

The crown also frequently took advantage of the presence in the *Casa de Contratación* at Seville of the funds called *bienes de difuntos*. These represented the property of intestates, and of those who died without heirs in the colonies, or on the voyage to or from America. The estates were wound up by royal officers appointed for the purpose, and the proceeds deposited with the colonial exchequer or forwarded to Spain, where advertisement was made for known or unknown heirs. In the sixteenth and seventeenth centuries the sums remitted on this account were very great, and, owing to the tardiness of claimants in appearing, accumulated in huge amounts at Seville, offering an irresistible temptation to the crown. Borrowings from the *bienes de difuntos* became so extensive that men in the Indies preferred to leave their estates to trustees with instructions to transmit to the heirs in Europe, or the latter to collect by their own agents, rather than entrust legacies to the medium officially established for this business. The crown in the seventeenth century sometimes offered interest at 10 per cent and even the salaries of the members of the Council of the Indies as security, but did not succeed in restoring confidence.

XV

❧❧❧

The Royal Exchequer

(II)

❧❧❧

The organization of the American exchequer in Hapsburg times was relatively simple, and it remained until the eighteenth century virtually unchanged. The collection of the revenues with few exceptions was in charge of individuals styled specifically the Royal Officials (*oficiales reales de hacienda,* or simply *oficiales reales*). In the beginning there were four in each colony, a treasurer, a comptroller (*contador*), a business manager (*factor*), and an inspector (*veedor*). The duties of treasurer and comptroller are fairly obvious. The factor disposed of the tribute in kind received from the natives, made purchases for the authorities, and in general attended to any commercial transactions in which the king's monies were involved. The *veedor* was overseer of the exchequer's interests at the mines and assay offices where the bullion was refined and the *quinto* subtracted from it. Later, at least after the middle of the sixteenth century, the office of *veedor* generally disappeared from the exchequer staff, and in many places that of *factor* as well. But there was always a treasurer and comptroller in the capital of every province, with deputies at the principal seaports, and if the province was very extensive, in other towns as well. Eventually important seaports like Vera Cruz came to have a separate treasury of their own. In the early years judicial proceedings instituted by the exchequer had to be pursued by the factor before the ordinary justices; but in the reign of Philip II the *oficiales reales* were given judicial functions with cognizance in first instance of all fiscal suits, appeal lying directly to the local *audiencia.*

Royal orders and decrees prescribed with great particularity the form in which the accounts and other records of the exchequer were to be kept. Every entry in the books of the treasurer and comptroller had to be attested by the signatures of all the *oficiales;* every deposit of money or bullion had to be made in their presence; and all public acts or communications had to be signed by them together. In each collection center or subtreasury the monies were deposited in a strongbox (*caja real*) heavily bound with iron and provided with three or four different locks, one key being in the possession of each of the *oficiales reales,* so that the box could not be opened except in the presence of all the officers or their deputies. In the course of time, with the increase in the number of taxes and the complexity of collection, some of the revenues were provided with an administration independent of the *oficiales reales,* although the proceeds were ultimately deposited with them. Such revenues were Indian tribute, the *cruzada,* seigniorage collected at the mints, the *alcabala,* the postal service, the more lucrative monopolies (quicksilver, salt, gunpowder, playing cards, and tobacco), and a few minor imposts.[1]

Most of the royal revenues were farmed out to the highest bidder, sometimes to the chief city or the district (*encabezamiento*), either for an annual lump sum or on a percentage basis. Others were collected directly by officers of the exchequer. Farming of the various taxes was the general rule under the Hapsburg kings and until after 1750. In the time of Charles III, and especially under the reforming influence of his great colonial minister, José de Gálvez, the tendency was to take the collection of taxes out of private hands and put it under the direct administration of the crown. Methods of accounting were vaguely adumbrated by numerous laws in the *Recopilación* and by subsidiary legislation of the eighteenth century. But as a matter of fact the systems employed differed widely in different areas, and continued so until the close of the colonial era. Beginning in 1785 the *Contaduría general de las Indias* in Spain made several attempts to provide uniformity by introducing double-entry bookkeeping, but with doubtful success.[2]

Officers with duties so important for the continued prosperity and security of the state, combining in themselves both administrative and judicial powers, should obviously be selected with the greatest care and diligence. Their places, however, like most others in the Indies, were before the end of the sixteenth century disposed of by sale to the highest bidder, and the incumbents frequently possessed few or none of the requisite qualifications. Indeed through their incapacity, ignorance, or peculation, the crown must have lost many times more than it gained from the sale of the offices involved.

Treasury officials might not absent themselves from the city in which they resided without license from the viceroy or *audiencia,* or from the province without leave from the king. They had to furnish bond for themselves and for their deputies, and any one of them or his surety might be held responsible in full for the default of any of his associates. They were forbidden to engage in trade, fit out ships, or operate mines,

---

1 Revillagigedo, *Instrucción,* par. 928-1226.
2 Herbert Ingram Priestley, *José de Gálvez, Visitor-general of New Spain,* 1765-1771, 81-2; Revillagigedo, *Instrucción,* par. 765-71.

sugar mills, or pearl fisheries, directly or through the intermediary of others, on pain of loss of office and forfeiture of their property; and after 1582 they might not marry any relative within the fourth degree of other officials in their district connected with the exchequer. They had also, at least from the time of Philip IV, to present an inventory of all their property, real or personal, when they entered upon their duties; for the law presumed, and not without reason, that if they subsequently grew rich it was at the crown's expense.

In Hapsburg times the crown always separated clearly the political and military functions of government from the administration of finnances. Consequently the *oficiales reales,* although of inferior rank to the governors, were in their own sphere of coordinate authority with them; and in some cases they might oppose actions which controverted their instructions or involved extraordinary expenditures. The inevitable result was frequent disputes and misunderstandings, especially growing out of favoritism displayed by the viceroys and governors toward relatives and friends.

Before long questions of general policy affecting the exchequer came to be discussed in each province by a *junta superior de real hacienda* meeting one afternoon in the week, and composed of the viceroy or governor, the *oficiales reales,* and the senior judge and the *fiscal* of the *audiencia.* After 1605 there was also added the senior auditor of the Tribunal of Accounts.[3] The custom was first introduced in Peru by Pedro de la Gasca in 1549, after the pacification of that region, and proved so satisfactory that it was soon (1554) applied also to New Spain. Money was drawn from the treasury by warrant signed by all the members of the junta. Extraordinary expenditures not specifically provided for in the instructions to viceroys and governors had to be referred to Madrid for approval before action might be taken, a course which always involved long delays and often endless bureaucratic red tape. In matters requiring immediate decision some of the earlier viceroys had been allowed to take the initiative, merely communicating their action to their subordinates and to the crown. After 1563 such questions had to be settled by majority vote in a general *acuerdo* of the *audiencia,* the *oficiales reales* taking part, and a full report sent to the king of the circumstances and the amount expended.[4]

---

3 Where there was no *audiencia* resident, the *oficiales reales* met with the governor of the province or his deputy. Under the intendant system at the close of the eighteenth century membership in the junta consisted of the viceroy as *superintendente de hacienda,* the regent, the *fiscal de hacienda,* the senior judge of the tribunal of accounts, and the senior *contador* or the treasurer of the royal exchequer, with in Lima the addition in 1796 of an *oidor* of the *audiencia.* (*Real ordenanza para . . . intendentes . . . de Nueva España,* art 4.)

4 Priestley says that in the seventeenth century (1627) action by the viceroy without the concurrence of the *audiencia* was restored (*José de Gálvez,* 77).

The crown was naturally concerned that those who represented its financial interests in the New World should be subject to a strict and regular audit. From the early days of the *Casa de Contratación,* officers on Hispaniola and neighboring islands were instructed to send reports of receipts and expenditures to that body; and the *Casa* to keep a copy of such records in a separate book apart. Among the 'New Laws' issued by Charles V in 1542-3 was one directing the *oficiales reales* to transmit at the end of each year to the Council of the Indies a general statement of the figures for each branch of the revenue, and a full and detailed report at the expiration of every three years. By the code of regulations issued for the colonial treasuries in 1554, the duty of receiving these accounts was imposed upon the president and two judges of the *audiencia,* or if there was no local *audiencia* upon the governor assisted by two of the *regidores.* The task had to be finished within two months after the New Year, the treasury officials losing their salaries for any time elapsing thereafter; and copies were remitted by the *audiencia* to the *Casa* at Seville, their final destination being the Council of the Indies. Deficiencies in the amounts found deposited in the coffers were to be made up within three days after the completion of the accounts, on pain of loss of office.[5]

The foregoing rules, however, were evidently not enforced, for in spite of reiterated orders and instructions there was plenty of laxity in the form and in the transmission of colonial ledgers. Audits were not taken regularly, and if taken were not always honest.

The newly-appointed viceroy of Peru, Francisco de Toledo, on his arrival at Panama in June 1569, found that the accounts of the oficiales reales there had not been properly audited since 1552; and he directed the books to be brought down to date and closed, under supervision of the audiencia, so that they might be sent to Spain. The sums involved were a matter of about 7,000,000 pesos. In 1591, again, orders were sent to the audiencia of La Plata (Upper Peru) to remit immediately to the king the exchequer accounts for the years 1573, 1576, 1577, and 1578; and in 1596 a royal letter enjoined greater strictness in this matter, on threat of heavy penalties.[6]

It was probably this situation, coupled with the increasing wealth and population of the trans-Atlantic provinces, their distance from the metropolis, and the difficulty of bringing guilty officers to justice, that prompted the innovations of 1605. Till then the Council of the Indies

---

5 Periodical reports of income and expenditure, by the week or month, might also be required by the viceroy or governor.

6 Haring, *Trade and Navigation between Spain and the Indies in the Time of the Hapsburgs,* 93.

had remained the final court of audit, where all the *oficiales reales* received their quittance. In that year, as stated before, three tribunals of accounts were erected in the New World, one in Mexico City for the viceroyalty of New Spain, one at Lima for the provinces of Peru, and a third at Santa Fe de Bogotá for the kingdom of New Granada. There was also a special *contador de cuentas* at Havana for the West Indian islands, and another at Caracas for the region of Venezuela. These tribunals were independent of the *audiencias* and other local authorities; they were empowered to audit all public accounts except those for the *alcabala,* tribute, and quicksilver, for which a separate *contaduría* had already been created; [7] and from their decision there was no appeal even to the Council in Madrid. They transmitted to the Council, however, an annual report together with copies in duplicate of all important papers they audited. The tribunal could also hear and decide extra-legal questions concerning treasury accounts, but suits at law were tried by judges of the *audiencia*. Three *oidores* designated by the viceroy or governor, together with the *fiscal,* held sessions in the tribunal's quarters, assisted by two *contadores* with 'consultative vote.' [8] *Oficiales reales* were required to send a report of receipts every six months to the tribunal, and a complete statement each year with the original warrants and other papers. If these were four months overdue, the *contadores* might dispatch an agent to get them at the *oficiales'* expense. Likewise at the end of each year one of the members of the *contaduría* was expected to make an examination and inventory of the principal treasuries or *cajas reales* to see that the contents tallied with the reports of the exchequer officer.

In most provinces the examination and adjustment of treasury records had fallen so far behind that even when Solórzano was writing in 1635 the tribunals had not succeeded in catching up, although the number of auditors had from time to time been considerably augmented. And some of the colonies, the Philippines, Guatemala, Panama, and Chile, were so far distant from the headquarters of the tribunals that within a few years it was deemed advisable to allow the local *audiencias* to audit the accounts, and send them either to Mexico and Lima or, as originally, to the *contaduría* of the Council of the Indies. Solórzano, who as a former judge of the Lima *audiencia* reveals a natural jealousy of the independence and widespread activities of these courts, gives the impression that they had done little to improve the general situation, and that the

---

7 The financial accounts of viceroys and governors taken by judges of residence were also exempt from the jurisdiction of the tribunals.

8 *Recopilación,* lib. VIII, tit. I, leyes 36, 63.

9 Owing to the distance from Lima of the important mining center of Potosí, the law required that a complete audit be made by a visiting *contador* from the tribunal every three years, a more superficial examination being entrusted annually to one of the judges of the *Audiencia* of Charcas.

auditors were too much concerned about social privileges and rights of precedence, and too little about the faithful and prompt execution of their arduous duties. This is a criticism that might easily be applied to all branches of administration in the Indies. In Gálvez's time, over a century later, although the tribunal in Mexico City was overstaffed, its labors were two or three years in arrears, and conditions under the second Revillagigedo were no better. Certain it is that disorders and irregularities of every sort continued in the collection and husbanding of the royal revenues, and that a large percentage of the king's financial resources in his colonies was diverted into private hands. It was for this reason that the system of *intendentes* was introduced by Charles III in the latter part of the eighteenth century.[10]

The supreme authority, below that of the king, in the organization, extension, and governance of the colonial exchequer, as in every other department of American government, lay before the eighteenth century in the Council of the Indies. This authority, however, was somewhat limited after 1557, when Philip II ordered the control of receipts and expenditures to be shared with the Council of the *Hacienda*.[11] While this centralized fiscal administration in Spain, it set up for the Indies two coordinate and mutually jealous powers, an arrangement which often caused exasperating delays and conflicts of jurisdiction. The India Council met at least one day in each week to discuss questions of financial policy and make appointments to treasury offices, and when occasion warranted two members of the Council of the *Hacienda* might be called in to assist. The monies from America were deposited at Seville with the treasurer of the *Casa de Contratación,* and were subject to draft by the *Hacienda* with the approval of the Council of the Indies.

Taxation in the American provinces was not unduly heavy as compared with that in Spain but the machinery of collection became incredibly costly and unwieldy. The financial system as a whole represented an accretion over several centuries of special levies created *ad hoc* to meet specific needs and once imposed continued indefinitely. There were few taxes of a general character, and any scientific basis of incidence or administration was wholly lacking. The endless variety of impositions, the number of independent administrations, the overlapping of jurisdictions, and the complexity of procedure made honest or effective government virtually impossible.

---

10 The Ordinance of Intendants of 1786 provided that the *cajas reales* be inspected on the first day of each month and their contents checked against the ledgers of the treasury officials. On the basis of this inspection the local subdelegates submitted monthly reports in quintuplicate to the *intendente,* who distributed copies to the viceroy, to the tribunal of accounts, and to the king. From these reports the annual statements were drawn up in the *contaduria,* which in turn were checked against year-end inspections and reports from the *cajas. (Ordenanza,* art. 234-7.)

11 See *ante,* p. 106. n. 13.

As Revillagigedo the younger remarked in the celebrated *Instrucción* to his successor,

It is also impossible for the taxpayer to have knowledge of every one of the contributions, to know clearly what he ought to pay, and how and why he ought to do so . . . [and he therefore all the more resents] the arbitrary methods of officials under a multitude of complicated rules, added to the unjust or improper manner in which subordinates are wont to conduct themselves.

All this is extremely difficult to remedy when there are so many exactions, some of them so complicated and so difficult to determine that their collection has to be left to the discrimination of the collector.

It would therefore be desirable to decrease considerably the number of the revenues . . . although it be at the expense of increasing somewhat the principal ones in order to indemnify thereby the royal exchequer for what it lost or failed to collect in suppressing the lesser.[12]

Of all the American colonies New Spain in the eighteenth century came to be much the richest and most productive. Especially after 1750, with the increase of population and the commercial and administrative reforms of the reign of Charles III, the revenues far surpassed those of any other reign. In the middle of the sixteenth century the gross revenues of New Spain had averaged just under a half million pesos a year, of which the *quinto real* supplied approximately 213,000 pesos, and the Indian tribute 138,000 pesos. One hundred and fifty years later, in 1688-96, the annual gross revenues were slightly over two million, of which 600,000 represented the *quinto*. The civil list consumed about 552,000 pesos, and subsidies to the West Indian islands and the Philippines over 825,000 pesos.[13] In the eighteenth century the average annual gross receipts of the treasury, about three and a half million in 1710, increased to six million in the middle of the century, to twelve million in 1775, to eighteen million in 1790, and to over twenty million in 1802.[14] The effects of freer trade within the empire, and of a more rigid enforcement under the *intendente* system of honesty and efficiency in the collection of revenues, were plainly evident. Yet the receipts as a rule were barely equal to the needs of the viceroyalty on the one hand, and the pressing demands of the government at Madrid on the other. There could be little or no surplus accruing to the benefit of the colonist. More often the treasury was in arrears.

---

12 *Instrucción,* par. 1367-9.

13 Haring, 'Ledgers of the Royal Treasurers in Spanish America in the Sixteenth Century,' *Hisp. Amer. Hist. Rev.,* II, 178, 186.

14 Priestley, op. cit. 383. In 1804 over 26 million pesos in silver were coined in the Mexican mint, the highest figure during the colonial era (J. M. Zamora y Coronado, *Registro de legislación ultramarina,* 3 vols., Havana, 1839, II, 444).

The public revenues as a rule were of two categories: the general funds, and those earmarked for transmission intact to Spain or at least for disposal by the crown. Among the latter were the receipts from the monopolies of quicksilver, playing cards, and tobacco, and from ecclesiastical tithes, the *cruzada,* and the *mesada* and *media anata.* The general funds were derived chiefly from the royalty on bullion, the *alcabala* including the taxes on spirits, Indian tribute, profits from the mint, and the *almojarifazgo.* In the years 1785-9 in New Spain they produced a net annual average of about nine million pesos, the special funds about 4.3 million, of which the tobacco monopoly alone supplied over three million. Of these earmarked revenues about 3.5 million were transmitted annually to Spain. From the general funds three million were absorbed in the subsidies (*situados*) to such fiscally dependent areas as Havana, Florida, Puerto Rico, and the Philippines, leaving about 5.8 million for the general operation of the viceregal government. The expenses of administration consumed four million, over half of it for the military budget, leaving a surplus of about a million and three-quarters which could be applied to outstanding government obligations.[15]

The earliest commercial transactions of the Spaniards in America were by barter, both with the Indians and among themselves. If any coined money was brought out by Columbus and his companions, it was so small in amount as to play a negligible role in trade. Even the semi-civilized natives on the continent had developed no system of exchange based upon the use of the precious metals as coins. Among the Indians of Mexico the Spanish conquerers found such articles as cacao beans, cotton textiles, and sometimes quills of gold dust used to supplement barter. Under the peculiar economy of the Inca empire no medium of exchange was called for. Consequently the Spaniards, whether on the islands or on the mainland, were forced to use gold or silver by weight, and to such an extent that the term *peso* (weight) came to be used generally as representing a monetary unit.

The crown, however, also endeavored to put into circulation silver and copper coins sent over from Spain. In Seville is a copy of a decree of 15 April 1505 ordering the officers of the *Casa de Contratación* to coin and ship to Hispaniola a million maravedís, half in silver and half in *vellon,* the silver real to circulate at a value of 44 maravedís; and later documents refer to similar remittances to meet the lack of currency in

---

15 Fonseca y Urritia, op. cit. I, XL-XLII. The public debt of New Spain in 1789 was about four million pesos.

The viceroy Branciforte reported in March 1797 that during the two years and eight months of his administration sixteen million pesos, or an annual average of six million, was remitted to Spain. 'Instrucción . . . a su sucesor D. Miguel José de Azanza,' in *Instrucciones a los vireyes de Nueva España,* Mexico, 1867-73, II, 536-7.

the colonies.[16] By selling silver reals at 44 maravedís when their legal
value in Castile was only 34, the crown made an excellent profit over the
risk and expense of shipment. And the real continued to circulate at
the higher rate until the end of 1538, when as a consequence of the
establishment of a mint in the Indies, its value on Hispaniola was arbitrarily reduced to 34 in conformity with the rules elsewhere.[17]

Apparently in the first flush of discovery of these new lands, the Catholic kings had intended to set up mints immediately to receive the
precious metals secured there. In the instructions to Columbus of 23
April 1497, we read:

Likewise it seems to us that the gold which may be obtained in the said
Indies should be minted, and coins of 'excelentes de la Granada' be
made from it, as we have ordered to be done in these our kingdoms,
since in this way cheating and sharp practice [cautelas] with the said
gold will be prevented in the said Indies, and to make the said money
we command that you take along the persons and dies and apparatus
of which you will have need.

Not until 1535, however, was a royal mint set up in America, and
meanwhile means of exchange remained extremely crude and confused.
As no facilities were provided for coining 'excelentes de Granada' (i.e.,
ducats, the standard gold coin of Castile after 1497) from the gold
gathered on the islands, the settlers resorted to an uncoined gold unit of
value approximating that of the *castellano,* the predecessor of the ducat
with which they were more familiar. It weighed one-fiftieth of a marc.
This was the celebrated *peso de oro de minas.* Herrera tells us that some
of the colonists cut small pieces of gold imitating the castellano or the
ducat, and even crude reals with the arms of the king. The castellano was
of a fineness of 23¾ carats, but the pesos de minas, doubtless owing to
the crude methods of assay and smelting, was considered to be of a fineness of about 22 or 22½ carats and its value was presumed to be 450
maravedís.[18] This unit of exchange was carried by the Spaniards from
the West Indies to Mexico, and later by way of Panama to Peru, and
remained for a long time in use in all parts of the Indies.

In New Spain in the early years, the situation was much more be-
wildering. Owing to the rudimentary means of testing the fineness of
gold in the jewels, ornaments, etc., constituting the most valuable part
of the plunder, that which passed for *oro de ley* was much closer to 18

17 Apparently in response to protests from the islanders, the crown extended the
old rate until 1552.

16 In 1519 the crown forbade anyone to send money to America without express
royal authorization.

18 Strictly speaking, if assays had been accurate the *peso de oro de minas* should
have been valued at 454 or 465 maravedís.

than to 22 carats. Moreover the weights used by the conquerers were probably at fault, for Bernal Díaz del Castillo tells us that they had to manufacture their own scales and weights to ascertain the value of the booty. He likewise remarks that the Spanish authorities in the beginning circulated gold at 3 carats less than the presumed legal fineness in order to aid the soldiers in paying their debts, and incidentally to defraud the merchants who had come to Vera Cruz to trade at a time of excessively high prices in the new colony. It was known as *oro común* or the *peso corriente* and was worth about three hundred maravedís. There also circulated a kind of gold largely mixed with copper which had been common among the Aztecs and which the Spaniards immediately found useful as a medium of exchange. The Indians doubtless found it profitable greatly to increase the supply. It was called by the Indian name, *tipuzque,* and was valued at about 272 maravedís. Moreover in the 'thirties the output of the Mexican silver mines began to be felt, silver became more common than gold, and was used more and more as a circulatory medium. It too was by weight and fineness reckoned in pesos de minas of 450 maravedís, sometimes called *pesos de plata ensayados,* but it was doubtless subject to the same irregularities as gold.

Coins minted in Europe meantime remained extremely rare, especially with relation to the increase and spread of the Spanish population on the mainland. And there were many complaints about the gold in circulation, the fineness or value of which it was impossible to know. Much of it was falsified and worth only half its presumed value. Eventually the emperor, moved by petitions from the colonists, ordered the payment of customs dues and judicial fines in New Spain to be made in *oro de tipuzque* so as to withdraw it from the country.

In view of this confusion, and in response to representations from the Bishop Zumárraga and the crown officials, the crown decided to establish mints in the New World. The viceroy Mendoza, in instructions received before his departure from Spain, was ordered to establish immediately such an institution, and ordinances for its governance were embodied in a *cédula* of 11 May 1535.[19] Silver and copper were to be coined, but not gold, the silver in pieces of 1, 2, 3, ½, and ¼ reals.[20] This real was to be valued at 34 maravedís, as in Spain, and only silver stamped as having paid the *quinto* might be used. Three reals were to be deducted from each marc of silver as remuneration to the staff,[21] and

---

19 *Col. doc inéd.,* 2nd ser., x, 264-71. The ordinances provided also for a mint at Santo Domingo on Hispaniola.

20 The 3-real piece was soon replaced by one of 4 reals.

21 Later one real was deducted as seigniorage for the crown, and two reals for the treasurer and the contractor who operated the mint (*Recopilación,* lib. IV, tit. 23, ley 7). During most of the colonial period seigniorage was collected twice, once at the royal smeltery and again at the mint. In the time of the second Revillagigedo, when the mints were administered by the crown, the deduction amounted to nearly 4 reals (*Instrucción,* par. 950).

an Indian pueblo was to be assigned to the mint as an *encomienda* to provide the labor as well as tribute toward the support of the mint officials. The first coins were probably issued in the spring of 1536.[22] Copper coins, of the value of 2 and 4 maravedís, were not ordered struck by Mendoza until 1542. After 1565 this coinage was discontinued, as it found no acceptance among the mass of the population, the Indians, who preferred to use the traditional cacao beans.

The viceroy proposed to the emperor the coinage of pieces of eight reals as equal in value to the current *pesos de oro de tipuzque*. Permission was granted in a decree of 18 November 1537, at the viceroy's discretion, but there is no evidence of the issue of such coins till the time of Philip II.[23] The silver peso of 8 reals or 272 maravedís, called variously *peso fuerte, duro real de á ocho*, became, however, the standard coin of the Spanish Indies. As the Spanish dollar or 'piece of eight' of trade the world over, it was the prototype of the United States silver dollar and of similar coins used in many of the Spanish American republics and in the Far East. Gold was not coined in America until the second half of the seventeenth century,[24] for the early Hapsburgs were very loath to see any gold bullion remain in the New World. The few gold pieces that appeared there must have been brought over by private individuals.

In Peru for thirty-five years after the conquest the monetary situation was the same as had prevailed in New Spain. For large transactions gold and silver circulated in bars, for small transactions in crudely stamped pieces of silver which were often debased by the Indians, and doubtless by Spaniards too, with a large proportion of copper and lead. Bullion was valued in pesos de minas of 450 maravedís, although the 'current silver' in circulation was worth only about 300. In the 'fifties and 'sixties the authorities frequently complained of the absence of coined money, and urged the establishment of a mint. Arequipa was recommended as a proper location, because it was on the route from Upper Peru to the sea over which the bullion traveled on its way to Panama, and because supplies of wood were available for fuel. A mint was finally set up in Lima and began operations in 1568. But it was far from the principal mining centers, not enough silver was offered to pay the cost of operation, and it was 'transferred' in 1572 to Potosí.[25] The Lima mint, how-

22 A. S. Aiton and B. Wheeler, 'The First American Mint,' *Hisp. Amer. Hist. Rev.*, XI, 204-5.

23 *Col. doc. inéd.*, 2nd ser., X, 332, 385; Aiton and Wheeler, loc. cit. 205, 214-15.

24 Cobo in his *Historia natural de las Indias*, completed in 1653, states (I, 300) that gold doubloons were being coined in New Granada.

25 Roberto Levillier, *Gobernantes del Perú*, 14, vols., Madrid 1921-6, I, 282, 487; III, 44, 198, 300. Juan de Matienzo *Gobienro del Perú*, Buenos Aires, 1910, pt. II, cap. 10. Manuel Moreyra Paz-Soldán, *Antecedentes españoles y el circulante durante la conguista e iniciación del virreinato*, Lima, 1941, 24-9, 50-56. André E. Sayous, 'La Circulation de métaux et de monnaies au Perou pendant le XVIe siecle,' *d'Econ, Pol.*, 1928, 1310-11.

ever, in reality operated sporadically until about 1590, and was permanently re-established a century later, in 1683.[26] In the interval all the coined silver came from remote Upper Peru, and its circulation in the rest of the viceroyalty was very deficient. Lima, the distributing center for most of the European trade of Peru and its adjacent provinces, seems especially to have suffered.

After 1536 in New Spain, and some thirty years later in Peru, silver coined in reals or pesos gradually superseded the peso de oro de minas as a unit of value. But the process was a slow one, and until well into the following century the imaginary unit continued to be used in buying and selling gold and silver bullion and in other large commercial transactions. Minted coins, as a matter of fact, circulated freely only in limited areas, in the European centers, in the vicinity of the mints, and along the principal trade routes. This was especially true of Peru. In areas distant from the centers of silver production, the colonists perforce continued to use the precious metals in small pieces by weight. Even in Upper Peru bar silver was in great demand to pay for imported European articles at Panama or Portobello, where it was preferred to the crudely stamped coins of the American mints.[27] With the increase of the ratio of gold to silver, the peso de minas reckoned in gold bullion was officially advanced in value, in 1578 to 556 maravedís, and later to 589 maravedís. Reckoned in silver, at least in Peru, it was in practice reduced in value, being considered as equivalent to 12½ reals or 425 maravedís.[28]

The operation of American mints before the eighteenth century was let out under contract to private individuals or to *compañias de fabricantes de moneda,* which paid to the crown the seigniorage tax and charged the silver merchants a fixed tariff for services rendered. Sometimes offices in the mint were sold by the crown to the highest bidder. In 1702, for instance, the post of treasurer-administrator was purchased in perpetuity by the Count of San Juan de Lurigancho for 80,000 pesos. Throughout the sixteenth and seventeenth centuries, however, the technique of refining the precious metals as well as of manufacturing coins

---

26 In the eighteenth century mints were established in Guatemala, Bogotá, Popayán, Santiago de Chile, Guanajuanto, and Guadalajara.

27 Sayous, op. cit. 1315.

28 Escalona y Agüero, lib. II, pt. I, cap. 12, par. 6; pt. 2, cap. I, par. 15; 'quinto de oro,' par. 5. *Recopilación,* lib. VIII, tit. 8, ley 11.

The viceroy Toledo (1569-81) in Peru had issued an order that when the *quinto* and the tribute of the Indians were paid in silver or reals, the pesos should be reckoned at only 12½ reals, or 425 maravedís, the difference representing the cost of coining the silver at the mint (Cobo, op. cit. I, 320). Philip II in 1592 extended the order to cover all payments of the treasury (*Recopilación,* lib. VIII, tit. 8, ley 8). This unit was called the *peso ensayado de tributos*: There was likewise in use in Peru an imaginary unit called the *peso ensayado* of 9 reals (306 marvedís).

remained very defective, and fraud was general in both the fineness and the weight of money. Owing to the crudeness of the originals, counterfeits by the Indians were common; and the clipping of coins was very general. This seemed to be especially true of the Peruvian vice-royalty, in which the coins issued from Potosí were notorious. There were repeated royal orders in the seventeenth century to collect all base or fraudulent coins at the mints, melt them down and re-issue them in conformity with the law, but the orders had little permanent effect.[29]

A radical reform was introduced in the eighteenth century by the ordinances issued by Philip V of 9 July 1728. The mints were taken out of the hands of private contractors, and were administered directly by the crown under a superintendent subordinate to the viceroy to whom he made annual report. Coinage on the individual account of miners or bullion merchants was discontinued, and thereafter the government purchased and coined all the output of the mines on its own account. By the new ordinances all coins must be round, stamped in what might be called a fly-wheel press (acuñados en molinos y volantes), and finished with milled edges to discourage clipping. The gold unit, the escudo, was made of equal weight and fineness with the silver real, each being cut 68 to the marc. As gold and silver were later (1750) fixed at a ratio of 16 to 1,[30] the escudo came to be worth two silver pesos of eight reals each. The new rules were put into practice almost immediately in New Spain (1732-3), but were not effective in Peru until 1748.[31]

In spite of the new regulations, minor adulteration of the coinage in American mints continued. New Spain was still flooded with clipped and sweated angular money minted before 1728, and with light gold pieces from Peru. Finally in 1752 Ferdinand VI instructed the viceroy to redeem the old money at par, i.e., at the expense of the crown, within a stated time limit. Foreign and counterfeit coins, however, and 'provincial' money or token silver shipped out from Spain, continued to be an insoluble problem. As British and Dutch interlopers extracted good coins from the Caribbean colonies in exchange for degraded foreign money, a special type of silver of lighter weight was issued by the

29 Manuel Moreyra Paz-Soldán, 'La Tesorería y la estadistica de acuñación colonial en la casa de moneda en Lima.' Cuadernos de Estudios, tomo II, no. 4, 13-23. A notorious case was that of the alcalde provincial of Potosí, Francisco Gómoz de la Rocha, found to have defrauded the mint of 472,000 pesos, and executed together with the assayer of the mint in 1654 (ibid. 19-20).

30 Somewhat higher than in Spain,, and creating a gold premium of about seven per cent. Between 1772 and 1786 Spanish coinage was progressively debased by the crown, and the ratio between gold and silver in Spain and in the Indies sank to 16.61 to 1. Earl J. Hamilton, 'Monetary Problems in Spain and Spanish America, 1751-1800,' Journ. Econ. Hist., IV, 32-5.

31 Manuel Moreyra Paz-Soldán, Apuntes sobre la historia de la moneda colonial en el Perú. El reglamento de la casa de moneda de 1755, Lima, 1938, 5-8.

Mexican mint after 1786, especially for Cuba and Caracas where contraband operations were most active.[32]

The Spanish American provinces always suffered from a scarcity of small silver and a complete absence of copper money or vellon for small change. The smallest silver piece issued by the mints was the half-real, and cacao beans continued to be used among the Indians for their petty transactions down into the nineteenth century. The retail merchants of Mexico City also issued tokens called *tlacos* as change in daily business, to the great loss and inconvenience of poor whites and Indians. Charles III in 1767 ordered the viceroy to prohibit these tokens, and in that year and later considered the advisability of coining vellon in the colonies. But the official ban on tlacos was never effective, and they continued to circulate in Mexico long after the end of the colonial regime. The minting of copper money encountered the persistent opposition of mercantile and financial interests represented in the *consulado,* and not until 1814 were vellon coins of 2, 4, and 8 maravedís put into circulation.[33]

---

32 Hamilton, loc. cit. 25-7, 37.

33 Ibid. 36, 38-9. In 1789 the Mexican mint was ordered to coin silver quarter-reals to relieve the situation, but they were too small for convenient use and were issued in inadequate quantities.

XVI

❧❧❧

The Spanish Commercial System

❧❧❧

The economic policy of the Castilian crown with regard to the colonies was in accord with the prevailing mercantilist ideas of the time. The ideal, then as now, was national power and self-sufficiency, although the means employed to achieve this end were generally somewhat different from those that operate today. National power meant military and naval power, supported by an abundance of money and command of certain essential products. And these were to be secured by a definite economic policy that involved the protection of certain industries and activities within the commonwealth at the expense of others. The accumulation of money was conditioned by the prevailing belief that gold and silver alone constituted wealth—the so-called bullionist theory. Each nation must keep what it had and get as much as possible from others. In the earlier and cruder stage this object was attained simply by prohibiting the export of the precious metals, a device that was never wholly effective, especially when trade with the Orient was involved. Later it was supposed to be accomplished by maintaining a favorable 'balance of trade.' The production of commodities that increased exports was therefore encouraged; certain other industries might be discouraged by restrictions or even prohibition. Mercantilism was essentially a protectionist system, aimed to secure the ultimate welfare of the community as a whole, but involving radical interference with private interests and aimed largely at export commerce.

From these concepts the old 'colonial system' was a natural development. Colonists were esteemed chiefly because they were potential sources of wealth and security to the mother country. They offered closed markets to Spanish manufacturers and agriculture, and supplied necessities such as cotton, dyes, and hides, or tropical luxuries such as sugar, cacao, and tobacco. But above all, the American provinces produced immense quantities of the precious metals. The crown therefore sought to create for Spain a monopoly of all trade and shipping with the Indies, as well as to engross most of the gold and silver from American mines. And so there gradually evolved under the early Hapsburgs a rigid and elaborate commercial system through whose operations a large part of the wealth of America might ultimately be syphoned back to Spain. All external trade of the colonies was reserved to the mother country, Spain furnishing them with all they required from Europe, shipped on Spanish vessels, and the colonies producing in general only raw materials and articles that did not compete with the products of Spain. The export of gold and silver to foreign countries was absolutely forbidden. This policy of colonial monopoly was pursued to the very end of the colonial regime. The bullionist principle in its earlier form was abandoned in the more enlightened days of the eighteenth century.

These precepts, followed by a relatively nonindustrial country like Spain that was in no position to fulfil its part of the colonial compact, led to results that in many cases were not foreseen, and in others were plainly disastrous. The industry of Castile, carefully fostered by Ferdinand and Isabella, was destroyed in the sixteenth and seventeenth centuries by the lack of any consistent and intelligible economic policy on the part of their royal successors. The Catholic kings themselves, blinded by religious fanaticism, had probably weakened Spain by expelling the Jews and the Moors, its ablest merchants and agriculturists. The Hapsburgs who followed them, by ruinous taxation to support an unending succession of expensive foreign wars, and by violent oscillations between free trade and protection in a vain effort to protect the Spanish consumer in a time of rising prices, brought Spanish industry and agriculture into complete decay. Eventually Spanish maritime power all but disappeared, and her trade became but a shadow of what it might well have been.

Spain consequently could not export her own manufactures to the colonies, when her declining industries were unable to supply her own needs. To make up the deficiency, both of goods and of capital, her merchants had recourse to foreign sources; and as the law forbade intercourse between the colonies and traders of other nations, Spanish merchants often became in effect merely intermediates, the agents or factors on a commission basis of foreign commercial houses to which often they lent their Spanish names in order to elude the law. The goods remained the property of the foreign merchant, and were shipped at his risk. In return for the manufacturers of Flanders, France, Italy, England, and Germany, Spain gave her own products—wool, wine, dried fruits—and the products of the Indies—sugar, cotton, hides, cochineal, dyewoods—but also, in spite of the law forbidding export, gold and silver bullion. Gold and silver also flowed out of the kingdom with the direct connivance of the crown to meet its obligations abroad, often in great sums, two hundred thousand or three hundred thousand ducats at a time.

The share of foreign merchants and foreign goods in the export trade to the American colonies became of increasing importance as time wore on, especially under the later Hapsburgs. Even before 1600 ships from the Hanseatic cities called in large numbers at Seville and its seaport Sanlucar, bringing textiles and other wares also from the Low Countries and England. French vessels were likewise increasingly common, and by the close of the Hapsburg era French merchants held a dominant position in the Seville market, followed closely by the Genoese and the Dutch.[1]

So in time the trade of Spain with America became a more or less passive machine, a device by which was canalized under royal control the supply of goods from the rest of Europe. It profited the merchant houses of Seville and Cadiz, but it contributed little to the development of industry or the enchantment of the well-being of the people as a whole. In 1608 the Council of the Indies informed the king that foreign interest in the fleets sent to the Indies amounted to two-thirds of the gold and silver which the royal armadas brought back to Spain.[2] A century later, we are told, foreign countries were supplying five-sixths of the manufactures consumed in Spain and nine-tenths of that American trade which the crown had sought so carefully to monopolize for its own subjects.[3] Years before, Pedro Farnández de Navarrete in his *Conservación de monarquías* had moaned: 'All that the Spaniards bring from the Indies, acquired after long, prolix, and hazardous navigations, and all that they harvest with blood and hard labor, foreigners carry off to their homelands with ease and comfort, building in their provinces most sumptuous palaces with the wealth of Spain.'

In Spain as in other European countries before the nineteenth century it was held to be axiomatic that colonial commerce should be the exclusive privilege of the merchants of the mother country. The policy

---

1 A French mémoire of 1691 stated that the French introduced every two years 20 million livres of goods into Cadiz, of which 12 million went out on the fleets to America. Of the later, 6 or 7 million were on the account of the French themselves, the rest on the account of the Spaniards and others who bought from the French. The author also remarked that profits on goods sold in the Indies were generally from 40 to 50 per cent. The following figures were given for the cargoes of the fleets returning from America:

> French share—13-14 million livres
> (about 4½ mililon pesos)
> Genoese share—11-12 million livres
> Dutch share—10 million livres
> English share—6-7 million livres
> Flemish share—6 million livres
> German share—4 million livres

Henri Sée, *Documents sur le commerce de Cadix*, Paris, 1927, 21 ff.

2 Irene A. Wright, 'Rescates, with Special Reference to Cuba, 1599-1610' *Hisp. Amer. Hist. Rev.*, III, 338 n.

3 Campillo wrote *c.* 1740 that nine-tenths of the precious metals from America went abroad, *Nuevo Sistema de gobierno económico para la América*, 8.

of Charles V was an exception. With a version more imperial in scope, or perhaps beholden to his foreign bankers in Italy and Germany, in 1526 he opened trade and navigation with America to all of his subjects within the Hapsburg dominions. The Welsers of Augsburg were especially active, with an agency or 'factory' at Santo Domingo, silver mines in New Spain, and after 1528 the province of Venezuela to settle and exploit. The great merchant-banking house of the Fuggers also had commercial interests and properties in America. Both they and the Welsers helped to finance the voyages of García de Loaisa and Sebastian Cabot sent by the crown to the Moluccas, and the Welsers had a hand in the expedition of Pedro de Mendoza to colonize the Rio de la Plata. But all this was of short duration. The colonial ventures of the Welsers proved to be a cruel and disastrous failure, and toward the close of Charles's reign the custom was insensibly renewed of excluding all strangers from the New World. From the time of Philip II a merchant, to engage in trade with the colonies, had by law to be of Spanish birth, or naturalized and domiciled in the peninsula, and only native Spaniards might be owners or masters of ships in the Indies navigation. Foreign merchants, even if they received a special royal dispensation, might trade only with their own capital, and Spaniards were forbidden to serve as a façade for unlicensed foreign mercantile operations.[4]

The penalty for infraction of these rules was forfeiture of the goods involved and of all the property of the culprits, not only of the foreigner who attempted to trade but also of the native who shielded him under a Spanish name. Under the circumstances reviewed above, however, absolute exclusion was difficult or impossible to maintain, and very early certain foreign-born residents secured the right of admission to the India trade.

As a matter of fact lines were drawn even more narrowly. Traffic with America became to all intents and purposes a monopoly in the hands of the larger commercial houses of Seville.[5] Not only was trade confined to this city, and to its neighbor and subsidiary, Cadiz, but it was also made difficult or inconvenient for the small merchant to have a direct share in it. From the middle of the sixteenth century no one might cross the Atlantic to trade, either on his own account or as a factor or supercargo, unless he loaded for the voyage goods of a certain minimum value —ultimately fixed at 300,000 maravedís or about 1,100 pesos. The original purpose of the rule was doubtless to prevent the emigration of persons who represented themselves falsely as exporting merchants. But

---

4 *Recopilación*, lib. ix, tit. 27, leyes 1, 3.

5 Except for the supply of Negroes to the colonies, which was widely distributed among concessionaires who were frequently of foreign orgin.

the result was practically to confine trade to the wealthier Andalusian firms.

The chief administrative agency for the regulation and development of this commerce was the *Casa de Contratación* or House of Trade established at Seville by a royal decree of 20 January 1503.

Seville was chosen as its residence, not because of superior maritime facilities, for Cadiz had much the better harbor, but probably because Seville happened to be the wealthiest and most populous city of Castile, of which the Indies were considered to be the exclusive possession ... as all trade with the New World was to pass through the *casa,* the control of this commerce was from the outset restricted to a single port for the whole of Spain. And for two centuries, in spite of the claims of other cities, in spite of protests from the colonies, and the well-intentioned efforts of Ferdinand's grandson the emperor, Seville retained her high distinction.[6]

The vested interests of its merchants were sufficient to bear down all opposition; and for the crown it seemed much easier and more economical to maintain in a single port the rigid supervision of trade and navigation that was contemplated from the outset.

The *Casa de Contratación* was also the earliest institution in Spain created specifically for the governance of the American empire. In the beginning it was without doubt planned to be the private trading house of the crown, corresponding with royal 'factories' in the New World—possibly in imitation of the *Casa da India* established by the Portuguese in Lisbon for the control of the spice trade with the Orient. If this was intended, it soon proved to be impracticable, and the *Casa* emerged as a government bureau, licensing and supervising all ships and merchants, passengers and goods, crews and equipment, passing to and from the Indies, and enforcing the laws and ordinances relating thereto.[7]

The *Casa* received and cared for all the revenues in gold, silver, and precious stones remitted to the crown by colonial treasurers, and collected the *avería* or convoy tax and customs and other duties. Transcripts were kept of official communications passing through the *Casa*

6 Haring, *Trade and Navigation between Spain and the Indies,* 7-8.

7 If direct exploitation of trade by the crown was originally designed, it was not the last time that the proposal was entertained. In the very beginning of the reign of Philip II several projects were put forward by Spanish capitalists to help ease the penury of the royal treasury. The crown was to go into partnership with the proponents on a capital basis ranging from 400,000 to a million ducats, three-fourths of which would be supplied by the king. A general trade was contemplated, in free competition with private enterprise, except for a monopoly of certain lines such as Negro slaves, quicksilver, and textiles; and factors were to be maintained in the principal industrial cities of the Continent. Needless to say, the king was in no position to advance the capital required.

to America, and of correspondence from America, about trade and finance, as well as of accounts of receipts and expenditures of the colonial treasurers. Its officers might propose to the king anything they deemed necessary for the organization and development of American trade.[8] The *Casa* therefore became a sort of special ministry of commerce, subordinate later to the Council of the Indies, and one of the principal outposts of the royal exchequer.

The personnel of the *Casa* consisted at first of a treasurer, a *contador* or a bookkeeper-secretary, and a *factor* or business manager, who were expected to meet for consultation and joint action morning and afternoon every day in the year except holidays. With increase in the volume and complexity of business, from time to time subordinate officials, secretaries, and legal counselors, were added, and the three original officers became executive heads of large departments. In 1514 the office of postmaster-general (*correo mayor*)[9] was created, and Philip II in 1579 added

---

8 They themselves were strictly forbidden to trade with the Indies on their own account, either directly or indirectly, on pain of heavy fines, forfeitures, or loss of office.

9 The post of *Correo mayor de las Indias* was conferred in perpetuity on Dr. Lorenzo Galíndez de Carvajal, a distinguished jurist and member of the Council of Castile, with responsibility for the dispatch and receipt of both official and private correspondence with the Indies, as well as for the service within the colonies and between the *Casa de Contratación* and the court. He exercised the office, however, through a deputy, usually one of the officials of the *Casa*. To what extent he appointed postmasters in the colonies does not appear. In 1570 he sold the Spanish services to the *correo mayor* of Seville, and thereafter they passed through various hands until in 1633 they were purchased by the Conde de Villamediana, *correo mayor general* of Spain. Finally in 1706 the crown expropriated this office and incorporated the Spanish postal service into the royal administration. After 1570 the function of *correo mayor* in the viceroyalty of Peru, covering all of Spanish South America, passed to a younger son of the original grantee, who had gone out to Peru with the viceroy Nieva; and it continued in the Peruvian branch of the Carvajal family until incorporated in the crown in 1768 in return for a pension and numerous honors and privileges. In New Spain the Carvajals never succeeded in having their claims recognized, and the post of *correo mayor* was first established by the viceroy Martín Enríquez as a vendable office in 1580. Its value fluctuated between 40,000 and 60,000 pesos. When in 1765 Charles III decided to make the post office in all the colonies a government service, existing private rights in New Spain were bought out by the state. In the captaincy-general of Guatemala the *correo mayor* had a similar history. The postal service in the colonies was gradually extended in the sixteenth and seventeenth centuries to include all the more important cities. The overland mails were usually carried by Indian or mulatto runners (*chasquis*), later by mounted postmen where the roads permitted, from one post to another on the principal highways. In Peru in the seventeenth century there were about 140 such posts. In the transatlantic service dispatch boats, light, swift sailing vessels of from 50 to 100 tons, accompanied the periodical fleets to America, and frequently returned alone to Spain with the latest news from the colonies. Between fleets similar vessels carried dispatches to and from the Indies, financed by the *avería*, or by contract with the *Consuldado*, or at times at the expense of the crown. Finally in 1764

that of president of the *Casa,* to coordinate the work of the departments and represent the *Casa* in external matters. From 1588 there was a purveyor-general of armadas and fleets with a staff of his own, and at the close of Philip's reign a *tribunal de la contaduría* or board of audit. In the seventeenth century appeared a commandant of the navy yard, a staff to superintend the purchase and testing of artillery and powder and to teach gunnery, and another to administer the convoy tax for the defense of the annual fleets.

A chief pilot (*piloto mayor*) was appointed as early as 1508, the first being Amerigo Vespucci, and under his direction there gradually developed a hydrographic bureau and a school of navigation, for the construction and validating of nautical charts and instruments, and for teaching and examining pilots for the Indies traffic. A 'professorship' of cosmography was established in 1552. One of the duties of the pilot major and his associates was to maintain a careful and systematic record of the results of geographical discovery and exploration, and a standard map, *padrón real,* was kept in the *Casa* to which all charts had legally to conform. This nautical school at Seville seems to have been the first of its kind in modern Europe, and for a long time it was an object of admiration by visitors from other lands. When Queen Elizabeth in 1563 appointed Stephen Borough to the office of chief pilot, it was without doubt in emulation of the Spaniards.

The *Casa* was also a court of law. Its officers very early attempted to exercise judicial authority over infractions of its rules and in disputes between merchants and mariners engaged in the American trade. Coming into conflict with the local judiciary of Seville, its competence was in 1511 defined by the crown to cover all civil suits growing out of the trade, and the crime of barratry as well. Its three officials were therefore referred to as *jueces oficiales.* Final shape as given to the *Casa's* jurisdiction by Charles V, who in 1539 granted it exclusive authority not only over infractions of its ordinances, but over local civil suits affecting the revenues of the crown, and over all crimes committed on the voyage to and from America, with appeal in important cases to the Council of the Indies.

A *fiscal* or prosecuting attorney was added to the *Casa's* staff in 1546, and such was the increase of judicial business that in 1583 a separate chamber, or *sala de justicia,* was created consisting of two, and later of three, justices. Thereafter the *Casa* comprised two quite separate branches, administration and justice, the president serving as the link between them. The erection at Seville in August 1543 of a *consulado,*

---

under the minister Grimaldi, was created the *Correos Marítimos,* a state-owned shipping enterprise. See Walter B. L. Bose, 'Organización del correo en España y en las Indias occidentales,' *Revista de correos y telégrafos,* Buenos Aires, no. 60, 1549-58.

or guild of merchants trading with America, had meantime somewhat reduced the number of civil cases. Its officers, a prior and two consuls,[10] elected annually by the merchants, took over the settlement of virtually all civil suits between members, including proceedings in bankruptcy. Their methods were simpler, cheaper, and more expeditious than those of the ordinary law courts, and they relieved the *Casa* of a great mass of judicial work.[10]

A guild organization similar to those established earlier in Burgos and Bilbao had been sought by the merchants engaged in the American trade for some years. And when in 1543 the crown, at the solicitation of these same commercial interests, issued decrees making the sailing of periodical convoyed fleets an obligatory rule, at the same time the Seville merchants received permission to incorporate as a guild. An important motive was without doubt the crown's dependence upon the merchants to finance the ships and armaments involved.[12] The *consulado*, or *Universidad de los cargadores a las Indias,* exercised a major influence upon the character of the American trade down to the second half of the eighteenth century. It arranged with the *Casa de Contratación* for the outfitting and dispatch of the fleets, and supplied its officers with expert advice on financial and commercial matters. Within a few decades it became virtually a closed corporation of a few great commercial houses enjoying a monopoly of traffic between Spain and its overseas empire. Through it the Seville merchants came to control the character and size of outbound cargoes, and to dictate at will prices in America. Through it they also made loans and extended other financials aids to the crown, often under duress or to secure special favors. In practice, therefore, if not in theory, this organization somewhat resembled the exclusive trading companies of the same period in Holland and England. Similar merchant guilds were later established in New Spain (1594) and Peru (1613), associations of the principal importers whose interests coincided with those of the merchant oligarchy in Andalusia.[13] The effect

10 In the eighteenth century there were three counsuls, two representing the merchants of Seville, one those in Cadiz. Neither foreigners nor their sons or grandsons might be elected to the office of prior or consul.

11 The ordinances of the *consulado,* drawn up in collaboration with members of the Council of the Indies, were published in 1556. For the *consulado's* support a small tax was levied on all goods exported to America, collected when the customs dues were paid. Only .05 per cent in the beginning, it was increased to .1 per cent in 1603, and so remained until its temporary abolition in 1712. The *consulado* also derived considerable revenues from the sale of notorial offices or *escribanías* connected with the fleets. Robert Sidney Smith, *The Spanish Guild Merchant. A History of the Consulado,* 1250-1700, Durham, N. C., 1940, 105.

12 Ibid. 91.

13 The *consulado* in Mexico City (*Universidad de los mecaderes de la Nueva España*) was created by royal decree of 15 June 1592, in response to petitions from the *cabildo* and the principal merchants, and the guild was formally organ-

was to diminish the supply of European goods in America and of American products in Europe. The colonies were kept chronically understocked, and had to pay exorbitant prices for all European commodities. It was one of the most serious obstacles to the growth in industry, in population, and in general well-being; and it had the inevitable result of encouraging a widespread contraband trade.

Overseas trade with America on the other hand involved large risks. Remittances on consignments sent out on the fleets were often long delayed, American markets might have a momentary surfeit of smuggled goods and be not at all lucrative. Dishonesty in agents or commission men was not uncommon. And under the Hapsburg kings the likelihood of sequestration of gold and silver shipped to Spain on private account was ever present. Consequently interest rates on borrowed capital for use in the Atlantic trade were generally high, sometimes as much as 30 or 35 per cent, especially as in case of disaster the loss fell entirely on the capitalist lender. Bankruptcies were therefore not uncommon in the history of Seville and Cadiz. With a very slow turnover of capital, and many and unusual hazards, the American trade was a speculative enterprise fit only for merchants with large funds and not too impatient of early returns.[14]

Not until the eighteenth century was an exclusive trading company, in the more usual form of a simple joint-stock organization, given trial in Spanish American commerce. The explanation for the absence of great corporations, it has been suggested, may be found in part in the prevalence in Spain of old Italian forms of business contracts, the *commenda* and the *societas,* both of them simple partnerships. In the beginning Spanish traders sold goods in American seaports personally or through factors or traveling agents, and smaller houses continued to do so. More powerful Seville houses, having constant and regular relations with the colonies, soon could afford to possess one or more agents resident in America, to carry on business for them or to send unprejudiced information. But partnership contracts seem generally to have been preferred, both for special missions to America and with resident merchants in the New World.[15]

ized in January 1594 (R. S. Smith, 'Antecedentes del Consulado de México, 1590-1594.' *Rev. Hist. Amer.* no. 15, 299-313). It was provided with ordinances based on those of Seville. Toward the close of the eighteenth century *consulados* were also established in Caracas and Guatemala (1793), Buenos Aires and Havana (1794), and Catagena, Santiago, Guadalajara, and Vera Cruz (1795). Smith *The Spanish Guild Merchant,* 16.

14 Cf. comments in *Le Parfait Négosiant* by Jacques Savary, Paris, 2 vols., 1763 II, ch. 49.

15 E. Sayous, 'Partnerships in the Trade between Spain and America and also in the Spanish Colonies in the Sixteenth Century,' *Jour. Econ. Bus. Hist.,* 1, 282-301.

Under Philip V in the eighteenth century strenuous efforts were made by the *consulado* at Cadiz to circumscribe the American trade even more closely within its own group, to the exclusion of foreign residents and even of Creoles. In 1729, perhaps as a reaction to the organization in the previous year of the Company of Guipúzcoa in the north of Spain, the *consulado* obtained from the crown a decree to the effect that shippers (*cargadores*) on the *flotas* and galleons must be active voting members of the guild; and active membership since 1623 had been limited to the sons and grandsons of Spaniards. The rule was not abrogated until 1742. In the same year, 1729, new regulations of the *consulado* prohibited Creole merchants in America from serving as agents or consignees of the exporting houses. And six years later a royal order forbade inhabitants of New Spain and Peru to remit gold or silver to Spain for investment in exports to America. True, this order was rescinded in 1738, but Creoles were still permitted to do business at Cadiz only through Spanish merchants matriculated in the Indies trade. And although the rule was formally revoked in 1749, it continued in practical effect until 1780.[16]

Another institution subordinate to the *Casa* was the *juzgado de Indias* in the neighboring city of Cadiz. Owing to the difficulties and dangers of the bar at Sanlucar at the mouth of the Guadalquivir, and the shallow channel of the river up to Seville fifty miles inland, ships after 1508 were permitted to lade at Cadiz or Sanlucar under supervision of an inspector from the *Casa*. In 1535 the crown appointed a permanent resident, *juez oficial,* at Cadiz, and ships and fleets returning from America were frequently allowed to make Cadiz their port, provided cargoes and registers were transported intact to Seville. This institution was throughout the sixteenth and seventeenth centuries a source of perennial jealousy and dispute. The *Casa* endeavored to confine exports from Cadiz to local products such as wine and wax, and keep the tonnage assigned to it as small as possible; but the superior advantages of Cadiz harbor, lower duties collected there, and the greater facilities offered for illicit trade, attracted foreign merchants and shipping more and more to it, and the *consulado* of Seville repeatedly tried to have the *juzgado* suppressed altogether.[17] Finally under the new Bourbon dynasty and the influence of more rational ideas from abroad, in 1717 the two cities exchanged roles. Both the *Casa de Contratación* and the *consulado* were transferred to the rival port, and to Seville was assigned the *juzgado de Indias.*[18] The Seville merchants struggled hard for several

16 Rafel Antúnez y Acevedo, *Memorias históricas,* 298-305.

17 Albert Girard, *La Rivalité commerciale et maritime entre Seville et Cadix jusqu' à la fin du XVIIIe siècle,* Paris, 1932, 43 ff.

18 The actual transfer was carried out in the following year. It was not without significance that a few days before the transfer was ordered, the intelligent and farsighted statesman, José Patiño, was appointed president of the *Casa.*

years to have the decision reversed, but common sense ultimately triumphed over traditionalism, and in 1726 the primacy of Cadiz was assured.

The *Casa* also had charge of trade with the Canary Islands and with the adjacent African coast. The Canaries early became a regular port of call on the outward voyage to the Indies, in 1534 islanders were permitted to engage in American commerce, and by the middle of the century ships were sailing directly from the Canaries to the New World. Early in the reign of Philip II, therefore, the crown saw fit to set up an organization similar to the *juzgado* of Cadiz in the three principal islands. Traders from Northern Europe were consequently attracted there —Frenchmen, Flemings, Englishmen, and Scots—and the presence of these foreign merchants gave occasion for illicit practices, and for a consequent limitation in the seventeenth century of the amount of tonnage permitted to the islands.

Only one serious attempt to break the monopoly of Seville was made before the eighteenth century. Charles V in January 1529, in an effort to encourage emigration and trade, issued a decree permitting ships to sail directly to America from certain other ports in the peninsula: Coruña, Bayona, Avilés, Laredo, Bilbao, and San Sebastian on the coast of Biscay, and Barcelona and Malaga on the Mediterranean. On the return voyage, however, the cargoes had to be landed at Seville and reported to the *Casa de Contratación*.

There is some evidence that exporting merchants in these northern ports availed themselves of this privilege, especially in Bayona and Coruña in Galicia. But it also appears that the municipal authorities were very lax in enforcing the many regulations governing the American trade. Ships were ill-conditioned, overloaded, carried forbidden passengers and goods, failed to pay *almojarifazgo,* or to call at Seville on the return voyage. Consequently Philip II, in response to protests from the Seville merchants, in December 1573 abrogated the privilege, although there seem to have been fraudulent sailings from the northern ports after that date.[19]

The policy of limiting trans-Atlantic commerce to the Andalusian cities of Seville and Cadiz was reflected in a similar policy in the Indies. There trade was concentrated at three points, Vera Cruz in New Spain, Cartagena in New Granada, and Nombre de Dios (later Portobello) on the Isthmus of Panama. The ends in view were doubtless greater ease in enforcing the regulations, preservation of the Seville monopoly, and prevention of contraband traffic. Caribbean seaports and the principal West Indian islands, however, were served by ships under special license; and for a short time trade was permitted between various Pacific

---

19 José Torre Revello, 'Puertos habilitados en España en el siglo XVI para comerciar con las Indias occidentales,' *Humanidades,* xxv, pt. 2, 353-62.

coast ports and the Philippine Islands. But before the close of the sixteenth century Seville's jealousy barred all from Oriental commerce except Acapulco in New Spain; and there it was permitted only to a very limited amount. Imports from the Orient might not be sent to Peru even as gifts! Trade from Europe to South America by way of Buenos Aires or round the Horn to the Pacific was also virtually prohibited until the more liberal days of Charles III. All of the southern continent except the Caribbean area must be supplied by way of the Isthmus of Panama, and thence down the Pacific to Peru and Chile. Traffic between various parts of the Indies in native products that competed with exports from Spain was also generally forbidden; and efforts were made to limit intercolonial trade in general. European merchandise allotted to inferior ports and islands might be distributed from one to another, but under no circumstances might it be carried to the major ports of Vera Cruz, Cartagena, and Portobello.

Partly to enforce this limited-port policy, but also to protect vessels from privateers and pirates during the recurring wars of the House of Austria, a fleet system was developed that remained officially in force for two hundred years. After 1526 merchant ships were forbidden to sail alone to or from the Indies. They most go in flotillas, and armed according to rules issued by the *Casa*. In 1537 apparently for the first time a royal armada was dispatched to the West Indies to insure the safe transport of gold and silver to Spain. It was the first of the great treasure fleets, and was commanded by Blasco Núñez Vela, the man who later went out as viceroy to Peru. Another armada was dispatched for treasure in 1542, under Martín Alonso de los Rios; and in the following year, at the solicitation of the merchants of Seville, decrees were issued making the sailing of vessels in semiannual, protected fleets a permanent and obligatory practice. The new orders were not in the beginning consistently observed, but from 1550 onward the system of periodical convoys between Spain and America was well established, although *registros* or special licenses for individual sailings to minor ports were occasionally granted.

It was in the years 1564-6 that the Indies navigation was given the organization it retained with little variation throughout the Hapsburg era. Two fleets were to be dispatched each year, one to New Spain and one to Tierra firme; the former to sail in the spring for the Gulf of Mexico, taking with it ships for Honduras and the islands; the other departing in August for the Isthmus of Panama, and convoying vessels for Cartagena, Santa Marta, and other ports on the northern coast of South America. Both were to winter in America, and concentrate at Havana in the following March, whence they were to sail together for Europe. The times of sailing did not remain so constant as this might imply, nor were annual fleets the invariable rule. But it was the ideal striven after, and sometimes achieved. From 1580 onward a year was frequently skipped, and toward the middle of the seventeenth century, as the monarchy declined in prosperity, the sailings became more and more irregular.

In Philip II's time it became more or less customary to send an armada of six or eight or more men-of-war with the Tierra firme fleet, on which were transported the enormous quantities of silver bullion exported from Peru when the yield of the Potosí mines was at its zenith. In the seventeenth century this was the invariable practice, so that the Tierra firme fleet came to be known collectively as the *Galeones,* from the type of war vessel composing its convoy. In contradiction the Mexican fleet became specifically the *Flota,* being defended only by two warships, a *capitana* and an *almiranta.* The number of merchantmen comprising the Indies fleets varied considerably, depending on the state of the American trade, the size of ships employed, and the security of the seas. It rose from between fifteen and twenty-five vessels in the middle of the sixteenth century, to between thirty and ninety toward the close. In the following century there was a gradual decline, both in total tonnage and in the number of vessels employed, the latter circumstance being partly accounted for by the increasing dimensions of ocean-going carriers. Veitia Linaje says that whereas the fleets formerly attained to a size of eight or nine thousand tons, in his own day if one of three thousand tons could be dispatched every two years it was accounted a miracle.[20]

The expense of maintaining convoys and other fleets for the protection of the Indies navigation was met by an assessment on exports and imports called the *avería.* The first recorded collection of this levy was in 1521, for the support of a small squadron of three or four armed caravels to patrol the waters between Spain, the Azores, and the Canaries. The *avería* was administered by a separate division of the *Casa de Contratación,* in collaboration with the *consulado,* which from time to time undertook by contract sole responsibility for its collection.[21] Assessment was based on the estimated cost of convoying each separate fleet,

20 Yet a French report of 1691 described the *Galeones* of that year as consisting of eight warships of 44-52 guns, besides two small *avisos,* and the *Flota* of sixteen armed merchant vessels totaling over eight thousand tons. (Sée, op. cit. 28.)

After Francis Drake's famous raid into the Pacific, bullion shipped from the Callao to Panama for transfer to the galleons at Portobello was also sent under convoy of one or more armed vessels called the Armada of the South Sea. The appointment of its officers and the arming of the ships were the responsibility of the viceroy at Lima. The receipt of the Peruvian bullion and its transshipment across the isthmus were under the immediate supervision of the *audiencia* and exchequer officials at Panama.

21 Haring, *Trade and Navigation between Spain and the Indies,* 67-82; Smith, *The Spanish Guild Merchant,* 97-100.

and the tax was collected when the merchandise was registered at the *Casa.* After the return from the Indies another estimate was made of all later expenses incurred, and that amount was assessed upon the return cargo. No articles escaped payment, even royal bullion and remittances by the colonial treasurers, except goods or money representing the wages of sailors and the profits of ship captains from freights.

The rate of the *averia,* especially in years when Spain was at war and the danger from foreign raiders increased, was apt to be very high. It also increased with the mounting practice of shipping gold and silver on the fleets *sub rosa* in order to escape payment of customs and other dues, the rate becoming correspondingly heavier on what was actually declared. In the seventeenth century under good management it might be as low as 6 per cent, but it sometimes rose to 30 per cent or higher, and together with the numerous tonnage and other dues [22] constituted a heavy burden upon American trade. Even at that, the *averia* administration frequently incurred enormous deficits. In 1660, when import duties on American commodities were abolished in return for an annual payment of 790,000 ducats apportioned among the interested merchants of America and Andalusia and the royal exchequer,[23] the *averia* also disappeared. From that time forward, and apparently until 1732, convoys were maintained entirely out of the royal treasury. In the latter year the Cadiz merchants agreed thereafter to contribute to this end 4 per cent of the value of all gold, silver, and cochineal imported from America.

In spite of minute regulation and supervision, evasion, with or without the connivance of the king's officials, was everywhere prevalent. Great numbers of unlicensed persons, both native and foreign, slipped out to America, and contraband trade at Seville and Cadiz flourished, as well as that carried on by foreigners directly with ports in the colonies. Ecclesiastics and royal officials took advantage of their exemption from payment of duties on articles they carried with them for their own use in America, to introduce large quantities of merchandise that found its way into the channels of trade. Monasteries and convents served as depositories and distributing centers for contraband goods.[24] Ships on the return voyage from the Indies put into other ports in Spain or into Portugal or France 'under stress of weather' in order to cover up fraudulent traffic. But it was the introduction of wares by the foreign interloper that had so disastrous an effect on the sale of goods from the

---

22 See *ante*, p. 281 and n. 19.

23 See *ante*, p. 280. Guillermo Céspedes del Castillo, *La Averia en el comercio de Indias,* Sevilla, 1945, 89-92.

24 *Cédula* of 2 February 1730 addressed to the authorities of New Spain (*Bol. Arch. Nac.,* Caracas, xxx, no. 120, 193-6).

Galeones and *Flotas,* and accounted chiefly for the reduction in the number and size of the fleets.

Repeatedly the galleon merchants [at Portobello], because of the reluctance of the Peruvian agents to buy, or of their unwillingness to pay any but very small prices, found themselves obliged to send their goods all the way to Lima to find purchasers . . . At the time of the fair of 1721 there had been nine Dutch vessels at Bastimentos, for whose goods the Peruvians had kept half of their money . . .[25]

There is also plenty of evidence that in Cadiz in the seventeenth and eighteenth centuries foreign merchants embarked goods upon the galleons directly from their own ships in the harbor, without registering them with the officials of the *Casa de Contratación;* and that on the return of the fleets from America they received the proceeds in bars of gold and silver by the same fraud. Of French returns from the Cadiz trade in the second half of the seventeenth century, three-fourths were said to be in gold and silver.[26]

There came to be organized at Cadiz a corps of professional bullion smugglers called *metedores.* In the words of the English consul there in 1738 they were 'made use of by merchants of all nations in carrying off their money for exportation, as also sometimes in the running and introducing that which comes to them from the Spaniish West Indies out of register.'[27] They usually were paid 1½ per cent of the value of the bullion involved, and 1 per cent of the value of coin. In 1696 the crown, helpless to prevent the illegal extraction of gold and silver from the country, finally capitulated, and issued a decree permitting the export of silver from Cadiz under license and on payment of a tax of 3 per cent. The concession was not effective, even though the rate was reduced in practice by special agreements with the foreign consuls, and it was withdrawn in 1700. Thereafter absolute prohibition of export was renewed, on pain of death.[28]

The crown as far back as the time of Philip II had sometimes tried to compromise by suspending the rules, permitting merchants to escape the penalty of confiscation by making declaration to the *Casa* of any goods or treasure which arrived from the Indies unregistered. At other times it recompensed itself for the loss of customs and other dues by imposing heavy fines or *indultos* on the whole body of merchants shar-

25 Vera Lee Brown, 'The South Sea Company and Contraband Trade,' *Amer. Hist. Rev.* XXXI, 673.

26 Albert Girard, *Le Commerce français à Séville et Cadix au temps des Habsbourg,* Paris, 1932, 454.

27 Consul Cayley to the Duke of Newcastle, 23 September 1738, quoted by Jean O. McLachlan, *Trade and Peace with Old Spain,* 1667-1750, Cambridge, 1940, 14.

28 Girard, op. cit. 197 ff.

ing in the cargo of the American fleets. They were paid by the *consulado* which reimbursed itself by taxing the merchants, half of the *indulto* being collected in Spain and half by deputies of the *consulado* in the seaports of the Indies. The *indulto* in the case of the galleons sometimes amounted to as much as a million ducats. This device was resorted to with increasing frequency in the seventeenth century. The *indulto*, imposed more or less arbitrarily by the Hapsburgs, became a regular payment during the War of the Spanish Succession and after, as a levy of 5 per cent (after 1730 raised to 9 per cent and occasionally doubled to 18 per cent) of the known value of the cargo.

The *indultos*, together with occasional 'gifts' or forced loans of from 200,000 to 500,000 pesos, constituted a heavy encumbrance upon the trade, and contributed to raise prices in America; but there is plenty of evidence that the foreign merchants, in spite of bitter complaints, continued to be attracted by large profits.[29] On the other hand, French and English naval squadrons occasionally appeared off Cadiz at the time of the arrival of the fleets from the Indies, to ensure reasonable treatment for their nationals by the Spanish government. In 1682, when relations betweeen France and Spain were strained because of French aggression against Luxembourg and the Spanish Netherlands, Louis XIV threatened to let loose the privateers in the West Indies, and even to seize several of the galleons as security for the safety of French property on the fleets returning from America.[30]

The most serious and widespread development of contraband trade, however, was in the colonies themselves. Illicit traffic was carried on by English, Dutch, and French interlopers, in the Caribbean countries, through Buenos Aires, and in the eighteenth century directly with the Pacific coast of South America. It was generally welcomed by the colonists, for it gave them access to a larger variety of goods at more reasonable prices than was obtainable through the mechanism of the Seville monopoly and the annual fleets.[31]

As pointed out in an earlier chapter, Buenos Aires was always an open door for this clandestine trade. Its location far from the centers of Spanish power in Lima and the West Indies, and close to the Portuguese in Brazil, made adequate control there almost impossible. And as the port was virtually closed in the interest of the galleon trade, the tempta-

---

29 In the eighteenth century French money loaned to entrepreneurs at St. Malo for investment in goods to be shipped to the Spanish colonies commanded as high as from thirty to fifty per cent. Henry Séo, 'Notas sobre el comercio francés en Cadiz . . . siglo XVIII,' *Anuario de hist. del derecho español*, II, 190.

30 Girard, op. cit., 278-9.

31 Goods of foreign origin exported to the colonies through Spain were subject not only to an import duty on entering the peninsula, but also to port dues, and the expense of loading, unloading, transportation, and storage; consequently the cost to the colonists was vastly increased.

tion was irresistible to secure by such means what was denied by Spain. An active local commerce with the coast of Brazil sprang up soon after the foundation of Buenos Aires.[32] And within twenty years the settlement was reported to the Council of the Indies to be the common resort of Portuguese, Flemings, Frenchmen, and Italians. Soon the Portuguese, including many Jewish *conversos,* were finding their way overland into Peru itself, to constitute a problem for the Inquisition there. From Buenos Aires wheat, hides, tallow, wine of Mendoza, and woolens of Tucumán were shipped out in return for sugar, conserves, Negro slaves, and miscellaneous merchandise obtained from or by way of Brazil. In response to appeals from the governor, and even from the *Audiencia* of Charcas, for an open port, the crown in 1602 accorded to the inhabitants of the Rio de la Plata the privilege for six years for exporting annually in their own vessels to Brazil, Guinea, and neighboring areas a limited amount of grain, tallow, and jerked beef. They might bring back any commodity they desired except slaves, provided the goods were not reshipped to any other province of the Indies. Entry into the colonies or departure of persons by that route was strictly forbidden, as was direct trade with Spain. The concession was renewed in 1608 and 1614. In 1618 it was somewhat altered, but still confined to an allowance of two vessels a year or not over one hundred tons each, sailing from Buenos Aires to Brazil, thence to Seville, and from Spain directly back to Buenos Aires. In short, direct importation from Brazil was now forbidden. Of commodities imported, a part might be transported overland to Peru, but only on payment of an additional duty of 50 per cent at an interior custom house set up in 1623 at Córdoba.[33]

Time and time again in the seventeenth century the colonists petitioned for a legalized outlet for their products, and as often the vested interests of Seville and Lima proved too strong. In the following century, and especially after the abolition of the galleons, vessels sailed more frequently from Cadiz under special license to provision the River Plate and adjacent provinces. And finally in 1778 this region was opened to free trade with the rest of the Spanish empire.

Meantime, and for two hundred years, Buenos Aires remained a favorite resort of the foreign interloper. The Brazilian trade—particularly it seems with Báia and Pernambuco, the wealthy sugar provinces of the north—was at its height in the first quarter of the seventeenth century, when the Spanish and Portuguese crowns were united, and before the renewal of the Dutch war drove Spanish shipping from the South At-

32 Roberto Levillier, *Antecedentes de política enconómica en el Rio de la Plata,* 2 vols,, Madrid, 1915, II, 378-408.

33 Ibid. II, 423. The shipment of slaves or the precious metals by this route was absolutely forbidden. The custom house was ordered to be moved in 1695 to Jujuy, ibid. 434-45.

lantic. In the time of Philip III it was stated (perhaps with some exaggeration) that as many as two hundred ships a year sailed from Lisbon or Oporto with textiles from English, French, or Flemish looms, which were carried to Brazil and thence to Rio de la Plata to be transported overland to Chile and Peru. Spanish merchants in Lima and Buenos Aires had correspondents in Brazil as well as in Europe, for they found that freights and other charges were less by way of the Rio de la Plata than by way of Panama.[34] After the Portuguese revolt of 1640, this Brazilian traffic almost ceased, and English and Dutch ships sailed directly to Buenos Aires for cargoes of hides and tallow. Acarete du Biscay, a Frenchman who visited Buenos Aires in 1658, reported twenty Dutch and two English ships in the river that had received permission from the governor to trade. Each was laden with from thirteen to fourteen thousand hides, besides vicuña wool and silver bullion. But he adds that the Council of the Indies seized and confiscated such parts of the cargoes as reached Spain, and deprived the governor of his post. Even after the Bourbon reforms of the eighteenth century, the contrabandists on the Rio de la Plata continued their illicit operations.

Another focus of contraband trade was in the Antilles, especially after the first quarter of the seventeenth century, when the English, French, and Dutch seized and settled the smaller islands skirting the eastern edge of the Caribbean Sea: Barbados, St. Christopher, Martinique, Tobago, etc. These islands became the center of a widespread system of illegal trade with neighboring Spanish colonies, the headquarters for the foreign interloper. Spain's commercial rivals had set up shop at the very doors of the Spanish Indies. Jamaica after its conquest by the English in 1655, and Curaçao after the Dutch seized it in 1634, were the principal resorts for this illicit traffic. The Jamaicans, from their central position in the West Indies, sold provisions, manufactures, and slaves, and received gold and silver which in turn enriched England and also supplied her North American mainland colonies with most of their hard money.[35]

English and Dutch sloops hovering off the Spanish coasts often did a risky business. Spanish coastguard vessels were not always to be ignored; sometimes they captured the interlopers and sent their crews as prisoners on the *flotas* to Spain. Nor were the traders always safe from their Spanish customers; for if the latter found that they outnumbered the visitors they were not above attempting to seize both ship and cargo. At other times the smugglers might have the unofficial protection of their own

---

34 Ch. Weiss, *L'Espagne depuis Philippe II jusqu'aux Bourbons*, 2 vols., Paris, 1844, II, 226-7: A. P. Canabrava, *O Comércio portugês no rio da Prata*, 1580-1640, São Paulo, 1944.

35 Curtis Nettels, 'England and the Spanish American Trade, 1680-1715' *Journ. Mod. Hist.*, March 1931, 1-32.

warships hovering in the neighborhood. In the eighteenth century New York and other North American ports developed a profitable trade with Havana, Puerto Rico, and Hispaniola; and English war vessels frequently sailed into Spanish harbors on the pretext of official business, but really to establish contact with the local merchants. Sometimes they themselves engaged in contraband and carried away silver in pesos or bullion.[36] Spaniards from Havana, Cartagena, and Portobello came to Jamaica and other islands in their own ships to exchange bullion and produce for slaves, textiles, and other manufactures, although in the eyes of Spanish authorities this was just as illegal. Governments on both sides connived at these practices. Spanish vessels received royal permission to call at foreign islands to buy slaves, and the English authorities winked at the export of goods to Spanish coasts although it contravened the Navigation Acts. In 1761 a commission in Spain reported to the king that the illicit trade of the English with Spanish America reached six million pesos a year.[37]

In order to encourage Spaniards to bring their products to the English islands (and also to legalize the trade of the mainland colonies in the produce of the Spanish and other foreign West Indies) Parliament passed an act in 1766 designating certain ports in Jamaica and Dominica as 'free ports,' i.e., where foreign vessels might exchange certain enumerated goods for others on payment of very nominal duties. Such a free port had been set up by the Dutch in St. Eustatius in 1737, and the Danes and the French were resorting to the same device in the 1760's. There is little evidence however, that it much diminished the contraband traffic with Spanish America.[38]

In the sixteenth and seventeenth centuries foreign capitalists, especially Portuguese and Italians, frequently secured contracts or *asientos* for the supply of Negroes from Africa to the Spanish colonies. This too facilitated contraband trade, for when delivering slaves to the West Indian islands or to ports on the mainland, they availed themselves of the opportunity to introduce merchandise as well, and frequently without the least obstacle. Officers and crews of the slave ships brought with them bales of merchandise which they sold on board the vessel or traded on shore at night to escape customs and other dues. Usually, of course, the captain had an understanding with the Spanish governor and the

---

36 Vera Lee Brown, 'Anglo-Spanish Relations in America in the Closing Years of the Colonial Era,' *Hisp. Amer. Hist. Rev.,* v, 377-82; 449-60.

37 Allan Christelow, 'Contraband Trade between Jamaica and the Spanish Main, and the Free Port Act of 1766,' *Hisp. Amer. Hist. Rev.,* xxII,, 312-13. The 'six million pesos' was probably merely a repetition of Ulloa (*Restalecimiento de fábricas,* etc., 1740), II, 29, who copied Uztáriz (*Teoría y práctica,* etc., 1724), cap. 29, who in turn referred to an English source of 1740.

38 Ibid. 334 ff.

exchequer officials covering their share of the profits. Sometimes Spanish passengers were illegally transported to Europe, carrying with them large amounts of gold and silver. Quantities of unregistered bullion thus found their way abroad both on the account of the *asentistas* and of private individuals. The former bought their slaves not only in Africa, but sometimes in Curaçao, Barbados, and Jamaica, and generally kept agents in Port Royal or Kingston. After the English by the Treaty of Utrecht in 1713 secured the privilege of the *asiento,* with the right to send each year one merchant ship of five hundred tons to Portobello, its abuse is one of the reasons usually assigned for the war between the two nations twenty-five years later.

Restrictions on intercolonial commerce between New Spain and Peru were likewise honored more in the breach than in the observance. Trade between the two viceroyalties was limited to the value of 200,000 ducats annually, sent in silver to Mexico in two ships of two hundred tons each, which returned with Mexican products but not China goods. Ships from Peru were absolutely forbidden to call at Acapulco, the Mexican terminus of the Philippine navigation, or to sail from Acapulco to Peru. Nevertheless trade flourished to an extent far beyond the limitations established by law, and contraband traffic in China goods to Peru was notorious.

Two circumstances combined to make this clandestine trade easy. One was the immense length of coastline on both Atlantic and Pacific sides of the American continent, a coast very sparsely settled, and effective surveillance over which was beyond the resources of any nation in the seventeenth and eighteenth centuries. Adequate policing except in certain limited areas was extremely difficult. The other circumstance was the venality of the Spanish governors and other officials in the Indies. They often tolerated and even encouraged the traffic, sometimes on the plea that the needs of the colonists demanded it. They not only accepted bribes, from the viceroy down to the customs officers of the ports, but they themselves often bought and sold contraband articles.

Such is the story of Spanish American commerce before the eighteenth century; on the one hand a stringent monopoly and a flood of restrictions inspired by 'bullionist' ideas, to prevent the diversion abroad of gold and silver coming from the New World; on the other, a flourishing illicit traffic by foreigners, through Seville and Cadiz, and directly with the ports of Spanish America. Whatever may have been the aims of the commercial system when first formulated, it proved inadequate to maintain or advance the prosperity either of Spain or of its American possessions. The productiveness of American mines concentrated the attention of the crown upon the precious metals. To the neglect of industry that alone would enable the realm to keep and absorb them, and caused it to try and enforce with increasing strictness a system that was patently unenforceable. So Spain saw her gold and silver escape her, her real wealth decline, her craftsmanship disappear, while her government was exhausted by imperialistic wars often dictated by dynastic ambitions or religious zeal. In spite of minute regulation, trade passed more and more into the hands of her rivals. Spanish shipping was reduced to a shadow of its former strength, and cargoes, vessels, and even crews were supplied from abroad.

The commercial and industrial decline of Spain under the Hapsburgs was but a reflection of political decline as well. Spain in the sixteenth century, under Charles V and Philip II, had been the most formidable power in Europe. Possessed of the most extensive colonial empire the world had ever seen, a vast Indian population, and bullion from the mines of Mexico and Peru—holding in the Dutch and Flemish Lowlands probably the richest revenue-producing area in Europe—firmly planted in the Western Mediterannean, with the great city of Barcelona, the islands of Sicily and Sardinia, the kingdom of Naples, and the duchy of Milan—champion of the Counter Reformation—backed by an infantry regarded as the staunchest and most formidable ever known—and finally, with the accretion of Portugal and its empire in Brazil and the Orient—at this pinnacle of power Spain seemed to have within her reach the hegemony of Christendom.

Yet already under Philip II the power and resources of Spain were an illusion. Charles, borrowing heavily from German and Italian bankers, had mortgaged mines and public utilities, and bequeathed to Philip a government that was well-nigh bankrupt, Philip engaging in an ambitious, pro-Catholic foreign policy, only fell more completely into the clutches of his creditors. By 1598 practically all sources of revenue in Spain were mortgaged, the mines and the fairs were in foreign hands, and the American revenues were pledged in advance. In the sevnteenth century voices were sometimes raised in Spain in criticism of the prevailing economic confusion, but they met with no responce in the council chambers of the crown. Spain progressively declined as a political and economic power, until under the imbecile Charles II the ruin was complete. Only under the new French dynasty of the Bourbons in the eighteenth century was there a slow, painful pilgrim's progress back to national sol vency.

XVII

◈◈◈

The Last Phase

◈◈◈

The black night of Spain's weakness and humiliation under Charles II was to usher in the dawn of recovery under the princes of the House of Bourbon. The speculative ideas of the Enlightenment that came to prevail among philosophers and publicists in eighteenth-century Europe penetrated as well into official circles in Spain, and resulted in important innovations in political administration and in trade. Serious attempts were made to balance the Spanish budget, to suppress the centrifugal forces of regionalism in the peninsula, to revive the navy, and to encourage trade both with Europe and with the provinces overseas. Colonial reforms did not begin as early, nor were they as complete or as well-rounded as those in Spain. Spanish traditionalism, and obstruction from those entrenched in the American trade, were hard to overcome. But especially after the middle years of the eighteenth century, under a series of intelligent and far-sighted ministers—Campillo, Aranda, Floridablanca, Gálvez—many of the old Hapsburg restrictions were gradually removed.

The system of *Galeones* and *Flotas,* in the last stages of decay at the death of Charles II, disappeared altogether during the early years of the War of the Spanish Succession. During the first five years no fleet at all sailed to the Caribbean; between 1706 and 1712 only four to New Spain and one to the isthmus, under convoy of French frigates. The needs of the colonists were meantime met by Spain's maritime foes, the English and the Dutch; also after 1703 by French merchant ships, chiefly from St. Malo, which a complacent allied government in Madrid permitted to sail around the Horn to the Pacific ports of Chile and Peru.[1] French traders soon dominated the commerce of the South Sea, and their goods were sold in Lima from 60 to 80 per cent cheaper than those which arrived by way of the fair at Portobello. Havana, Vera Cruz, Cartagena, and other West Indian ports were also centers of extensive

---

[1] A Spanish decree of 11 January 1701 permitted French ships to enter American ports to purchase provisions and other necessities—an open door to contraband trade. And during the later years of the war the Spanish government actually sold 'safe conducts' to French merchant ships to sail to its overseas possessions. George Scelle, *La Traite négrière aux Indes de Castille,* II, ch. 5.

French operations. Everywhere French and Spanish vessels went together almost indistinguishably, often under the auspices of the French
Guinea Company which in 1701 secured from Spain the *asiento* to supply during ten years 42,000 Negroes to the Spanish American colonies.
In fact it seems that the cost of the war on both sides, French and
Anglo-Dutch, was met largely with the gold and silver which came from
the Spanish colonies by way of contraband trade.

After the Peace of Utrecht these French activities gradually ceased,
and the old Spanish *flota* system was revived, at first at seems under
separate contract for each fleet with the Cadiz merchants. Finally by the
well-known *Projecto para galeones y flotas* of 5 April 1720,[2] an effort
was made to standardize it again. Fleets were to sail under convoy at
stated intervals, and must depart promptly on the day announced
whether all ships licensed to accompany it were ready or not. Sailing
times were prescribed, for the Galleons or Tierra firme fleet early in
September, for the Vera Cruz fleet early in June; and a maximum was set
for the number of days the fleets might tarry in each of the American
ports, Cartagena, Portobello, Vera Cruz, and Havana. In an attempt to
improve communications and keep the trade informed of current market
conditions, the *consulado* agreed to provide each year eight *avisos* or
dispatch boats, two sailing every three months to New Spain and the
isthmus, and supported by an additional 1 per cent on gold and silver
from the Indies.[3]

A small fleet sailed to New Spain at intervals of two or three years
between 1715 and 1736, and then because of war or threat of war in
Europe there was none at all for twenty years.[4] Only five fleets were
dispatched in the same period to Tierra firme. Indeed a royal order of
21 January 1735 suspended the Galleons altogether until goods sent out
on the fleet five years earlier were disposed of and contraband activities
curtailed. Single merchant vessels (*registros sueltos*) might be dispatched to Cartagena and Portobello when justified by market conditions, but thereafter the Galleons would be sent out only at a time and
under circumstances agreed upon by representatives of the Lima merchants at the court.[5] A fleet of seven merchantmen and two frigates did
sail in 1737 for the isthmus, but war intervened, and in 1740 all fleets

---

2 *Documentos para la historia Argentina.* Tomo v. *Comercio de Indias. Antecedentes legales* (1713-1778), 21 ff.

3 The service had first been provided for in a decree of 29 July 1718. Ibid. 118.

4 At the moment hostilities with England broke out in 1739 a *Flota* was ready to
sail, but its departure was suspended, and some of the goods were shipped on vessels
licensed for individual voyages. At the same time a loan of one million pesos was
exacted from the Cadiz merchant community. Henri Sée, *Documents sur le commerce
de Cadix*, 13-14.

5 Antúnez y Acevedo, *Memorias históricas*, appendix, LXXXIII-XCIII.

were suspended. Thereafter vessels departed alone under individual license from the crown for various ports in the Indies. Some of those which sailed to Buenos Aires had the right of *internación*, i.e., the privilege of dispatching goods over the Andes to Peru and Chile. The Galleons were never revived, the Portobello fair disappeared, and with it the prosperity and revenues of the Presidency of Panama. After 1740 ships were permitted to sail round the Horn directly to Peru, and thereafter scarcely a dozen vessels arrived annually on either side of the isthmus. In 1751 the *Audiencia* of Panama was suppressed.

The abolition of the fleets did not diminish frauds and other abuses. Contraband trade still flourished in America, to the prejudice as always of the export of goods via Cadiz. Indeed there were times when colonial markets were overstocked by the interlopers to their own disadvantage. So the Cadiz merchants, seeing no remedy but the restoration of trade on the old basis, actually welcomed the re-establishment of the Vera Cruz fleet and the limitation of supply to the colonies which this implied.[6] The Flota was restored by royal orders of 11 October 1754, on the basis of biennial sailings, although this regularity was never achieved. The first fleet was dispatched three years later, and occasional departures occurred till 1789 when the fleet system was again and finally abandoned. Thereafter New Spain enjoyed the same freedom which had been extended to the other American colonies decades earlier.

The monopoly enjoyed by the mercantile oligarchy of Cadiz and Seville was also curtailed by the organization of several privileged trading companies in the north of Spain. The first and most important was the *Real Compañia Guipuzcoana de Caracas,* created in 1728 with the privilege, later the monopoly, of trade with the coasts of Venezuela.[7] In 1734 a Company of Galicia was permitted to send two ships a year to Campeche, in 1740 was organized a Havana Company, and in 1755 a Barcelona and Catalan Company for trade with Hispaniola, Puerto Rico, and Margarita.

Even before 1700 the Spanish government had been increasingly concerned over the prostration of American trade, and listened to many and strange devices for its recovery. Subjects of the crown had advanced a number of projects for chartered companies on the model of the English and Dutch East India Companies, some of them providing for the retention of the fleet system unchanged, with the administration of colonial trade and navigation centered in a single private corporation. A

---

6 Henri Sée, 'Esbozo de la historia del comersio frances en Cádiz y en la America española en el siglo XVIII,' *Bol. Instit. Invest. Hist.,* Buenos Aires, ano VI, no. 34, 205.

7 Royal approval had been given to a small joint stock organization in 1714 to send several ships to Honduras and Caracas, but it was an immediate and calamitous failure. Roland D. Hussey, *The Caracas Company,* 1728-1784, Cambridge Mass., 1934, 43-8.

project of this sort, to which even foreigners were to be admitted, had been proposed in or about 1672 in the Council of the Indies. In 1687 and for a decade thereafter the Council had considered a proposal for a company in Flanders, to be granted the sole right to trade with Hispaniola and Puerto Rico, together with considerable political and judicial powers there. It might be open to all the king's vassals and even to capitalists of other friendly nations. None of these proposals had any real chance of acceptance under the Hapsburg regime. Lack of capital, or of confidence by prospective investors in the vagaries of Spanish officialdom, and the unremitting opposition of the Seville *consulado,* made failure inevitable. Not until two decades later, under a new dynasty and a new breed of royal advisers, was this foreign device of the chartered company accepted.[8]

In the second quarter of the eighteenth century, with the support of accomplished statesmen like José Patiño, the concept of the privileged trading corporation became very popular with business men and in the government. It seemed to be the one device capable of restraining the inroads of foreign trade with the colonies. Most of the companies were organized with capital from Catalonia and the Biscay provinces, and they were generally permitted to send ships to and from some specified northern port, the vessels calling at Cadiz on the return voyage. They were frequently obligated to build ships in their yards for the royal navy, arm small vessels to repress contraband, and transport supplies or furnish other small services without charge to the government. And in every case they received special privileges, if not a monopoly, in the trade with one of the more backward, less developed, areas of the American empire—areas with which Spanish trade was almost nil as the result of the old, canalized system of colonial commerce, and where the foreign interloper dominated the situation.

The government therefore appealed to the private interests of a limited group of capitalists, offered them commercial, and sometimes governmental, privileges in a certain region, in return for maintaining a police or coast guard service to eliminate the smuggler; hoping also that they would develop the latent resources of these backward areas in order to make their privileges more lucrative. Incidentally the device served also to stop the clamors of capitalists outside Andalusia for a share in colonial commerce.

All of the companies were financial failures, often because of bad management or government interference, except the Caracas Company,

---

8 Hussey, op. cit. 8 ff.

9 In 1785, the stockholders were reorganized to form the Philippine Company, and were granted a monopoly of trade between Spanish or American ports and the Philippine Islands by way of either Cape Horn or the Cape of Good Hope. Hussey, op. cit. 296-8.

which lasted until the eve of the French Revolution.⁹ In some respects its results were remarkable. Caracas at that time was the chief producer of cacao, and Spain was the largest consumer. Yet as most of the Venezuelan trade was in the hands of Dutch interlopers based upon the island of Curaçao, Spain had to buy much of her cacao from Holland. Not a single ship from Spain had entered the ports of La Guaira, Puerto Cabello, or Maracaibo during the years from 1706 to 1721,¹⁰ while eighteen or twenty Dutch ships regularly traded along that coast. The new company by policing the neighboring waters succeeded in eliminating a large part of the smuggling. The Spanish cacao trade doubled in volume, while the price in Spain fell by nearly a half. Before the eighteenth century only cacao had been grown in Venezuela for export; but other staples were introduced through the efforts of the Guipuzcoa Company: cotton in 1767, and indigo shortly thereafter. Tobacco, which had long been planted there, was increasingly cultivated, and became, with dyewoods, hides, and indigo, an important article of export. Some vested interests in the colony were doubtless hurt, and the company at times abused its monopolistic position. Nevertheless the prosperity of Venezuela as a Spanish American community really dates from the creation of this privileged company, whatever may have been the complaints of the colonists against it. The government of the province, formerly dependent upon an annual subsidy from the treasury of New Spain, almost immediately enjoyed a fiscal surplus.

Trade within the Spanish empire was still far from free, however. Most of it was still concentrated at Cadiz to the prejudice of other ports and other provinces of Spain, and at a few major seaports in America.¹¹ In the colonies the contraband activities of Spain's rivals continued unabated. Neither private trading companies nor tinkering with small details of the old commercial system had succeeded in eradicating this evil, or in appreciably improving either Spanish trade or the royal revenues. Slowly the conviction spread that free exchange among Spanish subjects on equal terms was the only means of lowering prices to meet the competition of the foreign interloper. Under Charles III in the second half of the century many of the remaining limitations were gradually removed. Possibly the crown was influenced by the example of what happened at Havana under English control in 1762. Till then the European trade of the island of Cuba had been almost nil, often confined to five or six ships a year. When the English captured Havana in the Seven Years' War, they threw the port open to all English vessels, and

10 José Gil Fortoul, *Historia constitucional de Venezuela* (2nd ed., 3 vols., Caracas, 1930), 96.
11 Bernardo de Ulloa states (*Restablecimiento de las fábricas y comercio español*, 1740) that the number of ships sailing each year with the cargoes from Spain to the Indies never exceeded forty.

in less than a year nearly a hundred ships entered the harbor. The need of imperial reorganization and defense, to which reference has been made in another connection, and consequently of increasing the prosperity and revenues of the empire, made this object lesson the more impressive.

Many of the major economic reforms under Charles III were foreshadowed in the celebrated work attributed to José Campillo y Cossío, *Nuevo Sistema de gobierno económico para la América,* apparently written just before his death in 1743, although not appearing in print until a half century later. Campillo, economist, statesman, minister of war and finance in 1741, bitterly criticized the economic backwardness of America, the miserable state of the Indians, and the small share that Spanish products had in colonial trade. Some of his proposals were a bit naïve, and more theoretical than practical in their approach to the problem, but his 'system' as a whole reflected a thoughtful study of the colonial experience of competing nations. Although urging that colonial manufactures be strictly limited in the interest of the mother country, he advocated distributing lands to the Indians tax free on condition that they were cultivated; training the natives as farmers and artisans, and providing agricultural credits; diminishing the widespread contraband traffic by freeing Spanish commerce from heavy taxation, by reducing customs duties on foreign goods, and by encouraging trade between the colonies; organizing a frequent overseas mail service; and limiting or abolishing the Cadiz monopoly and the system of periodically convoyed fleets.[12] These recommendations of Campillo were later substantially repeated by a royal commission which reported to the king early in 1765.

The first step had already been taken in 1764 when there was organized a monthly mail-packet service between Coruña and Havana, followed shortly by a bi-monthly service to Buenos Aires. In the following year trade with the West Indian islands (Cuba, Hispaniola, Puerto Rico, Trinidad, and Margarita), one of the most backward regions of the American empire, was thrown open to a number of important seaports of Spain.[13] Special license from the crown was no longer required, and the many old taxes on trans-Atlantic trade were replaced on most articles by a single payment in Spain of 6 or 7 per cent *ad valorem* to the crown.[14] Evidently the results exceeded expectations, for concessions of a similar

---

12 He also urged sending inspectors-general to the Indies to study *in situ* the economic evils that afflicted the colonies; attacked the disorders of the clergy, the excessive number of ecclesiastics, and the extraordinary accumulation of property in mortmain; and urged a policy of identifying socially Creoles and peninsular Spaniards, and opening up careers to the former in the army and in the government.

13 Cadiz, Seville, Alicante, Cartagena, Malaga, Barcelona, Santander, La Coruña, and Gijón.

14 See *ante*, p. 281.

nature were gradually extended to other parts of the empire: in 1768 to Louisiana,[15] in 1770 to Campeche and Yucatan, in 1776-7 to Santa Marta and Rio de la Hacha on the coast of New Granada, and by the famous *Reglamento* of 1778 [16] to all other American provinces except New Spain and Venezuela.[17] Moving forward with characteristic caution, regarding the new freedom as still in the experimental stage, the Spanish government apparently held these two prosperous areas in reserve in the interest of the royal exchequer. A certain number of tons for Vera Cruz were assigned each year to each qualified Spanish port from 1784 to February 1789, when special licenses and apportioned tonnage were abolished, and commercial relations with New Spain and Venezuela (the Caracas Company having disappeared) were made identical with those of the other American provinces. Meantime, in a series of decrees beginning in 1772, there had been further reduction of duties, and an increasing number of articles, Spanish and American, were placed on a free list.

What was more, many of the restrictions on intercolonial trade were at the same time removed. By 1774 Peru was permitted to trade more freely, although in American products only, with New Spain, Guatemala, and New Granada, and two years later Buenos Aires with Chile and the provinces of the interior.[18] Thus by the time of the death of Charles III, although American commerce was still reserved to Spain and to Spaniards, it was open to all important seaports and to all Spanish subjects. It was not free trade in our sense of the term, but thereafter any Spaniard might trade directly from any part of Spain with any part of the Indies. Finally in 1790 the *Casa de Contratación* at Cadiz was abolished, after a continuous and not undistinguished history of 287 years.

The results in general were remarkable. The trade of Cuba, which in 1760 required five or six vessels a year, in 1778 employed over two hundred. The export of hides from Buenos Aires rose from 150,000 to 800,000 a year. And in the decade between 1778 and 1788 the value of the whole

---

15 To conciliate the inhabitants of Louisiana, a colony acquired five years earlier from France, concessions were even more liberal. All articles exported to New Orleans, whether of Spanish or foreign origin, were duty free, and products of the colony imported into Spain paid only 4 per cent, later reduced to 2 per cent.

16 'Reglamento y aranceles reales para el comercio libre de España a Indias,' 12 October 1778, in *Documentos para la historia Argentina*, VI, 3-132.

17 At the same time four other ports were opened to American trade: Almería, Tortosa, Palma in the Balearis Island, and Santa Cruz de Tenerife in the Canaries. Vigo was added in 1783 and Grau in Valencia in 1791 (Antúez y Acevedo, op. cit. 37, 40 n.). The *Reglamento* included a detailed schedule of duties on all goods that might be exported to America.

18 *Doc. para la hist. Arg.*, V, 306-10; 373-4. The export of wine, raisins, olives, and almonds from Peru or Chile to the north was still prohibited, as was the shipment of gold, silver, fine textiles, and China goods from New Spain to the south.

trade with Spanish America is said to have increased about 700 per cent.[19]

The most noteworthy concession to the new spirit animating government policy was made in 1782. Louisiana, acquired two decades earlier from France, with a preponderantly French population accustomed to French goods, menaced at the same time by Anglo-American encroachment from the north, could not be adequately supplied by the commerce of Spain. If the prosperity of the province was to be maintained, to say nothing of its loyalty to the Spanish crown, commercial intercourse with some foreign nation seemed essential. And for many reasons trade with France was the natural choice. In fact during the war with England the colonial authorities in Louisiana had been forced to acquiesce in it. A royal decree of 22 January 1782, therefore, permitted ships belonging to Spanish subjects in Spain or Louisiana to sail with cargoes to New Orleans or to Pensacola directly from any port in France where a Spanish consul was resident, and to return with American products except gold and silver. The trade was subjected to a 6 per cent export and import duty in America, and 2 per cent additional on Spanish goods re-exported to other colonies. Trade was also permitted with some of the French West Indian islands in order to encourage the importation of Negro slaves. The concession was to last for ten years.[20] As a matter of fact two years earlier, to meet the demands of the sugar planters while the war was on with Great Britain, Spanish colonists about the Caribbean Sea and the Gulf of Mexico had received permission to buy Negroes from neighboring French colonies; and from 1789 even foreigners were allowed to supply Negroes free to the Spanish islands and later to the other colonies as well.[21] War in Europe in the last decades of the colonial era forced the Spanish government more than once to suspend temporarily the Spanish trade monopoly. Because of the increasing difficulty of supplying the colonies in Spanish ships during hostilities with England, a royal order of 18 November 1797 lifted the ban on trade in foreign vessels of neutral origin. The order was revoked in April 1799, but was renewed again in the years 1805-09.

The increasing freedom of commercial movement within the empire in the second half of the eighteenth century not only produced a greater volume of business; it operated to reduce prices in the colonies, discour-

---

19 The incidence of taxation upon Spanish colonial trade, however, still remained very unscientific. In import duties in Spain no distinction was made between raw materials intended for manufacturers and goods for immediate consumption. A variety of small tonnage dues and other minor taxes were still collected in American seaports, and the heavy sales tax or *alcabala* continued to the end of Spanish rule to hamper the economic prosperity of the colonies.

20 Antúnez y Acevedo, 37-8.

21 See *ante*, pp. 220-1.

age contraband trade, and probably to effect a wider distribution of wealth. The older monopolistic commercial houses, controlling imports on occasional fleets, had rested content with an understocked market, and expected to reap enormous profits from what was virtually a non-competitive business. With the increase of maritime traffic, especially in seaports earlier debarred from an active trade with Spain, a new class of merchants arose—both in Spain and in America— more numerous and endowed with enterprise and foresight not called for under a monopolistic regime, 'investing smaller sums [and] content with smaller profits.' [22] When vessels sailed alone at any time of the year, merchants could adapt themselves to meet the changing requirements of the American market more nearly as they arose, something impossible when supply was confined to fleets sailing at long intervals. And due to a more rapid turnover, they could sell more cheaply. Doubtless monopolistic practices persisted within the merchant fraternity, especially among commission agents in the seaports—as may happen even today. But the results of the new freedom in general must have been salutary for the community at large. Many lesser merchants who came out from Spain, moreover, used their profits to move into the domestic trade, and established themselves in the interior towns, to the mortification of the older vested interests.[23]

At the end of the colonial era most of the American provinces enjoyed greater prosperity and well-being than ever before. The Spanish colonies had always possessed vastly greater wealth than English America, and had achieved all the outward signs of opulence: imposing public buildings, universities, churches, hospitals, and populous cities which were centers of luxury, learning, and refinement.[24] The arts flourished, especially painting and silversmithing, in Mexico City, Quito, and Cuzco. There was a school of mines and a school of fine arts in Mexico City, and an astronomical observatory in Bogotá, before any such institutions existed in the English, French, or Portuguese colonies. Colonial literary culture was rich and varied, and men of letters, historians, mathematicians, poets, and priests composed many works in the New World. The viceroys were often men of education and personal distinction, some of whom dabbled in arts and letters and held literary salons in the viceregal palace.

The era of enlightenment under the Bourbons saw not only an allevi-

22 Priestly, *José de Gálvez*, 384-5.

23 The elder Revillagigedo complains of this situation as early as 1754. 'Instrucción . . . al Marqués de Amarillas,' in *Instrucciones que los vireyes de Neuva España dejaron a sus sucesores*, 2 vols., Mexico, 1867-73, 1, 16.

24 Mexico and Lima were larger cities in 1790 than Philadelphia and New York. When the North American Revolution began, the population of the thirteen colonies was still almost wholly rural, and almost entirely devoted to agriculture. There were only five cities or towns of more than 8,000 inhabitants.

ation of the age-long restrictions upon commerce, not only extensive changes in political and financial organization. Administration in the colonies was greatly invigorated, and the personnel of royal government tended markedly to improve. There is every evidence that Spanish America was quite as well governed as was Spain, and the weight of taxation was certainly no heavier. Increase of prosperity was reflected in increasing receipts of the royal treasuries, and in the increased productiveness of church tithes. The Indians had always had their staunch defenders among humanitarian judges and ecclesiastics, and although still an exploited race, in the eighteenth century their heavy burdens were gradually reduced. The horrors of the *mita* in the mines of Peru were largely mitigated, and the system of *corregidores* was by law everywhere abolished. Voluntary wage labor was supplanting forced labor, and working conditions of the aborigines tended generally to improve.

The last decades of the eighteenth century saw also a notable improvement in the comforts, conveniences, and elegancies of life, especially in the viceregal capitals and in other large cities—a sufficient witness to the increasing prosperity of the empire. In Mexico City the Alameda was doubled in length, the *quemadero* of the Inquisition was obliterated, new *paseos* were created and trees were planted. The principal streets were lighted and paved. The city was better policed. The water supply was increased by means of a handsome aqueduct carried on arches to the center of the city. Lima, after the terrible earthquake of 1746 in which only fifteen or twenty houses were left standing, was almost completely reconstructed and modernized.

There was also much new building. In the sixteenth and seventeenth centuries some splendid churches and convents had been erected. The eighteenth century saw not only many new churches in that peculiarly Spanish rendering of the later baroque, the churrigueresque, but also the construction of a number of fine private palaces and public nonecclesiastical edifices—in Lima the Torre Tagle palace and the mansion of La Perrichoei; in Mexico City the mint, the custom house, the tobacco factory, the school of mines, the Academy of San Carlos. And what was true of Mexico and Lima was true only in lesser degree of the principal provincial cities.

But progress and well-being did not produce a spirit of contentment among the colonists. The example of the independence of the United States, and the influence of eighteenth-century philosophic rationalism. both were disconcerting to the Creoles who became increasingly restless under a royal absolutism. And freedom of trade within the empire only engendered a desire for freedom to trade with the world at large. The opportunity was afforded by the wars in Europe during the French Revolution and the age of Napoleon. Whenever Spain and England were found in opposite camps, British naval power drove Spanish shipping from the seas, and maritime relations between Spain and her colonies were snapped. Ships and cargoes from industrial England flowed in to fill the vacuum thus created, and the colonists enjoyed the practical experience of cheap imported manufactures and enlarged markets abroad for their own raw materials.

Moreover political and social discrimination in the government of the empire still persisted. Royal patronage remained largely a monopoly of peninsular Spaniards, and Creoles continued to be excluded from high office in Church and State. The colonial system under the old regime *was* exploitation from the colonists' point of view; not so much for the benefit of the crown as for that of certain favored classes: Spaniards who formed the official caste in America, and the privileged merchants in the Iberian peninsula. The American colonists therefore came to consider their subjection to the metropolis more and more a liability rather than an asset.

Yet had there not been the circumstance of the wars in Europe, and had Ferdinand VII after his restoration seen fit to accord his subjects a moderate degree of political and economic liberty, the empire might for a time at least have been preserved. The wars of independence were essentially civil wars. One of the most striking features of the whole movement was the evidence of loyalty to Spain among a large part of the population. The bulk of the royalist forces in many regions were Spanish Americans, and in some provinces it was impossible to rouse serious or sustained opposition to the crown. The revolutions in America were the work of a comparatively few enlightened, keen-witted leaders, who in many areas represented the ambition of the educated Creole class to supplant the peninsular Spaniards in government and trade, and in whose hands the ignorant classes were a ready tool for the accomplishment of their aims. And the circumstance was not without significance for the later history of Spanish America. The same phenomenon was to be repeated endless times after independence was achieved, when republican governments became the pawn of selfish, rival political and military chieftains.

In the beginning the Creoles who contrived and led the revolutionary movements were most of them disinclined to break completely with Spain. They might easily have been conciliated by fair and open-minded treatment, by reasonable concessions of autonomy. The cry in the beginning was not 'Down with the king,' but 'Down with bad government.' The revolutions began, not as a deliberate revolt against Spain, but as an attempt to replace or reform a bad governmental and economic system; and it was occasioned, curiously enough, by the overthrow of the Spanish monarchy by Napoleon.

It gradually turned into a movement against Spanish authority through force of circumstances in Europe, by the agitation of a few radical leaders, and especially because of the unsympathetic or hostile attitude of successive governments in Spain itself. Only when it appeared that all parties in Spain, reactionary and liberal, were more or less indifferent to reform in the colonies, were the extremists able to win public opinion over to the idea of complete separation.

In fact, in both the English and the Spanish empire of those days the problem was fundamentally the same: to reconcile colonial liberty with imperial unity.[25] The Spanish American communities, like the thirteen English colonies of North America, had attained to a degree of maturity in their material and intellectual development, and to a feeling of separateness from Europe, which made the old colonial servitude seem intolerable. Both aspired to a position of equality within the empire. Could this higher status be achieved without resort to violence? Both England and Spain replied in the negative. And the result was secession.

---

25 Cf. Klaus E. Knorr, *British Colonial Theories*, 1570-1850, Toronto, 1944, 131-4.

❦❦❦

Bibliography

❦❦❦

The following bibliography makes no pretense to a completeness embracing everything that bears upon the topics referred to in the preceding pages. It does, however, aim to include important items of a general nature, and monographs and articles that, in the judgment of the writer, make some considerable contribution to an understanding of the subject. With few exceptions, older books are listed by their first edition.

For other bibliographies relating to Latin American colonial history, many of them of a specialized nature, the reader should consult the very formidable list compiled by Cecil Knight Jones, *A Bibliography of Latin American Bibliographies* 2nd edition, Washington, 1942, which contains over 6,000 entries and an excellent index. For a comprehensive coverage of current scholarly publications, an indispensable guide is the annual *Handbook of Latin American Studies,* a selected and annotated list prepared formerly under the auspices of the American Council of Learned Societies, and now by the Library of Congress.

GENERAL MISCELLANEOUS

CONTEMPORARY SOURCE MATERIALS

Acosta, José de, *Historia natural y moral de las Indias*. Sevilla, 1590.

Blair, Emma Helen, and James Alexander Robertson, eds., *The Philippine Islands*, 1493-1898. 55 vols. Cleveland, 1903-9.

Casas, Bartolomé de las, *Historia de las Indias*. Edición de A. Millares Carlo y estudio preliminar de L. Hanke. 3 vols. Mexico, 1951.

Colección de documentos inéditos para la historia de Ibero-América (title of vols. III, V-XII, XIV, *Colección* . . . Hispano-América). 14 vols. Madrid, 1927-32.

Colección de documentos inéditos relativos al descubrimiento, conquista y colonización de las posesiones españolas en América y Oceanía. 42 vols. Madrid, 1864-84.

(Abbreviated as *Col. doc. inéd.*, 1st ser.)

Colección de documentos inéditos relativos al descubrimiento, conquista y of vols. III, V-XII, XIV, *Colección* . . . Hispano-América). 14 vols. Madrid, 1885-1928.

(Abbreviated as *Col. doc. inéd.*, 2nd ser.)

Concolorcovo (Calixto Bustamante Carlos Inga), *El Lazarillo de ciegos caminantes desde Buenos Aires hasta Lima*. Guijon, 1773.

Cuevas, Mariano, ed., *Documentos inéditos del siglo XVI para la historia de México, Mexico*. 1914.

Diario de Lima de Juan Antonio Suardo (1629-1634). Publicado con introducción y notas por Rubén Vargas Ugarte. Lima, 1935.

Diaro de Lima (1640-1694). *Crónica de la época colonial de Josephe de Mugaburu y Francisco de Mugaburu (hijo)*. Lima, 1935.

Díez de la Calle, Juan, *Memorial, y noticias sacras y reales del imperio de las Indias occidentales*. Madrid, 1646.

Fernández, León, ed., *Colección de documentos para la historia de Costa Rica*. Vols. 1-3, San José, 1881-3; vols. 4-5, Paris, 1886; vols. 6-10, Barcelona, 1907.

Fernández de Navarrete, Martín, ed., *Colección de los viages y descubrimientos que hicieron por mar los españoles desde fines del siglo XV*. 5 vols. Madrid, 1825-37.

Fernández de Oviedo y Valdés, Gonzalo, *Historia general y natural de las Indias, islas y tierra firme del mar océano*. 4 vols. Madrid, 1851-5.

Fernández de Piedrahita, Lucas, *Historia general de las conquistas del Nuevo Reino de Granada*, Amberes, 1688.

Frézier, Amédée François, *Relation du voyage de la mer du Sud aux côtes du Chily et du Pérou, fait pendant les années 1712, 1713 et 1714*. Paris, 1716.

Gage, Thomas, *The English-American. A New Survey of the West Indies*, 1648. Ed. with an introduction by A. P. Newton. London, 1928.

Herrera y Tordesillas, Antonio de, *Historia general de los hechos de los castellanos en las islas e tierra firme del mar océano.* 4 vols. Madrid, 1601-15.

Jiménez de la Espada, Marcos, ed., *Relaciones geográficas de Indias.* 4 vols. Madrid, 1881-97.

Juan, Jorge, and Antonio de Ulloa, *Noticias secretas de América.* London, 1826.

—— *Relación histórica del viaje a la América meridional.* 4 vols. Madrid, 1748.

Latorre, Germán, *Relaciones geográficas de Indias . . . siglo XVI.* Sevilla, 1919.

Lizárraga, Reginaldo de, *Descripción y población de las Indias.* Lima, 1908.

López de Velasco, Juan, *Geografía y descripción universal de las Indias, recopilada desde el año 1571 al de 1574.* Madrid, 1894.

Nueva colección de documentos inéditos para la historia de España y de sus Indias. Publicanla don Francisco de Zabállburu y don José Sancho Rayon. 6 vols. Madrid, 1892-6. Vol. VI.

Páez Brotchie, Luis, *La Nueva Galicia a través de su viejo archivo judicial* (Biblioteca histórica mexicana de obras inéditas, XVIII). Mexico, 1939.

Paso y Troncoso, Francisco del, ed., *Epistolario de Nueva España, 1505-1818* (Biblioteca histórica mexicana de obras inéditas, 2nd ser., I-XVI). Mexico, 1939-42.

Peralta, Manuel M. de, ed., *Costa Rica, Nicaragua y Panamá en el siglo XVI, su historia y sus límites.* Madrid, 1883.

Pons, François Joseph de, *Travels in South America During the Years 1801 . . . 1804.* 2 vols. London, 1807.

Rodríguez Fresle, Juan, *El Carnero. Conquista y descubrimiento del Nuevo Reino de Granada.* Bogotá, 1859.

Scholes, France V., and Eleanor B. Adams, eds., *Don Diego Quijada, alcalde mayor de Yucatán, 1561-1565* (Biblioteca histórica mexicana de obras inéditas, XIV, XV). Mexico, 1938.

Solórzano Pereira, Juan de, *Política indiana.* Madrid, 1647.

Vázquez de Espinosa, Antonio, *Compendium and Description of the West Indies.* Tr. by Charles Upson Clark (Smithsonian Miscellaneous Collections, vol. 102). Washington, 1942.

Villa-señor y Sánchez, Joseph Antonio de, *Theatro americano, descripción general de los reynos y provincias de la Nueva España.* 2 vols. Mexico, 1746-8.

MODERN WORKS

Alamán, Lucas, *Historia de México.* 5 vols. Mexico, 1883-5. Vol. I.

Arias y Miranda, José, *Examen crítico-histórico del influjo que tuvo en el comercio, industria y población de España su dominación en América.* Madrid, 1854.

Bancroft, Hubert Howe, *History of Central America.* 3 vols. San Francisco, 1882-7.

—— *History of Mexico.* 6 vols. San Francisco, 1883-8.

Barros Arana, Diego, *Historia general de Chile.* 16 vols. Santiago, 1884-1902.

Bourne, Edward Gaylord, *Spain in America,* 1450-1580. New York, 1904.

Cánovas del Castillo, Antonio, *Historia de la decadencia de España desde el advenimiento de Felipe III al trono hasta la muerte de Carlos II.* 2nd ed. Madrid, 1910.

Cappa, Ricardo, *Estudios críticos acerca de la dominación española en América.* Vols. 1-19, 26. Madrid, 1889-97.

Carrera Stampa, Manuel, 'El Seguro social en la Nueva España,' *El Foro,* Mexico, 2ª época, II, 363-76.

Chacón y Calvo, José María, *Criticismo y colonización.* Habana, 1938.

Encina, Francisco A., *Historia de Chile desde la prehistoria hasta 1891.* 20 vols. Santiago, 1940-52. Vols. 1-5.

Flórez Estrada, Alvaro, *Examen imparcial de las disensiones de la América con la España, de los medios de su reconcilición, etc.* Cadiz, 1812.

García Pelaez, Francisco de Paula, *Memorias para la historia del antiguo reyno de Guatemala.* 3 vols. Guatemala, 1851-2.

Gil Fortoul, José, *Historia constitucional de Venezuela.* 2nd ed., 3 vols. Caracas, 1930. Vol. I.

Gómez de Orozco, Federico, *Relaciones histórico-geográficas de Nueva España* (El México antiguo, bd. III, heft ½). Mexico, 1931.

González Suárez, Federico, *Historia general de la república del Ecuador.* 7 vols. Quito, 1890–1903.

Haring, C. H., *The Buccaneers in the West Indies in the Seventeenth Century.* London, 1910.

Historia de la Nación Argentina (desde los orígines hasta la organización definitiva en 1862). Ricardo Levene, director general. 10 vols, in 14. Buenos Aires, 1936-50. Vols. I-IV.

Humboldt, Alexander von, *Political Essay on the Kingdom of New Spain.* 4 vols. London, 1811.

Keller, Albert Galloway, *Colonization and Colonies.* Boston, 1908.

Lowery, Woodbury, *The Spanish Settlements within the Present Limits of the United States.* 2 vols. New York, 1901-5.

Lewin, Boleslao, *Los León Pinelo; la ilustre familia marrana del siglo XVII ligada a la historia de la Argentina, Perú, América y España.* Buenos Aires, 1942.

Means, Philip Ainsworth, *Fall of the Inca Empire and the Spanish Rule in Peru: 1530-1780.* New York, 1932.

Merivale, Herman, *Lectures on Colonization and Colonies.* 2 vols. London, 1841-2.

Merriman, Roger Bigelow, *The Rise of the Spanish Empire in the Old World and in the New.* 4 vols. New York, 1918-34.

Milla, José, *Historia de América Central.* 2 vols. Guatemala, 1879-82.

Moses, Bernard, *The Establishment of Spanish Rule in America.* New York, 1898.

—— *South America on the Eve of Emancipation.* New York, 1908.

—— *Spain's Declining Power in South America,* 1730-1806. Berkeley, Cal., 1919.

—— *The Spanish Dependencies in South America.* 2 vols. New York, 1914.

Neasham, V. Aubrey, 'Spain's Emigrants to the New World,' *Hispanic American Historical Review*, XIX, 147-60.

Newton, Arthur Percival, *The European Nations in the West Indies, 1493-1688*. London, 1933.

Orozco y Berra, Manuel, *Historia de la dominación española en México* (Biblioteca histórica mexicana de obras inéditas, VIII-XI). 4 vols. Mexico, 1938.

Ots Capdequí, José María, *Instituciones sociales de la América española en el período colonial*. La Plata, 1934.

Parra-Pérez, C., *El Régimen español en Venezuela. Estudio histórico*. Madrid, 1932.

Parry, John H., *The Spanish Theory of Empire in the Sixteenth Century*. Cambridge, 1940.

Pereyra, Carlos, *La Obra de España en América*. Madrid, 1920.

Pérez Bustamante, C., 'Las Regiones españolas y la población de América (1509-1534),' *Revista de Indias*, II, no. 6, 81-120.

Picón-Salas, Mariano, *De la Conquista a la independencia*. Mexico, 1944.

Plaza, José Antonio de la, *Memorias para la historia de la Nueva Granada desde su descubrimiento hasta el 20 de julio de 1810*. Bogotá, 1850.

Priestley, Herbert Ingram, *The Mexican Nation, a History*. New York, 1923.

Rios, Fernando de los, 'Spain in the Epoch of American Colonization.' 'The Action of Spain in America,' *Concerning Latin American Culture*. New York, 1940, 25-78.

Rousseau, François, *Règne de Charles III d'Espagne*. 2 vols. Paris, 1907.

Serrano y Sanz, Manuel, *Orígenes de la dominación española en América* (Nueva biblioteca de autores españoles, XXV). Madrid, 1918.

Torre Revello, José, 'Esclavas blancas en las Indias occidentales,' *Boletín del Instituto de investigaciones históricas*, Buenos Aires, tomo VI, no. 34, 263-71.

Vargas Ugarte, Rubén, *Títulos nobiliarios en el Perú*. Lima, 1944.

Villacorta C., J. Antonio, *Historia de la capitanía general de Guatemala*. Guatemala, 1942.

Weiss, Charles, *L'Espagne depuis Philippe II jusqu'aux Bourbons*. 2 vols. Paris, 1844.

Yanes, Francisco Javier, *Compendio de la historia de Venezuela, desde su descubrimiento y conquista hasta que se declaró estado independiente*. 2nd ed. Caracas, 1944.

Zavala, Silvio, *La Filosofía política en la conquista de América*. Mexico [1947].
—— *New Viewpoints on the Spanish Colonization of America*. Philadelphia, 1943.

POLITICAL ADMINISTRATION

CONTEMPORARY SOURCE MATERIALS

La Administración de d. frey Antonio María de Bucarelli y Ursua . . . 46° virrey de México (Publicaciones del Archivo general de la nación, XXXIX, XXX). Mexico, 1936.

Beltrán y Rózpide, Ricardo, ed., *Colección de las memorias o relaciones que escribieron los virreyes del Perú.* 2 vols. Madrid, 1921-30.

Castillo de Bovadilla, Jerónimo, *Política para corregidores y señores de vassallos en tiempo de paz y de guerra.* 2 vols. Barcelona, 1616.

Instrucción reservada que el conde de Revilla Gigedo dió a su sucesor en el mando, marqués de Branciforte. Mexico, 1831.

Instrucciones que los vireyes de Nueva España dejaron a sus sucesores. 2 vols. Mexico, 1867-73.

León Pinelo, Antonio de, *Tablas cronológicas de los Reales consejos supremo de la Camara de las Indias occidentales.* 2nd ed. Madrid, 1892.

—— *Tratado de confirmaciones reales de encomiendas, oficios i casos, en que se requieren para las Indias occidentales.* Madrid, 1630.

—— *Un Manuscrito desconocido de Antonio León Pinelo.* Lewis Hanke, ed. Santiago de Chile, 1937.

Levillier, Roberto, ed., *La Audiencia de Charcas. Correspondencia de presidentes y oidores; documentos del Archivo de Indias,* 3 vols. Madrid, 1918-22.

—— *Audiencia de Lima. Correspondencia de presidentes y oidores; documentos del Archivo de Indias.* Tomo I, 1549-64. Madrid, 1922.

—— *Gobernación del Tucumán. Papeles de gobernadores en el siglo XVI; documentos del Archivo de Indias.* Madrid, 1920.

—— *Gobernantes del Perú. Cartas y papeles, siglo XVI; documentos del Archivo de Indias.* 14 vols. Madrid, 1921-6.

Manzano, Juan, ed., 'Un Documento inédito relativo a "Como funcionaba el Consejo de Indias."' *Hispanic American Historical Review,* XV, 313-45.

Memorial que trata de la reformación del reino dei pirú, compuesta por el sargento Juan de Aponte Figueroa, 1622 (Collección de documentos inéditos para la historia de España, LI, 521–62).

Memorias de los virreyes del Rio de la Plata. Nota preliminar de Sigfrido A. Radaelli. Buenos Aires, 1945.

Memorias de los virreyes que han governado el Perú durante el tiempo del coloniaje español. 6 vols. Lima, 1859.

Polo, José Toribio, comp., *Memorias de los virreyes del Peru, marqués de Mancera y conde de Salvatierra.* Lima, 1899.

Posada, E., and P. M. Ibañez, comp., *Relaciones de mando. Memorias presentadas por las governantes del Nuevo reino de Granada.* Bogotá, 1910.

Relaciones de los vireyes y audiencias que han gobernado el Perú. Vol. I, Lima, 1867; vols. II, III, Madrid, 1871–2.

Rodríguez Casado, Vicente, and Florentino Pérez Embid, eds., *Manuel de Amat y Junient del Perú, 1761–1776, memoria de gobierno.* Sevilla, 1947.

MODERN WORKS

Aiton, Arthur Scott, *Antonio de Mendoza, First Viceroy of New Spain,* Durham, N. C., 1927.

Alcázar Molina, Cayetano, *Historia del correo en América.* Madrid, 1920.

Basadre, Jorge, *El Conde de Lemos y su tiempo*. Lima, 1945.

Bose, Walter B. L., 'Organización del correo en España y en las Indias occidentales,' *Revista de correos y telégrafos*, Buenos Aires, no. 60, 1549–58.

——'Orígenes del correo terrestre en México,' *Revista de historia de América*, no. 23, 55–103.

——'Los Orígenes del correo terrestre español en el virreinato del Perú,' *Segundo congreso internacional de historia de América*, Buenos Aires, 1937, II, 72–5.

Bullón y Fernández, Eloy, *El Problema jurídico de la dominación española en América antes de las 'Relecciones' de Francisco de Vitoria*. Madrid, 1923.

Cardozo, Efraím, 'La Audiencia de Charcas y la facultad de gobierno,' *Humanidades*, XX, pt. I, 137–56.

Castañeda, C. E., 'The Corregidor in Spanish Colonial Administration,' *Hispanic American Historical Review*, IX, 446–70.

Chamberlain, Robert S., 'The *Corregidor* in Castile in the Sixteenth Century and the *Residencia* as Applied to the *Corregidor*,' *Hispanic American Historical Review*, XXIII, 222–57.

Cunningham, C. H., *The Audiencia in the Spanish Colonies as Illustrated by the Audiencia of Manila*, 1583–1800. Berkeley, Cal., 1919.

Fisher, Lillian Estelle, *The Intendant System in Spanish America*. Berkeley, Cal., 1929.

——*Viceregal Administration in the Spanish American Colonies*. Berkeley, Cal., 1926.

Góngora, Mario, *El Estado en el derecho indiano, época de fundación*, 1492–1570. Santiago, Chile, 1951.

González, Casanova, Pablo, 'Aspectos políticos de Palafox y Mendoza,' *Revista de historia de América*, no. 17, 27–67.

Hackett, Charles W., 'The Delimitation of Political Jurisdictions in Spanish North America to 1535,' *Hispanic American Historical Review*, I, 40–69.

Hanke, Lewis, 'La Libertad de palabra en Hispanoamerica durante el siglo XVI, *Cuadernos Americanos*, año V, vol. 26, 185–201.

Haring, C. H., 'The Genesis of Royal Government in the Spanish Indies,' *Hispanic American Historical Review*, VII, 141–91.

Hill, Roscoe R., 'The Office of Adelantado,' *Political Science Quarterly*, XXVIII, 646–68.

Levene, Ricardo, *Historia del derecho argentino*. Vols. 1–5, Buenos Aires, 1945–9.

Levillier, Roberto, *Don Francisco de Toledo, supremo organizador del Perú*, 1515–1582. 3 vols. Madrid, 1935–42.

Lohmann Villena, Guillermo, *El Conde de Lemos, virrey del Perú*, Madrid, 1946.

Mecham, J. Lloyd, 'The *Real de Minas* as a Political Institution,' *Hispanic American Historical Review*, VII, 45–83.

Ots Capdequí, José María, 'Algunas Consideraciones en tarno a la política económica y fiscal del estado español en las Indias,' *Revista de las Indias*, Bogotá, época 2, no. 6, 172–81.

——*El Estado español en las Indias*. Mexico, 1941.

——*Institutiones de gobierno del Nuevo reino de Granada durante el siglo XVIII*. Bogotá, 1950.

———*Nuevos aspectos del siglo* XVIII *español en América.* Bogotá, 1946.

Parry, John H., *The Audiencia of New Galicia in the Sixteenth Century, a study in Spanish Colonial Government.* Cambridge, 1948.

Pierson, William W., 'La Intendencia de Venezuela en el régimen colonial,' *Boletín de la Academia nacional de la historia.* Caracas, XXIV, 259–75.

Priestley, Herbert Ingram, *José de Gálvez, Visitor-General of New Spain,* 1765–1771. Berkeley, Cal., 1916.

Rubio Mañé, J. Ignacio, 'Jurisdicciones del virreinato de Nueva España en la primera mitad del siglo XVIII,' *Revista de Indias,* año VII, no. 25, 463–502.

Ruíz Guiñazú, Enrique, *La Magistratura indiana.* Buenos Aires, 1916.

Schäfer, Ernesto, *El Consejo real y supremo de las Indias.* 2 vols. Sevilla, 1935–47.

Torre Revello, José, *Ensayo biográfico sobre Juan de Solórzano Pereira* (Facultad de filosofía y letras. Publicaciones del Instituto de investigaciones históricas, XLIV). Buenos Aires, 1929.

———'Juan de Solórzano Pereira, nuevos datos para su biografía,' *Boletín del Instituto de investigaciones históricas,* Buenos Aires, tomo XVII, nos. 58–60, 1–29.

Velázquez, María del Carmen, *El Estado de guerra en Nueva España,* 1760–1808. Mexico, 1950.

Zavala, Silvio, *Las Instituciones jurídicas en la conquista de América,* Madrid. 1935.

LEGISLATION

CONTEMPORARY SOURCE MATERIALS

Aguiar y Acuña, Rodrigo de, *Sumarios de la recopilación general de las leyes, ordenanzas, provisiones, cédulas, instrucciones y cartas acordadas, que por los reyes católicos de Castilla se han promulgado . . . para las Indias occidentales.* Madrid, 1628.

Altamira y Crevea, Rafael, ed., 'El Texto de las leyes de Burgos de 1512,' *Revista de historia de América,* no. 4, 5–79.

Ayala, Manuel José de, *Notas a la Recopilación de Indias; origen e historia ilustrada de las Leyes de Indias.* Transcripción y estudio preliminar de Juan Manzano Manzano. 2 vols. Madrid, 1945–6.

Beleña, Eusebio Bentura, *Recopilación sumaria de todos los autos acordados de la real audiencia y sala del crimen de esta Nueva España.* 2 vols. Mexico, 1787.

Disposiciones complementarias de las leyes de Indias (Ministerio detrabajo y previsión. Publicación de la Inspección general de emigración). 3 vols. Madrid, 1930.

Encinas, Diego de, *Provisiones, cédulas, capitulos de ordenanzas, instrucciones y cartas . . . tocante al buen gobierno de las Indias y administración de la justicia en ellas.* 4 vols. Madrid, 1596.

Gobernación espiritual y temporal de las Indias (Col. doc. inéd., 2nd ser., vols. XX–XXV, Madrid, 1927–32).

'Las Ordenanzas de Felipe II sobre descubrimientos, población y pacificación de las Indias,' *Boletín del Archivo general de la nación*, vi, 321–60.

León Pinelo, Antonio de, *Autos, acuerdos y decretos de gobierno del real y supremo Consejo de las Indias*. Madrid, 1658.

Levillier, Roberto, ed., *Ordenanzas de don Francisco de Toledo, virrey del Perú, 1569–1581*. Madrid, 1929.

Matraya de Ricci, Juan, *El Moralista filaléthico americano o el confesor imparcial instruido en las obligaciones de su ministerio*. Lima, 1819. (Includes, pp. 259–596, a catalog of royal *cédulas* to the viceroyalty of Peru, 1680–1817.)

Maurtua, Victor M., *Antecedentes de la Recopilación de Yndias*. Madrid, 1906.

Montemayor y Córdova de Cuenca, J. F., *Recopilación dealgunos mandamientos y ordenanzas del gobierno de esta Nueva España heches por los Exmôs Señores vireyes y gobernadores de ella*. 2nd ed., Mexico, 1787. (Also included in Beleña.)

——*Recopilación sumaria de algunos autos acordados de la Real audiencia y chansillería de la Nueva España*. 2nd ed., Mexico, 1787. (Included in Beleña.)

——*Sumarios de las cédulas, órdenes y provisiones reales . . . para la Nueva España*. Mexico, 1678. (Included in Belena.)

Ordenanzas de la Junta de guerra de Indias. Madrid, 1634.

Ordenanzas del Consejo real de las Indias nuevamente recopiladas por el rey D. Felipe Quarto. Madrid, 1636. (Later eds., Madrid, 1681 and 1747.)

Ordenanzas reales del Consejo de las Indias. Madrid 1585. (Later ed., Valladolid, 1603.)

Ordenanzas reales para la Case de contratación de Sevilla, y para otras cosas de las Indias. Y de la navegación y contratación dellas. Sevilla, 1552. (Later eds., Madrid, 1585; Valladolid, 1604; Sevilla, 1647.)

Pardo, J. Joaquín, *Prontuario de reales cédulas, 1529–1599*. Guatemala, 1941.

Parry, John H., ed., 'The Ordinances of the Audiencia of New Galicia,' *Hispanic American Historical Review*, xviii, 364–73.

Pérez y López, Antonio Xavier, *Teatro de la legislación universal de España e Indias, por orden cronológico de sus cuerpos y decisiones no recopiladas, y alfabético de sus títulos y principales materias*. 28 vols. Madrid, 1791–8.

Puga, Vasco de, *Provisiones, cédulas, instrucciones de su Magestad*, etc. Mexico, 1563.

Real ordenanza para el establecimiento y instrución de intendentes de ejército y provincia en el reino de Nueva España. Madrid, 1786.

Recopilación de leyes de los reynos de las Indias. 4 vols. Madrid, 1681.

Zamora y Coronado, José María, *Biblioteca de legislación ultramarina en forma de diccionario alfabético*. 7 vols. Madrid, 1844–9.

——*Registro de legislación, ultramarina, y ordenanza general de 1803 para intendentes y empleados de hacienda en Indias*. 3 vols. Habana, 1839.

MODERN WORKS

Alcalá Zamora, Niceto, *Impresión general acerca de las leyes de Indias*. Buenos Aires, 1942.

Altamira y Crevea, Rafael, 'La Décentralisation législative dans le régime colonial espagnol (xvi⁰-xviii⁰ siècles),' *Bulletin du comité international des sciences historiques*, no. 43, 165–90.

——*Estudios sobre las fuentes de conocimiento del derecho indiano. Análasis de la Recopilación . . . de Indias de 1680.* (Facultad de derecho y ciencias sociales. Instituto de historia de derecho argentino. Estudios para la historia del derecho argentino, ii.) Buenos Aires, 1941.

——'La Legislación indiana como elemento de la historia de las ideas coloniales españolas,' *Revista de his⸱ ʳia de América*, no. 1, 1–24.

——*Manual de investigación de la historia del derecho indiano* (Instituto panamericano de geografía. Historia Comosión de historia. Manuales de técnica de la investigación de la historia y ciencias afines, i). Mexico, 1948.

(Earlier ed., *Técnica de investigación* etc., Mexico, 1939.)

——'El Manuscrito de la Gobernación espiritual y temporal de las Indias y su lugar en las historia de la Recopilación,' *Revista de historia de América*, no. 7, 1–38.

Jiménez de la Espada, M., 'El Código ovanindo,' *Revista contemporánea*, LXXXI, 225–45; 352–65.

Manzano, Juan, 'Un Compilador indiano, Manuel José de Ayala,' *Boletín del Instituto de investigaciones históricas*, Buenos Aires, tomo xviii, nos. 61–3, 152–240.

——'El Nuevo código de las leyes de Indias, projecto de Juan Crisóstomo de Ansoteguí,' *Revista de ciencias jurídicas y sociales*, xviii, 702–76.

Muro Orejón, Antonio, 'El Nuevo código de las leyes de Indias, projectos de recopilación legislativa posteriores a 1680,' ibid. xii, 287–339.

Ots Capdequí, José María, 'D. Manuel Josef de Ayala y la historia de nuestras legislación de Indias,' *Hispanic American Historical Review*, iii, 281–322.

——*Estudios de historia del derecho español en las Indias*, Bogotá, 1940.

——*Manual de historia del derecho español en las Indias y del derecho propiamente indiano.* 2 vols. Buenos Aires, 1943.

Peña Cámara, José de la, 'La Comulata de leyes de Indias y las ordenanzas ovandinas,' *Revista de Indias*, ii, no. 6, 121–46.

——'El Manuscrito llamado "Gobernación espiritual y temporal de las Indias" y su verdadero lugar en la historia de la Recopilación,' *Revista de historia de América*, no. 12, 5–72.

——'Las Redacciones del libro de la Gobernación espiritual. Ovando y la junta de Indias en 1568,' *Revista de Indias*, ii, no. 5, 93–116.

Torre Revello, José, *Noticias históricas sobre la Recopilación de Indias* (Facultad de filosofía y letras. Publicaciones del Instituto de investigaciones históricas, xlvi). Buenos Aires, 1929.

MUNICIPALITIES

CONTEMPORARY SOURCE MATERIALS

BUENOS AIRES. Archivo de la nación, *Acuerdos del extinguido cabildo de Buenos Aires*. 4 series. 83 vols. Buenos Aires, 1907–32.

BUENOS AIRES. Levillier, Roberto, ed., *Correspondencia de la ciudad de Buenos Ayres con los reyes de España*. 3 vols. Madrid, 1915–18.

CARACAS. Consejo municipal, *Actas del cabildo de Caracas*. Vols. 1–3, Caracas, 1943–50.

Cervantes de Salazar, Francisco, *Crónica de la Nueva España*. Madrid, 1914. Lib. IV, cap. 24, 25.

——*Mexico en 1554. Tres diálogos latinos traducidos por Joaquin García Icazbalceta*. Mexico, 1875.

Cobo, Bernabé, *Historia de la fundación de Lima*. Lima, 1882.

CORRIENTES (Arg.). Academia nacional de la historia, *Actas capitulares de Corrientes*. 4 vols. Buenos Aires, 1941–6.

CUZCO. Urteaga, Horacio H., and Carlos A. Romero, eds., *Fundación española del Cuzco y ordenanzas para su gobierno*. Lima, 1926.

HAVANA. Roig de Leuchseuring, Emilio, ed., *Actas capitulares del ayuntamiento de la Habana*. 2 vols. Habana, 1937.

JUJUY (Arg.). *Archivo capitular de Jujuy*. 4 vols. Buenos Aires, 1913–44.

LIMA. *Libros de cabildos de Lima*. Vols. I–XVI, Lima, 1935–48.

MEXICO. *Actas de cabildo de la ciudad de México*. 50 vols. Mexico, 1889–1916.

MONTEVIDEO. *Acuerdos del extinguido cabildo de Montevideo*. (Revista del archivo general administrativo, 1885–1922, continued as Archivo general de la nación.) 18 vols. Montevideo, 1885–1943.

QUITO. *Libros de cabildos de la ciudad de Quito*. 17 vols. Quito, 1934–41.

SAN JUAN (Puerto Rico). *Actas de cabildo de San Juan Bautista de Puerto Rico*, 1730–1750 [San Juan, 1949].

SANTIAGO DE CHILE. *Actas del cabildo de Santiago*. (Colección de historiadores de Chile, vols. 1, 17–21, 25–5, 28, 30–44, 46–7.)

SANTIAGO DEL ESTERO (Arg.). *Actas capitulares de Santiago del Estero*. (Academia nacional de la historia.) 5 vols. Buenos Aires, 1941–8.

TUCUMÁN (Arg.). Levillier, Roberto, ed., *Gobernación del Tucumán, correspondencia de los cabildos en el siglo XVI, documentos del Archivo de Indias*. Madrid, 1918.

TUCUMÁN (Arg.). Lizondo Borda, Manuel, ed., *Actas del cabildo*. Vols. 1, 2, Tucumán, 1939–40.

TUNJÁ (Col.). *Libro de cabildos de la cibdad de Tunja*. Vol. 1, 1539–42. Bogotá, 1941.

Vetancourt, Augustin de, *Tratado de la ciudad de México, y las grandezas que la ilustran despues que la fundaron españoles*. (Appended to *Teatro mexicano, descripción breve de los sucesos exemplares . . . del Nuevo mundo occidental de las Indias*. Mexico, 1698.)

MODERN WORKS

Alemparte R., Julio, *El Cabildo en Chile colonial*. Santiago, 1940.

Cervera, Manuel M., *Historia de la ciudad y provincia de Santa Fé*, 1573–1853. 2 vols. Santa Fe, 1907.

Dusenberry, William H., 'The Regulation of Meat Supply in Sixteenth Century Mexico City,' *Hispanic American Historical Review*, xxviii, 38–52.

Gálvez, José, *Estampas limeñas*. Lima, 1935.

García Juan Augustin, *La Ciudad indiana*. Buenos Aires, 1900.

Garretón, Alfredo, *La Municipalidad colonial, Buenos Aires desde su fundación hasta el gobierno de Lariz*. Buenos Aires, 1933.

González Obregón, Luis, *México viejo*, 1521–1821. Paris, 1900.

Kirkpatrick, F. A., 'Municipal Administration in the Spanish Dominions in America,' *Transactions* of the Royal Historical Society, 3rd ser., vol. ix, 95–110.

——*Regidores and Alcaldes Ordinarios* (MS.) 160 pp.

Kubler, George, 'Mexican Urbanism in the Sixteenth Century, *The Art Bulletin*, xxiv, 160–71.

Lafuente Machain, Ricardo de, *Buenos Aires en el siglo xvii*. Buenos Aires, 1944.

——*Buenos Aires en el siglo xviii*. Buenos Aires, 1946.

Montes de Oca, M. A., 'Cabildos coloniales,' *La Biblioteca, Buenos Aires*, iv, 28–60.

Ots Capdequí, José María, 'Apuntes para la historia del municipio hispanoamericano del período colonial,' *Anuario de historia del derecho español*, i, 93–157.

Pierson, W. W., 'Some Reflections on the Cabildo as an Institution,' *Hispanic American Historical Review*, v 573–96.

Porras Barrenechea, Raúl, ed., *Pequeña antologia de Lima* (1535–1935). Madrid, 1935.

Priestley, Herbert Ingram, 'Spanish Colonial Municipalities,' *California Law Review*, Sept. 1919.

Valle-Arizpe, Artemio de, *La Muy Noble y Leal Ciudad de México, segun relatos de antaño y hogano*. Mexico, 1924.

Zorraquín, Becú, Ricardo, *La Justicia capitular durante la dominación española* (Facultad de derecho y ciencias sociales. Instituto de historia del derecho argentino. Conferencias y comunicaciones, xvii). Buenos Aires, 1947.

INDIANS

CONTEMPORARY SOURCE MATERIALS

Agia, Miguel, *Servidumbres personales de indios*. [Tratado que contiene tres paraceres graves en derecho. Lima, 1604.] Edición y estudio preliminar de F. Javier de Ayala. Seville, 1946.

Campo y de la Rynaga, Nicolás Matías del, *Memorial apologético, histórico, jurídico, y político, en respuesta de otra . . . contra el repartimiento de indios . . . en Potosí,* etc. n.p., n.d.

——*Memorial histórico y jurídico, que refiere el origen del oficio de protector general de los indios del Perú,* etc. Madrid, 1671.

Documentos para la historia económica de México (Publicaciones de la Secretaria de la economía nacional). 12 pts. Mexico, 1933–8.

Gómez de Cervantes, Gonzalo, *La Vida económica y social de Nueva España al finalizar el siglo* XVI. Prólogo y notas de Alberto María Carreno (Biblioteca histórica mexicana de obras inéditas, XIX). Mexico. 1944.

Hanke, Lewis, ed., 'Un Festón de documentos lascasianos,' *Revista cubana,* XVI, 150–208.

León Pinelo, Antonia de, *Tratado de confirmaciones reales de encomiendas oficios i casos, en que se requieren para las Indias occidentales.* Madrid, 1630.

Loayza, Francisco, A., ed., *Juan Santos el invincible (manuscritos del año de 1742 al año de 1755.)* Lima, 1942.

Matienzo, Juan de, *Gobierno del Perú.* Buenos Aires, 1910.

Moreno, Gerónymo, *Reglas ciertas, y precisamente necessarias para juezes y ministros de justicia de las Indias, y para sus confessores.* Mexico, 1637.

Motolinia, Toribio, *Historia de los indios de la Nueva España.* Mexico, 1941.

Quiroga, Pedro de, *Libro intitulado Coloquios de la verdad, trata de las causas e inconvinientes que impiden la doctrina e conversión de los indios de los reinos del Pirú, y de los daños e males, e agravios que padecen.* Sevilla, 1922.

Rynaga, Salazar, Juan de la, *Memorial discursivo sobre el oficio de protector general de los indios del Pirú.* Madrid, 1626.

Vásquez, Genaro V., ed., *Doctrinas y realidades en la legislación para los indios.* Mexico, 1940.

Zavala, Silvio, 'Los Trabajadores antillanos en el siglo XVI,' *Revista de historia de América,* no. 2, 31–68; no. 3, 60–88; no. 4, 211–16.

——and María Castelo, *Fuentes para la historia del trabajo en Nueva España.* 8 vols. Mexico, 1939–46.

Zorita, Alonso de, *Breve y sumaria relación de los señores de la Nueva Espana* (Biblioteca del estudiante universitario, 32). Mexico, 1942.

MODERN WORKS

Amunátegui Solar, Domingo, *Las encomiendas indíjenas en Chile.* 2 vols. Santiago, 1909–10.

——*Historia social de Chile.* Santiago, 1932.

Arboleda Llorente, José María, *El Indio en la colonia.* Bogotá, 1948.

Aznar, Luis, 'Legislación sobre indios en la América hispano-colonial, cuestiones de criterio, periodos legislativos,' *Humanidades,* XXV, pt. 1, 233–74.

Basadre, Jorge, 'El Régimen de las mitas,' *Letras,* Lima, tercer cuatrimestre, 1937, 325–64.

Bayle, Constantino, *El Protector de indios*. Sevilla, 1945.

Belaunde Guinassi, Manuel, *La Encomienda en el Perú*. Lima, 1945.

Chamberlain, Robert S., 'Castilian Backgrounds of the Repartimiento-encomienda' (Carnegie Institution of Washington, Publication 509, 19–66).

Cline, Howard F., 'Civil Congregations of the Indians in New Spain, 1598–1606, *Hispanic American Historical Review*, xxvx, 349–69.

Feliú Cruz, Guillermo, and Carlos Monge Alfaro, *Las Encomiendas según tasas y ordenanzas* (Facultad de filosofía y letras. Publicaciones del Instituto de investigaciones históricas, lxxvii). Buenos Aires, 1941.

Gandía, Enrique de, *Francisco de Alfaro y la condición social de los indios. Rio de la Plata, Paraguay, Tucumán y Perú, siglos xvi y xvii*. Buenos Aires, 1939.

Hanke, Lewis, *Bartolomé de Las Casas, Bookman, Scholar and Propagandist*. Philadelphia, 1952.

——*Bartolomé de Las Casas, an Interpretation of his Life and Writings*. The Hague, 1951.

——*The First Social Experiments in America, a Study in the Development of Spanish Indian Policy in the Sixteenth Century*. Cambridge, Mass., 1935.

——'Pope Paul III and the American Indians,' *Harvard Theological Review*, xxx, 65–102.

——'The "Requerimiento" and its Interpreters,' *Revista de historia de América*, no, 1, 25–34.

——*The Spanish Struggle for Justice in the Conquest of America*. Philadelphia, 1949.

Ibot, A., *Los Trabajadores del rio Magdalena durante el siglo xvi*. Barcelona, 1933.

Kirkpatrick, F. A., 'The Landless Encomienda,' *Hispanic American Historical Review*, xxii, 765–74.

——'Repartimiento-encomienda,' ibid. xix, 372–9.

Kubler, George, 'Population Movements in Mexico, 1520–1600,' ibid. xxii, 606–43.

Marshall, C. E., 'The Birth of the Mestizo in New Spain,' ibid. xix, 161–84.

Mendizábal, Miguel O., 'Demografía colonial del siglo xvi, 1519–1599. Consecuencias demografícas del choque de la cultura occidental con las culturas indígenas de México,' *Boletín de la sociedad mexicana de geografía y estadística*, tomo 48, 2ª parte, 301–41.

Meza Villalobos, Néstor, 'La Política indígene en el siglo xvi, *Revista hiclena de historia y geografía*, no. 112, 35–50.

Miranda, José, 'La Tasación de las cargas indígenas de la Nueva España durante el siglo xvi, excluyendo el tributo,' *Revista de historia de América*, no. 31, 77–96.

Roys, Ralph L., *The Indian Background of Colonial Yucatan*. Washington, 1943.

Simpson, Lesley Byrd, *The Encomienda in New Spain; the Beginning of Spanish Mexico*. New ed. Berkeley, Cal., 1950.

——*Studies in the Administration of the Indians of New Spain:*

I *The Laws of the Burgos of 1512*; II. *The Civil Congregation* (Ibero-Americana, 7). Berkeley, Cal., 1934.

III. *The Repartimiento System of Native Labor in New Spain and Guate-*

mala (ibid. 13). Berkeley, Cal., 1938.

IV. *The Emancipation of the Indian Slaves and the Resettlement of the Freedmen,* 1548–1555 (ibid. 16). Berkeley, Cal., 1940.

Valcarcel Esparza, Carlos D., *La Rebelión de Tupac Amaru.* Mexico, 1947.

——*Rebeliones indigenas.* Lima, 1946.

Viñas Mey, Carmelo, *El Estatuto del obrero indígena en la colonización española.* Madrid, 1929.

Zavala, Silvio, *Contribución a la historia de las instituciones coloniales de Guatemala* (Jornadas, 36). Mexico, 1945.

——*La Encomienda indiana.* Madrid, 1935.

——'Las Encomiendas de Nueva España y el gobierno de don Antonio de Mendoza,' *Revista de historia de América,* no. 1, 59–76.

——*Estudios indianos.* Mexico, 1948.

——'Nuño de Guzmán y la esclavitud de los indios,' *Revista mexicana,* 1, 411–28.

——*Servidumbres naturales y libertad cristiana segun los tratadistas españoles do los siglos* XVI *y* XVII (Facultad de filosofía y letras. Publicaciones del Instituto de investigaciones históricas, LXXXIII). Buenos Aires, 1944.

Zorraquín Becú, Ricardo, 'La Reglamentación de las encomiendas en el territorio argentino,' *Revista de la facultad de derecho y ciencias sociales,* Buenos Aires, 3ª epoca, aña, 1, no. 1.

Zurkalowski, Erich, 'El Establecimiento de las encomiendas en el Perú y sus antecedentes,' *Revista histórica,* Lima, VI, 254–69.

NEGROES

MODERN WORKS

Carrancá y Trujilla, Raúl, 'El Estatua jurídico de los esclavos en las postrimerías de la colonización española,' *Revista de historia de América,* no. 3, 20–59.

Feliú Cruz, Guillermo, *'La Abolición de la esclavitud en Chile.* Santiago, 1942.

King, James F., 'Evolution of the Free Slave Trade Principle in Spanish Colonial Administration,' *Hispanic American Historical Review,* XXII, 34–56.

Molinari, Diego Luis, *La Trata de negros. Datos para su estudio en el Rio de la Plata* (Prólogo al tomo VII de Los Documentos para la historia argentina). Buenos Aires, 1916.

Saco, José Antonio, *Historia de la esclavitud de la raza africana en el nuevo mundo y en especial en los paises américo-hispanos.* 2 vols. Barcelona, 1879–93.

Scelle, Georges, *La Traite négrière aux Indes de Castille.* 2 vols. Paris, 1906.

Zavala, Silvio, 'Relaciones históricas entre indios y negros en Iberoamérica,' *Revista de las Indias,* Bogotá, no. 88, 53–66.

THE CHURCH

CONTEMPORARY SOURCE MATERIALS

Aguayo Spencer, Rafael, ed., *Don Vasco de Quiroga. Documentos.* Mexico, 1939.

Alegre, Francisco Xavier, *Historia de la Compañía de Jesús en la Nueva España.* 3 vols. Mexico, 1841-2.

Arriaga, Pablo Joseph de, *Extripación de la idolatría del Perú.* Lima, 1621.

Autos de fe la inquisición de México con extractos de sus causas, 1646-1648 (Documentos inéditos o muy raros para la historia de México, xxvii). Mexico, 1910.

Betancurt i Figueroa, Luis de, *Derecho de las iglesias metropolitanas i catedrales de las Indias, sobre que sus prelacias sean proveidas en los capitulares dellas, i naturales de sus provincias.* Madrid, 1637.

El Clero de México durante la dominación española, según el archivo archi episcopal metropolitano (Documentos inéditos o muy raros para la historia de México, xv). Mexico, 1907.

Conway, G. R. G., ed., *An Englishman and the Mexican Inquisition,* 1556-1560. Mexico, 1927.

Descripción del arzobispado de México hecha en 1570 [por Alonso de Montúfar, arzobispo de México] *y otros documentos.* Mexico, 1897.

Documentos inéditos referentes al ilustrísimo señor don Vasco de Quiroga Biblioteca histórica mexicana de obras inéditas, xvii). Mexico, 1940.

Fita y Colomer, Fidel, 'Fray Bernal Boyl—documentos inéditos,' *Boletín de le Real academia de la historia,* xx, 160-77.

——*Fray Bernal Boyl, o, El primer apóstol del Nuevo mundo. Colección de documentos raros e inéditos.* Madrid, 1884.

Frasso, Pedro, *De regio patronatu indiarum.* 2 vols. Madrid, 1677-9.

García Icazbalceta, Joaquín, ed., *Nueva colección de documentos para la historia de México.* 5 vols. Mexico, 1886-92.

González Dávila, Gil, *Teatro eclesiástico de la primitiva iglesia de las Indias occidentales, vidas de sus arzobispos, obispos, y cosas memorables de sus sedes.* 2 vols. Madrid, 1649-55.

Hernaez, Francisco Javier (ed., *Colección de bulas, breves y otros documentos relativos a la iglesia de América y Filipinas.* 2 vols. Bruselas, 1879.

La Inquisición de México, sus orígenes, jurisdicción, competencia, etc. (Documentos inéditos o muy raros para la historia de México, v). Mexico, 1906.

Los Judios en la Nueva España (Publicaciones del Archivo general de la nación, xx). Mexico, 1922.

Levillier, Roberto, ed., *Organización de la iglesia y órdenes religious en el virreinato del Perú en el siglo* xvi, *documentos del Archivo de Indias.* 2 vols. Madrid, 1919.

——*Papeles eclesiásticos del Tucumán, documentos originales del Archivo de Indias.* 2 vols. Madrid, 1926.

Libro primero de votos de la inquisición de México, 1573-1600. Introduction by Edmundo O'Gorman. Mexico, 1949.

Méndez Arceo, Sergio, 'Documentos inéditos que ilustran los orígenes de los obispados Carolense (1519), Tierra Florida (1520) y Yucatán (1561),' *Revista de historia de América,* no. 9, 31-62.

Mendieta, Gerónimo de, *Historia eclesidstica indiana*. Mexico, 1870.

Parras, Pedro Joseph, *Gobierno de los regulares de la América*. 2 vols. Madrid, 1783.

Peña Montenegro, Alonso de la, *Itinerario para parochos de indios*. Madrid, 1668.

Procesos de Luis re Carvajal (el mozo) (Publicaciones del Archivo general de la nación, XXVIII). Mexico, 1935.

Remesal, Antonio de, *Historia de la provincia de S. Vicente de Chyapa y Guatemala de la orden de nṙo glorioso padre sancto Domingo*. Madrid, 1619.

Ribadenayra y Barrientos, Antonio Joachín de, *Manual compendio de el regio patronato indiano*. Madrid, 1755.

Torquemada, Juan de, *Monarquía indiana. 3 vols*. Madrid, 1723.

MODERN WORKS

Bayle, Constantino, 'España y el clero indígena de América,' *Razón y fe*, XCIV, 213–25; 521–35.

Bolton, Herbert E., 'The Mission as a Frontier Institution in the Spanish American Colonies,' *American Historical Review*, XXIII, 42–61.

Borah, Woodrow, 'The Collection of Tithes in the Bishopric of Oaxaca in the Sixteenth Century,' *Hispanic American Historical Review*, XXI, 386–409.

——'Tithe Collection in the Bishopric of Oaxaca, 1601–1867,' ibid. XXIX, 498–517.

Cuevas, Mariano, *Historia de la iglesia en México*. 4 vols. Mexico, 1921–6.

Dercome, Gerard, *La Obra de los Jesuitas mexicanos durante la época colonial, 1572–1767*. 2 vols, Mexico, 1941.

Desdevises du Dezert, G., *L'Eglise espagnole des Indes à la fin du XVIIIᵉ siècle*. Paris. 1917. (Reprinted from *Revue hispanique*, XXXIX, 112–293.)

——'L'Inquisition aux Indes espagnoles à fin du XVIIIᵉ,' *Revue hispanique*, XXX, 1–118.

Fernández, Justino, and Edmundo O'Gorman, *Santo Tomás More y 'La Utopia de Tomás Moro en la Nueva España.'* Mexico, 1937.

García Icazbalceta, Joaquín, *Don fray Juan de ʋumárraga, primer obispo y arzobispo de México*. Mexico, 1881.

Graham, R. B. Cunninghame, *A Vanished Arcadia being Some Account of the Jesuits in Paraguay, 1607 to 1767*. London, 1901.

Hernández, Pablo, *Misiones del Paraguay, organización social de las doctrinas guaraníes de la Compañía de Jesús*. 2 vols. Barcelona, 1913.

Jimémez Rueda, Julio, *Herejías y supersticiones en la Nueva España*. Mexico, 1946.

Lea, Henry C., *The Inquisition in the Spanish Dependencies*. New York, 1908.

Legón, Faustino J., *Doctrina y ejercicio del patronato nacional*. Buenos Aires, 1920.

Leonhart, Carlos, 'Acción educadora de los Jesuitas españoles en los paises que formaron el virreinato del Rio de la Plata,' *Estudios* XXIV, 17–23, 115–31, 186–94, 268–80.

Leturia, Pedro, 'Der heilige Stuhl und das Spanische Patronat in Amerika,' *Historisches Jahrbuch*, XLVI, 1–71.

Loughran, Elizabeth Ward, 'Did a Priest Accompany Columbus in 1492?' *Catholic Historical Review*, XVI, 164–74.

——'The First Episcopal Sees in Spanish America,' *Hispanic American Historical Review*, X, 167–87.

——'The First Vicar-Apostolic of the New World,' *Ecclesiastical Review*, 9th ser., II, 1–14.

——'The Marquis's Hospital,' *Mid-America*, XIV, 39–47.

——'A Mexican Millionaire Philanthropist,' *Thought*, VII, 262–78.

Medina, José Toribio, *Historia del tribunal del Santo oficio de la inquisición de Cartagena de las Indias*. Santiago, 1809.

——*Historia del tribunal del Santo oficio de la inquisición en Chile*. 2 vols Santiago, 1890.

——*Historia del tribunal del Santo oficio de la inquisición de Lima* (1569–1820). 2 vols. Santiago, 1887.

——*Historia del tribunal del Santo oficio de la inquisición en México*. Santiago, 1905.

——*La Primitiva inquisición americana* (1493–1569). Santiago 1914.

——*El Tribunal del Santo oficio de la inquisición en las provincias del Plata*. Santiago, 1899.

Metraux, Alfred, 'The Contribution of the Jesuits to the Exploration and Anthropology of South America,' *Mid-America*, XXVI, 183–91.

Ricard, Robert, *La Coquête spirituelle du Méxique, essai sur l'apostolat et les méthodes missionairès des ordres mendiants en Nouvelle Espagne, de 1523 à 1572*. Paris, 1933.

Scholes, France V., *Church and State in New Mexico, 1610–1670* (Historical Society of New Mexico. Publications in History, VII, XI). Albuquerque, 1937, 1942.

Southey, Robert, *History of Brazil*. 3 vols. London. 1810–19.

Steck, Francis Borgia, *Ensayos históricos hispanoamericanos*. Mexico, 1940.

——*El Primer Colegio de América, Santa Cruz de Tlalteolco*. Mexico, 1944.

Streit, Robert, *Bibliotheca missionum*. Vols. I-XI, Munster, 1916–38.

Vergara, M. A., 'El Hospital colonial de Jujuy en los siglos XVII y XVIII,' *Boletín del Instituto de investigaciones históricas*, Buenos Aires, tomo XIII, nos. 49–50, 11–39.

Watters, Mary, 'The Colonial Missions in Venezuela,' *Catholic Historical Review*, XXIII, 129–52.

Zavala, Silvio, *Ideario de Vasca de Quiroga*. Mexico, 1941.

EDUCATION

CONTEMPORARY SOURCE MATERIALS

La Bula In Apostolatus Culmine del Papa Paulo III (Publicaciones de la Universidad de Santo Domingo, XXVII). Ciudad Trujillo, 1944.

Calancha, Antonio de la, *Historia de la universidad de San Marcos hasta el 15 de Julio de 1647*. Lima, 19921.

Constituciones de la real y pontífica universidad de México. 2nd ed. Mexico, 1775.

Osores, Félix, *Historia de todos los colegios de la ciudad de México desde la conquista hasta 1780*. Mexico, 1929.

Plaza y Jaen, Christoval Bernardo de la, *Crónica de la real y insigne universidad de México de la Nueva España desde el año de 1553 hasta el de 1687*. 2 vols. Mexico, 1931.   ,

Salazar y Zevallos, Alonso Eduardo de, *Constituciones, y ordenanzas antiguas, añadidas, y modernas de la real universidad y estudio general de San Marcos de la Ciudad de los Reyes del Perú*. Lima, 1735.

MODERN WORKS

Alegría, Paula, *La Educación en México antes y despues de la conquista*. Mexico, 1936.

Bayle, Constantino, *España y la educación popular en América*. Madrid, 1934.

Cháneton, Abel, *La Instrucción primaria en la época colonial*. Buenos Aires, 1936.

Dávila Condemarin, José, *Bosquejo histórico de la fundación de la insigne universidad mayor de San Marcos de Lima, de sus progresos y actual estado*. Lima, 1854.

Eguigeren, Luis Antonio, *Catálogo histórico del claustro de la universidad de San Marcos, 1576–1800*. Lima, 1912.

Fuenzalida, Grandón, Alejandro, *Historia del desarrollo intelectual en Chile 1541–1810)*. Santiago, 1903.

García Icazbalceta, Joaquín, *La Instrucción pública en la ciudad de México durante el siglo XVI*. Mexico, 1893.

Garro, Juan M., *Bosquejo histórico de la universidad de Córdoba, con apéndice de documentos*. Buenos Aires, 1882.

Lanning, John Tate, *Academic Culture in the Spanish Colonies*. New York, 1940.

MacLean y Estenós, Roberto, 'Escuelas, colegios, seminarios y universidades en el virreynato del Perú,' *Letras*, Lima, primer cuatrimestre de 1943, 14–63.

Méndez y Mendoza, J. de D., *Historia de la Universidad centrale de Venezuela*. 2 vols. Caracas, 1911–24.

Parra, Caracciolo, *Filosofía universitaria venezolana, 1788–1821*. Caracas, 1933.

Priestley, Herbert Ingram, 'The Old University of Mexico,' *University of California Chronicle*, XXI, no. 4.

Villarán, Manuel Vicente, *La Universidad de San Marcos de Lima. Los orígines: 1548–1577*. Lima, 1938.

Whitaker, Arthur P., ed., *Latin America and the Enlightenment*. New York, 1942.

LITERATURE, SCIENCE, AND SCHOLARSHIP

CONTEMPORARY SOURCE MATERIALS

Fernández del Castilo, Francisco, *Libros y liberos del siglo* XVI (Publicaciones del Archivo general de la nación, VI). Mexico, 1914.

Ruiz, Hipólito, *Travels of Ruiz, Pavón and Dombey in Peru and Chile* (1777–1788). *With an Epilogue and official Documents Added by Augustin Jesús Barreiro*. Tr. by B. E. Dahlgren (Field Museum of Natural History, Botanical Series, XXI). Chicago, 1940.

MODERN WORKS

Alonso, Amado, 'El Descubrimiento de América y el idioma,' *Humanidades,* XXX, 117–28.

Barreda, Laos, Felipe, *Vida intelectual del virreinato del Perú*. 2nd ed. Buenos Aires, 1937.

Carbia, Rómulo D., *La Crónica oficial de las Indias occidentales*. Edición definitiva. Buenos Aires, 1940.

Dunbar Temple, Ella, 'Periodismo peruano del siglo XVIII, "El Seminario crítico," ' *Mercurio peruano,* XXV, 428–61.

Flores, Francisco A., *Historia de la medicina en México*. 3 vols. Mexico, 1886–8.

Furlong, Cardiff, Guillermo, *Bibliotecas argentinas durante la dominación hispánica*. Buenos Aires, 1945.

——*Los Jesuitas y cultura rioplatense*. Montevideo, 1933.

——*Los Jesuitas y la imprenta en la América latina*. Buenos Aires, 1940.

——*Orígenes del arte tipográfico en América, especialmente en la República Argentina*. Buenos Aires, 1947.

García Icazbalceta, Joaquín, *Bibliografía mexicana del siglo* XVI. Mexico, 1886.

González Casanova, Pablo, *El Misoneísmo y la modernidad cristiana en el siglo* XVIII. Mexico, 1948.

González Suárez, Federico, *Memoria histórica sobre Mutis y la expedición botánica de Bogotá en el siglo décimo actavo* (1782–1808). Quito, 1888.

Gredilla, A. Federico, *Biografía de José Celestino Mutis con la relación de su viaje y estudios prácticos en el Nuevo reino de Granada*. Madrid, 1911.

Henríquez Ureña, Pedro, *Literary Currents in Hispanic America*. Cambridge, Mass., 1945.

Iguíniz, Juan B., *La Imprenta en la Nueva España*. Mexico, 1938.

Jiménez Rueda, Julio, *Historia de la cultura en México, el virreinato*. Mexico, 1950.

Leonard, Irving A., 'Best Sellers of the Lima Book Trade, 1583,' *Hispanic American Historical Review,* XXII, 5–33.

——*Books of the Brave*. Cambridge, Mass., 1949.

——*Don Carlos de Sigüenza y Góngora, a Mexican Savant of the Seventeenth Century*. Berkeley, Cal., 1929.

———'A Great Savant of Colonial Peru, Don Pedro de Peralta,' *Philological Review*, XII, 54–72.

———*Romances of Chivalry in the Spanish Indies*. Berkeley, Cal., 1933.

———[Articles on the book trade to the Spanish Indies] *Hispanic Review*, II-XI, passim.

Lohmann Villena, Guillermo, *El Arte dramático en Lima durante el virreinato*. Madrid, 1945.

Martínez Durán, Carlos, *Las ciencias médicas en Guatemala, origen y evolución*. Guatemala, 1941.

Maza, Francisco de la, *Enrico Martínez, cosmógrafo e impresor de Nueva España*. Mexico, 1943.

Medina, José Toribio, *La Imprenta en Lima* (1584–1824). 4 vols. Santiago, 1904–7.

———*La Imprenta en México* (1539–1821). 8 vols. Santiago, 1907–11.

Millares Carlo, Augustín, *Dr. D. Juan José de Eguiara y Eguren, prólogos de la Biblioteca mexicana*. Mexico, 1944.

Quesada, Vicente G., *La Vida intelectual en la América española durante los siglos XVI, XVII y XVIII*. Buenos Aires, 1910.

Ramos, Samuel, 'El Movimiento científico en la Nueva España,' *Filosofía y letras*, Mexico, tomo 3, no. 6, 169–78.

Rickett, Harold William, *The Royal Botanical Expedition to New Spain, 1788–1820, as Described in Documents in the Archivo de la Nacion* (Chronica Botanica, vol. 11). Waltham, Mass., 1947.

Romero, Carlos A., *Los Orígenes del periodismo en el Perú, de la recalión al diario*, 1594–1790. Lima, 1940.

Torre Revello, José, *El Libro, la imprenta y el periodismo en América durante la dominación española* (Facultad de filosofía y letras. Publicaciones del Instituto de investigaciones históricas, LXXIV). Buenos Aires, 1940.

———'Noticia sobre José Eusebio de Llano Zapata, historiador peruano del siglo XVIII,' *Revista de historia de América*, no. 13, 5–39.

———*Orígenes de la imprenta en España y su desarrollo en América española*.

Valton, Emilio, *Impresos mexicanos del siglo XVI*. Mexico, 1935.

Vargas, José M., *La Cultura de Quito colonial*. Quito, 1941.

Zavala, Silvio, 'Sobre la política lingüística del imperio español en América,' *Cuadernos americanos*, año V, no. 3, 159–66.

THE FINE ARTS

MODERN WORKS

Anderson, Lawrence, *The Art of the Silversmith in Mexico, 1519–1936*. 2 vols. New York, 1941.

Angulo Iñíguez, Diego, *Historia de arte hispanoamericano*. Vols. 1, 2, Buenos Aires, 1945–50.

Buschiazzo, Mario J., *Estudios de arquitectura colonial hispanoamericana*. Buenos Aires, 1944.

Cossío del Pomar, F., *Pintura colonial (escuela cuzqueña)*. Nueva edición. Cuzco, 1928.

Furlong Cardiff, Guillermo, *Músicos argentinos durante la dominación hispánica*. Buenos Aires, 1945.

Hernández de Alba, Guillermo, *Teatro del arte colonial, primera jonarda en Santa Fe de Bogotá*. Bogotá, 1938.

Kelemen, Pál, *Baroque and Rococo in Latin America*. New York, 1951.

Kronfuss, Juan, *Arquitectura colonial en la Argentina*. Buenos Aires, n.d.

Kubler, George, *Mexican Architecture of the Sixteenth Century*. 2 vols. New Haven, 1948.

Mariscal, Federico E., *La Patria y la arquitectura nacional*. Mexico, 1915.

Moreno Villa, José, *La Escultura colonial mexicana*. Mexico [1942].

Navarro, José Gabriel, *Artes plasticas educatorianas*. Mexico, 1945.

———*Religious Architecture in Quito*. New York, 1945.

Noel, Martin S., *Arquitectura virreinal* (Estudios y documentos para la historia del arte colonial, vol. 1). Buenos Aires, 1934.

Pereira Salas, Eugenio, *Los Orígenes del arte musical en Chile*. Santiago, 1941.

Pizano Restrepo, Roberto, *Gregorio Vázquez de Arce y Ceballoz*. Paris, 1926.

Revilla, Manuel G., *El Arte en México*. 2nd ed. Mexico, 1923.

Romero de Terros y Vinent, Manuel, *Las Artes industriales en la Nueva España*. Mexico, 1923.

Torre Revello, José, *Aristas pintores de la expedición Malaspina* (Estudios y documentos para la historia del arte colonial, vol. 2). Buenos Aires, 1944.

———'Los Bailes, las danzas y las máscaras en la colonia,' *Boletín del Instituto de investigaciones históricas*, añn IX, no. 46, 434–54.

———*La Orfebrería colonial en hispanoamerica y particularmente en Buenos Aires*. Buenos Aires, 1945.

Toussaint, Manuel, *Arte colonial en México*. Mexico, 1948.

Vargas, José María, *El Arte quiteña en los siglos XVI, XVII y XVIII*. Quito, 1949.

Weismann, Elizabeth Wilder, *Mexico in Sculpture, 1521–1821*. Cambridge, Mass., 1950.

Wethey, Harold E., *Colonial Architecture and Sculpture in Peru*. Cambridge, Mass., 1949.

TRADE AND INDUSTRY

CONTEMPORARY SOURCE MATERIALS

Acarete du Biscay, *An Account of a Voyage up the River de la Plata and Thence Overland to Peru*. London, 1698.

Antúnez y Acevedo, Rafael, *Memorias históricas sobre la legislación y gobierno del comercio de los españoles con sus colonias en las Indias occidentales*. Madrid, 1797.

Barba, Enrique M., 'La Organización del trabajo en el Buenos Aires colonial, constitución de un gremio,' *Labor del centro de estudios históricos* [Universidad nacional de La Plata], 1944, 22–152

Barrio Lorenzot, Francisco del, *El Trabajo en Mexico durante la época colonial, ordenanzas de gremios de la Nueva España* ... *con introducción* ... *de Genaro Estrada.* Mexico, 1920.

Campillo y Cosío, Joseph del, *Nueva sistema de gobierno económico para la América.* Madrid, 1789.

Comercio de Indias (Facultad de filosifía y letras. Documentos para la historia argentina, v-vII). Buenos Aires, 1915–6.

Fabila, Manuel, comp., *Cinco siglos de legislación agraria en México* (1493–1940). Vol. 1, Mexico, 1941.

García del Prado, J., *Compendio general de las contribuciones y gastos que ocasionan todos los efectos* ... *que se trafican entre los reynos de Castilla y América.* Madrid, 1762.

Gutiérrez de Rubalcava, Joseph, *Tratado histórico, político y legal de el comercio de las Indias occidentales* etc. 1ª *parte: Compendio histórico del comercio de las Indias.* Cadiz, 1750.

Mercado, Tomás de, *Summa de tratos y contratos.* Sevilla, 1571.

Nifo, Manuel Deogracias, *Noticia de los caudales, frutos, y efectos que han entrado en España de la América en el féliz reynado de* ... *Carlos III.* Madrid, 1788.

Savary, Jacques, *Le Parfait Négociant ou instruction général pour tout ce que regarde le commerce* ... 2 vols. Paris, 1763.

Sée, Henri, *Documents sur le commerce de Cadix.* Paris, 1763.

'El Trabajo industrial en la Nueva España a mediados del siglo xvII, visita a los obrajes de paños en la jurisdicción de Coyoacán, 1660,' *Boletín del Archivo general de la nación,* xI, 33–116.

Ulloa, Bernardo de, *Restablecimiento de las fábricas y comercio español.* 2 vols. Madrid, 1740.

Uztáriz, Gerónimo de, *Teoría y práctica del comercio y de la marina.* Madrid, 1724.

Vásquez, Genaro V., ed., *Legislación del trabajo en los siglos xvi, xvii y xviii, relación entre la economía, las artes y los oficios en la Nueva España.* Madrid, 1938.

Veitia Linaje, Joseph de, *Norte de la contratación de las Indias.* Sevilla, 1672.

Zavala, Silvio, ed., *Ordenanzas del trabajo, siglos xvi, y xvii.* Mexico, 1947.

MODERN WORKS

Arcila, Farías, Eduardo, *Comercio entre Venezuela y México en los siglos xvii y xviii.* Mexico, 1950.

——*Economia colonial de Venezuela.* Mexico, 1946.

Artiñano y de Galdácano, Gervaiso de, *Historia del comercio con las Indias durante el dominio de los Austrias.* Barcelona, 1917.

Borah, Woodrow, *Silk Raising in Colonial Mexico* (Ibero Americans, no. 20). Berkeley, Cal., 1943.

Brown, Vera Lee, 'Anglo-Spanish Relations in America in the Closing Years of the Colonial Era,' *Hispanic American Historical Review,* v, 327–483.

——'The South Sea Company and Contraband Trade,' *American Historical Review*, XXI, 662–78.

Bruman, Henry J., 'Early Coconut Culture in Western Mexico,' *Hispanic American Historical Review*, XXV, 212–23.

Caillet-Bois, Ricardo R., *Ensayo sobre el Rio de la Plata y Revolución francesa* (Facultad de filosofía y letras. Publicaciones del Instituto de investigaciones históricas, XLIX). Buenos Aires, 1929.

Canabrava, A. P., *O Comércio, português no Rio da Prata*, 1580–1640. (Faculdade de filosofía, ciências e letras, Boletim XXXV). São Paulo, 1944.

Carrera Stampa, Manuel, 'The Evolution of Weights and Measures in New Spain,' *Hispanic American Historical Review*, XXIX, 2–24.

Céspedes del Castillo, Guillermo, *Lima y Buenos Aires, repercusiones económicas y políticas de la creación del verreinato del Plata*. Sevilla, 1947.

——*La Avería en el comercio de Indias*. Sevilla, 1945.

Chevalier, Francois, 'Les Cargaisons des flotes de la Nouvelle Espagne vers 1600,' *Revista de Indias*, Madrid, añn, IV, 323–30.

Christelow, Allan, 'Contraband Trade Between Jamaica and the Spanish Main, and the Free Port Act of 1766,' *Hispanic American Historical Review*, XXII, 309–43.

——'Great Britain and the Trades from Cadiz and Lisbon to Spanish America and Brazil, 1759–1783,' ibid. XXVII, 2–29.

Coni, Emilio A., *Agricultura, comercio e industria coloniales (siglos XVI-XVIII)*. Buenos Aires, 1941.

Dahlgren, Erick Wilhelm, *Les Relations commerciales et maritimes entre la France et les de Pocéan Pacifique*. Vol. 1. Paris, 1909.

García Icazbalceta, Joaquín, 'La Industria de la seda en México,' (*Opúsculos Varios*, 1, 125–61).

Girard, Albert, *Le Commerce français à Séville et Cadix au temps des Hapsbourg, contribution à l'étude du commerce étranger en Espagne aux XVIe et XVIIe siécles*. Paris, 1932.

——*La Rivalité commerciale et maritime entre Séville et Cadix jusqu'à la fin du XVIIIe siécle*. Paris, 1932.

Guthrie, Chester L., 'Colonial Economy. Trade, Industry, and Labor in Seventeenth-Century Mexico City,' *Revista de historia de América*, no. 7, 103–33.

Hamilton, Earl J., *American Treasure and the Price Revolution in Spain, 1501–1650*. Cambridge, Mass., 1934.

——'American Treasure and the Rise of Capitalism, 1500–1700,' *Economica*, no. 27, 338–57.

Haring, C. H., *Trade and Navigation Between Spain and the Indies in the Time of the Hapsburgs*. Cambridge, Mass., 1918.

Hernández de Alba, Guillermo, 'Ensayo sobre la evolución histórica de la propiedad en Cundinamarca,' *Boletín de historia y antiguedades*, vol. 29, no. 338, 1079–89.

Hussey, Roland D., *The Caracas Company, 1728–1784*. Cambridge, Mass., 1934.

Lafuente Machain, R. de, *Los Portugueses en Buenos Aires (siglo XVII)*. Madrid, 1931.

Lee, Raymond L., 'Grain Legislation in Colonial Mexico,' *Hispanic American Historical Review*, XXVII, 647–60.

Levene, Ricardo, *Investigaciones acerca de la historia económica del Virreinato del Plata*. 2 vols. La Plata, 1927–8.

Loosley, Allyn C., 'The Puerto Bello Fairs,' *Hispanic American Historical Review*, XIII, 314–35.

McLachlan, Jean O., *Trade and Peace with Old Spain, 1667–1750*. Cambridge, 1940.

Márquez, Miranda, Fernando, *Ensayo sobre los artífices de la platería en el Buenos Aires colonial* (Facultad de filosofía y letras. Publicaciones del Instituto de investagaciones historicas, LXII). Buenos Aires, 1933.

Miranda, José, 'Notas sobre la introducción de la mesta en la Nueva España,' *Revista de historia de América*, no. 17, 1–26.

Montoto, Santiago, 'D. José de Veitia Linaje y su libre; Norte de la Contratación,' *Boletín del Centro de estudios americanmistas de Sevilla*, nos. 44–5, 1–24.

Moreyra Paz Soldán, Manuel, 'El Comercio de exportación en el Pacifico a principios del siglo XVIII,' Universidad católica del Perú, Instituto de investigaciones históricas. Cuadernos de estudios, II, no. 5, 248–85.

——*El Tribunal consulado de Lima*. Lima, 1950.

Nelson, George H., 'Contraband Trade under the Asiento, 1730–1739,' *American Historical Review*, LI, 55–67.

Nettels, Curtis, 'England and the Spanish American Trade, 1680–1715,' *Journal of Modern History*, III. 1–32.

Pares, Richard, *War and Trade in the West Indies, 1739–1763*. New York, 1936.

Romero, Emilio, *Historia económica y financiera del Perú, antiguo Perú y verreynato*. Lima, 1937.

Sayous, André E., 'Les Changes de l'Espagne sur l'Amérique au XVIe siècle,' *Revue déconomie politique*, 41e année, no. 6, 1417–43.

——'La Circulation de métaux et de monnaies au Pérou pendant le XVIe siècle,' ibid. 42e année, no. 5, 1300–17.

——'Les Débûts du commerce de l'Espagne avec l'Amérique (1503–1518),' *Revue historique*, CLXXIV, 185–215.

——'Partnerships in the Trade Between Spain and America and also in the Spanish Colonies in the Sixteenth Century,' *Journal of Economic and Business History*, I, 282–301.

Reales Ordenanzas para la dirección, régimen y gobierno del importante Cuerpo de minería de Nueva España. Madrid, 1783.

MINING

CONTEMPORARY SOURCE MATERIALS

Arniaz y Freg Arturo, 'D. Fausto de Elhuyar y de Zubice,' *Revista de ristoria de América*, no. 6, 75–96.

Cobb, Gwendolin B., 'Supply and Transportation for the Potosi Mines, 1545–1640,' *Hispanic American Historical Review*, XXIX, 25–45.

Hamilton, Earl J., 'Imports of American Gold and Silver into Spain, 1503–

1660,' *Quarterly Journal of Economics*, XLIII, 436–72.

Haring, C. H., 'American Gold and Silver Production in the First Half of the Sixteenth Century,' ibid. XXIX, 433–74.

Howe, Walter, *The Mining Guild of New Spain and its Tribunal General*, 1770–1821. Cambridge, Mass., 1949.

Lexis, Wilhelm, 'Beiträge zur Statistik der Edelmetalle,' *Jahrbücher für Nationalökonomie und Statistik*, XXXIV, 361–417.

Lohmann Villena, Guillermo, *Las Minas de Huancavelica en los siglos XVI y XVII*. Sevilla, 1949.

Maffei, Eugenio, and Ramón Rua Figueroa, *Apuntes para una biblioteca española de libros . . . y manuscritos relativos al conocimiento y explotación de las requezas minerales y a las ciencias auxiliares*. 2 vols. Madrid, 1871.

Mendizábal, Miguel O. de, 'Los Minerales de Pachua y Real del Monte en la época colonial,' *El Trimestre oconómico*, VIII, 253–3009.

Restrepo, Vicente, *Estudio sobre las minas de oro y plata de Colombia*. 2nd ed. Bogotá, 1888.

Soetbeer, Adolf, *Edelmetall-Produktion und Werthverhältniss zwischen Gold und Silber seit der Entdeckung Amerikas bis zur Gegenwart*. Gotha, 1789.

Tamayo, Jorge L., 'La Minería de Nueva España en 1794,' *El Trimestre económico*, X, 287–319.

Wagner, Henry R., 'Early Silver Mining in New Spain,' *Revista de historia de América*, no. 14, 49–71.

West, Robert C., *The Mining Community in Northern New Spain: the Parral Mining District* (Ibero-Americana, 30). Berkeley, Cal., 1949.

Whitaker, Arthur P., 'The Elhuyar Mining Missions and the Enlightenment,' *Hispanic American Historical Review*, XXXI, 557–85.

——*The Huancavelica Mercury Mine*. Cambridge, Mass., 1941.

THE EXCHEQUER

CONTEMPORARY SOURCE MATERIALS

Alsedo y Herrera, D. de, *Memorial . . . del consulado de la Ciudad de los Reyes . . . sobre diferentes puntos tocantes al estado de la real hacienda, comercio . . .* Lima (–), 1726.

Briceño-Iragorry, ed., *Orígenes de la hacienda en Venezuela (documentos inéditos de la época colonial)*. Caracas, 1942.

Documentos relativos al arrendamiento del impuesto o renta de alcabalas de la ciudad de México y distritos circundantes. Introducción por Ricardo Torres Gayban (Archivo histórico de hacienda, IV). Mexico, 1945.

Elhuyar, Fausto de, *Indagaciones sobre la amonedación en la Nueva España*. Madrid, 1818.

Escalona y Agüero, Gaspar de, *Gazophilatium regium perubicum*. Madrid, 1647.

Fonseca, Fabián de, and Carlos de Urrutia, *Historia general de real hacienda escrita . . . por orden del virrey, conde de Revillagigedo*. 6 vols. Mexico, 1845–53.

Levillier, Roberto, ed., *Antecedentes de política económica en el Rio de la Plata*. 2 vols. Madrid, 1915.

'Nuevo método de cuenta y razón para la Real hacienda en las Indias, 1784,' *Revista de la biblioteca nacional*, Buenos Aires, IV, 267–318.

Ordenanzas generales, dadas por su magestad a oficiales reales, para la administratión, recaudación, y cobro de su hacienda, buen regimiento, y instrucción, y custodia de sus caxas, 3 July 1573 (in Escalona y Agüero, ed. 1775, lib. II, pt. 2, 304ff.)

Ordenanzas para el govierno de la labor de monedas que se fabicaren en la real casa de moneda de México. Madrid (?), 1750.

Ordenanzas reales para el gobierno de los tribunales de contaduría mayor en los reynos de las Indias. Valladolid, 1666.

Primeras ordenanzas reales para el gobierno de los tribunales de quentas, que en los reynos de las Indias, ciudades de los Reyes en el Perú, México en la Nueva-España, Santa Fe en el Nuevo Reyno de Granada, se han fundado por orden del rey muestro señor, 24 August 1605 (in Escalona y Agüero, ed. 1775, lib. II, pt. 2, 318 ff.).

Rezbaf y Ugarte, Joseph de, *Tratado del real derecho de las medias-anatas seculares y del servicio de lanzas a que están obligados los títulos de Castilla*. Madrid, 1792.

Segundas ordenanzas reales para los tribunales de quentas de las Indias, 17 May 1609 (ibid. 331 ff.).

Sluiter, Engel, ed., 'Francisco López de Caravantes' Historical Sketch of Fiscal Administration in Colonial Peru, 1533–1618,' *Hispanic American Historical Review*, XXV, 224–56.

MODERN WORKS

Aiton, Arthur S., and Benjamin W. Wheeler, 'The First American Mint,' *Hispanic American Historical Review*, XI, 198.

Burzio, Humberto F., *La Ceca de la villa imperial de Potosí y la moneda colonial* (Facultad de filosofía y letras. Publicaciones del Instituto de investigaciones históricas, LXXXVIII). Buenos Aires, 1945.

Gallardo y Fernández, Francisco, *Origen, progresos y estado de las rentas de la corona de España, su gobierno y administración*. 8 vols. Madrid, 1805–1808.

Hamilton, Earl J., *La Monnaie en Castile*, 1501–1650. Paris, 1932.

——'Monetary Problems in Spain and Spanish America, 1751–1800,' *Journal of Economic History*, IV, 21–48.

Haring, C. H., 'The Early Spanish Colonial Exchequer,' *American Historical Review*, XXIII, 779–96.

——'Ledgers of the Royal Treasurers in Spanish America in the Sixteenth Century,' *Hispanic American Historical Review*, II, 173–87.

Herrera, Adolfo, *El Duro: estudio de los reales de a ocho*. 2 vols. Madrid, 1914.

Mariluz Urquijo, José M., 'El Tribunal mayor y audiencia real de cuentos de Buenos Aires,' *Revista de la facultad de derecho y ciencias sociales,* Buenos Aires, año VI, no. 23.

Moreyra Paz-Soldán, Manuel, *Antecedentes españoles y el circulante durante la conquista e iniciación del virreinato.* Lima, 1941.

———*Apuntes sobre la historia de la moneda colonial en el Perú. El reglamento de la casa de moneda de 1755.* Lima, 1938.

———'La Casa de moneda de Lima en su primera fundación,' *Revista universitaria católica del Perú,* X, 54–65.

———'La Tesorería de la casa de moneda de Lima bajo juro de heredad y comprada por los condes de San Juan de Lurigancho,' *Revista histórica,* Lima, XV, 106–42.

———'La Tesorería y estadística de acuñación colonial en la casa de moneda de Lima,' Universidad católica del Perú, Instituto de investigaciones históricas, Cuadernos de estudios, II, no. 4, 3–56.

Ots Capdequí, Josá María, 'El Tributo en la época colonial,' *El Trimestre económico,* VII, 586–615.

Peña Cámara, José de la, *El 'Tributo,' sus orígenes, su implantación en Nueva España.* Sevilla, 1934.

Sucre Reyes, José, 'Sistema tributario durante el período colonial,' *Biletín de la cámara de comercio de Caracas,* año XXXI, no. 355–6, 8849–58, 8884–91.

Zavala, Silvio, 'Apuntes históricos sobre la moneda del Paraguay,' *El Trimestre económico,* XIII, 126–43.

Index

Academia de las nobles artes de San Carlos de la Nueva España, 234
Acapulco, 250, 262, 304, 312
Acarete du Biscay, 310
Acordada, 123-24
Acosta, José de, 219
Acuerdo, 124, 281
Adelantado, 19-22, 69, 128, 152
Agriculture, 11-12, 206-08, 235-43
Aguiar y Acuña, Rodrigo de, 104
Alamán Lucas, 115, 155, 177, 196, 198, 203, 248, 249
Alba de Liste, Luis Henríquez de Guzmán, Conde de, viceroy of Peru, 65
Albuquerque, Francisco Fernández de la Cueva, Duke of, viceroy of New Spain, 277
Albuquerque, Rodrigo de, 42
Alcabala, 20, 254, 261, 268-70, 277, 280, 283
Alcaide, 21
Alcaldes de barrio, 151
Alcaldes de la hermandad, 150-52
Alcaldes de la mesta, 151
Alcaldes del crimen, 120
Alcaldes mayores, 56, 59, 67, 128-32, 265, 273n
Alcaldes ordinarios, 15, 16, 17, 150-52, 155, 156, 157, 254, 265, 273n
Alcaldes provinciales, 152n, 272
Alexander VI, Pope, 7, 167, 265
Alfaro, Francisco de, 62
Alférez real, 150, 154, 272
Alguacil mayor, 20, 150, 154, 271
Alhóndigas, 254
Almodovar, Friar Lucas de, 217
Almojarifazgo, 20, 258, 261-63
Alzate, José Antonio, 223, 230

Amalgamation of silver ores, 244-45
Amat y Junient, Manuel de, viceroy of Peru, 133, 222
Ansótegui, Juan Crisótomo, 106
Antilles. *See* West Indies
Antioquia, 90
Aquinas, St. Thomas, 216
Aragon, government of, 2, 6
Arbitrios, 158
Arbol de justicia, 149
Arequipa, 289
Aristotle, in the universities, 216, 222
Arizpe (Sonora), 80
Armada, the Great, 276-77
Armada de barlovento, 269
Army in the colonies, 115-16
Asiento of Negroes, 204-05, 312-13, 316
Assemblies, provincial, 160
Astronomical observatory (Bogotá), 223-24
Atahualpa, Juan Santos, 200
Audiencia, 15n, 16, 17, 51, 56, 70, 99, 106, 120, 157, 240, 264, 280, 281, 282, 283
    functions of, 77-78, 110-11, 120-22, 124-25
    president of, 77, 120-25
    pretorial, 120-25
    size of, 120
    appeals from, 121, 157
    regent of, 122-23
    importance of, 126-27
Audiencia, of Buenos Aires, 87, 92
    Caracas, 93
    Charcas, 85, 86-87, 92, 282, 300
    Chile, 87-88
    de los Confines, 75. *See also*

Guatemala
  Cuzco, 93
  Guatemala, 75, 76
  La Plata. *See* Charcas
  Lima, 75, 83-87, 106, 111, 144
  New Galicia, 73-74
  New Granada, 84, 85, 86
  New Spain, 72-75, 144, 244, 248
  Panama, 75, 83-84, 90, 316
  Quito, 85-87
  Santo Domingo, 15, 16, 17, 73n, 74, 77-79, 83-84, 90, 158
Auditor de guerra, 115
Augustinians, 181
Autos acordados, 124
Avería, 297, 305-06
Aviadores, 246
Avila, Francisco de, 219
Avilés, 303
Avisos, 315
Ayala, Manuel Josef de, 105n
Ayuntamiento. See Cabildo
Azara, Félix de, 225

Bahama Islands, 12
Baía, 309
Bancos de plata, 246
Banda Oriental, 91, 186
Banks in the colonies, 178-79, 247, 248-49
Barbados, 310, 312
Barcelona, 303
Barros Arana, Diego, 176
Bartolache, José Ignacio, 230
Bayona, 303, 304
Bienes de difuntos, 278
Bilbao, 303
Bobadilla, Francisco de, 9-10, 39, 138, 140, 142-43
Bolton, Herbert Eugene, 188
Bonilla, *Licensiado,* visitor-general, 145
Bonpland, Aimé, 225
Books, importation of into the colonies, 226-28
  license to print, 227

Borough, Stephen, 299
Botanical expeditions to America, 218, 222-24, 225n
Bourbon kings, reforms by, 89, 92-93, 107-08, 314
  See also Intendencias
Boyl, Friar Bernal, 169-70
Bravo de Saravia, Melchor, 87
Brazil, frontier with Spanish America, 90-92
  a council of the Indies for, 106-07
  trade with, 308, 309-10
Breve . . . doctrina christiana en lengua mexicana y castellana, 229
Bucareli, Antonio María, viceroy of New Spain, 119, 246
Buenaventura, 84, 86
Buenos Aires, city of, 89-90, 91, 150, 250, 304, 315, 320, 321
  contraband trade in, 89-90, 308-10
Buga, 86
Bullion, remittances of to Spain, 249-51
  seizure of by the crown, 278
  merchants, 259, 290-91
  smugglers, 307
Burgos, Laws of, 44-45, 64

Caballero y Góngora, Antonio, viceroy of New Granada, 222
Cabildo, 16, 104, 111, 147-65, 239, 252
  composition of, 151-52
  how chosen, 152-57
  functions of, 156
  revenues of, 158
  abierto, 160-61
  Indian, 162-63, 185-86
  relations with the governor, 163, 164
Cabildo of Mexico City, 52, 155, 175, 238
  Buenos Aires, 156

Guadalajara, 163
Cabot, Sebastian, 296
Cacao, 237, 318
  beans (Indian currency), 286,
    288, 291
Caciques, 57n, 67, 162, 264
Cadiz, 295, 296, 297, 302-03, 307,
    308, 309, 316, 317, 318
Caja de comunidad, 162-63
Caja real, 280
Cajamarca, 86
Calancha, Antonio de la, 219
Caldas, Francisco José de, 223, 231
Calderón de la Barca, Pedro, 227
Cali, 86
California, 73, 74, 75, 80
Campeche, 316, 320
Campillo y Cossío, José, 319
Canary Islands, 235-36
  See also Trade, colonial
Cañete, Andrés Hurtado de Men-
    doza, Marquis of, viceroy of
    Peru, 116, 117
Cañete, García Hurtado de Men-
    doza, Marquis of, viceroy of
    Peru, 154
Captaincy-general of Chile, 93
  Cuba, 79
  Guatemala, 76
  New Granada, 76, 79, 83, 84-85
  Santo Domingo, 79
  Venezuela, 93
Captains-general, 71-72
  functions of, 110-13, 115-16, 122
  tenure of, 116
  salaries of, 117
Capuchins, 184
Caracas, 90, 156, 206, 292, 318
Caracas Company. *See Real com-
    pañía guipuzcoana de Caracas*
Carolense, diocese, 170
Cartagena, 83, 90, 189, 304, 305,
    315
Casa da India, 297
Casa de Contratación, 94, 96n, 99,
    103, 107, 199, 207, 226, 236,
    250, 257, 278, 282, 284, 287,
    288-309 *passim,* 321
  personnel of, 298
  judicial functions, 299
Casa de fundición, 258
Casos de corte, 15, 121
Castellano (a coin), 288
Castile, government of, 2-3
Castilla del Oro, 76
  See also Panama
Castillo de Bovadilla, Gerónimo,
    114
Catalan Company, 316
Catalonia, 317
Catholic Kings, 138, 142, 152, 167,
    264, 270
  See also Ferdinand II *and*
    Isabella
Catorce, mines of, 245
Cauca River, valley of the, 84, 86
Celaya, 233
Celis, Isidoro, 222
Central America, 72, 73-76, 260
Cerralvo, Rodrigo Pacheco Osorio,
    Marquis of, viceroy of New
    Spain, 277
Cervantes de Salazar, Francisco,
    213
Cervera, Manuel, 157
Cevallos, Pedro de, viceroy of
    Buenos Aires, 91, 92
Chachapoyas, 86
Chancillería, 73
Chapetón, 195n
Charcas. *See* Presidency of Charcas
Charles II, king of Spain, 97, 314
Charles III, king of Spain, 91, 92,
    105, 107, 108, 134, 136, 169,
    246-49, 251, 261, 280, 284, 285,
    292, 298n, 319
Charles IV, king of Spain, 105, 108
Charles V, Holy Roman emperor
    (Charles I, king of Spain), 45,
    46-47, 94, 152, 158, 161, 203,
    235, 249, 257, 270, 278, 296,
    300 303, 304

Chasquis, 298n

Chiapas, 76

Chihuahua, 80

Chile, 83, 89, 203, 236, 244, 283, 304, 309, 313, 321

Chuquisaca. *See* La Plata

Church in America, 42, 166-94
  royal control of, 167-69
  first bishoprics, 170-71
  economic aspects of, 176-78

Churrigueresque, architectural style, 233

Cieza de León, Pedro, 219, 221

Cimarrones, 206

Classes in colonial society, 197-99, 201-03

Clement VII, Pope, 170, 181

Clergy in America, worldliness among, 173, 190-93

Clergy in Spain, 2, 166

Coahuila, 75

Cobo, Bernabé, 215, 219

Cofradías, 181, 182, 192, 252

Colegio del Rosario, 223

Colegio de San Ildefonso, 212

Colegio máximo of St. Peter and St. Paul, 212

Colegios, 208, 216
  See also Education, secondary

Colleges, university, 214

Colonia, del Sacramento, 91, 186

Colonization, work of private enterprise, 18-22, 25
  before and after the discovery of America, 26-27
  compared with that of England, 41 ff.
  motives of, 43 ff.

Columbus, Bartholomew, 10, 20n

Columbus, Christopher, 1, 3-4, 12-13, 14, 39, 94, 169, 235, 286, 287
  privileges of, 7, 14-15
  viceroy and admiral of the Indies, 8-9
  law suits of, 12-19 *passim*

Columbus, Diego, 2nd viceroy and Admiral of the Indies, 12-18, 43, 77, 78, 138, 276

Columbus, Diego, 4th Admiral of the Indies and 2nd Duke of Veragua, 19n

Columbus, Luis, 3rd Admiral of the Indies and Duke of Veregua, 18, 19

Comisario general subdelegado de la santa cruzada, 267

Compañías de fabricantes de moneda, 290

Compañías de palacio, 115

Company of Galicia, 316

Compostela (New Galicia), 74

Comuneros, War of the, 158

Concepción (Chile), 88

Conchillos, Lope de, 42

Condorcanqui, José Gabriel, 200

'Congregations,' 65

Consejo de cámara de las Indias, 109

Consulado, 120, 123, 125, 253, 269, 300-01n
  of Seville, 300-01, 306, 307, 308, 315, 317
  at Cadiz, 302

Contador de cuentas (Havana and Caracas), 283

Contaduría general de las Indias, 280

Contraband trade. *See* Trade, colonial

Conversos. See New Christians

Convictorio of San Carlos, 222

Convoys. *See* Fleets

Copiapó, 88

Copper coinage, 289, 292, 293

Coquivacoa, 14n

Córdoba, Pedro de, 44

Córdoba (Argentina), 89, 309

Corregidores, 4, 16-17, 56, 59, 128-32, 133, 151, 163, 198, 264
  relations with the *cabildo,* 131-32

Corregidores de indios, 58, 65n, 67, 68, 132-34
Correo mayor de las Indias, 298, 298n
'Correos Maritimos,' 298n
Cortés, Hernando, 2, 7-8, 10, 43, 47, 48, 72, 73, 78, 111, 143, 146, 152, 181, 191, 221, 235
Cortés, Martín, 237
Cortes of Cadiz, 108
Coruña, 303, 304, 320
Cosmographer of the Council of the Indies, 95
Costa Rica, 76
Council of Castile, 95, 97, 101
Council of the Hacienda, 101, 284-85
Council of the Indies, 18, 94-109, 283, 284, 295, 298, 300, 310, 317
  increase of personnel, 95-97
  relation to other councils, 97, 97n, 100, 101
  administrative functions, 97-98
  judicial functions, 98-282
  committees of, 99-100
  defects of, 99-100
  last years of, 108-09, 110-12, 114
Cozumel, 76, 171
Craft guilds, 251-53
Creoles, excluded from high office, 194-95
  shortcomings of, 196-97
Croix, Carlos Francisco de, Marquis of, viceroy of New Spain, 144
Cromberger, Juan, 229
Cromwell, Oliver, 79
Cronista mayor. See Historian
Crown, legal relationship with the American provinces, 3-6
  title to dominion in the Indies, 5-7
Cruillas, Joaquín Monserrat, Marquis of, viceroy of New Spain, 276

Cruz, Alonso de la, 228
Cruz, Sor Juana Inés de la, 221
Cruzada, 267-68, 280
Cuatequil. See Repartimiento of Indian labor
Cuba, 161, 206, 236, 292, 321
Cuerpo de la minería. See Real cuerpo de minería
Cumaná, 46, 90, 93n
Cura doctrinero, 162, 167
Curaçao, 310, 312, 316
Curacas. See Caciques
Currency in the colonies, 287-92
Customs duties. See Almojarifazgo
Cuzco, 86, 232, 233

Darién, 15, 170, 235
  See also Panama
Dávila, Pedrarias, 13, 75, 235
Dehesas, 159
Depositario general, 150, 153, 272
Derecho de fundidor, ensayador y marcador, 260
Derecho de unión de armas, 269
Desdevises du Dezert, G., 169, 193
Diario de Lima, curioso, erudito, económico y comercial, 230
Diario de México, 231, 232
Diario literario de México, 230
Díaz del Castillo, Bernal, 221, 288
Díez Venero de Leiva, Andrés, 84
Doctrina, 183, 192
Doctrineros. See Cura doctrinero
Dombey, Joseph, 225n
Dominica, 311
Dominican friars, 44, 46, 53, 171, 201, 208, 210, 212, 222, 237
Don Quijote, 227
Duns Scotus, John, 216
Duro (a coin), 289
Dutch trade with the Spanish colonies, 310, 311, 318

Echave, Baltásar de, 232
Education in the Spanish colonies, 208-18

primary, 209, 211, 212
secondary, 210-11, 212
Ejido, 158, 162
El Nuevo Luciano de Quito, 224
Elhuyar, Fausto de, 247, 248, 249
Emigration to America, 199, 207-09
Eccomenderos
  absenteeism, 42, 46
  military obligation of, 43
  residence of, 52, 55
Encomiendas, 11-12, 20, 20n, 40, 41n, 57, 99, 110, 121, 198, 199
  attempts to abolish, 47, 49, 53
  right of inheritance of, 48, 49, 52, 53, 54
  not landed estates, 57
  gradual disappearance of, 66-67
English trade with the Spanish colonies, 310-11, 314, 319
Enlightenment, eighteenth-century, in Spanish America, 222, 223, 224, 314
  in Spain, 314
Enríquez, Martín, viceroy of New Spain, 59, 118, 243, 299n
Entails, 240
Ercilla, Alonso de, 221
Escala espiritual para llegar al cielo, 228
Escalona y Agüero, Gasparo de, 219
Escribano, 15, 151, 153, 154, 270, 271
Escudo (a coin), 292
Esparragosa, Dr. Narciso, 218
Exchequer, colonial, 13, 256-78
  receipts of, 257
  organization of, 279-85; *see also* Intendencias
Expedición botánica, 223
'Exploitation colonies,' 28-31

Factor of the royal exchequer, 264, 280

of the *Casa de Contratación*, 298
Falkland Islands, 92
Farfan, Dr. García, 217
'Farm colonies,' 27-31
Ferdinand II, king of Aragon, 2, 11-12, 13, 15, 44, 45, 152, 167, 203, 235, 258, 265, 276, 294
Ferdinand VI, king of Spain, 292
Ferdinand VII, king of Spain, 105, 108
Fernández de Navarrete, Pedro, 295
Fernández de Oviedo y Valdés, Gonzalo, 9, 235
Fernández Piedrahita, Lucas, 219
Fiel ejecutor, 150, 153, 254
Figueroa, Rodrigo de, 45, 46, 263
Fine arts in the colonies, 232-34
Fiscal, 56, 95, 120
Fleets, system of periodical, 304-07, 314-16
Florida, peninsula of, 73, 79
Flota, 305, 314-16
Focher, Juan, 210
Foreigners in the colonies, 11, 199, 224-26
  See also Trade, colonial
Franciscan friars, 11, 172, 175, 181, 184, 201, 209, 210, 212
Franklin, Benjamin, 223
'Free ports' in the West Indies, 311
Freedmen, 203
French Royal Guinea Company, 205, 315
French trade with the Spanish colonies, 308, 314-15
Friars, 172-76
  and the secular clergy, 174-75
  rivalry between creoles and peninsulars, 175
  See also Dominican, Franciscan, Hieronymite, Mercedarian friars
Fuggers, 296

Gaceta de México, 230
Gachupín, 195n
Gage, Thomas, 202
Galeones, 305, 314-16
Galíndez de Carbajal, Lorenzo, 95, 298n
Gálvez, José de, 80, 107, 143-44, 163, 246, 248, 276, 280
Gálvez, Matías de, viceroy of New Spain, 178
Gaona, Juan de, 200
Garay, Francisco de, 78
García de Castro, Lope, governor of Peru, 132
García de Loaisa, Francisco, Cardinal-archbishop of Seville, 95
Garzaron, Francisco, visitor-general, 145
Gasca, Pedro de la, 281
Gattinara, Mercurino de, grand chancellor of Castile, 95n
Gazeta de Goathemala, 230
Gazeta de literatura de México, 230
German miners in Spanish America, 244, 248
Gil, Jerónimo Antonio, 234
Gobernador intendente. See Intendentes
Gobernadores, 128-32, 133
Gold, production of, 12, 243, 244, 249, 257
    coinage, 289, 291
González Dávila, Gil, 172, 276
Gouvenot, Laurent de, 203
Government in America, characteristics of, 112-15
    See also Viceroys, Audiencia
Gracias a Dios, 76
Gran Chaco, 86
Grand chancellor of the Indies, 95
Grazing industry, 237-38, 257
    See also Mesta
Gregory VIII, Pope, 267

Guadalajara, 75, 277
Guanajuato, 244, 245
Guatemala, 75, 76, 77, 269, 283, 298n, 321
Guatemala City, 156
Guayana, 90, 93n
Guayrá, province of, 184
Guiena, Gabriel de, Bishop of Bari, 171
Guilds. See Consulado, Craft guilds, Real cuerpo de minería, Mesta
Guinea, 309
Gunpowder monopoly, 275
Guzmán, Nuño de, 72, 74
Gypsies, 189

Hacienda real. See Exchequer
Haenke, Thaddeus, 225n
Havana, 207, 305, 310, 314, 319, 320
Havana Company, 316
Hawkes, Henry, 237
Hernández, Francisco, 96, 217n
Herrera, Juan de (architect), 233
Herrera y Tordesillas, Antonio de, 95n, 97
Heyn, Admiral Piet, 278
Hidalguías, 198
Hieronymite friars, 44-46, 64, 203, 235, 263
Hispaniola, 7-8, 11, 15, 79, 161, 187, 236, 257, 276, 282, 287, 310, 316, 317
História de España vindicada, 220
Historian of the Council of the Indies, 95, 97
Hojeda, Diego de, 221
Honduras, 75, 79, 305
Hospital of the Immaculate Conception, 180, 181-82
Hospitals, 11, 179, 180, 181-82
'Hospitals of Santa Fe,' 179
Huancavelica, 259

Humboldt, Alexander von, 141, 176, 177, 187, 225, 236, 245

Ibáñez de Ibarra, Pero, 42
Independence movement in America, 108, 161, 165, 222, 324-26
Indian College (Harvard), 211n
Indians, policy toward, 10, 11-12, 38ff.
  kidnapping of, 12, 42, 66
  tribute of, 39, 50, 52, 58, 66, 263-64, 265, 277, 280, 283, 285
  forced labor of, 39, 40-42, 44-46, 48, 52, 53, 57-59
  slavery of, 40, 49, 49n, 50, 52, 53-54, 63, 64
  decline of numbers in West Indies, 43
  reduced to village life, 45n, 46, 64
  Yanaconas, 49-50
  declarations of Pope Paul III concerning, 50-51
  emancipation of slaves, 51, 53
  protective legislation for, 43-45, 51, 55, 60-63
  legal assistance to, 56, 110, 121
  use of as carriers, 57n
  wages of, 60, 63n
  ill-treatment of, 60, 61n, 66
  and free labor, 62
  in Chile, 63-64
  condition of in Peru, 65-66
  Araucanians, 88
  conversion of, 172, 173
  Guaraní, 184, 187
  social status of, 190-91
  revolts of, 191
  admission to the clergy, 191
  education of, 209-12, 215
Indultos, 307
Inquisition, 189-91
Intendencias, 134, 164, 265, 286
  reasons for, 135-36
Intendentes, 266, 284

Isabella, queen of Castile, 2, 4, 39, 94, 152, 167, 203, 236, 258, 265, 294
Italian trade with the Spanish colonies, 308, 311

Jaequin, Nikolaus von, 225n
Jamaica, 18, 79, 205, 310, 311, 312
Jesuits, 169, 172, 175, 178, 184, 191, 222, 229
  colleges of, 209, 212, 214
  See also Missions
Jesús Nazareno. See Hospital of the Immaculate Conception
Jews in the colonies, 10, 189, 190
Jiménez de Cisneros, Cardinal Francisco, 24, 45, 95, 203, 213
Jiménez de Quesada, Gonzalo, 84, 221
Jiménez Paniagua, Fernando, 104
Jimeno, Rafael, 235
Juan, Jaime, 96
Juana, queen of Castile, 12
Jueces de comisión. See Pesquisidores
Jueces repartidores, 59
Juez de la acordada, 123
Juez de residencia. See Residencia
Julius II, Pope, 167
Junta Central in Spain (1809), 108
Junta de diezmos, 266
Junta de guerra de Indias, 100, 115
Junta superior de real hacienda, 124, 136, 164, 281
Justicia mayor, 151
Juzgado de bienes de difuntos, 125
Juzgado de Indias, 302-03
Juzgado general de indios, 56, 59, 121

La Antigua, 76
La Araucana, 221
Labor problems. See Indians,

Negroes, 'Exploitation colonies,' *Encomiendas*
La Cristiada, 221
La Guaira, 318
Land tenure, 240-43
Landa, Diego de, bishop of Yucatan, 173
Lanning, John Tate, 222
La Plata (Upper Peru), 85, 86
Laredo, 303
La Rodoguna, 222n
Las Casas, Bartolomé de, 6-7, 8-9, 11, 44, 46-47, 51, 56, 203, 207, 235
Las Cuevas monastery, 18
Las Primicias de la cultura, 224
Latifundia in the colonies, 177, 240-42
Law in the Indies, 100-06
Legaspi, Miguel de, 72
Legislation. *See* Law in the Indies, *Recopilación*
León Pinelo, Antonio de, 104, 105, 219
León y Gama, Antonio de, 222
Lerma, Francisco de Rojas de Sandoval, Duke of, 100
Letrados, 97
License to emigrate to America, 199
Lima, 99, 189, 290, 313
Lima fundada, 220
Limpieza de sangre, 197, 198, 215
Linares, Fernando de Alencastre, Duke of, viceroy of New Spain, 177
Line of Demarcation. *See* Tordesillas
Literature in the colonies, 220-22, 225-28
Llano Zapata, José Eusebio, 222
Loaisa, García de, 296
Loans or subsidies to the crown, 276-78
Loaysa, Cardinal García Jofré de, 18

Loefling, Peter, 225n
López, Dr. Pedro, 180
López de Gómara, Francisco, 236
López de Salcedo, Diego, 75
López de Velasco, Juan, 76, 95n
Los Rios, Fernando de, 166
Los Rios, Martín Alonso de, 305
Louisiana, 79, 135, 320, 321

Magdalena River, valley of the, 84
Magellan, Strait of, 83, 88
Malaga, 303
Malaspina, Alejandro, 225n
Mamelucos of São Paulo, 91
Mangino, Fernando José, 235
Manila Galleon, 263
Manufacturing industry in the colonies, 242-43, 251-53
Maracaibo, 90, 93n, 318
Margarita, 93n, 316
Marquina, Félix Berenguer de, viceroy of New Spain, 216
Martín, Esteban (printer), 228
Martinique, 215
Matienzo, Juan de, 101-02, 118n, 219
Mayorazgos, 198, *See also* Entails
Mayordomo (municipal official), 150
Mayorga, Martín de, viceroy of New Spain, 235
Medellín, 83
Media anata, 66, 273-74
Medical science in the colonies, 217-18
Medina, Bartolomé de, 244
Mendieta, geronimo de, 175
Mendoza, Antonio de, 1st viceroy of New Spain, 12, 71-72, 111, 116, 117, 118, 143, 210, 212, 217, 244, 245, 263, 268, 289
Mendoza, Pedro de, 19, 296
Mendoza (Argentina), 88
Menéndez, de Avilés, Pedro, 206
Mercantilism and Spanish policy, 293-94

Mercedarian friars, 172, 184
Mercurio peruano, 230
Mercurio volante, 222, 230
Mercury. *See* Quicksilver
Merriman, Roger Bigelow, 6, 140
Mesada, 273-74
Messia de la Cerda, Pedro, viceroy
    of New Granada, 222
Mesta, 120, 125, 239
Mestizos, 201-02
    education of, 211-12
Metedores. See Bullion smugglers
Mexico City, 108, 189, 252
Michoacán, 244
Military service in the colonies,
    11-12, 43, 115-16
Militia, colonial, 115, 116
Minaya, Bernardino de, 50
Miners' guild. *See Real cuerpo de
    minería*
Mines operated for the crown, 42,
    259
Mining, 10-11, 82-83, 241-51, 258-
    61
    codes, 244, 245, 246, 247
Minister of Marine and Indies,
    107
Mints in the colonies, 120, 123,
    287, 290-92
    of Mexico, 251, 271, 289, 292
    of Peru, 289-90
Missionary Colleges, 184
Missions, 91, 182-89
    shortcomings of, 186-88
    as a pioneering agency, 188-87
Mita, 59, 60-63, 64*n,* 66*n,* 67
Mitayos, 59
Mixton War, 43
Mociño, José Mariano, 225*n*
Mogrobejo, Toribio, Archbishop
    of Lima, 192
Moluccas, 296
Monardes, Nicolás, 238
Monasteries, 168, 172, 174, 175-76,
    193, 208
    See also Friars

Monclova, Melchor Portocarrero
    Laso de la Vega, count of,
    viceroy of Peru, 215
Monopolies, 274-76, 280
Montaña, Dr. Luis, 218
Montejo, Francisco de, 19
Montepio, 252
Monterey, 75
Montesclaros, Juan de Mendoza y
    Luna, Marquis of, viceroy of
    Peru, 145, 193*n*
Montesinos, Antonio de, 43, 44
Montevideo, 91
More, Sir Thomas, 179
Moreno, Ignacio, 222
Moreto y Cavaña, Augustín, 227
Moses, Bernard, 148
Motolinía, Toribio de, 173, 219,
    237
Moyabamba, 86
Mulattoes, 203, 215, 253
Municipalities, common lands of,
    12
    in Spain, 147
    in Spanish America, 146-50, 159
    See also Cabildo
Mutis, José Celestino, 223, 224

Nebrija, Antonio de, 226
Negrete, Juan, 213
Negroes, 46*n,* 203-07, 215, 253, 322
    uprisings of, 206-07
New Biscay, 73, 74
New Castile, 83
New Christmas, 189, 190, 308
New Galicia, 72, 73, 79
    audiencia of, 73-74, 121
New Granada, 75, 83, 84, 203, 206,
    244, 321
    emerald mines in, 259, 283
New Laws of Charles V, 51-53, 75,
    83, 84, 98, 143
    opposition to, 52
New Leon, 74, 80
New Mexico, 73, 74, 80
New Orleans, 321

New Santander, 74, 80
New Spain, 22, 96, 161, 189, 236, 237, 257, 268, 283, 288, 292, 296, 305, 312, 315, 316, 318, 320, 321
viceroyalty of, 71, 72-81
revenues of, 285-86
New York, 310
Nicaragua, 74, 75, 83
Nicuesa, Diego de, 14
Nieva, Diego López de Zúñiga, Count of, viceroy of Peru, 54, 87
Niño, Fernando, Archbishop of Granada, 171
Nombre de Dios, 304
Nordenflicht, Thaddeus von, 248
Notaries, 14. *See Escribanos*
Nuestra Señora de la Caridad (school), 212
Nuevo Sistema de gobierno económico para la América, 319
Núñez de Landecho, Juan, 76
Núñez Vela, Blasco, viceroy of Peru, 52, 83, 143, 305

Obrajes, 61, 61n, 66, 242, 243
Oficiales reales of the exchequer, 151, 279-83
Oidores, 120
restrictions upon, 125-26
Ojeda, Alonso de, 14n
Olive culture, 236-37
Ondegardo, Juan Polo de, 219
Ordinance of Intendants, 266
Oro de tipuzque, 288, 289
Ovando, Juan de, 96, 98n, 103
Ovando, Nicolás de, governor of the Indies, 10-13, 14, 14n, 15n, 39, 44, 64, 138, 180, 189, 203, 237, 263, 265, 268, 276

Pablos, Juan, 229
Pachuca, 244
Padilla, Juan de, 65
Padrón real, 299

Paita, 86
Palafox y Mendoza, Juan de, Bishop of Puebla, 174
Palmeo, 262-63
Panama, 13, 15, 75, 83, 206, 283, 304, 305
city of, 169, 282
See also Audiencia
Paraguay, 86, 89, 90, 92, 158
See also Missions
Partido, 63n
Pasto, 83
Patagonia, 92
Patiño, José, 317
Patio process. *See* Amalgamation
Patriarch of the Indies, 171
Patronato Real, 50, 167-69, 171
Paul III, Pope, 50
Paulistas, 184
Pavón, José, 225n
Pearl fisheries, 260
Penas de cámara, 158
Penas de casados, 197
Pensacola, 321
Peonage, 62, 66
Peralta Barnuevo, Pedro de, 220, 221n
Pérez de Marchena, Juan, 169
Periodicals in the colonies, 230
Pernambuco, 309
Peru, 93, 161, 203, 236, 237, 257, 289, 304, 305, 308, 309, 312, 315, 317, 320
See also Viceroyalty of Peru
Peso corriente, 288
Peso de oro de minas, 288, 290, 291
Peso de plata ensayado, 288
Peso ensayado de tributos, 290n
Peso fuerte, 289
Pesquisidores, 3-4, 9, 78, 143
Peter of Ghent, 173, 180, 209-10, 232
Philip I, king of Castile, 12
Philip II, king of Spain, 96, 104, 153, 189, 217, 242, 245, 257,

270, 277, 278, 284, 304, 305, 307, 313

Philip III, king of Spain, 100, 257, 277, 309

Philip IV, king of Spain, 100, 172

Philip V, king of Spain, 292, 293

Philippine Islands, 1, 72, 96, 189, 237, 250, 263, 283, 285, 304, 312

Piezas de Indias, 204

Piloto mayor, 299

Pinzón, Vicente Yáñez, 14*n*

Piura, 86

Pius V, Pope, 174

Pizarro, Francisco, 43, 111

Playing cards, monopoly of, 275

Pliego de mortaja, 124

Ponce de León, Juan, 14, 19

Pons, François Josephe de, 155

Popayán, 83, 86, 90, 150

Porco, mines of, 244

Portobello, 304, 315, 316

Portuguese in the Spanish colonies, 204-05, 208, 308, 311

Postal service, colonial, 123, 280, 298, 298*n*

Postmaster-general. *See Correo mayor de las Indias*

Potosí, 233, 289, 290
mines of, 65, 82, 94, 244, 250, 305

Presidency, 71
of Charcas, 83, 86-87, 92
Quito, 86-87, 90
Chile, 89
Panama, 84, 89, 90

President of the *audiencia*, 122, 124-25

Prices, control of, 254-55

Printing press in America, 186, 228-29

Privateers in the West Indies, 206-07

Procurador de indios, 56

Procurador general, 16, 150, 152

Projecto para galeones y flotas, 315

Propios del consejo, 158

Protector of the Indians, 44, 47, 52, 56

Protestants in the colonies, 189

Protomedicato, 120, 123, 218

Protomédico, 96, 217-18

Provincias Internas, commandancy general of the, 79-80

Puebla de los Angeles, 170, 233

Puerto Cabello, 318

Puerto Príncipe, 89

Puerto Rico, 206, 236, 310, 316, 317

Puga, Vasco de, *Cedulario* of, 104

Querétaro, 184

Quicksilver, monopoly of, 245, 275, 283
mines, 259

Quinto real, 259-60, 285

Quiroga, Vasco de, Bishop of Michoacán, 174, 179, 184

Quito, 83, 90, 217, 232, 269

Races in Spanish America, 197-207

Ramírez de Fuenleal, Bishop Sebastián, 78, 210, 264

Ramírez de Quiñones, Pedro, 86

Real Compañía Guipuzcoana de Caracas, 316, 318

Real corporación de la mesta. See Mesta

Real cuerpo de minería, 120, 123, 246-49

Real de á ocho, 289

Real de minas, 247

Real del Monte mines, 63*n*, 244

Receptor de penas, 150, 153

Recopilación de Leyes de los reynos de las Indias, 25, 101-03, 104-06

Recurso de fuerza, 121

Regañón de la Habana, 230

Regent. *See Audiencia*

Regidores, 14, 150-64 *passim,* 271, 282
Registros, 305, 315-16
Reglamento of 12 October 1778, 263, 320
Relaciones de indios, 96-97
Relaciones of the American viceroys, 12
Repartimiento of Indian labor, 59-63, 63*n*
Repartimientos of Indians, assignment of, 15, 15*n*, 39, 41, 41*n* *See also Encomiendas*
Repartimiento of merchandise, 67, 133, 137
Requerimiento, 6
Residencia, 12, 16-17, 84, 137, 138-42, 143
Revillagigedo, Juan Vicente de Güemes Pacheco de Padilla, 2nd Count of, viceroy of New Spain, 119, 124, 159, 193, 253, 273, 276, 285
Ricardo, Antonio (printer), 229
Rio de la Plata, 83, 86, 89, 91, 203, 235, 296, 309
Rio Grande do Sul, 91
Rio Hacha, 78, 320
Rivero, Mariano, 222
Rodríguez de Fonseca, Juan, 44, 94-95, 171, 184
Rodríguez Fresle, Juan, 219
Rodríguez Mendoza, Toribio, 221
Rojas Antonio de, Archbishop of Granada, 170
Roldán, Francisco, 9
Ruiz, Hipólito, 225*n*

Sahagún, Bernardino de, 210, 219
St. Augustine (Florida), 73*n*
St. Christopher, 310
St. Eustatius, 311
St. Malo, 313
Sale of offices, 143-45, 270, 298*n*
Salt, monopoly of, 258, 275
San Francisco, 75

San Juan (Argentina), 88
San Juan de Letrán (school), 212
San Juan de Lurigancho, Count of, 290
San Luis Potosí, 163
San Sebastián, 303
Sanlucar, 295, 302
Santa Cruz de la Sierra, 86
Santa Cruz de Tlaltelolco (school), 210-11
Santa Cruz y Espejo, Francisco Javier Eugenio de, 224
Santa cruzada, 125
Santa Fe de Bogotá, 84, 85, 90, 99
Santa Marta, 90, 305, 320
Santiago de Chile, 88, 146, 155
Santiago de los Caballeros de Guatemala, 76
Santo Domingo, 11, 12, 13, 14, 16, 17, 18, 19*n*, 206, 296
Schäfer, Ernesto, 94, 141
Scholarship in the colonies, 219-20, 222
School of Mines, 223, 233, 247, 249
Sciences, natural, in the colonies, 96-97, 217-18, 222-26
Seigniorage, 247, 280, 288*n*
Semanario del nuevo reyno de Granada, 231
Seminario convictorio, 208
Seminario de San Telmo, 263
Sessé, Martín, 225*n*
Seven Years' War, 91, 115-16, 135, 319
Seville. *See Casa de Contratación*
Sheep industry in Spain, 147 in the colonies. *See Mesta*
Sigüenza y Góngora, Carlos de, 220, 221
Silk culture, 237-38
Silver. *See Mining*
Silver coinage, 288-92 *passim*
Simpson, Lesley Byrd, 59, 61*n*
Sinaloa, 75
Sindico, 150
Slavery, Negro, 202-07

[369]

Smuggling. *See* Trade, colonial
*Sociedades económicas de amigos
    del país,* 222, 223, 231
Solórzano Pereira, Juan de, 104,
    105, 114, 122, 132, 139, 140,
    144, 145, 219, 284
South Sea Company, 204-05
Spain, intellectual life in, 24-25
    recovery of in 18th century, 26
    economic policy of, 294-97
    decline of, 251, 256, 312-13
Spaniards, national idiosyncrasies
    of, 23-26
Spanish Succession, War of the,
    278, 314-15
Subdelegados, 134, 135, 137, 163-
    64, 265
Sugar-cane culture, 11, 203, 234
Superintendente, general, 135
Superunda, José Manso de Vel-
    asco, Count of, viceroy of
    Peru, 215

Tabasco, 75
Taxation in the colonies, 257-78,
    280
Tello de Sandoval, Francisco, 52,
    53, 143
Texas, 74, 80
Textile factories. *See Obrajes*
Theatre in the colonies, 227-29
Tirso de Molina, 228
Tithes, ecclesiastical, 14, 167, 176,
    257, 264-67
Tlacos, 292
Tlaxcala, 171
Tobacco, 237
    monopoly of, 276, 281
Tobago, 310
Toledo, Francisco de, viceroy of
    Peru, 50, 56, 64, 86, 87, 101,
    111, 118, 119, 120, 132, 213,
    243, 244, 259, 264, 269, 282,
    290n
Toledo, María de, 12, 18
Tolsá, Manuel, 234

Tonnage dues, 263
Tordesillas, line of, 7n, 14, 90
Torquemada, Juan de, 65, 219
Trade, colonial, 293-313
    commodities of, 239-40
    contraband, 88-89, 291-92, 306-
        12, 314-15, 316, 318, 319
    foreign share in, 294, 296, 303,
        306-12, 317, 318, 322; *see also
        Asiento*
    limited to a few ports, 296-97,
        304
    monopoly of, 294, 296-97, 301,
        302
    with the Canary Islands, 303
    freedom of under Charles III,
        263, 320
    increase in the eighteenth cen-
        tury, 321, 322
Trade, intercolonial, 237, 261-62,
    304, 312, 320-21
Trading companies, 301-02, 316-18
Treasure-trove, 258
Treasuries, colonial. *See Exche-
    quer*
Treaty of Tordesillas, 7n
    San Ildefonso, 92
    Utrecht, 312
Tresguerras, Francisco Eduardo,
    234
*Tribunal del protomedicato gen-
    eral,* 218
Tribunals of Accounts, 99, 120,
    123, 281, 283, 298
Tribute. *See* Indians
Tributos vacos, 54n
Trinidad, 93n
Trujillo (Peru), 237
Tucumán (province), 86, 89, 90,
    92, 162
Tupac Amaru II, rebellion of, 66,
    93, 200

Ulloa, Antonio de, 65, 141, 225
Unánue, Dr. Hipólito, 218
Universidad de los cargadores a

las Indias. See Consulado
Universities, 212-17
    Salamanca, 24
    Alcalá de Henares, 24
    Mexico, 73, 213, 222
    Guatemala, 77, 214
    Lima, 86, 119
    La Plata, 86, 214
    Santo Domingo, 212-13
    San Marcos, 213, 215, 222
Upper Peru, 89, 289-90
Urabá, 14n

Valdivia, Pedro de, 88, 146, 221
Valencia, Friar Martín de, 209
Valenciana, Conde de, 245
Valera, Blas, 219
Valero, Baltásar de Zúñiga, Marquis of, viceroy of New Spain, 144-45
Vásquez de Arce y Ceballos, Gregorio, 233
Vásquez de Ayllón, Lucas, 18
Vásquez de Coronado, Francisco, 8, 74, 143
Veedor de hacienda, 280
Vega, Garcilasso de la (El Inca), 219
Vega Carpio, Lope Félix de, 228
Veitia Linaje, Joseph de, 306
Velasco, Luis de, 2nd viceroy of New Spain, 54, 116, 117
Velázquez, Diego de, 44-45, 78
Velázquez, y León, Joaquin, 222
Venezuela, 46, 78, 158, 296, 316, 318, 320
Vera Cruz, 304, 315, 320
Vera Cruz, Alonso de la, 213
Veragua, duchy of, 13, 14, 19, 19n
Vértiz y Salcedo, Juan José de, viceroy of Buenos Aires, 92
Vespucci, Amerigo, 299
Viceroyalty of Buenos Aires, 90, 91-92, 205
    New Granada, 79, 90
    New Spain, 22, 71, 72-81

Peru, 22, 71, 82-84 283
    See also Buenos Aires, New Granada, New Spain, Peru
Viceroys, 117-19
    residencia of, 17
    functions of, 110-13, 115-16, 122
    tenure of, 116-17
    salaries of, 117
    restrictions upon, 126
Vida del pícaro Guzmán de Alfarache, 227
Villa Manrique, Alvaro Manrique de Zúñiga, Marquis of, viceroy of New Spain, 144
Villaseca, Alonso de, 178
Visita, 137, 142-46
    general, 142, 144-45
    'specific,' 145-46
Visitador-general, 142
Visitadores, 3-4, 80, 84, 99, 107
Voyage aux régions équinoxiales du nouveau continent, 225

Welsers, 19, 296
West Indies, 203, 207, 235, 249, 257, 260, 277, 285, 304, 320
    European rivalries in, 78-79
    contraband trade with, 310-11
    See also Santo Domingo
Wine, production of, 236-37

Yanaconas. See Indians
Yapuguay, Nicolás, 186
Yucatan, 170, 320

Zacatecas, mines of, 244, 245
Zapata, Luis, 95
Zavala, Silvio, 62, 208
Zea, Francisco Antonio, 223
Zorita, Alonso de, 59
Zuazo, Alonso, 45
Zumárraga, Juan de, 1st bishop and archbishop of Mexico, 47, 56, 173, 174, 180, 212, 228, 288